The

Black Elk

Reader

Black Elk at Manderson, South Dakota, 1947

Photograph by Joseph Epes Brown.
Courtesy National Anthropological Archives, Smithsonian Institution.

The
Black Elk
Reader

Edited by CLYDE HOLLER

 Syracuse University Press

The paper used in this publication meets the minimum requirements of American National Standard for Information Sciences—Permanence of Paper for Printed Library Materials, ANSI Z39.48-1984.∞™

The following permissions are gratefully acknowledged: from the University of Nebraska Press, to quote from *Black Elk Speaks* and *The Sixth Grandfather,* from Luther Standing Bear's *My People the Sioux,* John Neihardt's *When the Tree Flowered,* and Thomas E. Mails's *Fools Crow;* from the John G. Neihardt Foundation, to quote from "A Sender of Words: Essays in Honor of John G. Neihardt," edited by Vine Deloria Jr.; from nila northSun, to quote from her poem "Stupid Questions," which was published in *Returning the Gift: Poetry and Prose from the First North American Native Writers Festival,* edited by Joseph Bruchac, and published by the University of Arizona Press; from Grove Press, to quote from *Ohitika Woman,* by Richard Erdoes and Mary Brave Bird; from the University of Oklahoma Press, to quote from *Black Elk: Holy Man of the Oglala,* by Michael F. Steltenkamp, and *The Sacred Pipe: Black Elk's Account of the Seven Rites of the Oglala Sioux,* edited by Joseph Epes Brown; from Princeton University Press, to quote from *The Collected Works of C. G. Jung,* edited by Herbert Read, Michael Fordham and Gerhard Adler, volume 7, copyright © 1972, volume 18, copyright © 1975, by the Bollingen Foundation.

Library of Congress Cataloging-in-Publication Data
The Black Elk reader/edited by Clyde Holler.
     p.   cm.
     Includes bibliographical references and index.
     ISBN 0-8156-2835-8 (cloth : alk. paper)—ISBN 0-8156-2836-6 (pbk. : alk. paper)
     1. Black Elk, 1863–1950. Black Elk speaks. 2. Neihardt, John Gneisenau, 1881–1973. 3. Oglala Indians—Biography. 4. Oglala Indians—Religion. 5. Teton Indians. I. Holler, Clyde.
E99.O3 B483 2000
978'.004975'0092—dc21
[B]   99-086250

Manufactured in the United States of America

Contents

Part Two

Textuality, Cultural Appropriation, and Outright Theft

Part Three

Philosophical, Theological, and Religious Studies Perspectives

Part Four

Reading about Black Elk

Contributors

Raymond A. Bucko, S.J., is Associate Professor of Anthropology in the Department of Sociology and Anthropology at Le Moyne College. His writings include *The Lakota Ritual of the Sweat Lodge: History and Contemporary Practice* and the introduction to the new edition of Joseph White Bull's *Lakota Warrior.*

Ross Enochs received his doctorate in religious studies with a concentration in the history of Christianity from the University of Virginia. He is Assistant Professor of Religious Studies at Marist College in New York. He is the author of *The Jesuit Mission to the Lakota Sioux: Pastoral Theology and Ministry, 1886–1945.*

Gregory P. Fields is Assistant Professor of Philosophy at Southern Illinois University–Edwardsville.

Ruth J. Heflin is Assistant Professor at Kansas City Kansas Community College. She is the author of *I Remain Alive: The Sioux Literary Renaissance,* which is forthcoming from Syracuse University Press.

Clyde Holler's work on Black Elk includes "Lakota Religion and Tragedy: The Theology of *Black Elk Speaks,*" "Black Elk's Relationship to Christianity," and *Black Elk's Religion: The Sun Dance and Lakota Catholicism.*

Frances W. Kaye is editor of the *Great Plains Quarterly* and Professor of Literature at the University of Nebraska.

George W. Linden is Professor of Philosophy Emeritus at Southern Illinois University–Edwardsville. His writings on Black Elk and Lakota culture include "Warrior and Mystic: Nicholas Black Elk and John G. Neihardt," "The Dethronement of Yata," and "*Black Elk Speaks* as a Failure Narrative" (with Fred Robbins).

Hilda Neihardt is the author of *Black Elk and Flaming Rainbow: Personal Memories of the Lakota Holy Man and John Neihardt,* an account of the 1931 and 1944 interviews with Black Elk, which she attended along with her father, John G. Neihardt. She is Chairman of the Board of the John G. Neihardt Foundation.

Amanda Porterfield is Professor of Religious Studies at the University of Wyoming. Her books include *Female Piety in Puritan New England: The Emergence of Religious Humanism, Mary Lyon and the Mount Holyoke Missionaries, The Power of Religion: A Comparative Introduction,* and *The Transformation of American Religion* (forthcoming).

Julian Rice has written five books on Lakota culture: *Before the Great Spirit: The Many Faces of Sioux Spirituality, Ella Deloria's "The Buffalo People," Ella Deloria's "Iron Hawk," Deer Women and Elk Men: The Lakota Narratives of Ella Deloria,* and *Black Elk's Story: Distinguishing Its Lakota Purpose.* He lives in Boca Raton, Florida.

Paul B. Steinmetz, S.J., received a Ph.D. in the anthropology of religion under Åke Hultkrantz at the University of Stockholm, Sweden. He is the author of *Meditations with Native Americans, Pipe, Bible, and Peyote among the Oglala Lakota: A Study in Religious Identity,* and *The Sacred Pipe: An Archetypal Theology.*

Michael F. Steltenkamp is Associate Professor of Anthropology and Religious Studies at Wheeling Jesuit University. He is the author of *Black Elk: Holy Man of the Oglala* and *The Sacred Vision: Native American Religion and Its Practice Today.*

Dale Stover is Professor of Religious Studies at the University of Nebraska–Omaha. He is the author of "Eurocentrism and Native Americans," "The Other Side of the Story: Indigenous Interpretation of Contact with Europeans," and "Religious Freedom, Native American: Legal and Philosophical Context" in *The Encyclopedia of Native American Legal Tradition*.

R. Todd Wise is an instructor in the Department of Religion at Augustana College. He is an enrolled citizen of the Muscogee tribe. His writings on Native American religion include "Native American *Testimonio:* The Shared Vision of Black Elk and Rigoberta Menchú" and "Mary Brave Bird Speaks: A Brief Interview" (with Christopher Wise).

Alexandra Witkin–New Holy is Assistant Professor at the Center for Native American Studies at Montana State University–Bozeman. Her writings on the Lakota include "Possibilities for Accommodating Contradictions: Developing Lakota Theology and Its Classroom Applications" and "The Heart of Everything That Is: *Paha Sapa,* Treaties, and Lakota Identity."

Introduction

The more we learn about Black Elk, the more controversial he becomes, a development that would hardly have seemed possible twenty years ago. In those happy days, practically everyone accepted Frank Fools Crow's assessment of Black Elk as the greatest of the Lakota holy men (Mails 1979, 53), and Plains anthropologists accepted *Black Elk Speaks* and *The Sacred Pipe* as authentic revelations of aboriginal Lakota consciousness.[1] The situation today, after a little critical scholarship, is somewhat different. Leading anthropologists now question whether these same texts are authentic, and there seem to be rumblings of disapproval of Black Elk—or at least of scholarly interest in him.[2] Perhaps this is due in part to the fact that the more we learn about Black Elk, the more his romantic image as an old-time Lakota holy man seems compromised by Christianity. In any case, it has become painfully clear that some people greatly prefer the nineteenth-century traditionalist who was constructed by Neihardt and Brown to the real Black Elk, the twentieth-century religious leader in dialogue with Christianity.

Nonetheless, Black Elk remains important, albeit for rather different

1. Not that Black Elk never had his critics. One dissenting voice was John (Fire) Lame Deer's, who is reported to have called him a "catechism teacher" and a "cigar-store Indian" (Matthiessen 1983, xxxvii).

2. The most outspoken critic is William K. Powers, who argues that *Black Elk Speaks* obscures rather than illuminates Lakota religion (1990c, 136), referring to it flatly as one of the "fabrications of the white man" (149). He also states that elderly Lakotas who knew Black Elk would "wonder why all the fuss" (137). For his part, Raymond J. DeMallie may have retreated somewhat from his defense of Neihardt as "an extraordinarily faithful spokesman for Black Elk" (1984a, 51). He now suggests that because "almost everything we know about Black Elk comes to us secondhand" (1997, 245), it is difficult to assess his significance and religion.

reasons than he seemed important twenty years ago, when he was regarded primarily as a passive informant on his people's past. This is so whether one finally agrees with Fools Crow or with the latest deconstruction of the Black Elk myth as a gigantic fraud perpetuated by the ever nefarious white man. In either case, his influence has been enormous, and, as the essays in this volume demonstrate, there is still much to be learned from studying Black Elk and the texts associated with him. Although those texts can no longer be read as a cry from the depths of pristine Lakota consciousness, in my view they stand revealed as something vastly more important, the record of a great Lakota holy man's response to the sweeping economic and cultural change of his times and to the challenge presented by an invasive religion backed by a hostile government.

Approve or disapprove of Black Elk's involvement with Christianity, his influence is indisputable. For one thing, it is impossible to imagine the revival of Native American religion without *Black Elk Speaks,* and there is hardly a single traditional religious leader who has not appealed to Black Elk for authentication of his own practices and teachings. For another thing, Black Elk's teachings have an undeniable beauty and power that has made them attractive far beyond their original cultural horizon. As several of the articles in this volume demonstrate, his influence on mainstream American thought and culture has been profound. Assessing and appreciating that influence is—or ought to be—separate from approving or disapproving his Christianity as well as from assessing his degree of commitment to it.

As a leader of an oppressed people, Black Elk is comparable in some ways to Martin Luther King Jr., whose Christianity both influenced the direction in which he led his people and provided the means by which he led them. In view of Black Elk's militant posture during the Ghost Dance disturbances, another great American, Malcolm X, provides a contrasting example of an American political leader whose inspiration was essentially religious. As a leader of his people during a time of considerable troubles, Black Elk had to confront Christianity and the intellectual challenges posed by the aggressive missionization of the Lakota. One can admire Black Elk's commitment to his people and appreciate his significance in American culture without necessarily approving his involvement with Christianity. To study Black Elk in his historical context and point to his influence on American thought and culture is very different from implying that Lakotas should do as Black Elk did and join the Catholic Church. Despite the recent scoffing at scholarly fascination with Black Elk, which seems in part motivated by disapproval of his Christianity, I believe he should be studied and respected as a great American whose courage was incomparable and whose choices should be understood in their historical context.

Today Black Elk stands at the intersection of many scholarly disciplines. Some of the fascination is due to the controversies that surround him, which are not so much over the facts of his life, but over the interpretation of his thought and the appropriation of his legacy. The debate over the texts that are associated with him is particularly instructive because they have been examined from the perspective of many disciplines—anthropology, literature, religion, philosophy, history, and ethnic studies. There is in this literature a wide variety of approaches and conclusions, making Black Elk scholarship a model case of the ways in which disciplinary perspectives—and personal commitments—affect scholarly conclusions. Many disciplines are interested in Black Elk because his life and work are central to many vital scholarly issues and subjects. Among other things, a proper understanding of Black Elk is essential to the study of (1) American religion, (2) Lakota religion and culture, (3) the worldwide resilience and revitalization of traditional religion and culture, (4) religious change and adaptation, and (5) ethnic American literatures and indigenous autobiography. As one of the best-documented and most influential Native American leaders of the twentieth century, Black Elk's shadow falls in a number of different directions. Ignore him at your peril if you are interested in American thought and culture.

Part of the fascination for the study of religion is that a living oral tradition surrounds Black Elk. As a key figure in the revival of traditional religion, Black Elk's legacy has been appropriated by practically every contending religious and political faction in native America. As most religionists are aware, an enormous amount of scholarly energy has been devoted to debating and reconstructing the functioning of the oral tradition that preserved the teachings of Jesus until they were fixed in written form. The Black Elk tradition provides a fascinating parallel that illuminates the ways in which the teachings of a great religious master are appropriated and adapted by his successors.

The scholarly debate over his true religious allegiances is also instructive. How did Black Elk resolve the differences between Lakota religion and Christianity, and how did he come to embrace a way of thinking that was so different from his own? Or did he? And was it? Considered from this point of view, Black Elk represents the human side of the process of syncretism, the coldly clinical term for the mutual interaction between religions. The Lakota themselves are a model case of religious change, survival, and evolution, and Black Elk's life reflects the way in which a great Lakota religious leader came to grips with those changes on a personal and intellectual level.

Black Elk's teachings also present a deeper challenge to Western ways of thinking and speaking about religion. Although the discipline of anthropology has long focused on native America, the scholarly study of religions has tended to ignore it, focusing instead on the study of the world religions, which are similar to Christianity in their reliance on sacred texts. To the extent that it remains an oral tradition, Lakota religion presents a considerable challenge to the scholarly study of religion, stretching the methods and approaches generally employed in the humanities. As a living religion, the Lakota wisdom tradition that Black Elk represents also constitutes a deep challenge to Western ways of understanding human life and the cosmos, constituting a uniquely American perspective on ultimate truth.

Black Elk's life is eventful and fascinating in itself, and it remains one of the best textual windows into the old Lakota world. For readers who may be encountering Black Elk for the first time, I have provided a brief sketch of his life and times at the end of this introduction.

The Essays in This Volume

When Syracuse University Press asked me to prepare this book, I wanted to make the project as inclusive as possible, and I invited everyone I could locate who had previously published on Black Elk, because my idea was to have a full and frank exchange of views representing the entire spectrum of interpretations of Black Elk. I also placed a call for papers on the op-ed page of *Indian Country Today* and on various subscriber groups on the Internet. I am pleased to say that the resulting volume represents an unusually broad range of scholarly disciplines, personal perspectives, and conclusions, which is especially instructive because the reader will be plunged directly into the controversies that surround Black Elk today. I have imposed no ideological requirements on my contributors, several of whom differ sharply with my own methods and conclusions.[3] There are new statements here by many of the established authorities on Black Elk, as well as groundbreaking work by young scholars who I believe will make their mark.

In the remainder of this section, I briefly introduce the various essays and make necessary remarks about the editing of this volume.

From the perspective of literary studies, Ruth J. Heflin argues that Black Elk's freedom of choice has been underestimated. She reads *Black Elk Speaks* itself as a modernist text experiment or collage, a literary form chosen by Neihardt to imitate as closely as possible the multivocality of Black Elk's actual performance. In *I Remain Alive: The Sioux Literary Renaissance,* which is also to be published by Syracuse University Press, she argues that Black Elk's work and that of other Sioux writers, including Charles A. Eastman, Gertrude Bonnin, and Ella Deloria, constitute an *Oyate* literary renaissance.

In a revised version of his essay on *Black Elk Speaks,* R. Todd Wise makes a completely different contribution to the discussion of its genre by comparing it to the *testimonio* as exemplified by *I Rigoberta Menchú: An Indian Woman from Guatemala.* In the course of his essay, Wise brings to bear a philosophical critique informed by engagement with postcolonial perspectives, revealing surprising parallels between *Black Elk Speaks* and recent "Third World" literature.

Amanda Porterfield considers the means by which *Black Elk Speaks* has entered not only the college curriculum, but the religious consciousness of Americans as a whole, producing a situation in which Black Elk's "belief

---

3. For this reason, this is not an appropriate forum to answer my critics, although I will say that the central thrust of my early work was to disentangle Neihardt's and Black Elk's judgment on the validity and viability of traditional Lakota religion and lifeways (1984a) and to demolish the anthropological understanding of Black Elk as an informant, a passive source of information on the past rather than an active creator of the Lakota present (1984b). With respect to my later work, I am still a little skeptical of anthropological assertions of proprietorship over native America. I do appreciate the opportunity afforded by the postmodern critique to restate one of my fundamental theses, which is that the perceived opposition between Black Elk's traditionalism and his Christianity is largely a product of colonial consciousness.

in the importance of his vision and its relevance for the world has been rather spectacularly confirmed." In pointing to the ways in which transcendentalist spirituality has framed the reading of *Black Elk Speaks,* she interprets Black Elk's thought as the maturation of American transcendentalism. Along the way, she points to the advantages of using *Black Elk Speaks* in the classroom and discusses Black Elk's reconceptualization of both Christianity and traditional religion in *The Sacred Pipe.*

In a revised version of his essay, Julian Rice argues that though *Black Elk Speaks* was effective in introducing Lakota culture to the white world, it obscured or failed to communicate many of the Lakota meanings of the dreams and ceremonies that it described, which can be recovered only through a detailed study of Lakota symbols in their cultural context. As an example of what such a study would entail and reveal, Rice examines the Lakota perception of the horse, the predominant symbol of transformation in Black Elk's vision. By examining the symbolism of the vision as an intricate variation on a set of complex conventional symbols, Rice encourages us to "look through both Black Elk and Neihardt to a Lakota wisdom tradition more profound than any single instrument or interpreter."

In the first of two essays in this volume, George W. Linden writes to defend Neihardt against his recent critics, including Julian Rice. Drawing on his personal experience of Neihardt as one of his teachers, Linden argues for the fundamental integrity of *Black Elk Speaks,* describing Neihardt as a mystic, not an "apostolic apologist."

In her contribution, Hilda Neihardt shares some of her memories of the original Black Elk interviews, which she attended with her father and sister in 1931. Responding to questions posed by R. Todd Wise, she discusses Neihardt's intentions in writing *Black Elk Speaks* and gives her point of view on the critical issues surrounding the Black Elk texts. She also tells of her plans to compile a book in which Black Elk's family members are allowed to speak. Finally, she clarifies some of the points covered in her recent book on the Black Elk interviews, *Black Elk and Flaming Rainbow,* and addresses the differences between her estimate of the religious convictions of Black Elk's daughter, Lucy Looks Twice, and that offered by Michael F. Steltenkamp.

Michael F. Steltenkamp provides a retrospective on his revisionist biography of Black Elk, *Black Elk: Holy Man of the Oglala* (1993). Saying that he at first embraced the portrait of Black Elk as an unspoiled traditionalist, Steltenkamp explains how he came to see this image as a harmful stereotype that required correction. Arguing that he did not rely too heavily on the recollections of Lucy Looks Twice because they were collaborated by others who knew Black Elk, Steltenkamp portrays Black Elk as a Lakota Catholic with a broad religious repertoire: he could sing sacred songs in both Latin and Lakota and could pray the rosary en route to the top of a hill to chase away a thunderstorm.

From the perspective of religious studies, Dale Stover reassesses Black Elk in the light of postcolonial theory by describing four successive "retellings" of the Black Elk story. The first three correspond to various modes of colonizing discourse while the fourth constructs Black Elk as "the postcolonial Indian." In the process, Stover discusses the retellings of Neihardt and Brown, drawing on the work of Greg Sarris and George Tinker for his theoretical foundation.

Frances W. Kaye explores the ethics of cultural appropriation through a comparison of *Black Elk Speaks* with Nathaniel Hawthorne's *Marble Faun*. During the course of her discussion, she situates *Black Elk Speaks* as a thirties text, of a piece with the public iconography of the times. Drawing on her teaching experiences, she concludes that the ethics of reading *Black Elk Speaks* is perpetually charged. Appropriating Black Elk's teaching obligates the reader to not simply "take the rituals and run" but to give something meaningful back to the community that has created them.

Writing as a philosopher, Gregory P. Fields examines the account of the sweat lodge ceremony *(inipi)* in *The Sacred Pipe,* comparing it to historical and contemporary practice. As a contribution to the growing debate on the authenticity of this text, Fields argues that Brown's account is credible in the light of the evidence, in the process casting light on the distinction between text and tradition and on Black Elk's religious syncretism.

Writing from the perspective of ethnic studies, Alexandra Witkin–New Holy explores the connections between Lakota spirituality and the Black Hills, pointing out that the full enactment of Black Elk's vision on earth required the journey to the Black Hills that formed the climax to the Neihardt interviews. She also elucidates metaphors that are central to Lakota religious discourse, including *cangleska* (the circle or hoop) and *hocoka* (the center), relating them both to Black Elk's vision and to the contemporary struggle to regain the Black Hills.

In a revised version of his classic essay, George W. Linden, a philosopher with a long-standing interest in the Lakota, writes perceptively of the Lakota worldview, comparing and contrasting it with others both East and West. Readers who are new to the subject should note that "Dakota," as used in this essay, refers to the Sioux people as a whole.

Writing as a philosopher, R. Todd Wise contributes to the current discussion of text and textuality by analyzing the implications of approaching Black Elk's vision as literature. Drawing on the theoretical work of Eugen Drewerman, Wise argues that symbolic comprehension requires us to move beyond the historical-critical method to a deeper level of participation in the text. Through a survey of the various ways in which the vision has been interpreted by the academic community, Wise argues for a constructivist approach and against any closed or final interpretation.

Writing as a theologian with considerable experience among the Lakota, Paul B. Steinmetz, S.J., examines Black Elk's religion from the point of view of recent developments in Catholic missiology, concluding that traditional religion and Christianity fulfill each other and arguing for the sincerity of Black Elk's belief in both. In the course of the discussion, he refines his model of the Ecumenist II position and conceptualizes conversion not as the substitution of one religion for another, but as "mutual fulfillment." Steinmetz's contribution to the discussion can be understood more fully in the light of the theology of missions that he develops in his recent book *The Sacred Pipe: An Archetypal Theology.*

Drawing on the archival research underlying his book on the Jesuit mission to the Lakota, Ross Enochs argues the revisionist thesis that the Jesuits, far from repressing traditional religion and culture wholesale, practiced "missionary adaptation" by accepting and encouraging the aspects of Lakota religion and culture that they perceived as good. In stressing the continuity between traditional Lakota beliefs and Catholicism, Enochs points to similarities in the concepts of ritual, sacrifice, justification, the dead, and reconciliation, relating retreats to vision quests and Catholic Congresses to Sun Dances. For Enochs, Black Elk did not need to experience a complete change of worldview to become a Catholic, although he did reject some beliefs that he formerly held and accept others that were new.

Although bookmaking logic demands that it close the book, anthropologist Raymond A. Bucko's bibliographic essay provides a brief introduction to the study of Lakota culture as well as a sensitive guide to the issues surrounding cultural appropriation. I urge readers who may be unfamiliar with this discussion to turn to it first for the help it will provide in situating Black Elk in the overall context of these issues. Although good bookmaking also required that his bibliography be merged with the works cited for the other essays in this volume, this should not be allowed to obscure the work that he has done in compiling and annotating this guide to the further study of Black Elk and Lakota culture.

It should be noted that in editing this volume, I have not taken the usual step of regularizing the Lakota orthography. The various essays encompass a broad range of historical periods and situations. The Lakota spoken around the sweat lodge today is different from the older Lakota discussed in Julian Rice's essay, and it strikes me as anachronistic to conform one to the other. Although this leads to some variability in the spelling of terms, this should not present a problem as long as they are sounded.[4]

Brief Sketch of Black Elk's Life and Times

The bare facts of Black Elk's life can be fairly quickly told, and they are not in serious scholarly dispute.[5] It is considered appropriate for a Lakota holy man to live a long life, and Black Elk's life spanned a significant period in his people's lives and in American history. His formative years were spent living the old nomadic life, making his life story one of the best windows

4. It is also worth noting that one key term carries different connotations depending on how it is spelled. When the early missionaries translated "God," they appropriated the existing Lakota term for the godhead, spelling it as one word. When "Wakantanka" is encountered, it thus tends to imply monotheism or a Lakota Christian context or both. On the other hand, when "Wakan Tanka" is encountered, the reference may well be to a plurality of spirits. (In *The Sacred Pipe*, Joseph E. Brown chose to hyphenate the term—"Wakan-Tanka"—which has been retained in quotations from that source.)

5. The primary sources for Black Elk's biography are *Black Elk Speaks* itself and Raymond J. DeMallie's reconstruction of the interviews on which they are based, *The Sixth Grandfather*. The main secondary sources are DeMallie's introduction (1984c) and commentary to that volume and Michael F. Steltenkamp's *Black Elk: Holy Man of the Oglala*. William K. Powers's contrarian—and largely undocumented—contribution is also of value (1990c). I survey the secondary literature in the first chapter of *Black Elk's Religion*.

on the old Lakota world. If, as Neihardt reports, he was born in 1863, he was born in the year of the Battle of Gettysburg, the turning point in the Civil War. If, as seems more likely, he was born in 1866 (Holler 1995, 39 n), he was born in the first year after the Civil War. Although the war probably did not affect Black Elk and his people unduly, the peace certainly did because when the war was over, the attention of the nation turned to western expansion. At the same time, the attention of the army turned to Indian fighting, and some of the famous Civil War generals, including Sherman and Sheridan, became equally famous Indian fighters.[6] These years were momentous for the Lakota, for they marked the beginning of the end of native autonomy. By 1866, the old nomadic life the Lakota had lived was nearly gone, and they were being forced rapidly toward the mainstream of American culture. This year also saw the first outsider observations of the Sun Dance, marking the beginning not only of the reservation period, but also of more than a century of scholarly interest in—or intrusion into—Lakota religion.

Given the way in which he remembers it, we may suppose that Black Elk's early years were happy years, relatively unmarked by overt oppression. As a young boy, he must have experienced at least the afterglow of the glory days of the Lakota, when they enjoyed hegemony over a large portion of the Plains, which was supplied with an abundance of food in the form of the buffalo. Despite this abundance, life was not necessarily easy for the Lakota. They had plenty of enemies, and shortages of food were common during the harsh Plains winters. But the summers were devoted to festivals, togetherness, and feasting—and to the Sun Dance—and at least some of Black Elk's evident nostalgia for the old free days of the Lakota must be attributed to the fact that he actually lived them.

Still, these days included constant skirmishing with the army, because Black Elk was a member of Big Road's band, which hunted in the territory west of the Black Hills, where the establishment of the Bozeman Trail in 1864 led to contact and conflict with the whites (DeMallie 1984a, 3). As a youngster, Black Elk was no stranger to war, and he was present at the high-water mark of Lakota military resistance against the white invaders, the Custer Fight or the Battle of the Little Big Horn where Custer was

---

6. It is important to emphasize this point, because I have found that many people erroneously assume that the Plains Indian wars took place before the Civil War.

killed in 1876. Although too young to really participate in the fighting, Black Elk scalped a fallen soldier from Reno's command, shooting him in the forehead with a pistol afterward (DeMallie 1984a, 183). Crazy Horse was instrumental in that fight, and when he was captured and subsequently killed at Fort Robinson in 1877, Black Elk and his people fled to Canada, where they remained for about three years (6).

Perhaps, had he been older at this time, Black Elk would have received renown as a warrior. But three years earlier than the Custer Fight, and in the same general vicinity, Black Elk fell sick and received the vision that marked him for a vocation as a holy man (DeMallie 1984a, 111–42). This vision, which Black Elk shared with John Neihardt in an elaborated form, has become famous as his "Great Vision," an acknowledged masterpiece of religious literature. According to his friend Standing Bear, Black Elk was sick for a period of twelve days, falling sick all at once (143).

In 1881, Black Elk enacted the first portion of his vision as the Horse Dance, which was both a public announcement of his vocation as a holy man and an indication of the high esteem in which he was held by the elders of his tribe, for it was rare for the Lakota to accept new rituals.[7] That the ritual persisted as part of the tradition is attested by Fools Crow's remark that he was a dancer in the last "true and holy" Horse Dance in 1931 (Mails 1979, 79). Perhaps some of Black Elk's character can be seen in the fact that the Horse Dance is not among the important rites discussed in *The Sacred Pipe*. In any case, at this very early age—fifteen, if he was born in 1866—Black Elk seems already to have been marked for greatness.[8]

In the same year that Black Elk enacted the Horse Dance, some of the last great Sun Dances also took place. The storm that had been gathering was about to break, for the government banned the Sun Dance in 1883, ushering in five decades of vigorous repression of Lakota religion and ritual (Holler 1995, 110–38). Because the practice of native medicine was outlawed as well, the profession Black Elk had entered two years previ-

---

7. This was a model case of the Lakota mechanism for generating and accepting new rituals, because Black Elk shared his vision with an older medicine man and accepted his advice (DeMallie 1984a, 214). This model—individual inspiration and community control—is also depicted in Black Elk's account of the Sun Dance in *The Sacred Pipe*.

8. Black Elk says in his narrative that he was seventeen, but it is likely that this number was provided by Neihardt, reckoning forward from a birth date of December 1863.

ously could no longer be practiced legally. It is likely that he practiced it anyway, because the private practice of medicine was inherently harder to repress than the large public spectacle of the tribal Sun Dance. However, the ban certainly hurt the holy men economically, for the Sun Dance was their major source of income. In these years, the tide was running decisively against traditionalism, and Black Elk must have felt its effect, for in 1887 he enlisted with Buffalo Bill's Wild West Show, a forerunner of the cultural appropriation deplored by traditionalists today. In order to join the show, he was required to become an Episcopalian. Although we do not know if Black Elk was disaffected with his medicine practice at this time, he seems to have joined the show in part to learn more about the whites and their religion.[9] In any case, while traveling with Buffalo Bill, Black Elk and his compatriots had many experiences that were unusual for nineteenth-century Lakotas, including a command performance for Queen Victoria.

It is certainly possible that when Black Elk joined Buffalo Bill, he wanted to learn more about the whites and accommodate himself to them. But things took a rather different turn when Black Elk returned from Europe to the Pine Ridge Reservation in 1889, for the Ghost Dance was stirring among the Sioux, and—at least on his own account—he quickly became its leader (DeMallie 1984a, 266). The Ghost Dance, the first major pan-Indian religious phenomenon, has been characterized by anthropologists as a revitalization movement, an attempt to revive traditional culture through ritual and dance. The Lakota Ghost Dance seems to have functioned in part as a substitute for the banned Sun Dance, with the people dancing in a circle around the sacred pole, seeking visions of their departed ancestors. Implicit in the mythology of the dance was the return of the buffalo and the old happy days—as well as the disappearance of the whites or their influence over native America.

During the Ghost Dance disturbances, Black Elk was a militant, inciting the people to fight with the troops (DeMallie 1984a, 268) and pre-

---

9. After returning to Pine Ridge, Black Elk wrote in *Iape Oaye,* a newspaper published under missionary auspices, that "of the white man's many customs, only his faith, the white man's beliefs about God's will, and how they act according to it, I wanted to understand" (DeMallie 1984a, 9–10).

sumably favoring the breakout to the Bad Lands that subsequently took place. Unfortunately, this breakout led to the massacre at Wounded Knee in December 1890, during which elements of the Seventh Calvary slaughtered Big Foot's band, which had surrendered. Black Elk was present at this fight, and was wounded in the side while rallying his people on horseback.

Although we can be sure that the failure of the Ghost Dance and the events at Wounded Knee were deeply felt by Black Elk, we know very little of what he was actually thinking and doing between 1890 and 1904 because the 1931 Neihardt interviews end with the massacre at Wounded Knee. With the Sun Dance underground, he seems to have concentrated on healing, on his medicine practice. In 1904, however, Black Elk accepted Catholicism and shortly afterward became very active as a catechist. As discussed in several articles in this volume, the precise meaning of Black Elk's acceptance of Christianity is a point of considerable scholarly dispute.

In 1931, another turning occurred when Black Elk gave an account of his early life to a white poet, John G. Neihardt, which subsequently became the world-renowned classic in religion, *Black Elk Speaks*. In part because it focuses entirely on his life before becoming a catechist, the accuracy of Neihardt's portrait of Black Elk is a key point of scholarly dispute. But there is no doubt that it horrified most of the reservation Jesuits with whom Black Elk worked when it was published in 1932. As Christopher Vecsey's archival work makes clear, when Black Elk was overrun by a wagon in 1933, extreme unction (the last rites) was withheld until a written recantation of the book was obtained. According to Vecsey, the publication of *Black Elk Speaks* effectively ended the Jesuit experiment with native catechists (1997, 277–78), so Black Elk presumably did himself out of a job by collaborating with Neihardt.

Perhaps in part for this reason, Black Elk subsequently worked for the Duhamel Sioux Indian Pageant, a seasonal tourist attraction on the road between Rapid City and Mount Rushmore. (His son, Ben, was associated with Mount Rushmore itself for many years, and he was featured on postcards sold in the gift shop.) At the twice-daily shows, Black Elk was the main attraction, demonstrating rituals including the offering of the pipe, healing, and the Sun Dance (DeMallie 1984a, 64–65). As might be expected, scholarly estimates of his intentions in enacting these demonstrations differ, but there are some indications that Black Elk may have regretted his Catholicism in his later years (Holler 1995, 11, 25).

Black Elk's later years also saw two significant authorial collaborations. In 1944, Neihardt returned to Pine Ridge and interviewed Black Elk for a book that was to become *When the Tree Flowered*. These interviews focused more on tribal history and memory than on Black Elk's personal story, perhaps one reason they have been relatively neglected by scholars. This neglect is unfortunate, because this material adds much to our knowledge of Black Elk and his teaching.[10] During the winter of 1947–1948, he also collaborated on an account of Lakota ritual with Joseph Epes Brown, *The Sacred Pipe*, the authenticity of which is a growing topic of scholarly controversy.

Black Elk died in 1950. His death was accompanied by an unusual celestial display, which has been movingly described by a Jesuit brother, William Siehr (Steltenkamp 1993, 132–34).

---

10. DeMallie has included the transcript of the 1944 interviews in *The Sixth Grandfather* (1984a, 299–409). In some ways, this is a more authoritative text than the 1931 material because it was produced in the field on a typewriter by Hilda Neihardt. It has thus not required the level of emendation necessary for the 1931 interviews, which were reconstructed in part from shorthand notes.

PART ONE

Black Elk Speaks in Literary and Historical Perspective

1

Black Elk Passes on the Power of the Earth

Black Elk's Purpose and Use of Lakota Literary
Tradition in Creating *Black Elk Speaks*

RUTH J. HEFLIN

John G. Neihardt and Nicholas Black Elk created an interstitial text, *Black Elk Speaks,* interweaving both Lakota and Euro-American literary and cultural influences from both their lives. Although Neihardt's contributions to the book have been extensively investigated, what is lacking most in literary discussions about *Black Elk Speaks* is an examination of Black Elk's literary choices. Black Elk chose to convey his sense of Lakota culture, especially his personal vision, to a larger audience. Why? What considerations went into making the choice to pass on his powerful vision? What considerations went into his choice of Neihardt as his collaborator or amanuensis?

Black Elk was more shrewd in his selection of collaborator than he has been given credit for. Black Elk probably did not want his story to end up like so many other Indian stories, as an essay in some anthropological journal or as a book with little literary value other than the fact it contains the life history of an Indian holy man. Black Elk knew anthropologists were avid collectors of personal and tribal lore, having rejected at least one anthropologist's request to record his story (J. Neihardt 1979, xvi; H. Neihardt 1995, 12–13). Black Elk had probably heard of the success *Oyate* writers such as Dr. Charles A. Eastman and Gertrude Bonnin were experiencing in transmitting traditional *Oyate* stories and ideas to the wider world.[1] Is it too outrageous to speculate that Black Elk understood the potential, and lasting, impact of a story with literary value as opposed to one collected by an anthropologist? Was Black Elk consciously looking for a larger audience and a more influential transmitting medium, recognizing the power of the written word because of his knowledge of the Bible's power given Christianity's scope around the world?

Black Elk was, after all, a Catholic catechist who read and who preached from a Lakota Bible in Lakota to other Lakotas. He probably could have written his story in Lakota. But he was probably also aware of the widespread impact of written stories in English. He was also well traveled and had conversed with other men and women trained in spiritual, practical, and literary interpretations of the Bible. Although he had remained on the reservation, he also knew the reservation's structures—including the influences on younger generations by day schools and boarding schools. As an observant, intelligent man, he would have been able to discern—even through the filter of reservation living—what was important to Euro-Americans and what was becoming important to the Lakota.

He knew stories not only had to appear to be truthful for Euro-Americans to appreciate them, but also had to be well told. As Rice points out, Black Elk "must have known of the white man's need to have an absolute predetermined truth from his 30 years as a Catholic catechist. Stories of the oral traditions express the 'subjective' truth of the teller's inspiration which can be wrapped in many bundles of which those preserving the people's life are true, and those inflating the teller or flattering the listener are false" (1989, 47). Black Elk could have refrained from writing his story in Lakota because of concerns about being able to publish it, as well as the skepticism he would have encountered from being an Indian, and a seemingly presumptuous one from a Lakota perspective, who asserted that his story was important enough to tell in his own, alien

---

1. The term *Oyate*, which means "the People," will be used instead of the derogatory term *Sioux* to indicate the nation as a whole. References to Black Elk's specific culture, Lakota, will be couched in terms of the Oglala Lakota or simply the Lakota. The terms *American Indian* and *Euro-American*, both of which gloss over the plethora of cultures within them, will be used when more generalized references are needed to indicate culture.

to most publishers, language. Telling one's personal story without being invited to tell it was against Lakota custom.

Yet, Black Elk knew his story was important not only to himself, but also to his people, as well as to the world. He knew he had a good story to tell and he knew he could tell it well. The literary value inherent in looking for a believable, well-told story is not unique to Euro-Americans, and it is presumptuous to assume it is. Charles Eastman's reverent descriptions of famed storyteller Smokey Day,[2] and Ella Deloria's vivid descriptions of the effect a mesmerizing storyteller, Woyaka, has on his audience (1988, 50–57), as well as Waterlily's ability to captivate her children with tales (82–83), demonstrate the *Oyate* appreciation of a story well told.

As James Clifford points out, many ethnographers have observed methods, from blatant to subtle, by which "their research was directed or circumscribed by their informants" (1988, 44), so "that indigenous control over knowledge gained in the field can be considerable, and even determining" (45). It is highly plausible that Black Elk would reject one potential amanuensis for a better one—one who was not only a recognized poet, but also a man who was familiar with native ways of living and thinking (H. Neihardt 1995, 38). The facts that Neihardt could tell a good story and was familiar with Lakota culture would have become clear to Black Elk within the first hour or so of their meeting. A spiritual connection, if one really existed, would have been a bonus and would have helped reassure Black Elk that his decision to reveal his life story, and his sacred vision, to this particular person was the right choice.

Although many critics acknowledge Black Elk's communal efforts in telling his stories to Neihardt, most dismiss Neihardt's initial pursuit and final gathering of Black Elk's stories as only those of a Westerner trying to pin down, for his own purposes, an individual's life story. However, Neihardt did not set out to preserve Black Elk's story, but to gather information on the Messiah movement for his epic poem *A Cycle of the West*. There is ample evidence that he, too, knew a good story when he heard one and knew the potential for a good book when he found one (H. Neihardt 1995, 18).

2. See *Indian Boyhood* (1902), pp. 115–53, and all of *Wigwam Evenings: Sioux Folk Tales Retold* (1990).

Perhaps one reason Black Elk felt a kinship with Neihardt was because Neihardt spoke a kind of ritual language, stemming from a trained aesthetic appreciation for language that Black Elk recognized, something like the *hanbloglaka* (the term Black Elk used to describe Neihardt's mission to be an epic poet) used by those interpreting visions, in which Black Elk was trained. Both men, then, were trained with particular, perhaps similar, aesthetic concerns for language. Like the *Oyate* ritual language, Euro-American literary terms are not standardized, "but . . . contain some lexical items which [are] mutually intelligible between" those trained to use it (W. Powers 1975, 65). William K. Powers tells us that Lakota "sacred persons were distinguishable from the common people not only by their ability to interpret sacred knowledge," just as literary scholars interpret texts, but also "by their ability to communicate . . . in a special language unintelligible to the uninitiated . . . although [there is] no evidence that there was a conscious attempt by sacred persons to exclude common people from sacred discourse" (64), which can also be said, for the most part, about literary scholarship. Perhaps it was Neihardt's Euro-American literary training that prepared him for his being able to speak as one *wakan* man to another in something like *Oyate wakan* language.

Regardless of his intentions, many critics see Neihardt's motivations as purely Western and Black Elk's as purely Indian. Albert Stone, for instance, sees Black Elk's culture as clearly Indian, meaning communal, and Neihardt's as Western, meaning individually driven (1982a, 158)—believing Neihardt "surrendered himself to his Indian subject" (157–58). H. David Brumble sees *Black Elk Speaks* as a product of two personalities and two cultures (1988, 12) and only allows that an Indian is capable of conceiving of more than one self—one tribal, one individual—after the influences of Euro-American autobiography become familiar to them (146). Arnold Krupat believes, simultaneously, that Indian writers must suppress their communal natures to write (1989, 134), but that they find it impossible to suppress those other (communal) voices completely (145). David Murray asserts that *Black Elk Speaks* "blends the historical and the spiritual to present a moving account of a world-view in which all aspects of existence are integrated into a whole but which seems ultimately powerless to present the remorseless disintegrating forces of white civilization. This gives Black Elk's account an epic sweep and grandeur untypical of autobiographies, in that the individual becomes almost incidental, even though fully realized and human" (1991, 71). For most of these scholars, cultural differences simply get in the way of examining Indian as-told-to narratives, so that they turn out to be something exotic and foreign, instead of the examples to the world that every autobiography can be. All writers, Western or not, speak to audiences. Autobiographers pass on their lives—which have been touched by so many others that they actually reveal multiple voices and, often, points of view, in repassing through their life stories—to a larger community.

The modernists were not the first writers to utilize polyvocal narratives, nor were they the first to intermix "primitive" rituals and symbols into more familiar literary structures. But they were the first group of writers to advocate drawing on the "more primitive" aspects of our cultures—from T. S. Eliot's drawing on symbolism from Jesse Weston's *From Ritual to Romance* to a plethora of writers who "reached into the presence of the past and reinvented the Indian at the heart of this continent's humanity [so that] the resurrected noble savage, reduced by a factor of sixteen since 1492, would rise above the ruins of anarchic Manifest Destiny on literary wings" (Lincoln 1991, xvii). *Black Elk Speaks*, then, is the quintessential modernist text: mixed narratives in experimental combinations—playlike structures based on corroborative speakers to create polyvocal narratives next to poetry and chants, dramatic monologue, sacred symbolism, mythology, and ritual, with several drawings inserted for clarity and milieu. Yet, whereas the intermixture of narratives and the use of sacred symbols and myths—"the quintessential forms of man's expression and interpretation of himself and his experience" (May 1960, 13 n)—was a way for modernists to revitalize the power of their writings, for Black Elk it was a fulfillment of his social and sacred responsibilities.

Black Elk Speaks has similarities to his *Oyate* predecessors' works. Like the other writers' autobiographical works, *Black Elk Speaks* is largely chronological. And, like the other life stories, it contains chosen glimpses of Black Elk's life intermingled with information about general *Oyate* history. This interstitial quality, wherein the *Oyate* writers who are products of both cultures freely draw from both cultures, is strongly evident in all their works—from Eastman's *Indian Boyhood* to Ella Deloria's *Dakota Texts*.

In a more complex manner than the other writers probably encountered,[3] Black Elk and Neihardt's textual choices involved at least five levels. First, Black Elk had the visions that Black Road, the shaman who first introduced Black Elk to the world of *wakan* language and images, interpreted. Although the symbols in Black Elk's vision were undoubtedly common Lakota images/icons, making his vision similar to others, such as White Bull's half a century earlier, the events in the vision were different enough to evoke a particular mission for Black Elk (DeMallie 1984a, 85). The vision, as commonly held by the Lakota, specifies directions or obligations the seer must follow or suffer the consequences for his inaction. Before Black Elk told his vision to Black Road, he lived in constant fear of the Thunder Beings and told Neihardt, "I knew all the time I had something to do but I couldn't figure out what it was that I was to do that I didn't do" (213). Black Elk could not act without Black Road imparting his *wakan* knowledge and interpreting the vision's meaning for the younger man.

Second, Black Elk chose Neihardt, "with the same sense of mission and awareness of the permanency of the white man's records," as his traditional spiritual successor, just as "he would have passed his spiritual knowledge by word of mouth to a younger man of the tribe" (Holly 1979, 121), in effect controlling " 'the use of sacred knowledge by restricting its use to responsible parties bound by the ties of kinship, discipleship, and religious obligation' " (Rice 1989, 27). What has largely been ignored about Black Elk's choice of transmission is the fact that he chose his son Ben to be the interpreter. Ben, who does in part become a successor to Black Elk's sacred duties (Holler 1995, 32; H. Neihardt 1995, 114), would have been the natural selection as Black Elk's traditional spiritual protégé. Perhaps one possible reason Black Elk seizes the opportunity to tell his story to Neihardt is because Ben is readily available to act as translator. Perhaps be-

---

3. How much control individual Indians had in the production of their books has been a point of contention concerning the works' "authenticity." "As-told-to narratives" are often regarded as less than "authentic," with some critics going out of their way to give credit to Euro-American "amanuenses" who do not deserve such credit. So, here I admit I am discounting arguments that Elaine Goodale Eastman had more than an editing role in Charles's books, because there is no proof Elaine did more than type Charles's manuscripts (see pp. 61–66 of my dissertation, "Examples for the World"). There is little substantial proof, as well, that E. A. Brininstook, Clyde Champion, and Prof. Melvin Gilmore gave Luther Standing Bear more than editing assistance.

cause of the ongoing government prohibition of traditional religious practices, and perhaps because of the possibility that Ben's acculturation into Christian attitudes would have made Black Elk concerned that Ben would refuse the obligation of such succession, Black Elk realized that an opportunity had come for him to transmit his knowledge, almost surreptitiously, to his son.

We must remember that Ben was present during all the interviews, dances, and ceremonies performed by Black Elk for Neihardt in the 1930s. Even if Ben did not embrace all of his father's vision or the traditional Lakota beliefs imparted to him during the interviews, he was almost certainly impressed with them (H. Neihardt 1995, 53). By interpreting through Ben, Black Elk maintains the Lakota ritual of using oral tradition to pass down sacred knowledge; even if Neihardt were to get it wrong, Ben would remember.

We must also remember that, for cultures based largely on oral traditions, the *performance* of the text is its publication. Black Elk, for his part, really needed nothing more than a chance to perform his duties and pass on his vision to the safekeeping of the next generation.

Third, Black Elk decided what to reveal, even when answering direct questions from Neihardt, using his "intuitive selection of significant memories . . . not [as] a factually accurate 'history' but storytelling in the same sense that a fiction writer purifies, sweats away irrelevance to tell a story that is good as well as true" (Rice 1989, 33). Repeatedly, Hilda Neihardt emphasizes that even Ben and Standing Bear had not previously heard all of Black Elk's vision (1995, 36, 50). Although there were parts of his life Black Elk chose not to mention, such as details of his life as a Catholic, everything he tells demonstrates the intricate ties of religion and life to the traditional Lakota.

Fourth, Neihardt clarified wording and meaning through repetition of the ideas that were then verified by Black Elk after Ben countertranslated the English back into Lakota. Although undoubtedly tedious, the repetitious countertranslating demonstrated to Black Elk that Neihardt really did want to understand what Black Elk was telling him. As observant as Black Elk surely was, he probably also noted the kinds of information that most struck Neihardt's attention. Ultimately, both Black Elk and Neihardt placed enormous trust in Ben to be as accurate in his translations as possible.

And fifth, Neihardt chose what parts of the stories to include in the book and how to arrange them with, according to DeMallie, a serious attempt at retaining the already musical (a literary quality) and authoritative elements of Black Elk's words (1984a, 51–52). There was probably also some additional editing on the part of the publishers. It is important to emphasize that Black Elk, despite Neihardt's intervention in selecting, organizing, and emphasizing, was responsible for the choice of most of the book's content. In fact, Neihardt did an excellent job of melding Western lyricism with *Oyate* literary traditions, striking a balance between Euro-American and *Oyate* literary traditions that parallels Black Elk's balance between Catholicism and traditional Lakota religion.

Although Neihardt does trim material and consolidate phrases for clarity, he seems to give in to the temptation to make Black Elk an important figure, as Charles Eastman and Luther Standing Bear both try to do for themselves, by making him appear more influential than he probably really was. As a result, he sometimes takes Black Elk's words literally. For instance, when Black Elk relates his first vision from Ghost Dancing, he describes two men he meets in a land of plenty. In *Black Elk Speaks,* the *hanbloglaka* passage reads: " 'We will give you something that you should carry back to your people, and with it they shall come to see their loved ones.' I knew it was the way their holy shirts were made that they wanted me to take back. . . . [W]hat I brought back was the memory of the holy shirts the two men wore. . . . So the next day I made ghost shirts all day long and painted them in the sacred manner of my vision" (J. Neihardt 1979, 243). The transcripts from the interviews indicate that the day before this dance, Black Elk prepared himself to join the Ghost Dancing, of which he had been skeptical to this point, by dressing "in the sacred clothes" (DeMallie 1984a, 259). During his vision, the transcripts read, "I could see two men coming toward me. They were dressed with ghost shirts *like I was dressed.* . . . what I brought back was the memory of what they had shown me and I was to make an exact copy of it. *This* ghost shirt was to be used always in the ghost dances. So I started the ghost shirt. . . . I made the first two shirts according to what I saw in the vision. . . . I worked all day making shirts. . . . I wanted all the people to know the facts of this vision" (emphasis mine; DeMallie 1984a, 261–62). Did Black Elk begin the *idea* of wearing the ghost shirts, or did he start this one particular design of the ghost shirt?

DeMallie cites James Mooney's reference to the first recorded Euro-American sighting of the ghost shirts, wherein a schoolteacher claims a woman, Return from Scout's wife, created them—shirts for the men, dresses for the women—after she saw them in a vision (Mooney 1973, 916). To explain the different accounts, DeMallie merely speculates that "it seems likely that several of the ghost dancers had had visions relating to sacred regalia for the ceremony" (1984a, 262 n. 9). It is possible that both visions, Black Elk's and Return from Scout's wife's, were embellishments on the sacred clothing, which Black Elk mentions having put on to prepare for his first participation in the dance, already being worn by the ghost dancers. In any event, Black Elk's recollection of his initial participation in the dancing, soon after which he designed his particular ghost shirts, happened in the spring of 1890, and the schoolteacher reported that Return from Scout's wife had had her vision of them in October 1890. Black Elk could have been the original instigator of the ghost shirt phase of the Ghost Dance religion.

Mooney has a more plausible explanation, however. He notes that "the protective idea in connection with the ghost shirt does not seem to be aboriginal. The Indian warrior habitually went into battle naked above the waist" so that "the warrior should be as free and unencumbered in movement as possible. The so-called 'war shirt' was worn chiefly in ceremonial dress parades and only rarely on the warpath." Mooney believes that the ghost shirt originated in the same area of the country that the Ghost Dance religion did, so that the garment "may have been suggested by the 'endowment robe' of the Mormons, a seamless garment of white muslin adorned with symbolic figures, which is worn by their initiates as the most sacred badge of their faith, and by many of the believers is supposed to render the wearer invulnerable" (1973, 790). He points out as well that only the *Oyate* attached war connotations to the shirts, calling them bulletproof, whereas other tribes either wore them as peace symbols or forsook wearing them because of the connotations of war that developed with the ghost shirts after the *Oyate* began using them (791).

Neihardt made the choice to emphasize the idea that Black Elk was the originator of the idea of the ghost shirts. But Neihardt makes another textual choice, which had to be more difficult, about the ghost shirts. Later, when Black Elk speaks of the Wounded Knee massacre, the transcripts show graphically how the shaman believed in the bulletproof nature of his shirt, and his sacred bow, which is never pointed out as a bullet-proofing device in *Black Elk Speaks*. Neihardt had to ask himself if a Euro-American audience would believe Black Elk's statement that, as Black Elk tells it in the transcripts: "I could feel the bullets hitting me but I was bullet proof. I had to hang on to my horse to keep the bullets from knocking me off. I had the sacred bow with me. . . . I had to hold my bow in front of me in the air to be bullet-proof but just as I had gotten over the hill after completing my charge, I let my bow down and I could feel some bullets passing through my ghost dance shirt near my hip" (DeMallie 1984a, 273–74). Although Neihardt mentions the bow, he eliminates Black Elk's connection with its ability to make him bulletproof, eliminating altogether Black Elk's stated belief that the sacred things he did made him invulnerable to bullets, making the event sound more like luck than sacred power: "I just held the sacred bow out in front of me with my right hand. The bullets did not hit us at all" (J. Neihardt 1979, 258).

Neihardt does the opposite with Black Elk's wounding. He makes it more dramatic and supplies information earlier in the description of the event than Black Elk does in the transcripts. Neihardt's version, clearer than Black Elk's, yet still relating to the sacred, says, "All this time the bullets were buzzing around me and I was not touched. I was not even afraid. It was like being in a dream about shooting. But just as I had reached the very top of the hill, suddenly it was like waking up, and I was afraid. I dropped my arms and quit making the goose cry. Just as I did this, I felt something strike my belt as though some one had hit me there with the back of an ax. I nearly fell out of my saddle, but I managed to hold on, and rode over the hill" (1979, 266). The more repetitive, clearly more oral version in the transcripts reads, "as I fled toward the hill I could hear the bullets hitting my clothes. Then something hit me on the belt on the right side. I reeled on my horse and rode on over the hill. . . . I should have kept on coming like that with my hands up. I was in fear and had forgotten my power. I had forgotten to make the goose sound there and to keep my hands up. I doubted my power right there and I should have gone on imitating the goose with my power and I would have been bullet-proof. My doubt and my fear for the moment killed my power and during that moment I was shot" (DeMallie 1984a, 277–78). Notably, Neihardt maintains the accuracy of Black Elk's actions, but restructures the telling, eliminating repetition (an oral tradition for emphasis) and clarifying the consequences of the actions more immediately for a more readable (though perhaps less musical), dramatic effect. He has not changed the action in Black Elk's story, but he has, significantly, downplayed the sacred powers Black Elk believed in. This choice was probably very conscious on Neihardt's part, since his Euro-American audience probably would have labeled the sacred powers supernatural and unbelievable, or at least suspect.

Although Neihardt does not necessarily change facts, he changes emphasis often. For instance, Black Elk has second thoughts after he has mounted his horse and is on his way to investigate the shooting going on at Wounded Knee. Neihardt's version reads, "I took only my sacred bow, which was not made to shoot with; because I was a little in doubt about the Wanekia religion at that time, and I did not really want to kill anybody because of it" (1979, 264).

The transcript of Black Elk's words reads, "I just thought it over and I thought I should not fight. I doubted about this Messiah business and therefore it seemed that I should not fight for it, but anyway I was going because I had already decided to. If [I] turned back the people would think it funny, so I just decided to go anyway" (DeMallie 1984a, 272).

Neihardt's version reduces the strength of Black Elk's doubt because he probably felt a Euro-American audience would not believe any of the sacred things Black Elk mentions if he so easily doubts the Ghost Dance religion—which, after all, is more Christian than the Lakota traditional religion, thus might be more understandable and believable to the predominantly Christian readers (and might be one of many reasons so many non-Indians feared the Ghost Dance religion, which professed a Messiah). Neihardt might also think his readers would also "think it funny" if the book's "hero" was to be depicted as wishy-washy. Black Elk's decision not to fight, because he comes from a warrior society, would have cast aspersions on his manhood to many non-Indians, who probably rarely made clear or direct connections between war and spiritual callings. Neihardt's version, though not quite the truth, keeps Black Elk and his wavering belief in the Ghost Dance religion from looking foolish in Euro-American eyes for his deciding not to fight and for only carrying a ceremonial bow into a battle where army bullets are massacring his people.

Neihardt adheres strictly to other Lakota literary concerns, however. As Rice points out, "by having four narrators at the beginning, even though Black Elk assumes the place of principal narrator later on, the appropriately respectful invocation for spiritual assistance has been made" (1989, 43). Such a ritual is important to legitimize the strength and power asked for from *Wakan Tanka*, but also to demonstrate that Black Elk has "not forgotten any spirit or power or charm. Any slight omission might bring down on his luckless head the wrath of the incensed deity" (Daugherty 1927, 152).

The speakers strengthen Black Elk's powers as a storyteller, as well as corroborate the events of which he tells. In the same manner, Standing Bear's illustrations in the original edition, many of which are in color, act as corroborative information, serve to illustrate events in the visions that might not be easy for non-Indians to imagine, and demonstrate Lakota symbolism. They also supply the visual drama, albeit poorly, that would have been present in Black Elk's telling of and performance of the vision. The first color drawing, for instance, depicts the tipi made of a flaming rainbow, his adopted name for Neihardt, in which he met the six sitting Grandfathers, the powers of the world, all waiting to offer Black Elk some aspect of themselves to aid his and his people's spiritual needs.[4] Above the tipi, thunderclouds seethe with lightning and a spotted eagle and crow fly unharmed. Outside the tipi, the two spirit warriors, complete with eagle wings, stand guard, ready to take Black Elk, depicted as a small boy with a bow and arrow, on to the next phase of his vision (J. Neihardt 1979, following p. 22). The more difficult concept of the center of the earth, at Harney Peak in the Black Hills of South Dakota, is depicted in color as well. Harney Peak, a mingling of black, greys, and reds, supports Black Elk and a spotted eagle, representing the sky spirits and *Wakan Tanka*, on his sorrel pony. Above them fly geese from the North. Behind Black Elk, the *waga chun*, or the cottonwood tree, is budding out, symbolizing the rebirth of the *Oyate*'s powers. To the left, the Grandfather of the West sits astride a black horse with an arrow ready to strike like lightning, as Standing Bear's representation of the Thunder Beings. Directly below is the Grandfather of the South riding a buckskin and carrying the flowering

4. Traditionally, there are six Lakota grandparents—the sixth of which is Grandmother Earth. This perspective adds interesting questions: Did Black Elk change the gender of the sixth power because he associates himself with it and did not want to emasculate himself to a Euro-American audience? Is the change in gender significant at all?

stick, which he promised Black Elk would flower as the Lakota tree of life, once order has been restored. To the far right, the Grandfather of the North rides a bay pony and carries a rod with red particles spewing from it, possibly representing the winds and their healing powers. On the bottom right, the Grandfather of the East rides a sorrel pony and carries the sacred red stick that has a starlike red spot on the end whose fragments touch the "good red road" encircling the Black Hills known as *Ki Iyanka Ocanku*, the Sacred Race Track, representing the Sacred Hoop of the Lakota Nation (Goodman 1992, 7; J. Neihardt 1979, following p. 76).

Besides clarifying difficult images for non-Indian readers, Standing Bear also demonstrates traditional Lakota methods of recording stories, even showing the book's readers how to write the name Black Elk in pictograph, with a black elk's head above a man's head with a line descending from the elk to the man's mouth (J. Neihardt 1979, 195).

Standing Bear's illustrations, as well as Black Elk's and his corroborating friends' dramatic monologues, not only adhere to *Oyate* literary traditions—from traditional types of stories to traditional techniques such as repetition, indirection, and the use of personal sacred symbols—but also contribute to the modernist textual experiment that is *Black Elk Speaks*. The book unfolds almost like a play, with the drawings acting like stage directions, becoming substitutes for the dramatic elements of the vision's presentation as tribal ceremony. This playlike quality is as close as Neihardt can get to imitating Black Elk's performance. Neihardt's insertion of explanatory notes, such as the one on page 89 defining "coup," also add further dimension to the book. Prose mingles with poetry, as Black Elk reveals his sacred songs and chants, creating, as Rice puts it, "a 'bundle' of Lakota words which in turn become a bundle of English words" (1989, 47), or a modernist collage.

Through the melding of Lakota and Euro-American literary traditions, through the giving and comparing of traditional Lakota and Christian philosophies, and through a joining of purposes—both literary, both forms of cultural inheritance—Black Elk and John Neihardt strike an important and culturally significant balance in the rendering of *Black Elk Speaks* for a largely Euro-American audience. Black Elk could have assumed, observing firsthand the tremendous push for acculturation and assimilation of Indians, that the audience his book would reach would eventually come to include Indians. In essence, then, Black Elk used Neihardt to achieve his visionary mission to pass on the power of the earth, a.k.a. the Sixth Grandfather, who Black Elk had been told through his vision was himself, representing "the spirit of mankind" (DeMallie 1984a, 141), obliged to reach out to his people and to anyone else who was interested.

Louis Owens argues, in discussing American Indian novels, that the movement (which for him is an "irreversible metamorphosis") "from oral, communal literature to the written commodity of published work . . . represents a necessary 'desacralization' of traditional materials, a transformation that allows sacred materials—from ritual and myth—to move into a secular world of decontextualized 'art' " (1992, 11). To Owens, putting the sacred on paper is like the public viewing of traditional dances; it becomes hokey and less powerful, in essence stealing something from the communal culture.

Similarly, Kenneth Lincoln reports that "tribal peoples may be justifiably apprehensive of a written form of literature that fixes spiritual ideas. Peter Nabokov reminds us that the first Cherokee shamans to adapt Sequoyah's 1921 syllabary of eighty-six characters, the earliest known 'talking leaves' north of the Rio Grande, hid their transcriptions in trees and attics, fearful of exploitation. Their fears were not unfounded, given the many anthropological misunderstandings and abuses of sacred tribal materials" (1983, 25).

Black Elk was probably aware of these kinds of fears and attitudes toward revealing sacred information. There are many indications that Black Elk was rebuffed to some degree for having "conspired" with the outsider, Neihardt, in revealing information about what many assume to be purely Lakota or *Oyate* ideas. But, as Clyde Holler points out, "Each tribe had its own religion, its own origin myth, and its own stories. Each holy man had his own vision, which directed both his storytelling and his ritualizing. Each holy man tells the old stories differently, in accord with his vision" (1995, 213). Although many of the historical facts in *Black Elk Speaks* were events that happened to the *Oyate* as a group, the visions, the sacred part of the book, are all exclusively Black Elk's in the sense that he was the one who had them. Even in traditional Lakota belief, only Black Elk had the power to decide whether or not to pass on his vision and its powers. He also decided to whom to pass them.

Although he was supposed to use the power from the visions for the good of his people, he did not want to fulfill one particular command. In 1900, he was supposed to use "the soldier weed, a destructive power that would wipe out his enemies—men, women, and children," to create "such wholesale destruction, so he gave it all up and became a Catholic" (DeMallie 1984a, 14). A kind of reluctant "messiah," Black Elk was not willing to harm people with his "soldier weed" because he worried he would "probably have killed the women and children of the enemy," which for a trained Lakota warrior was the most despised part of warfare (DeMallie 1984a, 136).

Just as it is more probable that Black Elk envisioned the design for a particular set of ghost dance shirts, ones that came from the symbols of his own visions, it is also probable that Black Elk understood that his visions were exactly that, his visions. He was still able to exercise his prerogative as a Lakota—choice. He chose not to fulfill all of the mandates of his original vision. He recognized the dilemma of having followed the wrong vision during the Ghost Dancing because, as Neihardt said so eloquently for him, "It is hard to follow one great vision in this world of darkness and of many changing shadows. Among those shadows men get lost" (J. Neihardt 1979, 250). Black Elk chose to reveal those visions to a man in whom he had the confidence necessary to entrust them, even though he knows he has given away his power by giving away his vision (206).

Unfortunately, we will never know for certain if Black Elk was satisfied with how the book itself turned out, or with the influence it has had. I doubt he would have been surprised that the power of his words have lived on because Black Elk understood the power and the limits of language: "Of course there was very much in the vision that even I can not tell when I try hard, because very much of it was not for words. But I have told what can be told" (J. Neihardt 1979, 205). Although there is no record of Black Elk having said those exact words, Neihardt makes it abundantly clear that even his powers of writing are poor compared not only to the power of Black Elk's vision, but also to the power of Black Elk's telling and performance of it.

The other major modern *Oyate* writers, such as Charles Eastman, Gertrude Bonnin, Ella Deloria, and Luther Standing Bear, never returned to their native ways of living as completely or successfully as Nicholas Black Elk did. Perhaps because he was a full-blood and was never educated in a white man's school, he never felt the drive to compete with others for

fame and material things, a "lack" that kept him near Manderson, South
Dakota, his whole life. Perhaps because Black Elk owned a piece of his
people's sacred land, near what he continued to think of as the Center of
the World, Harney Peak, he chose to stay there. Perhaps because Black Elk
had more fully embraced both cultures' religions and found a productive
way to use both the power of conversion and the power of his visions for
his people, he remained closest to his home ground.

Eastman, Bonnin, Deloria, and Standing Bear all acted in various ways
and with different energies as advocates for Indian rights and to promote
understanding between races. But it was Black Elk who most effectively
spoke of and performed the act of passing on his knowledge to future generations—not necessarily to perfectly preserve his knowledge, but to see
that his medicine visions were available to his people, and could perhaps,
in the process, be effective in making life better for all. In a manner similar
to his writing *Oyate* predecessors, Black Elk's Lakota-trained literary
choices, combined with Neihardt's knowledge of Euro-American literary
traditions, produced a truly modern, interstitial literary text, and helped to
cap off a highly successful *Oyate* literary renaissance.

2

Speaking Through Others

Black Elk Speaks as Testimonial Literature

R. TODD WISE

The oft-quoted statement of Adorno that after Auschwitz there could be no more poetry presents an honest dilemma for today's Orpheus.[1] Because Auschwitz was understood as the purification and culmination of Western cultural development in Nazi Germany, and because art played a role in the objectifying tendencies of this evil atrocity, post-Auschwitz art forms would require new directions in order to survive as art. Poets today have attempted to address this crisis in similar ways by redeeming "speech from the silence of pain" and by illustrating "God's existence in the face of His apparent disappearance" (Forché 1993, 39). In the wake of Nietzsche's death of God and the technologies of death and war, today's Orpheus plays a lyre that is "without strings" and his song is a music from silence (Hassan 1971). The current "crisis" of Orpheus shares certain similarities with the historical context of *Black Elk Speaks*. Constructed forty years following a Lakota Auschwitz at Wounded Knee, Nicholas Black Elk of the Oglala Lakota surprised many with a word that seemingly erupted from silence. His speech appeared in 1932 following the aftermath of un-

This essay is a revised version of the author's essay "Native American Testimonio," which appeared in *Christianity and Literature* 45, no. 1 (1995) and is reprinted with permission.

1. Orpheus is the classical model of the poet. Although his prehistory has ties to shamanism, Orpheus has come to be associated with the art of producing harmony between man, animals, God, and nature. In Western tradition Orpheus appears in art, music, drama, and poetry. For a discussion of the Orpheus myth in comparison with Native American traditions, see Wise (1999).

speakable atrocities, both before and after Wounded Knee. This chapter explores ways in which Black Elk's literary efforts parallel recent attempts to "give voice" to those people silenced by tyranny and colonial oppression. Attention is directed to the specific arrangement of recorder and witness and how this approximates the self-conscious goals of the *testimonio*.

The fields of "Third World" and "postcolonial" literature are representative of the contemporary interest to resurrect a voice from those voices silenced by a dominant culture. As a largely antigeneric genre, the *testimonio* stands somewhere between literature and anthropology, offering an arrangement that paradoxically brings those people marginalized or decentered by writing back to the literary center (Gugelberger and Kearney 1991; Beverley 1993). As a method, the *testimonio* stresses the difference between the culturally "housed" and the "unhoused" *(unheimlich)* through an interview format that separates the speaker from the ethnographer/author who transcribes the narrative. The "unhoused" or "uncanny" or both voice serves as an actual "witness" or "testimony" to events that have occurred, but an institutionally based transcriber constructs the text for a foreign (and sometimes hostile) audience. The arrangement is a deliberate attempt to preserve the nomadic status of the "other" who speaks to the reader from a place exterior to the code or sign of the text.[2] *Testimonio* scholars have compared these speeches from silence to a rhizome.[3] In contrast to the Occidental metaphor of the acorn that births a forest (that is, academic historical culture), Georg M. Gugelberger in particular has embraced the idiomatic and ephemeral passing of the rhizome fruit or blossom as the poignant metaphor for a new genre. For Gugelberger, the *testimonio*'s power consists in its uncanny ability to resist the hegemonic pressures of traditional academic definitions of liter-

---

2. Deleuze suggests that nomads speak from orientations that are not constant. "Egypt had its Hyksos, Asia Minor its Hitites, China its Turco-Mongols . . . the Hebrews had their Habiru, the Germans, Celts, and Romans their Goths, the Arabs their Bedouins." Although the nomad is "inorganic" to academic colonial cultures, it is "more alive" precisely because it is "inorganic" (1993, 168).

3. In contrast to the traditional conceptions of the literary text in terms of "tree" logic or genealogy, Deleuze elevates the "antigenealogy" of the rhizome above a conservative and hierarchical model of tree and descent (1993, 28). Rhizomes are not connected by roots to other rhizomes, and they are periodically hidden from all view during a seasonal dormant period.

ature. Because a "housed" insider introduces an unhoused "Third World other," a witness is preserved in spite of the inherent colonialism of language and literature (Gugelberger and Kearney 1991, 5–6).

Most scholars have suggested that testimonial literature arose in the 1960s during the Cuban Revolution and in cultural spaces sometimes referred to as the Third World. Cuban Miguel Barnet's *Autobiography of a Runaway Slave* (1967) is probably the best-known example. Subsequently important expressions of testimonial witness developed in Bolivia, Guatemala, Nicaragua, El Salvador, Honduras, and more recently India and Africa. Academic critics such as Gugelberger, Kearney, and Beverley have documented how the *testimonio* arose as a way of giving written voice to the voiceless, often preliterate individuals who were powerless to speak under colonial oppression. Though one finds an occasional passing reference to earlier testimonial literature before this date, literary scholars have not given serious attention to literature that precedes the Cuban Revolution according to the terms of this newly emergent genre. This has been particularly evident with Native American literature on the North American continent prior to the 1960s. The lack of attention directed to "testimonial" works in North American aboriginal cultures may be related in part to the fact that works before the late 1960s have often been discounted as merely "*testimonio*-like" (Beverley 1993, 71).

Although authors have focused their attention on countries outside the North American continent, there are many examples of testimonial witness from the indigenous communities of North America. In their search for atrocities abroad, some North American writers may overlook the local foreign witness in their own geographic vicinity. Such a word may appear tucked away in a reservation ghetto or housed in a controlled multiculturalism, long since commodified for a self-serving capitalistic society. It may make sense for some to look far and away for a message on Western colonialism. This chapter seeks to counter such a perspective by establishing the literary productions of Black Elk as clear examples of testimonial literature before the "official" birth of this genre. Nicholas Black Elk was involved directly in at least two major works presented in the testimonial format of recorder and witness, *Black Elk Speaks* (1932) and *The Sacred Pipe* (1953) and in several productions after his death stemming from these original meetings. DeMallie's *Sixth Grandfather* (1984a) is a recent addition to Black Elk's original message. There are many similarities between the literature written from Black Elk's testimony and the current testimonial productions outside North America. However, the primary similarity is that Black Elk did not write one word of these texts.

Black Elk Through Others

A hallmark of the testimonial genre is that the decentered or marginalized other speaks as a representative of a larger social class or group. *I Rigoberta Menchú: An Indian Woman from Guatemala* is an acknowledged model of *testimonio* literature.[4] In contrast to what Hans Robert Jauss has identified as the *Ichform* of the self-made protagonist of the Western novel, the problematic hero who stands in antagonism against his community, Menchú speaks in the name of her people (Beverley 1993, 74). She is not the author in the sense of the narcissistic autobiography, but an exemplary member of a group. She self-consciously addresses the individualism of literary culture in her opening paragraph. "My story is the story of all poor Guatemalans. My personal experience is the reality of a whole people" (Menchú 1993, 1). Menchú, who was a proved social activist and winner of a Nobel Peace Prize, credentials her message as a *testimonio* with these remarks.

This work is not merely just another version of the "native informant" of ethnography, since Menchú consciously constructs the narrative that is to be told. She is the narrator speaking to an intellectual who is a representative from a separate cultural tradition. The reporter who writes the text is a "compiler" or "activator" who faithfully records through a

---

4. Not surprisingly, recent scholarship has challenged the accuracy of Menchú's account. As a representative from academic culture, David Stoll (1998) recently reported some discrepancies in Menchú's account uncovered through his interviews with Quiché people. In this article, I stress the unhoused or uncanny quality of the testimonial report. We can raise questions and answer back to the *testimonio* witness, but we should exercise some caution in trying to reconstruct an emic situation as an etic observer. Although not sui generis, the emic point of view of the *testimonio* is from a privileged standpoint. A foreign witness reports a gestalt of his or her own existential situation, and there is a poetic use of historical facts that shape the "voice" conveyed to the literary community. Black Elk and Menchú's accounts both preserve exemplary structures of historical experiences, which are not detached from their own subjectivity. Neither can we expect their witness to match the philosophy of the historical-critical method of a dominant culture, nor should we replace our attempts at etic reconstruction with the authentic perspective of the *testimonio*'s other.

process of slow questioning to check the accuracy of what is heard. The reporter and the *testimonio* narrator collaborate in a kind of solidarity, frequently for the explicit purpose of addressing social injustice. The compiler is not to "transform" language for "better" readability, but to stay faithful to the actual speech, leaving in repetitions. Although the order of narrative units is often arranged by the compiler, the actual narrative is wholly composed by the narrator. The "truth effect" of the arrangement produces an anonymity and a polyphony of other voices. As an entire literary genre, the *testimonio* is representative of numerous other "Indian" peoples with similar communal values, celebrating a broad movement of "peasant" resistance and international solidarity (Beverley 1993, 97).

Spivak has noted that narrators such as Rigoberta Menchú cannot be strictly regarded as subaltern, because the subaltern actually cannot address the literary canon. We are to take the more self-aware witness of persons such as Menchú as "organic intellectuals" who are familiar with the language and metonymy of the self in Western tradition. The *testimonio* narrator is often familiar enough with literature to be aware of textual violence. Frequently unknown to a dominant culture, the complicity of literature with forms of colonial and imperialist oppression are painfully known to the subaltern peoples who are able to read what has been written about them. Benjamin reflects this awareness when he writes that "there is no document of civilization which is not at the same time a document of barbarism" (1968, 256). From the maps created by the first European to define "America" to the plethora of texts that have overlaid native voices, many aboriginal persons have affirmed that it has been a distinctly European Adam who has thoroughly renamed all facets of literary reality.

Black Elk Speaks may not be recognized initially for its *testimonio* qualities. Arnold Krupat and Julian Rice have critiqued Neihardt's rendition of Black Elk as approximating Northrop Frye's definition of the Western romance hero, "superior in degree to other men" and, most particularly, "to his environment" (Rice 1991, 24). Indeed, it does appear that Black Elk addresses us in 1932 with a less obvious communal and representative voice. The following introduction is offered in the opening paragraph of *Black Elk Speaks:*

> My friend, I am going to tell you the story of my life, as you wish; and if it were only the story of my life I think I would not tell it; for what

is one man that he should make much of his winters, even when they
bend him like a heavy snow? So many other men have lived and shall live
that story, to be grass upon the hills.

It is the story of all life that is holy and is good to tell, and of us two-
leggeds sharing in it with the four-leggeds and the wings of the air and all
green things; for these are children of one mother and their father is one
Spirit. (J. Neihardt 1979, 1)

The clause "as you wish" refers to the factual arrangement between Black
Elk and John G. Neihardt, who requested the interview. Black Elk speaks
and Neihardt writes. Black Elk apparently alludes to other men, the "two-
leggeds," who have lived the same story as himself. Black Elk also explains
that his story is connected to others and to the living environment of
which he speaks (that is, the "grass," "four-leggeds," "air," "green
things," and "Spirit"). That Black Elk could not read English, that no
texts are cited by him, and that he speaks for others through an ethnographer all signal the "*testimonio*-like" dimensions of his narrative. What
might be missing, however, upon first glance is that the "other men" reflected by Black Elk's account are his own Lakota people. A reader unfamiliar with the concerns of the testimonial genre may wonder whether
Black Elk is speaking for "other" people who are not Lakota or whether he
is alluding to a universal "human" other. Because DeMallie has noted that
the above paragraph is actually Neihardt's rendition of what Black Elk
might have said but never did, we may need to look more closely into
Black Elk's point of reference.

Recent writings on *Black Elk Speaks* draw attention to the universalizing interpretations of Black Elk's spoken testimony. Raymond J. DeMallie
and Julian Rice have both pointed to a "Platonizing" of certain aspects of
Black Elk's actual speech. Rice, drawing from DeMallie's earlier analysis of
the verbatim transcripts and of Neihardt's edited text, shows clear indications that Black Elk's orientation in a specific ethnic context was "univer-
salized" to speak to "everyman" or a "common human spirit." Rice
critiques Neihardt for an "ethnocidal" tendency at certain key junctures in
Black Elk Speaks. Pointing to Neihardt's own stance as an unabashed lover
of German romantic poetry and professor of literature at the University of
Nebraska, Rice argues that Neihardt's understanding of Black Elk's
Lakota orientation was affected by his interest in transcendentalism. Rice

notes this passage from *Black Elk Speaks:* "Crazy Horse dreamed and went into the world where there is nothing but the spirits of all things. That is the real world that is behind this one, and everything we see here is something like a shadow from that world" (Rice 1991, 27; J. Neihardt 1979, 85). DeMallie has pointed out that this was Neihardt's embellishment and was not something Black Elk or a Lakota would actually say (1984a, 51, 77). The well known belief of Plato that the everyday world is a copy of archetypal Forms seems to loom behind such a statement. Rice clarifies that the Lakota's relationship to the other world is parallel to the everyday, that the goal is to embody spiritual power and not to encourage a permanent separation from it.[5]

Rice further states that Neihardt's emphasis as a Christian poet may also indicate a cultural bias in favor of a Christian tradition of physical expansion in the name of God (that is, Manifest Destiny). This might be deduced from a position Neihardt took in *The Song of the Messiah,* where the Messiah movement was pictured as a benevolent transition to Christian enlightenment. In *The Divine Enchantment,* Neihardt finds analogies of Hindu to Christian cultures, but notes that such parallels are intended to show the greater maturity of Christianity (J. Neihardt 1900; Rice 1991, 22). Neihardt's writings may have embellished the parallels of other religious perspectives, as in the case of Black Elk, in order to highlight the greater maturity of the Christian faith. This background may explain some of Neihardt's interest in the Black Elk project, as well as the historical criticism offered by scholars such as Rice for his periodically not acknowledging the ethnicity of Black Elk's narrative.

A further consideration for a less explicit presentation of Black Elk's difference as an "unhoused" other has to be that neither Neihardt nor Black Elk were writing/speaking to the specifications of any new "testimonial genre" or to the theoretical biases that have shaped its historical concerns. Matters that are now typical of testimonial literature, such as the preservation of ethnic distinctiveness in order to discover the oppression

---

5. The difference between literature and ritual may play into this discussion. Neihardt, as a literary man, may not have had training in or awareness of ritual process. Hilda Neihardt intimates that he had a unusual reluctance to dance (1995, 49, 87). The involvement in ritual experience and the embodiment of spiritual power has a hermeneutical vantage point all its own, that is, "somatic knowing" (Laeuchli 1992).

of a particular people, were less known or valued during the construction of *Black Elk Speaks* in the 1930s. As a product of his era, Neihardt may have lacked the awareness and specific focus of the later testimonial ethnographers. Clifford confirms this tendency through the history of ethnography in general. Whereas earlier ethnographers were participant observers who carried away a fixed text for an expert interpretation, ethnographers today stress that every discourse is linked to a specific context and that every use of "I" presupposes a "you." Because ethnographic writing is never completely free of the shared perspective of all language events, there is a more self-conscious attempt by contemporary ethnographers to directly quote rather than transform the language of the other. Neihardt admits that he "transformed" the language of Black Elk at several points, and DeMallie has identified the significant areas (DeMallie 1984a, 52–58). Testimonials after 1970 are in general more self-conscious about contextualization, to prevent objectifying a piece of dialogue for a later misapplication, and attempt to remain faithful to the precise wording of the narrator.

Although the opening remarks attributed to Black Elk may be read in a "universalist" or "transcendentalist" sense, the "many people" and the "two-leggeds" should be understood with Black Elk's Lakota purpose and context in mind. These are his people that he speaks for out of his own community and not any or every person. Black Elk states "You have heard what I have said about *my people*" in the final portion of his interview with Neihardt (emphasis added; DeMallie 1984a, 293). He told Neihardt that he had been appointed by his "vision to be intercessor for my people . . . so it was up to me to do my utmost for my people and everything that I did not do for my people, it would be my fault—if my people should perish . . ." (294). Black Elk self-consciously distinguished his position and his people from the white man during the interviews. Prior to the coming of the white man, Black Elk stated that the "four leggeds and the wings of the earth and the mother earth were supposed to be relative-like and all three of us lived together on mother earth" (288). A transition from this picture of harmony takes place in the next paragraph of the interview where Black Elk states, "But from time to time the white man would come on us just like floods of water, covering every bit of land we had and probably someplace there is a little island where we were free to try to save our nation, but we couldn't do it. We were always leaving our lands and the flood devours the four-leggeds as they flee. When we get to the island the water is all around us and today I feel very sorry—I could just cry—to see my people in a muddy water, dirty with the bad acts of the white people" (289). Black Elk goes on to differentiate his position from that of the white man when he states, "I think there will be a great punishment for the whites in the future as a result of this" (289).

The universalizing tendency in *Black Elk Speaks* is not Lakota, according to DeMallie and Rice, because Lakota culture is based on a unification of mind, body, and environmental context. Lakota belief does not distinguish between abstract spirit and concrete matter, or between spirit and intellectual self. These are Western accruements, particularly post-Descartes (Yuasa 1987). There are no universal others, only the others who extend from his people. Black Elk speaks with the testimony of his people, not for himself alone but for the Lakota.[6] Although Black Elk's message can not ever be fully separated from Neihardt's presentation or from the specific context in which it arose, it is important to remember that he speaks to us momentarily at the margins, outside rugged Western individualism, unhoused and nomadic to literary culture.

Ethnic Distinctiveness and Testimonial Genre

The critical analyses by DeMallie and Rice raise fascinating questions about the historical validity of *Black Elk Speaks*. Has Black Elk's unique voice been replaced by a Western romanticism? Beverley has noted an immediate risk of integrating testimonial literature into the dominant canon by missing the radical difference presented in this literary mode. Pointing to the work *I Rigoberta Menchú* being placed on the required reading list at Stanford University, Gugelberger has also warned that the testimonial could become more "canon fodder" as a commodified monument for the "teaching machine." When testimonial literature becomes sanctioned by the academic "industry" as a familiar voice, it risks losing its rhizomatic

---

6. That Black Elk himself considered his vision relevant to other people outside his Lakota context is without question. What is certain is that Black Elk did not apply his vision to any "universal other," but to any specific persons who might take the time to listen to what he had said. Black Elk assumes throughout his meeting that others who are not Lakota would be able to understand what he is saying.

and unhoused qualities. "The goal for literature," writes Gugelberger, is "not to integrate Third World literary works into the canon, but to identify with the 'wretched of the earth' . . . to look into what is really going on in the world . . . to learn about our limitations" (1991, 506).

DeMallie and Rice's critique of Neihardt echo these concerns in their separate attempts to highlight the distinctive Lakota reference point of Black Elk. When the radical difference of the testimonial witness is ignored, colonization and harm continue through the sanctioning powers of academic intention. The *raison d'être* of the *testimonio*, on the other hand, is to give voice to the voiceless, as noted by Gugelberger and Kearney. Scholars of the *testimonio* have stressed the daunting risk incurred by jumping too quickly from idiosyncratic utterance to the "universals" of mainstream culture and perspective. Beverley rightly notes that testimonials need to be preserved first and foremost as "foreign agents," or "nomadic others," to the dominant literary code and canon (1993, 90). Several scholars argue that Neihardt's "Platonizing" may have contributed to a weakening of Black Elk's own *foreign* voice. Because how one reads a text is as important as what it says, we may wonder about the popularity of *Black Elk Speaks*. Has Black Elk's message become too institutionalized, too well known to be heard for its "uncanny" witness?

Critics should assume neither that more sophisticated and contemporary writers/ethnographers have surpassed Neihardt's allegedly "ethnocidal" tendencies when approaching the Third World subject, nor that more recent writings about Black Elk will not further obscure the confrontation of the "housed" with the "unhoused." It helps that Black Elk speaks to us through others, keeping us alert as we attempt to establish his position. Fredric Jameson has offered a guide to address the continual risk of losing the foreign subject of literary works such as the *testimonio* when he states that the "real is what hurts" (1981, 102). The testimonial militantly resists being read without a truthful or moral reference, and insists upon the acceptance of human otherness. It refuses to dismiss the "real" or the historical. There is the preservation of "you write what I speak"; there is the nomadic other who is outside the literary reference point; and there is the silence of what is not said. But, most important, there is the shared horror of real-life description that ultimately resists being reduced to literary representation alone. The postmodern reader must not only acknowledge signs and codes but also experience the clenched fist, the tight neck, and the sick feeling in the stomach when faced with a suffering other. This form of awareness helps to preserve Black Elk's unique message.

Black Elk and His Message

The testimonial narrator speaks from a place silenced by oppression. Testimonial literature in general arose in response to the inadequacy of existing forms to represent subordinate or subaltern peoples (Beverley 1993, 92). As with Menchú, Black Elk's voice appears historically within a largely hostile signifying system. Both Menchú and Black Elk were well aware of the futility of active military resistance against the dominant culture(s), even though they supported such actions at points. Several examples are given by each of their own personal misery and indignation following military resistance. While Menchú notes the killing of her mother, father, and brother, Black Elk describes several grim battles resulting in the death of loved ones. Although Black Elk participated in military activity during his early life, his attention at the time of *Black Elk Speaks* is to a different battlefield. The fight against colonialism had grown mostly away from military actions to the protection of the code and symbol in his living culture. Like most testimonial literature, Black Elk's literary efforts grew out of a Christian, mostly Roman Catholic, milieu, where the use of Christian metaphor, code, and symbol was frequently employed. Although Christianity, with its formal commitment to a "text" and tradition, is not indigenous to native cultures, acceptance and use of Christianity is frequently found in the testimonial witness.

For example, there is a similar involvement in Catholicism for both Menchú and Black Elk. Like Menchú, Black Elk professed himself to be a strong adherent to Christian belief and practice. Menchú and Black Elk were also each catechists in the Roman Catholic Church. Much more than passive members, both served as actual missionaries in the promotion of Catholic ritual and teaching. Their public and vocal adherence to Christian tenets presents a natural question with respect to their testimonials. Does an allegiance to Christianity diminish their status as "foreign agents" who stand outside the dominant literary culture, a trademark of the testimonial genre, particularly when Christianity is a part of the dominant culture? Does Menchú and Black Elk's Christianity betray their assimilation to dominant cultural codes and symbols?

Burgos-Debray evokes George Devereux's term "disassociative acculturation" in the opening of Menchú's work to describe her use of dominant cultural forms. Disassociative acculturation is "an attempt to revive the past by using techniques borrowed from the very culture one wishes to reject and free oneself from" (Menchú 1993, xvii). Menchú addresses the wrongs done to her people by the Spanish colonists, who "dishonored our ancestors' finest sons, and the most humble of them. And it is to honor these humble people that we must keep our secrets" (13). Additionally, Menchú informs us that the *ladinos,* or descendants of Spanish colonists, "exploit us, oppress us, and discriminate against us" (123). However, even in the midst of this oppression, Menchú does not fail to support the use of the same Bible and Catholic tradition that was an essential "weapon" of Spanish colonial rule against her people. Menchú not only goes against her people's tradition of speaking Spanish in order to use the colonizer's own language as a "weapon," but also employs the Bible, including its traditions and metaphors, as a "a weapon" against the dominant Christian culture (130–35). In addition, Menchú does not fail to identify the cause of her people with biblical heroes such as Judith, Moses, and David, and she willingly condones violence in the manner of the early church fathers through "just war" ethics. A particularly impressive application of the Bible occurs with her use of the figure of Judith. In this story the Israelites believe that Judith is a traitor until she proves her worth. By consorting with an enemy king and then cutting off his head, she encourages Israel and causes enemy troops to retreat. Menchú self-consciously uses signs and codes such as these, drawn from Christian sources, as weapons to protect her Quiché heritage and purpose.

Did Black Elk follow a similar example in his involvement with Catholicism? Recently, Black Elk's Catholicism has been touted by Michael F. Steltenkamp as pivotal to understanding Black Elk's own message, but with differing conclusions. His Christianity has been carefully debated by several writers. On the one hand, numerous witnesses and verbatim accounts suggest that Black Elk remained a devout Catholic from the time of his conversion in 1904 to his death in 1950. Steltenkamp points out that the promotion of Lakota belief and culture in *Black Elk Speaks* and *The Sacred Pipe* presents a distorted view of Black Elk, who was a devout Catholic for more than thirty years. The publication of these works came after years of Catholic belief and, by some reports, after he had facilitated some four hundred conversions in his capacity as a catechist. Several Jesuits who knew Black Elk as a churchman compared him to Saint Paul, who initially opposed the Church but became a zealous supporter of it (Enochs 1996, 80). The Jesuit fathers who had known and worked with Black Elk through the years were very much surprised that "old Nick," known by his baptized name of Nicholas, could have produced such a profound exposition of Lakota (that is, "pagan") beliefs. The emphasis Black Elk seems to have given in his literary works continues to cause "surprise" for many today. Enochs has recently laid blame for the nonmention of Black Elk's Christianity in *Black Elk Speaks* solely on Neihardt, "who provided a distorted view because he failed to show that Christianity had a great impact" (85). The two quid pro quo letters of 1934, constructed by Black Elk as a payment for extreme unction, appear to highlight a concern by Black Elk himself to be considered a sincere Catholic Christian (Vecsey 1997, 277–78). There have been many reactions from Christian individuals who would dismiss the Lakota religious emphasis of Black Elk's literary works as complete misrepresentation.

Such a position does not square with other accounts that indicate that Black Elk felt he had "made a mistake in rejecting [the old religious ways] for Christianity" near the end of his life (DeMallie 1984a, 72; Rice 1991, 8–9). Before passing away, Black Elk told his daughter, Lucy Looks Twice, that "The only thing I really believe is the pipe religion" (H. Neihardt 1995, 119). The views of Steltenkamp and Enochs are in contrast to that of Rice. Far from being an embellishment of Lakota belief, Rice charges that *Black Elk Speaks* is filled with Neihardt's "Christian platonizing."[7] Although Steltenkamp and Enochs stress that Black Elk was a bicultural Christian, Rice emphasizes that Black Elk spoke in his last years as a way of protecting Lakota culture but that this was effectively masked by Neihardt's editorial additions. Rice sees a contrast between "inner" belief and a mere sociofunctionalist involvement with Christianity (1991, 2). He concludes, "Drawing on a wide range of religious metaphors, some of them Christian, Black Elk spoke to protect the people" (153). Did Black Elk self-consciously use his Christian involvements to protect? Noting the Lakota nature of Black Elk's later testimonial works, particularly *The Sa-*

7. Rice states that *Black Elk Speaks* perhaps will be "relegated to the ranks of nineteenth century curios, reflecting white misconceptions of Indians" (1991, 14).

cred Pipe, DeMallie argued that Black Elk made a conversion of expedience to Catholicism (DeMallie 1984c, 15, 27, 58). DeMallie claims that the assault on tribalism had been unavoidable with the inundation of Christian missionaries on the reservation and that Black Elk went underground and hid his true intentions. DeMallie and Rice see Black Elk as using Christianity throughout his life in service of a more profound Lakota purpose. This use of disassociative acculturation would be a classic example, similar in some respects to the case of Menchú.

The perplexing relationship of Black Elk to his Catholicism allows no less than three alternatives for his Catholicism. He was either: a sincere Catholic who returned to Lakota religion after the Neihardt interviews; a consistently active and committed Catholic who never turned back; or an ingenious, syncretic Lakota-Christian (Rice 1991, 8). It may be that all these alternatives are partially true because there is development and nuance within the life of virtually any individual. Several recent authors have identified a bicultural and dual religious nature to Black Elk. Although Holler has described Black Elk as a "creative theologian" with a "theological bi-culturalism," I have previously pointed to the pragmatic goals of a "healer" who strove to stay in contact with his immediate environment and the psychic structures of an evolving community (Holler 1995; Wise 1995a). The great-granddaughter of Black Elk, Charlotte Black Elk, also supports the view of dual religious participation. She stated that Black Elk often "tricked" the priests into thinking he was a thorough convert, but that he also was a believing Catholic (Vecsey 1997, 278).

The dual religious stance of Black Elk as both a sincere Catholic and a sincere Lakota believer fits with many other *testimonio* witnesses, as in the case of Rigoberta Menchú. Did Black Elk, like Menchú, use his Catholic beliefs as a "weapon" in defense of his Lakota heritage? Although Black Elk's testimony could not be expected to carry the same clarity of intention as later *testimonio* narrators who have been influenced by a "postcolonial" literary perspective, his testimonial purpose is present just the same. His description of the "butchering at Wounded Knee" of "women and children and babies, who had never done any harm and were only trying to run away" (J. Neihardt 1979, 262; DeMallie 1984a, 35–36, 274–75), engenders the same disgust in the reader.[8] Although Black Elk was versed

---

8. DeMallie's report of Black Elk's phrasing carries its own impact. "I got up on the top [of] the hill and it was terrible! Soldiers were standing there mowing the women and

and pious enough to be accepted and appreciated as a catechist in the Catholic Church, remaining a devout Catholic by many reports for more than thirty years, he was also an astute articulator of Lakota religion. It is certain that both his Catholicism and his Lakota religion were matters of ultimate concern both before and after his literary testimony. It is also certain that he used these involvements to protect his people.

The essential similarity of *Black Elk Speaks* with later *testimonio* narratives would be an identification of his witness with social injustice, because social oppression is a mainspring of the *testimonio* genre. Was Black Elk's message a judicial witness? The historical context leading up to Black Elk's *testimonio* seems to leave little doubt that Black Elk's entire context was under duress. Some of the violence against his people is so foundational that it is necessary to be reminded of the wider historical context. From the very start, the "Requiremento," "Encomienda," the "Doctrine of Discovery," and "Manifest Destiny" were all used as legal justifications for Christian colonists' claims on indigenous lands and peoples of North and South America. As beginning legal doctrines, these texts profoundly shaped future governmental decisions in the United States. The case of *Johnson v. McIntosh* in 1823 is a chief example that established the ownership of reservations in the hands of the federal government and not of the Native Americans who inhabited them, setting a stage for the arrangement at Pine Ridge (Pommersheim 1995, 40–43).[9] Such federal decisions illus-

---

children down! [*There I stood and cried.*] So I decided that I must defend my people . . . I depended on my vision . . . I did all I could do to defend my people. It was hopeless. So I decided to take it just as it was. It was a butchering and I cried because I couldn't defend my people in time" (DeMallie 1984a, 36).

9. The three key decisions by order of appearance are *Johnson v. McIntosh*, *Cherokee Nation v. Georgia*, and *Fletcher v. Peck*. The first laid groundwork regarding title to the land. The title or deed to the land was placed by Marshall in the hands of the discovers, which merely placed a previous policy within federal legal practice. From this decision, federal law recognized that discovery gave exclusive rights to the land. From Marshall's view, Native Americans never had any independent natural law–based right to full sovereignty of American soil, because Marshall's entire legal framework was from the position of acquisition that was transferred from European powers to the United States during the Revolutionary War. The "Marshall Trilogy" legally established the right to title in the hands of the discover or conquer. In *Fletcher v. Peck*, Marshall proclaimed that "it has never been doubted that the United States, or the several States had a clear title to all the lands." To this day, the United States has legal title to all native lands, in part because of the *Cherokee Nation v. Georgia* decision that relegated tribal sovereignty to a mere "domestic dependent" status. In this way,

trate that the devastating "Christian/pagan" distinction was not merely a private belief, but was a foundational building block for both ecclesiastical and secular law. Williams has tracked a solid historical connection between the early "Christian Discovery" doctrines and the American legal restriction of native people to the Papal Bulls of the Roman Catholic Church. The Bull "Romanus Pontifex" sent by Pope Nicholas V in 1452 is an example. The Bull exhorts the king of Portugal to go to the western coast of Africa and "capture, conquer, and subjugate the Saracen [Muslims] and pagans, and other enemies of Christ wherever they exist, together with their kingdoms . . . and bring their persons into perpetual slavery" and to take all their possessions and their property (Ehler and Morrall 1967, 146–53).[10] This position of the fifteenth-century Church was a foundational premise for the Christian voyagers in the treatment of Indians, setting in place a legal basis for later court decisions (R. Williams 1990, 71). The Protestant colonialists carried similar legal precedents extending from the Crusades, where the Christian warrior-knight was supplanted by the Christian merchant-adventurer in the westward expansion (130).

The encroachment of ecclesia, of "settlers," and of American governmental rule had specific consequences during Black Elk's own lifetime. The early German Jesuits' initial interest in the Lakota was to explicitly alter the fundamental conditions of Lakota existence in order to "graft" or apply Christianity (Vecsey 1997, 265–70). Although Chief Red Cloud embraced the Catholic presence early, it was in part to maintain peaceful relationships with non-Indian families and the growing mixed-blood descendants (265–66). The placement of missionary outlets on Pine Ridge carried its own brand of coercion. The missionaries located on Pine Ridge consciously worked with the federal government at points to undermine

---

European discovery doctrines were permanently etched in American legal practices (R. Williams 1990, 312–17).

10. It is important to contextualize the "Romanus Pontifex" as a response to the brutal treatment and threat given by the Muslims that preceded the fall of Constantinople in 1453. It is also important, however, to not let the historical context of the Bull overshadow a moral and judicial evaluation. Another Bull titled "Inter Caetera Divinae" of Pope Alexander VI in 1493 is of interest, because it built on the policy set forth in the "Romanus Pontifex." This Bull transferred the imperialistic policies set forth on Western Africa by Pope Nicholas V to the Americas, effectively blessing from the "plentitude of Apostolic power" the "conquering" of "pagan" Native America.

traditional Lakota relations from the beginning. The Church forbade the "drum, the flute, the pumpkin-shells and sacred dances and songs" (including the Sun Dance!) (269). Although many Lakota natives valued the helpful aspects of Christian mission, and have critiqued one-sided "mission bashing" as too simplistic, there are examples of the Church's role in contributing to a cultural oppression. The priests encouraged strict and "severe" punishment of the children who would return to traditional ways, and embraced a boarding-school policy that separated children from their parents (288–90).[11] Although the Catholic Church accepted many catechists, the Lakota men were thought to be too "unstable" for the priesthood. To date, the Catholic Church has ordained one Lakota to the priesthood in its one hundred–plus years of missionary contact—a Brulé Lakota named C. P. Jordan. They have not produced a single Oglala Lakota priest (276).

There were other influences not directly related to the Church setting. Although the encroaching settlers nearly extinguished the buffalo in the mid-1880s, the sacred animal and main staple for the Lakota, the U.S. government applied binding legal contracts that were not able to be honored. The loss of *Paha Sapa* (the Black Hills) to the Lakota, the Garden of Eden or birth place of the first man and woman in Lakota belief, came when the federal government unlawfully reneged on the 1868 treaty. In addition, the governmental ban on the Sun Dance, the most sacred of Lakota religious practices, began in 1883 and extended throughout Black Elk's lifetime. With these and a host of other oppressive conditions and events (such as Wounded Knee), is it really difficult to imagine that Black Elk spoke under conditions of oppression and social injustice?

In retrospect, it is somewhat miraculous that his message was sent out at all. The Great Depression produced a unique situation during the time of Black Elk's interviews. The shock of trying to economically survive created a new influence for the Native American. Roosevelt's New Deal pol-

---

11. In *Other People's Children: Cultural Conflict in the Classroom* (1995), Lisa Delpit documents the disability incurred by children who are not allowed to learn through their own language and culture. A learning style that does not fit with the neurolinguistic patterns of children contributes to emotional and learning deficits. Research supports teaching children first about their own culture. Material that is taught from outside their culture should also be taught first in their own language.

icy of attempting to stimulate the economy by investing federal money
translated into the "Indian New Deal" under John Collier of the Bureau
of Indian Affairs. Following on the coattails of the Merriam Report
(1928), which laid blame for the deplorable reservation conditions at the
feet of federal allotment policy, Collier was able to stimulate native traditions and religious beliefs with federal dollars on a platform of "cultural
pluralism" (Olson and Wilson 1986, 101). This turn of events was truly
remarkable in light of the earlier enforced Christian farmer model of the
Dawes Severalty Act. Although later critiqued for "paternalism," the gov-
ernmentally enforced promotion of native practices was undoubtedly felt
by Black Elk in 1932, creating a less threatening context. Collier's efforts
were short-lived, however, in the wake of World War II, when cultural pluralism sounded "socialistic" and "unpatriotic" to the public and un-
Christian to the Church (131*ff.*).

Understanding how Black Elk's "truth" telling came under cultural
duress helps us to see how his literary efforts were attempts of social activism. Another way of grasping this aspect is to see Black Elk's efforts as a
confession. Gallegher recently identified a historical relation of the *testimonio* genre to the ritual of confession and the history of confessional literature. The literary genre of confession has significant ties to Western
Christian religious practices that include a testimony, such as a historic
confession or creed, and an admission, as in the act of admitting guilt
(1995, 97). Postmodern writers have stressed the relationship of power in
the confessing act. In his *History of Sexuality,* Foucault stated that all narrative is an attempt to gain mastery over the reader through a deferred closure. He also stated that confessions give the confessor some power over
those people who hear the confession. By giving the "truth" about oneself, there is a power relationship established between the confessor and
his audience. When we hear and sympathize with Black Elk, for example,
we are caught in a sense by his text. His testimony bears some similarities
to a confession for us, through Neihardt. Not only does he tell us that he
is an "intercessor for my people" (DeMallie 1984a, 294), he expresses to
us some of his own sorrow or guilt, that he had "fallen away thus causing
the tree never to bloom again" (295). A power relationship is established
for the reader. We are attracted not only by his sense of guilt, shame, or
sorrow, but also by our own as extensions of a cultural drama that has contributed to the torment of a people. Black Elk in fact helps us on this as-

pect when he confesses a dominant culture guilt. "We [Lakota] made a mistake when we tried to get along with the whites. We tried to love them as we did ourselves. On account of this we are now in misery" (290).

Nietzsche raised an issue regarding self-deception when we question a subject about himself. He asked, how are we to know that these reporters are not interpreting themselves falsely for their own benefit? (1967, 272). Gallegher wrote that it is actually the confessional element in relation to a community that argues against deception. Testimonies and confessions are spoken in reference to a community of others, presenting the confessor with the opportunity of speaking a "truth." That it is a contextual truth presented in a specific setting to a specific audience and for a particular purpose defines and limits the "truth" shared.[12] Although Clyde Holler (1995) rightly argued against any sophisticated form of self-deception by Black Elk, it is also clear that Black Elk did not tell us everything about his life. Who could do that? Although we should not doubt that what he did tell us was a truthful and honest account, offering his word in reference to his community, we may wonder about what Black Elk did not choose to share. The practice of keeping a secret is in fact a chief characteristic of the *testimonio* production. In the concluding words to her own testimony, Menchú stated, "I'm still keeping secret what I think no one should know. Not even anthropologists or intellectuals, no matter how many books they have, can find out all our secrets" (1993, 247). Although Black Elk does not explicitly remind us of this rather obvious fact, his use of silence may help us to understand some of the discrepancy between the Neihardt interviews, the quid pro quo letters, and the Brown project. The usefulness of a secret as a boundary or protective device does not have to imply any form of deception and insincerity. Black Elk chooses to stress certain aspects of his life and not others, contextually shaping and defining the message he wants told.

This chapter highlights the genius of Black Elk as an activist for his people. His use of a literary method from the dominant culture is a brilliant cultural achievement for the Lakota, similar in many respects to Devereux's

12. For a discussion of some of the implications of confession, truth telling, and the Roman Catholic tradition, see Wise (1995b).

disassociative acculturation. Because Lakota culture evolved like any other culture, it is doubtful that his literary communication was intended to "reject" all dominant cultural forms, as with a strict use of disassociative acculturation. It is likely that Black Elk spoke to protect not a pristine "original" culture, but an evolving one. The early adaption of the horse culture, of non-native hair and clothing styles, and of Christianity are among many aspects in the changing cultural dynamic of the Lakota. Although his testimony does not carry the sharp, more self-conscious activism of more recent testimonies, there is a clear judicial witness. An originator and advocate in a time when there was no *testimonio* genre, Black Elk stayed true to his Great Vision by speaking in order to protect his people. Through the juxtaposition of the contemporary *testimonio* genre to Black Elk's literary efforts, this essay reveals a similar witness against dominant culture oppression that is familiar to "Third World" and "postcolonial" literature. Such similarities contribute to the solidarity among other indigenous communities in the pursuit of native rights, a mainstay of the testimonial literature.[13]

13. Efforts have been made in the last few years to increase solidarity between the natives of Guatemala and the Lakota of South Dakota. Alberto Orozco Ayquichi, a training and education official of the Guatemalan grassroots organization CONIC, recently spoke at the Sinte Gleska University and Oglala Lakota College. His trip to South Dakota was cosponsored by the South Dakota Peace and Justice organization (SDPJ) and by the Lakota Studies Department of Sinte Gleska University. His visit took him to the Cheyenne River, Rosebud, and Pine Ridge Reservations from October 30 to November 3, 1995. He came to educate "the indigenous people of Indian Country within the borders of South Dakota" about his Mayan culture and to learn more about the native life in South Dakota. In return, a solidarity trip to Guatemala by Lakota people was performed in the summer of 1996 by the SDPJ center of Porcupine, South Dakota.

3

Black Elk's Significance in American Culture

AMANDA PORTERFIELD

Thanks to the work of scholars represented in this book, we have come a long way in understanding the religious and historical significance of Nicholas Black Elk. Pointing to his "creative and courageous confrontation with Christianity and with the challenges of modernity," Clyde Holler called him "the greatest religious thinker yet produced by native North America." With regard to his specific contributions to Lakota religion, Holler emphasized Black Elk's leadership in two areas, the creation of "an authentic Lakota Christianity" and the revitalization of traditional Lakota religion. As a convert to Catholicism and a catechist in the Roman Catholic Church, Black Elk identified points of commonality between Christianity and Lakota religion and showed how Christianity could be embraced without sacrificing Lakota identity. As the principal visionary behind the modern revitalization of Lakota religion, Black Elk worked to reinvigorate the Sun Dance, and to reinstate it as the centerpiece of Lakota religion. Today, Lakota traditionalists follow his version of the Dance (Holler 1995, xix, 223).[1]

By enabling us to better appreciate Black Elk's place in Lakota religious history, the work of Holler and others also lays the groundwork for understanding Black Elk's significance in the larger contexts of American culture and American religious history. Without minimizing his significance as a Lakota religious leader, we can build on the work of these scholars as we begin to outline Black Elk's relationship to American culture, and his contribution to its transformation.

Many Americans without any ancestral ties to native tribes have incor-

---

1. Also see Rice 1991 and Steltenkamp 1993.

porated reverence for Native American teachings into their own religious lives through pilgrimages to contemporary Lakota Sun Dances that carry Black Elk's influence and, more commonly, through reading *Black Elk Speaks,* the popular rendition of Black Elk's life by the Nebraska poet John Neihardt, and *The Sacred Pipe,* Black Elk's interpretation of Lakota ritual as recounted to Joseph Epes Brown. Among the millions of people who have taken religious studies courses in U.S. colleges since the 1970s, *Black Elk Speaks* has been one of the most familiar and commonly read texts. It has played a crucial role in the burgeoning interest in native religions in the United States, and this interest has altered the face of mainstream religions, contributing to their "greening" with regard to concern for environmental issues, and to their respect for Native American people as authorities on the relationship between spiritual insight and attentiveness to the natural world.

Focusing on Black Elk as a religious authority within American culture, this essay points to long-standing cultural trends that prepared the way for acceptance of his authority. The essay also points to aspects of his authority that are new. The essay considers Black Elk's fame as a religious visionary in the context of deep-seated tendencies in American culture to regard the natural world as a vehicle for religious experience, and to regard Indians as noble savages who enjoy an original relationship with the spiritual powers of nature, free of the corruptions of civilization. The essay will also argue that, as an exemplar of environmental stewardship and ecospirituality, Black Elk has contributed significantly to the transformation of Native Americans from being religious outsiders to being religious authorities within American culture. Black Elk has functioned as a catalyst of a religious transformation in American culture in which romantic images of Indians have become insufficient and problematic, and in which Native Americans have themselves become religious experts and teachers.

In *Black Elk Speaks,* Neihardt viewed Black Elk as a tragic figure, and he treated the story of Black Elk's life as a description of a noble way of life that had vanished forever. Neihardt did not appreciate the tenacity of Black Elk's faith in Lakota religion, or take seriously his commitment to its future contribution to the world. He took Black Elk's story of having a vision as a child with absolute literalness, and assigned the relevance of that vision to a culture of the past. Neihardt never considered the possibility that Black Elk's vision developed over the course of his lifetime, or that telling the vision to Neihardt was a significant part of its development and realization. He never considered the stories Black Elk told him about the vision and its impact on the life of his people as a statement about the ongoing vitality of Lakota culture.

Neihardt's attitude toward Black Elk and his vision conformed to the perspective on Native American cultures that predominated in the 1930s, when Neihardt wrote *Black Elk Speaks*. In the early twentieth century, a new approach to the study of Native Americans took hold under the leadership of the German American Franz Boas. Boas and his influential students (including Ruth Benedict, Gladys Reichard, Elsie Clews Parsons, Frank Speck, and Alfred Kroeber) approached Native American societies as internally coherent cultural systems in which religion played a central role. Their emphasis on culture as a relative, internally coherent phenomenon marked a significant advance over anthropological theories prevailing at the turn of the century. These older theories presupposed normative concepts of culture as something one had more or less of (as in, "she is a highly cultured person") and involved racist arguments about the cranial structures of different peoples around the world that defended the supposed moral and intellectual superiority of Anglo-Saxon people.[2]

But though the cultural relativism of Boasian anthropology represented an important step forward, it carried certain romantic assumptions about tribal cultures that made it difficult to see them historically, and to recognize the complex relationships at work between cultural change and cultural vitality. Boas and his followers worked at recording the symbols of these cultural systems with a strong sense of urgency born of the belief that Native American cultures could not survive the onslaught of modern civilization, and were moving rapidly toward extinction. Like Neihardt, these anthropologists were far more interested in native cultures as they were presumed to have existed before contamination by Western culture than in culturally complicated lives of twentieth-century Native Americans, or in the creative efforts Native Americans made to work with the forces of Western society, to build bridges between their cultures and Western society, and to enable their cultures to survive and even flourish.

But even though Neihardt framed Black Elk's story in terms of his own romantic and tragic vision of the past, many aspects of the story are

2. See Stocking 1968, 1989, and 1996.

authentic. Over the course of numerous sittings in 1931, Black Elk described the events of his life to Neihardt, who had come to Black Elk seeking firsthand material about the old ways of the Lakota people, and about the Ghost Dance, a pan-Indian religious movement embraced by many Lakota people at the end of the nineteenth century. The stories that Black Elk produced for Neihardt were translated by Black Elk's son Ben, and recorded in shorthand by Neihardt's daughter Enid, who put her notes in chronological order and prepared a typescript for Neihardt's use (Holler 1995, 4).

Thus, *Black Elk Speaks* is not *Hiawatha*. In contrast to Longfellow's poem, which has only a tenuous basis in Native American reality, *Black Elk Speaks* is based on Black Elk's own account of his life. Moreover, the ongoing interpretive effort to disentangle the voices of Neihardt and Black Elk calls attention to Neihardt's romanticism and works to distinguish it from Black Elk's own perspective. Studying *Black Elk Speaks* today often involves a process of becoming aware of savagist preconceptions and sifting through them, as well as immersion in a Native American story.

Black Elk Speaks in the Context of American Culture since the 1960s

Some of the first steps in considering Black Elk's place within the larger context of American culture were taken by the anthropologist Alice Beck Kehoe, in *The Ghost Dance: Ethnohistory and Revitalization*. Kehoe discussed the role of the Ghost Dance in the 1890 massacre of Big Foot's band of Lakota people beside Wounded Knee Creek in South Dakota, and traced the legacy of this event into the twentieth century, focusing especially on the armed occupation of the Wounded Knee massacre site in 1973 by members of the American Indian Movement (AIM). Members of this Red Power group styled themselves as a new warrior society and brought together young Indians from different tribes in a struggle for Indian rights.

Black Elk's influence on AIM activists in the 1970s was considerable. Because many of the activists were raised in urban settings and knew little about the religious traditions of their ancestors, they turned to *Black Elk Speaks,* and to Black Elk's disciple, the Lakota holy man Fools Crow, for assistance in developing the religious aspect of their movement.[3] The concept of pan-Indian spirituality developed by AIM activists in turn drew considerable attention from other young people across America who were disaffected by the policies of the U.S. government in Vietnam and by what they perceived as the racism and general complacency of middle-class American culture. Even before the occupation of Wounded Knee in 1973 and the media attention it attracted to AIM, hundreds of religious seekers had visited Indian reservations looking for spiritual inspiration and instruction, and as Kehoe notes, "*Black Elk Speaks* blossomed in the jeans pockets of these pilgrims" (1989, 90). AIM's unofficial endorsement of the book contributed to its popularity.

As *Black Elk Speaks* became something of an icon for countercultural activists and religious seekers, it was also picked up by instructors in religious studies courses as a means of introducing students to Native American religions. Native American religions had not played much part in the study of American religion, or in any other part of the academic study of religion, until that time. But in the late sixties and early seventies, religious studies instructors were drawn to Native American religions as a result of several factors: publicity about Indian rights associated with AIM and Wounded Knee; growing interest in alternative religions and alternative forms of spirituality; and a surge in scholarly publications focusing on the history of mistreatment of Indians by the U.S. government, on popular stereotypes about Indians that legitimated that mistreatment, and on the connection between the history of U.S. policies toward Indians and the

---

3. In describing this influence, Kehoe writes, "By late 1969 . . . AIM had a national structure of chapters in cities with substantial Indian populations. Its leaders were constructing an ideology affirming an Indian identity supported by Indian religion, which turned out to be basically Oglala Lakota, thanks to the handy paperback *Black Elk Speaks* and the willingness of several Oglala *wicasa wakan* to assist the neophytes. Leonard Crow Dog, from Rosebud Reservation, became active in AIM, and Frank Fools Crow, from Pine Ridge, welcomed AIM members as he did others seeking spiritual guidance and blessing in the Oglala manner." Kehoe goes on to note that though Leonard Crow Dog and other AIM leaders "have been viewed as ambitious politicians," Frank Fools Crow, "born in about 1890, is respected as a legitimate traditional Oglala leader who saw a responsibility to intercede when events involving his people called for godly (that is, *wakan*) wisdom" (1989b, 76.)

debacle in Vietnam.[4] Because of its usefulness as both an introduction to Native American religions and as a commentary on American insensitivity to indigenous peoples, *Black Elk Speaks* became part of the mainstream curriculum in American higher education.

For many instructors in religious studies, a steady increase in awareness of the complexities involved in reading *Black Elk Speaks* added to its instructional value. Because of several helpful analyses of Neihardt's strategies, and because of increased familiarity with the original notes based on Neihardt's interviews with the holy man, it became increasingly difficult to teach *Black Elk Speaks* as a straightforward description of old-time Lakota religion as Black Elk remembered it, or as an accurate presentation of Black Elk's outlook on the future.[5] Although Neihardt's editorial strategies obscured both the originality of Black Elk's religious outlook and his commitment to the ongoing vitality of Lakota religion, heightened awareness of Neihardt's editorial hand not only made classroom discussion of *Black Elk Speaks* more critically sophisticated, but also called attention to the significance of Black Elk's contributions to Lakota religion, and enhanced appreciation of him as a religious leader.

In addition, analysis of *Black Elk Speaks* leads easily to discussions about the authenticity of words attributed to other religious founders and visionaries. Seen in comparative context, the issues involved in Neihardt's representation of Black Elk's words are not unlike those involved in the representation of Jesus' words in the New Testament, or Mohammed's words in Islamic *hadith*, or Siddhartha Gautama's words in early Buddhist sutras. Although the issues involved in interpreting *Black Elk Speaks* are similar to the ones involved in interpreting other religious texts, many instructors find *Black Elk Speaks* a good place to begin addressing these issues because the text itself is relatively recent, and scholarly criticism of it is not so extensive or impenetrable that it cannot be handled within a semester.

As well as being useful in the comparative study of religion, *Black Elk Speaks* is instructive as a story about America. First and most obviously, it

4. See Berkhofer 1976 and 1978, Slotkin 1973, Rogin 1976, and Drinnon 1980.

5. See Kehoe 1989, Holler 1984a, Linden 1984, Linden and Robbins 1984, and McCluskey 1972.

is a story about the mistreatment of the Lakota people by the U.S. government in the late nineteenth and early twentieth centuries, and the valiant efforts Black Elk and others made to preserve their religion and culture against the hostile forces arrayed against them. But as a story about America, *Black Elk Speaks* is not only an indictment of the stupidity and cruelty of Americans who made native lives miserable, and is not only a tribute to the valor of a relatively small ethnic group who defended their religion and culture against great odds. As this essay hopes to show, it is also a story about the relevance of Black Elk's vision for all Americans. Taken not just as a narrative contained within the cover of a book, but as a story that includes the interpretative community of its readers, Black Elk is also a story about the planting and development of native ideas within the religious imaginations of millions of Americans.[6]

Despite Neihardt's effort to present Black Elk's story as an account of a noble religion that was sadly but inevitably doomed by the onset of modern culture, Black Elk's belief in the importance of his vision and its relevance for the world has been rather spectacularly confirmed. To the extent that *Black Elk Speaks* has functioned as a catalyst for widespread appreciation of Native American cultures, and more specifically for widespread interest in Lakota culture as a leading exemplar of Native American cultures and the ecospirituality they exemplify, Black Elk's goal of revitalizing Lakota religion, and of promoting its relevance for modern life, has surely been attained. Through Black Elk and his interpreters, the religious outlooks of many Americans have begun to coincide with, and to become instructed by, those outlooks of Native Americans.

Black Elk in the Context of Long-standing Trends in American Cultural History

The popularity of *Black Elk Speaks* over the last thirty years signals some important shifts in American thought, but at the same time, it can also be understood in the context of American cultural traditions that involve fascination with Indians and efforts to identify with them. Although their political treatment at the hands of American colonists and representatives of

6. For discussion of reader-response theory, which defines a text to include the reactions and interpretations of its readers, see Mailloux 1982, Fish 1980, and Eco 1979.

the U.S. government has often been brutal, Native Americans have also been admired for centuries. It is worth noting that the numbers of these admirers have increased as threats of Native American warfare have declined, and as industrial and technological changes have distanced people from the proximity to nature associated with Indian life. The unprecedented attractiveness of Native Americans today coincides with relatively low levels of overt hostility between native groups and other Americans, as well as with extraordinarily high levels of concern about natural environments and their degradation.

But positive images of Indians go back a long time. Like others before and since his time, the seventeenth-century founder of Rhode Island, Roger Williams, compared the moral characters of Native Americans and Europeans and found the latter wanting. With regard to the Narragansett Indians he lived with, Williams wrote,

> God gives them sleep on ground, on straw,
> On sedgy mats or board:
> When English softest beds of down
> Sometimes no sleep afford.
>
> I have known them leave their house and mat
> To lodge a friend or stranger,
> When Jews and Christians oft have sent
> Christ Jesus to the manger (P. Miller 1970, 64).

Such relatively positive images of Indians as simple and wholesome contrasts to more privileged representatives of Western civilization were heavily outweighed by negative images of Indian cruelty, filthiness, and stupidity until the end of the French and Indian Wars in 1763, when the threat of Indian attack east of Ohio dramatically declined. Beginning in the late eighteenth century, images of Indians as noble savages gained popularity as numerous historians, playwrights, novelists, poets, and visual artists drew romantic portraits of the charms of Indian life as part of a deliberate effort to create a literary and artistic culture that would distinguish America from Britain and Europe. The Indian warrior came to symbolize the fierce pride, spirit of independence, down-to-earth intelligence, and natural skillfulness believed to characterize the proud citizens of the new American republic.[7]

In the nineteenth century, the transcendentalist movement contributed both directly and indirectly to this romantic view of Native Americans. In celebrating Indians for their practical knowledge about the natural world, and for their supposedly immediate and childlike acquaintance with nature's spiritual powers, transcendentalists played a leading role in shaping romantic stereotypes about Native Americans. They also helped to shape these stereotypes indirectly by fostering an intellectual and emotional climate that celebrated nature as a primary source of religious experience.[8]

As a religious and philosophical movement, American transcendentalism grew out of the concept of transcendental idealism advanced by the eighteenth-century German philosopher Immanuel Kant. Kant argued that all our perceptions and reasonings are contingent on prior intuitions about the nature of reality, and that our perceptions and reasonings are features of our experience rather than copies of things outside ourselves. The American transcendentalists were influenced by the highly personalized and poetic interpretations of this argument advanced by Goethe, Wordsworth, Coleridge, Carlyle, de Staâl, and Cousin, all of whom equated intuition with religious impulse. Their celebration of intuition encouraged American transcendentalists to view religious institutions as having a stultifying effect on religious inspiration, and to recommend individual encounters with the sublimities of nature as the best means to that inspiration.

American transcendentalism also had earlier roots in Platonic thought, and especially in the Platonic idea that material reality reflects or embodies ideal truths. For centuries, this Platonic idea exerted profound

7. See Albert Keiser's still-classic work (1933). Also see Pearce 1988, which was first published in 1953 as *The Savages of America: A Study of the Idea of Civilization.*

8. In an important book, Catherine Albanese discusses transcendentalism as a well-known and influential instance of the "nature religion" that runs through and helps to shape American culture. Albanese understands "nature religion" as a term that encompasses various groupings of religious belief and practice that are organized around symbolism about the natural world. Thus, "nature religion" is a name for "a symbolic center and the cluster of beliefs, behaviors, and values that encircles it" (1990, 7).

influence on Christian thought through allegorical interpretations that conceptualized natural events as signs of Christian truths. But this train of thought was limited by the belief, epitomized by the influential Christian theologian Augustine, that Adam and Eve's fall into sin created disorder in the natural world, and that nature awaited supernatural rehabilitation to reflect the perfection it had at the time of Creation. The Augustinian emphasis on the natural world being infected by sin was an important ingredient in the religious outlook that the English Puritans brought with them to America. It helped shape the Puritan tendency to view Native Americans as savage beasts whose proximity to nature (and ignorance of Christ) led them to devil worship.[9]

Throughout the eighteenth century and much of the nineteenth, the heavy emphasis on sin laid by spokesmen for Puritan culture was overtly challenged by religious liberals, and also softened internally through gradual shifts in theological innuendo carried out by more conservative thinkers. These challenges and changes contributed to the emergence of American transcendentalism, and to its positive view of nature as a source of spiritual inspiration. In varying degrees, the transcendentalist outlook defined the work of some of America's best and most influential writers, including Ralph Waldo Emerson and Henry David Thoreau.

Emerson advocated the idea that nature was a living bible of spiritual revelations and signs. In the opening passage of his famous essay "Nature," first published in 1836, he recounted his personal experience of nature's role as a conduit for religious experience. This essay, and the type of experience it promoted, came to epitomize American transcendentalism. "Crossing a bare common, in snow puddles, at twilight, under a clouded sky, without having in my thoughts any occurrence of special good fortune, I have enjoyed a perfect exhilaration. I am glad to the brink of fear. . . . Standing on the bare ground,—my head bathed by the blithe air, and uplifted into infinite space,—all mean egotism vanishes. I become a transparent eye-ball; I am nothing; I see all; the currents of the Universal Being circulate through me; I am part or particle of God" (1983, 10).

For readers steeped in American literary culture, this form of religious experience has provided a context in which to appreciate Black Elk and his

9. For further discussion of this tendency, see both Kibbey 1986 and Jennings 1975.

vision of the spirit world. Emerson's account of his religious experience
and vision is different in several respects from the account of Black Elk's
experience of *Wakan Tanka* recorded in *Black Elk Speaks*: the specifics of
Black Elk's vision, including the Six Grandfathers and all their accompa-
nists, are different, and the concern to ritually dramatize the parts of the
vision is different. But the experience of being struck by the divine out-of-
the-blue is similar, as is the experience of becoming identified with the divine while finding an absence of "all mean egotism." Moreover, both
visionaries experience the divine working through the natural world like a
hand in a glove. Thus, Black Elk hears the Grandfathers talking to him
through birds and clouds, and is often prompted by these natural signs to
recall his vision of the spirit world and its continuing importance. Similarly, Emerson's observation of snow puddles at twilight catapults him
into the presence of God, and he is often prompted by natural events to recall the omnipresence of God, of which he perceives these events to be
signs.

Although the transcendentalist formula cannot fully capture Black
Elk's vision, it has helped to frame the reading of *Black Elk Speaks* and to
establish the groundwork for its popularity. This comparison is not to suggest that Black Elk was familiar with the writing of Emerson or of other
transcendentalists, but rather that their writings exemplify a form of religious expression that is a hallmark of the culture of American literary expectation that many of Black Elk's readers have inhabited. Additional
examples of this form of religious expression can be found in the writings
of numerous other American authors, including Henry Wadsworth
Longfellow, Francis Parkman, James Fenimore Cooper, Emily Dickinson,
Walt Whitman, and more recently Annie Dillard, Wendell Berry, Peter
Matthiessen, Gary Snyder, and N. Scott Momaday. As it entered the mainstream culture of American higher education, *Black Elk Speaks* acquired a
readership schooled to appreciate accounts of personal experiences of God
in nature celebrated by these and other arbiters of American literary taste.
The book's success is partly a result of its resonance with a religious formula already famous in American literature.

But this reason is not the one commonly understood for using the
book in religious studies courses. *Black Elk Speaks* has been taught as a college text because it emphasizes the religious dimensions of Lakota culture,
the differences between Lakota culture and Western society, and the ef-

forts made by the Lakota people to resist Americanization. Indeed, the book's thrust with respect to American society is distinctly countercultural. But counterculturalism is an important element of American culture itself and one that has been closely linked to experiencing God in nature.

For Emerson, emphasis on nature as the principal vehicle for religious experience was not only a call to celebrate nature and explore its religious opportunities, but also a protest against his own culture and its reliance on the institutions of the past. "Our age is retrospective," complained the sage of Concord at the beginning of *Nature.* "It builds on the sepulchers of the fathers. It writes biographies, histories, and criticism. The foregoing generations beheld God and nature face to face; we, through their eyes. Why should not we also enjoy an original relation to the universe?" Emerson chided the cultural leaders of his own day for attempting to institutionalize the ideas of earlier generations, and for failing to live with their freshness of spirit and openness to new ideas. "Embosomed for a season in nature, whose floods of life stream around and through us, and invite us by the powers they supply, to action proportioned to nature. . . . Let us demand our own works and laws and worship" (1983, 7).

Although Emerson's words may be exceptional in their lyricism, the revolutionary attitude they convey toward the past, and toward the institutions of the present, is typically American. Along with its corollary celebration of nature as an alternative to the corruptions of civilization, and as a conduit for authentic spiritual inspiration, this deeply ingrained American tendency toward cultural iconoclasm helped to define the milieu in which the indictment of American culture in *Black Elk Speaks* has won affirmation.

Of course, Black Elk's identity as a Native American is crucial to the popularity of his story and to its countercultural appeal. The positive reception accorded *Black Elk Speaks* can be understood, in part, as an extension of the image of Indians as noble savages that has often functioned as a symbol of resistance to civilization and affinity with nature. Cooper's Chingachgook and Longfellow's Hiawatha exemplify this image, and helped to prepare the way for the celebrity of *Black Elk Speaks.*

But a great deal more is going on in the appreciation of *Black Elk Speaks* than a simple confirmation of the stereotype of Indians as symbols of countercultural protest, natural wisdom, and spiritual insight. For all its romantic packaging by John Neihardt, the book still contains an authentic Indian voice reporting on something other than a stock antagonism between nature and civilization. But if *Black Elk Speaks* breaks through the preconceived image of the noble savage, the effort to make that breakthrough is itself a force with significant precedent in American literary culture.

Concern to hear the voices of real Native Americans, and to break through romantic stereotypes of savagism, can be traced back at least to Henry David Thoreau. Although the concept of the noble savage played a major role in organizing Thoreau's own self-concept, the very intensity of his effort to be like an Indian led him to fill his notebooks with information about how Indians actually lived. His effort to be like an Indian also led him to seek out—and hire—Indians as guides to nature.

In *Thoreau and the American Indians,* Robert F. Sayre comments that Thoreau "had Indians on the brain" (1977, 97). Sayer prefaced his chapter on *Walden* with a quotation from *Black Elk Speaks,* and described Thoreau's life at Walden Pond as a vision quest aimed at seeing the Pond as Indians must have seen it in earlier days. Sayre illustrates his argument with a passage from Thoreau's journal in which the naturalist recorded the sudden thrill he felt upon hearing a robin sing. Suddenly he heard the robin "even as he might have sounded to the Indian, singing at evening upon the elm above his wigwam, with which was associated in the red man's mind the events of an Indian's life, his childhood. Formerly, I had heard in it only those strains which tell of the white man's village life; now I heard those strains which remembered the red man's life, such as fell on the ears of Indian children" (97). Later, in *Walden,* Thoreau condensed his commentary on the robin's song and burnished it to an exquisite degree: "I heard a robin in the distance, the first I had heard for many a thousand years, methought, whose note I shall not forget for many a thousand more,—the same sweet and powerful song of yore" (97).

If *Walden* exemplifies Thoreau's embrace of savagism, his subsequent writings about his travels in Maine trace his relinquishment of that romantic construct. The catalyst in this process was a Penobscot Indian named Polis, whom Thoreau hired as one of his guides. In his funeral eulogy for Thoreau, Emerson identified Polis as one of the three people who most influenced the naturalist in his later years—the other two were John Brown and Walt Whitman. Thoreau was sufficiently interested in Polis to be made uncomfortably aware of the disparity between Polis's behavior and the kind of pious attitude toward nature he presumed was typical of Indians and had hoped to observe. Polis resisted isolation and loved society much more than did Thoreau. He was less hostile to civilization, more devoted to Christianity, and less romantic about nature than Thoreau, who was offended by his guide's relish for killing and eating moose. Perhaps most important, Polis taught Thoreau that Native American religious beliefs and cultural customs were diverse, and could not be lumped together as "Indian." As Sayre writes, "Thoreau overcame savagism in his recognition of Polis as a person, and as a person who illustrated the depth and diversity of *the Indians*" (184).[10]

Much the same process has occurred in interpretations of Black Elk. From Neihardt's portrait of him as a tragic, almost iconic figure representing the irreconcilability of Indian culture and Western civilization to more recent discussions of Black Elk as a person active in both contexts, interpretations of the man have worked against expectations of savagism and toward recognition of him as an individual who illustrates the depth and diversity of Native American people. Some of the same issues that led to the complexification of Thoreau's perceptions of Polis have also been involved in the process of awakening to Black Elk's individuality. As their students have learned to better understand them, both Black Elk and Polis have come to be seen as less hostile to Western culture than they had been assumed to be, and much more likely than previously assumed to be devoted to Christianity.

Black Elk Speaks and the Re-creation of American Culture

As Thoreau's changing attitude toward Indians illustrates, the struggle to break through savagism is not new, and thus our current efforts to understand Black Elk and his influence have important precedent. What *is* new about Black Elk is the religious authority commonly attributed to his voice, and the fact that this authority is accepted both by Americans with

10. "But Thoreau," Sayre adds, "it must be considered, wrote of Polis as 'the Indian,' even after addressing him as 'Polis.' " On the other hand, Thoreau addressed Polis in a way that was more respectful than convention would have dictated, though Polis addressed Thoreau in a way that was "more intimate and less respectful than convention" (Sayre 1977, 184).

ancestral ties to Lakota culture and by many Americans without such ties. This shared recognition of Black Elk's religious authority involves more than the assimilation of Lakota people to American culture. It is one of the harbingers of a new American culture reflecting the influence of Lakota values, as well as Anglo-Protestant and other Western ones.

This is not to say that American culture is a simple blend, or that American religious history can be reduced to just one story line. However, the more we become aware of the complexity of American culture and the more our awareness of the diversity of American stories proliferates, the more our awareness of historical interconnections increases. This growing appreciation of religious and cultural interconnections in the past is stimulated by the increasing diversity of our own religious situation. As the abundance of different religious options increases today, as interreligious communication and borrowing intensify, and as people move from one religious orientation to another with increasing ease and participate more often in more than one religion at a time, we become more alert to the existence of these tendencies in the past and to their development over time. With this increased alertness to religious interaction and cross-fertilization, it is becoming increasingly more awkward and difficult to consider Native American religions in a category separate from other religions in North America.

In addition, Native American religious leaders can no longer be so easily defined, as they once were, by perceptions not of their making. They are no longer the "Other" about whom normative Americans construct imagery through which to define themselves and organize their culture. This is not to say that imaginative appropriations of Indians have ceased in American culture, but simply that such appropriations are often challenged now and, even more important, that the actual religious voices of Native Americans are now more often heard and respected.

At the same time, however, the self-expressions of Native Americans have not gone untouched by romantic American images of nature and savagism. Black Elk and other Lakota Indians joined Buffalo Bill's Wild West Show, Onondaga and Mohawk Indians accepted roles in the film version of Cooper's *Deerslayer*, and the voice of AIM activist Russell Means played one of the leading voices in the Disney film, *Pocahontas*. In addition to participating in such public displays of savagism for purposes of entertainment, art, and financial gain, Native Americans have also accepted savagism, more or less depending on individual circumstance, as part of their self-conceptions. Of course, no individual is the lone creator of his or her identity, and Native Americans are hardly unique in shaping themselves out of the expectations that others have for them. In the case of Black Elk, a similar point can be made. American idealism about Indians contributed to the development of his understanding of his religious vision and its importance for American culture.

In addition to absorbing varying amounts of the savagist idealism of American culture, the majority of Native Americans have been deeply influenced by Christianity, and many accept some form of this religion as their own. Black Elk is not unique in valuing both Christianity and the religious traditions of his native ancestors, or in seeing them as complementary or mutually inspiring. Although it is true that some Native Americans who belong to very strict Protestant churches do reject their ancestral traditions as forms of heathenism, many others bring expectations of give-and-take to both their ancestral traditions and Christianity.

The Sacred Pipe is a particularly clear example of this syncretic give-and-take. It represents a later stage in Black Elk's development of his vision, a stage in which that vision has become a theology. With the theology of *The Sacred Pipe* in mind, we are better equipped to understand both Black Elk's voice in *Black Elk Speaks* and the nature of his impact on American culture.

Two and one-half years before his death in August 1950, Black Elk gave an account, "The Seven Rites of the Oglala Sioux," through his bilingual son Benjamin to Joseph Epes Brown, a student of both Native American religions and comparative mysticism. In the text he published after Black Elk's death, Brown included footnotes of his own devising that compared various aspects of Lakota religion with Sufi, Baha'i, and Hindu mysticism, but the main text stayed sufficiently close to Benjamin Black Elk's translation of his father's words for the 1971 Penguin Books edition to identify Black Elk as the author on the book's spine, and for Brown to state in the accompanying biographical sketch: "This volume I really consider to be his work and his contribution to the Sioux."

Additional evidence of the text's relative purity comes from the fact that *The Sacred Pipe* does not obscure Black Elk's hopefulness about the ongoing vitality of Lakota religion, as Neihardt's *Black Elk Speaks* did. For example, in the chapter "Tapa Wanka Yap, the Throwing of the Ball," the seventh and culminating rite in Black Elk's discussion of the rituals associated with the sacred pipe, the ball symbolizes *Wakan Tanka,* which Black Elk identifies both as God and as the universe. The ritual itself is a sacred game representing "the course of a man's life" and also a metaphor for Black Elk's own handling of Lakota religion. The last paragraph in the book reads, "At this sad time today among our people, we are scrambling for the ball, and some are not even trying to catch it, which makes me cry when I think of it. But soon I know it will be caught, for the end is rapidly approaching, and then it will be returned to the center, and our people will be with it. It is my prayer that this be so, and it is in order to aid in this 're- covery of the ball,' that I have wished to make this book" (J. Brown 1974, 138).

The exact nature of the rapidly approaching end, mentioned here at the conclusion of *The Sacred Pipe,* is ambiguous, and perhaps deliberately so. At one level, Black Elk seems to imply that the end of the Lakota people's scrambling for survival, and the end of their despair and the be- ginning of their return to a religiously centered life, may be near. At an- other level, he may be invoking a Christian view of the end as culmination and fulfillment of historical time brought about by the return of God. At still another level, he may be interpreting this Christian end in terms of the Lakota concept of world cycles, and suggesting that the current world cycle is coming to an end and a new one beginning.

This confounding of Christian and Lakota mythology is suggested even more clearly at the outset of the book. In the foreword, Black Elk refers to the Christian belief "that God sent to men His son, who would restore order and peace upon the earth; and we have been told that Jesus the Christ was crucified, but that he shall come again at the last Judgment, the end of his world or cycle." Acknowledging his own acceptance of these Christian ideas, Black Elk goes on to say that God is equally incarnate in White Buffalo Cow Woman, who first appeared in the form of a calf and then, as a woman and benefactor, bestowed upon the Sioux people the sa- cred pipe, the central symbol and means of communication between the Sioux people and God. She "will appear again at the end of this 'world,' a coming which we Indians know is now not very far off" (J. Brown 1974, xx).

Belief in God is central to both traditions, Black Elk stresses, and the Lakota people "know the one true God" that Christians also worship. He is concerned to help the Lakota people see the importance of maintaining and developing their religion, and to help make that religion a primary resource for a new world order encompassing all the earth and its people. Thus, the purpose of his book is twofold, "to help my people in understanding the greatness and truth of our own tradition," and "to help in bringing peace upon the earth, not only among men, but within men and between the whole of creation" (J. Brown 1974, xx).

As Holler and others have recognized, Black Elk not only saw Lakota religion and Christianity as complementary, but also reconceptualized Lakota religion in light of Christian thought and expectation. In constructing the basic design for *The Sacred Pipe*, he chose seven rites from a larger collection of rituals practiced by the Lakota Sioux, thus replicating the exact number of sacraments in Roman Catholicism. As a Catholic, Black Elk understood the sacraments as rites through which the presence and power of God became manifest, and this understanding seems to inform his explanation of the meaning of the Oglala rites. Thus, in his description of "Inipi, the Rite of Purification," Black Elk emphasized that the central elements in the rite—the rocks, the water, and the willows that make the sweat lodge frame—are all material forms of the spiritual power of God. In his explanation of the symbolic meaning of the elements of *inipi*, one can hear echoes of what he heard Catholic priests say about the meaning of the sacraments, and of what he might have said in his role as a Catholic catechist. For example, "When we use the water in the sweat lodge we should think of *Wakan-Tanka* who is always flowing, giving His power and life to everything; we should even be as water which is lower than all things, yet stronger even than the rocks" (J. Brown 1974, 31).

In reconceptualizing Lakota religion in terms of Catholic experience and theology, Black Elk equates *Wakan Tanka* with the Christian God, and presents White Buffalo Cow Woman as a figure analogous to Jesus. Thus, he appropriates the Christian concept of the Incarnation to argue that she, like Christ, came to earth as a living embodiment of God. At the same time, Black Elk is not simply remodeling Lakota concepts into parallel versions of Christian concepts, but also reconceptualizing Christianity through the prism of Lakota religion. Although drawn from both traditions, his theology is first and foremost a Lakota theology.

As a theology based primarily in Lakota belief and practice, Black Elk's system of thought in *The Sacred Pipe* is heavily influenced by Christianity, but is also predicated on the idea that Christianity has serious shortcomings. From Black Elk's perspective, Lakota theology fosters awareness of these shortcomings and offers means of overcoming them. Thus, he reverses the modern Christian idea that Christianity represents the fulfillment of other religions, and that other religions should be respected as partial expressions of truth, or stages on the way to culmination in Christ. With its overriding focus on human beings, and its blinders to the natural world as principal arena of divine manifestation and the context of human life, Christianity is the partial truth, and Lakota theology its fulfillment. "We should understand well," Black Elk tells his readers, "that all things are the works of the Great Spirit. We should know that He is within all things: the trees, the grasses, the rivers, the mountains, and all the four-legged animals, and the winged peoples; and even more important, we should understand that He is also above all these things and peoples. When we do understand all this deeply in our hearts, then we will fear, and love, and know the Great Spirit, and then we will be and act and live as He intends" (J. Brown 1974, xx).

One of the important implications of this theology is its revision of Christian ideas about sin. On the one hand, emphasis on the need for forgiveness, belief in the importance of humility, and attention to the role of suffering as a means of attaining insight and purification are as strong in Lakota religion as they are in Christianity, and Black Elk promotes cultivation of these things. But on the other hand, he does not accept the idea that the natural world is fallen and corrupt, that flesh is inherently sinful, or that spiritual purification requires a renunciation of nature or flesh. From Black Elk's perspective, what requires forgiveness and purification through suffering is inattention to, and lack of respect for, the *wakan,* or holiness, present in the natural world.

Although Christian thought in the United States was already moving away from medieval and Puritan associations between nature and sin, Black Elk contributed to this process, and also to increasingly widespread acceptance of a countervailing association between nature and grace. In addition to helping to foster this greening of American Christianity, Black Elk's theology also represents the maturation of American transcendentalism. Like transcendentalism, it stresses the importance of personal religious experience and intuition. And it looks to nature for experience manifestation of the divine. But Black Elk's theology is less countercultural, less hostile to Christianity, more prosocial, and more community oriented than transcendentalism. As a theology accessible to and embraced by people raised in transcendentalism, it represents an overcoming of transcendentalism's savagism. But most important, Black Elk's theology also represents the religious achievements and religious authority of Native Americans, and the emergence of their religious thought as a highly respected element of American culture.

4

Akicita of the Thunder

Horses in Black Elk's Vision

JULIAN RICE

The process of spiritual transformation may be the most compelling "theme" of *Black Elk Speaks,* just as it is the supreme experience of *Lakol wicoh'an* (Lakota ways) in ceremonies, dances, songs, and oral narratives. Some illuminating interpretations of the holy man's visionary experience and ceremonial descriptions have been contributed by Castro (1983), Lincoln (1983), and Sayre (1971). But for the most part these critics approach the book as if it were primarily an English-language literary work by John Neihardt. A deeper understanding of the *hanbloglaka* (vision talk) of *Hehaka Sapa* (Black Elk) is made possible through the study of specific Lakota symbols in such richly detailed sources as those compiled by Ella C. Deloria, Densmore, and Walker. These works can provide an implicit comparative context. And in *The Sixth Grandfather,* his edition of the original manuscript upon which Black Elk's "autobiography" was based, Raymond J. DeMallie reveals an explicit misunderstanding between Black Elk and Neihardt: "Neihardt conceived of the project as writing Black Elk's life story, whereas Black Elk conceived of it as making a record of the Lakota religion" (1984a, 62). If the message of Black Elk's vision is to be received with sincere respect, readers must remember that Black Elk is not the author of his visions. The *woksape* (wisdom) that Black Elk "speaks" is larger than any one person's *wookahnige* (understanding) and was sent through Black Elk by the spirits. DeMallie's extensive editing pinpoints

This essay appeared in a slightly different version in *Melus* 12, no. 1 (1985) and is reprinted with permission.

Neihardt's alterations of Black Elk's report. Although the revelation speaks to all humanity, it was given to a specifically Lakota consciousness, and its symbolic associations can flourish only when rooted in the matrix of Lakota culture.

Neihardt faithfully recorded much of Black Elk's narration, but he also made some obscuring deletions and additions because he did not realize the fundamental meaning of certain parts of his material. He may not have felt it necessary to understand more of Lakota culture than he learned directly from Black Elk, and he trusted his mystical rapport with the *wicasa wakan* (holy man) to provide as much truth as was spiritually valid.[1] He was quite explicit about his intent to transform the narrative "so that it could be understood by the white world" (McCluskey 1972, 239). Unfortunately, much of that understanding remains blurred by Neihardt's romantic refusal to confront history and cultural difference: "I am not interested in *Indians* as *Indians*—only as people in a particular situation. Human nature in the grip of fate—not Indian nature as curiosity—interests me. And their poetry interests me because it is human and poetry" (Castro 1983, 79).

As an interpreter of Lakota culture, Neihardt failed to communicate many of the Lakota meanings of the dreams and ceremonies he transcribed. It has recently become possible for readers of *Black Elk Speaks* to understand the visionary chapters in ways that Neihardt did not convey and Black Elk felt no need to explain. DeMallie's *Sixth Grandfather* reprints the stenographic record as Black Elk spoke it without Neihardt's poetic revision. A study of the record in conjunction with *Black Elk Speaks* reveals that Neihardt's changes were made from aesthetic considerations in an Anglo-Christian literary context. The comparison also reveals that in sustained sections of the narrative, including the *hanbloglaka* (vision talk), Neihardt made only superficial changes. *Black Elk Speaks* is still a reliable introductory text. Nevertheless, a detailed study of Lakota symbols must precede any sincere attempt to understand a revelation given by the spirits to a Lakota individual in his own language (Sayre 1971).[2]

1. See Black 1969, McCluskey 1972, and Whitney 1976.
2. Sayre illustrates the limitations of interpretation from a "universal" perspective. He distinguishes between specifically Lakota symbols such as buffalo, geese, and elk, and symbols with universal significance such as the cup of water, the arrows, and the flowering sticks that can be catalogued in any monolithic system (Freud's, Jung's, Frazier's, and so on).

A representative beginning can be made by examining the Lakota perception of *sunkawakan* (the horse), the predominant animal of transformation in the Great Vision and the Horse Dance. Although the different colored horses in *Black Elk Speaks* represent the characteristics of the four directions, the horse as an animal species is an *akicita* (messenger), or potential embodiment of the *tonwan* (physically manifest power)[3] of only one direction—the Thunder Beings of the West. DeMallie points out that the Great Vision is a Thunder Being vision but that Neihardt minimized this to avoid duplicating the dog or *heyoka* vision (also brought by the Thunder Beings), and to censor entirely the *iwizilya akicita* (soldier weed) given to Black Elk by a black horse rider (Thunder Being), who first becomes a gopher and then becomes the herb itself. These transformations imply that the scourging power of the weed exists in many possible forms. It is not necessarily confined to a single destructive agent such as a nuclear weapon (Castro 1983, 79). War was a physical reality to the old Lakota just as it continues to be in the world today, but at the same time it is still a profound metaphor in Lakota public expression from powwows to sacred ceremonies. For the Lakota the war horse symbolized spiritual confidence. Accordingly, they made their horses receptive to the Thunder power by elaborately painting them before battle:

> The whole flank behind the one line and the shoulder and leg in front of the other line are covered with small circular markings, giving a somewhat dappled effect. These marks represent either cloud forms or hailstones; in either case, they are closely associated with thunder power . . . as the thunderbird rides the storms in safety, as the eagle, the hawk, the raven—related to the spirit bird—in the swiftness of their flight and the strength of their endurance escape the rain of hailstones and rise

---

Sayre then concentrates on the "process by which the symbols are generated and passed on and in their value to the culture" (1971, 517). This approach can stimulate interest in reading books about Indians, but it will not necessarily deepen sensitivity to Indian symbolic expression, which should be understood in its own complex context, whether tribal or pan-Indian contemporary. Sayre makes a Lakota *hanbloglaka* (vision-talk) acceptable to an academic audience by discovering that it was "a supreme fiction" that Black Elk used "in *order* to unite people" (534). But shouldn't we also consider the possibility that the vision is a supreme reality and that Black Elk is its speaker, not its author?

3. See Walker 1980 (230), and 1917, 1982, and 1983.

above the ferocity of the whirlwind, so may the bearer of these symbols go safely through battle.[4] (Blish 1967, 65)

Because the horses of the North, the East, and the South are also decorated with lightning streaks in Black Elk's Great Vision and Horse Dance, the connection between the powers of destruction and enlightenment is established at the outset. An explosive emergence of sound and light begins the Lakota cycle of maturation. Rigorous stages in the development of wisdom form the sequence of expression in several major ceremonies. Sun Dancers are thrown to the ground, pierced, and required to dance attached to the sacred center by thongs. But this "captivity" is inseparable from the sacred tree that is the source of joy and renewal. Spiritual completion is accomplished by "the release" when the bonds break through the dancers' flesh shortly before they return to the people who have always been with them just outside the circle. The thongs attach the dancers to a sacred center, so that upon release that same center will hold everyone in a hoop of generosity and mutual sacrifice. The ritual repeats a dynamic change of recognition and a simultaneous alteration of reality because some of the people will live in the company of spirits where no spirits had formerly been after each Sun Dance has been performed. When the ordeal ends, forgetfulness of one's true identity also ends. The tree, the thongs, the suffering, and "war" are valued, even loved. The dancer's scars are never boasted, but they become a lasting mnemonic of how a transformed understanding is brought about through sacrifice.

Just as the Sun Dance can be as trying to behold as to perform, so the horses in the Great Vision and in the Horse Dance "looked beautiful; but they looked fearful too" (J. Neihardt 1979, 165). The terrible aspect of an animal so familiar to everyday Lakota life probably stems from the horse's sudden appearance on the Plains as the *sunkawakan* (sacred dog), and from the exhilaration of risk in the buffalo hunt and in war. The speed of a horse is inseparable from the flow of energy and emotion in a skilled rider. Together they move like a *wakinyan* (Thunder Being). Returning from a successful raid, warriors painted their faces black, the color of the Thunder

4. See Blish 1967 for a number of pictographs employing these symbols.

spirits whom they kinetically resembled.[5] Densmore transcribes a horse song that communicates this connection, "*kola / mitasunke / kinyan yan / inyanke lo*" (friend / my horse / flies like a bird / as it runs) (1918, 299). The simile "like a bird" may be mistranslated here. *Kinyan* means something that flies, not necessarily a bird in the specific sense of *zintkala*. The Lakota spirits of the thunder are also (collectively) "something that flies" *Wakinyan* (*wa* = something, *kinyan* = flies), and the term *Thunderbird* in the case of the Lakota is somewhat misconceived. The Thunders represent potency and potentiality. They begin a process that culminates in electrifying manifestations of tree-splitting destruction or life-giving rain. Atmospheric percussion transformatively becomes the rumbling thunder of a *cega* (drum), the abundant hail of a *wagamuha* (rattle), the neighing of a *sunkawakan* (horse), and the words of a *walowan* (singer): "*anpao / hinape / cinhan / sunkawakan wan / hotonwe*" (daybreak appears / when / a horse / neighs) (300).

Similarly, in *Black Elk Speaks* the inception and completion of an expression are represented by the same animal of the Thunder *(sunkawakan)*, and the predominant metaphor of manifestation in Lakota culture was that of war. Densmore's transcription of the Thunder or *heyoka* vision of Lone Man opens with the dreamer's report of hearing thunder from the west becoming "the sound of hoofs, and I saw nine riders coming toward me in a cloud, each man on a horse of a different color" (1918, 159). Nine riders then come from each of the other directions and the men tell him, as Black Elk was also told, to kill an enemy and thereby become "a member of their company" so that he might "always call on them for help in time of need." Although these riders come from four directions, they are all Thunder Beings.

Not every Thunder dreamer had the power to present a Horse Dance. In a *Sunkawakan Wacipi* the dreamer exercises the advanced ability to allow the entrance of just enough fear to evoke courage and cooperation in participants and beholders. The most significant difference between the Horse Dance reported by Frank Fools Crow and that of Black Elk is that

---

5. Black Elk told Brown that the black face paint of returned warriors revealed shame: "we wish to hide our faces from *Wakan-Tanka*" (Brown 1974, 92 n). But he told Neihardt in 1944, "when we whip Germany, we will all black our faces" (DeMallie 1984a, 317), presumably to signify a wholehearted gratitude to the Thunder.

Fools Crow's horses are wild.[6] Their dangerous disposition is transformed
by a man whose name suggests a special affinity for horses: "A fire was
built next to the corral, and Poor Thunder made a medicine by taking
some red-hot ashes and mixing them with the smoke. The horses had
never been ridden and at first were frightened and unruly, stomping and
rearing. But when Poor Thunder took his medicine over to the corral and
let the wind blow it through the rails and across the horses they calmed
down in moments and were no longer wild" (Mails 1979, 79).

Then in the dance each rider covers his face with a black cloth he can
see through. Black is the color of the western powers, and the beholders
may now "see through" the Thunders' terrible aspect to their creative op-
eration. Poor Thunder begins the process. His is the power of initiating a
progressive growth through the Lakota virtues that flower in *woksape* (wisdom). His horse is therefore black, the color of inception: "Poor Thunder
went to the black horse and petted it. Then without the aid of a bridle, halter, rope, or anything else, he climbed on top of it" (Mails 1979, 79). Poor
Thunder's beginning manifests the first of the Lakota virtues, *woohitika*
(courage), making it possible for the other riders to successively mount
their horses. Once the sudden dramatic act of *woohitika* has brought the
riders astride, they must manifest *wawacintanka* (fortitude) by not losing
their nerve and allowing the horses or their own excitement to bolt.

But a spiritual ceremony does more than display the virtues of the participants. The purpose of the ceremony and of the virtues is to bestow
awareness on the beholders through the power of the third virtue, *wacantognaka* (generosity). Courage and fortitude prepare the way for the pivotal event, the visible arrival of the spirits. Singing, the articulate act of
evocation, must precede this visitation: "Then the singing began, and the
horses started dancing, really dancing. I was so excited I could hardly
stand it" (Mails 1979, 80). The spirits of the Thunder now enter into the
horses. Certain animals can contain specific spirits to become the *tonwan*
or embodied power of these spirits. The eagle is the *akicita* of the sun, and
the meadowlark is the *akicita* of the south wind. The Thunders make
themselves known through many things that fly such as the swallow, the
dragonfly, or the butterfly, but among the *sitoblayanpi* (four-legged be-

6. For additional variations, see Blish 1967 (39), Laubin and Laubin 1977 (360–62),
and Wissler 1912 (97–98).

ings), the *Wakinyan* clearly favor the horse: "It had been a sunny day, but huge black clouds formed in the sky. Thunder began to boom, and about ten yards ahead of us, lightning started to strike. Amazingly the horses did not bolt and run. Whinnying and snorting, making all of the strange sounds horses can make, they danced straight toward the lightning. As they did so, the lightning moved in a semicircle, and we followed it while it kept striking ahead of us in a broad flashing curtain of light. Not once did the wild horses run away or even turn their backs" (80).

The horses reveal an acceptance of difficulty, challenge, and threat, making prayers effective after fear has been dispelled: "Poor Thunder and I started to sing and pray, and the storm and the lightning split in two, as though the curtain of light were torn in half from top to bottom. The power of our prayer did this" (Mails 1979, 80). The prayers are potent because the riders have regarded the threat of the storm and the wildness of the horses with courage and respect. They hold no illusions of favored safety, however. After the ceremony the horses were *watogla* (wild) "once again and they took off running as fast as they could go" (80). Fools Crow emphasizes the unpredictability of existence in general represented by the wild horses and the Thunder Beings they temporarily contained: "there was a great amount of thunder and lightning, and it was a terrifying time. The performance of the horses was truly amazing" (80). The terror makes the miracle possible. Terror is the seed spread by the Thunder Beings, and it grows incrementally into *woohitika* (courage), *wawacintanka* (fortitude), *wacantognaka* (generosity), and *woksape* (wisdom).

Such fullness of vision is usually preceded by sacrificial emptiness—fasting in the ceremonies, poverty in the oral narratives. At the beginning of the fifty-third story of Ella Deloria's *Dakota Texts* poverty has prepared a man to receive power to strengthen his people who reveal themselves to be spiritually poor by their selfishness. Although they have an abundance of meat and other necessities because they have camped all winter near "plenty of buffalo," they do not provide even one strong horse to a poor man and his wife to allow them to come along. The couple subsists for a time on scraps of bone and meat strewn around the abandoned campsite until one day the man ascends a hill, as men do when they seek a vision, though he is seeking only rest from gathering wood. Nevertheless, he suddenly perceives the physical form through which the spirits will reward his virtue and his will to live. A black-spotted stallion comes over the eastern horizon to take a drink in a lake, after which it lies down, rolls, and goes back toward the east until it disappears. Although the horse comes from the east, its black markings identify its *tonwan* as that of the west, and its spots represent the hail. When the horse rolls and arises, it performs a symbolic cycle of death and renewal, after drinking the healing water of the lake, much as the black stallion of Black Elk's dream rolls and arises after Black Elk extends his healing herb toward it. The cup of water in Black Elk's vision is a gift of the western spirits, and their power for regeneration is symbolized by water, usually in the form of rain but in lakes and streams as well.

A little gray bird immediately arrives to give the man a special medicine that, like that of Poor Thunder in Fools Crow's Horse Dance, will have power to convert a wild horse, or an immature understanding, into a being whose full energies are concentrated into serving the people. To accomplish this, the man must impart his own spiritual power to a mediating symbol, as Black Elk does when his Great Vision is enacted in the Horse Dance. In the oral narrative the horse's head is first caught in a rope as the people's attention is caught in the hoop of a ceremony. Then the man chews a medicine root brought to him by the spiritual messenger, the gray bird, and after rubbing some on himself, he blows the rest on the horse's nose, so that the horse stands still and quietly lets a rope be put around his neck. A willingness to serve the people is realized through the usual sequence of transmission—a spirit sends a messenger (the gray bird) to a man who, through a symbolic medium, changes the life of the beholder (the horse). The effect of the medicine as a spiritual medium also strengthens the mare the man already owns and makes her fertile. From a humble receptiveness to mystery, and from a will to unstinting generosity, three miraculously swift colts are born that are a source of delight and confidence to the whole tribe. But the invigoration of mysterious favor can be dissolved by simple jealousy. When someone tries to cut the picket line outside the man's lodge, the horse articulately alerts the man to the thief's intention to "cause our death." The disappearance of a *wakanyan* (sacredly lived) harmony is always imminent. The man emerges to return the people to a sense of self-protectiveness:

> Sunka wakan kin lena aimayahahapikta ca wicabluhasni ye lo. Niyes oyate kin iniwastepikta un lena wicabluha cas un wayakuwapi ca nicinca

wotapi k'u; na nakuns ozuye ca wicanunpi na un wicohan wasteste sloy-
ayapi k'u. Sunka wakan kin lena wowacinyepi ca nazinpe lo.

[I do not keep these horses in order that you shall insult me through
them. I keep them for the sole purpose of bringing good to the tribe, and
in that spirit, I lend them to you to hunt meat for your children, as you
know; you have also used them freely in war and, as a result, have
achieved glory. These horses stand here to serve.] (E. Deloria 1972,
258–59)

Supernatural power must be used only to defend and nourish the nation. If any individual tries to selfishly exploit a blessing conferred on the
whole people, such as the sacred pipe, then all the people suffer. The influence of such antigenerative greed is noxiously contagious. The people
need to breathe in an atmosphere of generous symbolic expression or they
will be *watogla* (wild) and *itanyesni* (useless). The Thunder horse recalls
the consequences of forgetting gratitude and generosity:

Oyate kin le el taku iyuha ogna tanyan yaunpikta ca micinca op
migluota na un iniwastepi ke, wichoh'an sica wan el hiyu ca wanna
hehanyelakte lo. Ca ake sicaya yaunpikta tka he tuwa t'euye-wacinpi kin
he e ca oyate wawicakiyusice lo.

[In order that you in this tribe might be fortunate in all things, I and
my young have multiplied; and from that, you have benefited in the past;
yet now, because an evil thing has entered the tribe, this source of good
shall stop. You must go back to your former state when things were hard
for you, all because that one who tried to kill us has by his act brought it
upon the entire tribe.] (E. Deloria 1972, 259)

Only the fundamental details of living in a sacred manner are visible in
a story where man, like a vision-seeker, sees *wi hinape cin ogna taku hi-
napin* (something coming over the horizon) after a long period of deprivation. Among the *Wakan Tanka* (most powerful of the *wakan* spirits;
tanka means "huge") the initiation of life in a pure space was the task of
the *Wakinyan*, the flying ones who live in the west. They create many
forms of life that they strengthen in the rigors of atmospheric and emotional storms. These storms are always in process at various stages of an individual's life, or on different places on the earth among varying forms of
life. The *Wakinyans'* appearance is terrible to behold because it conveys

the insecurity of any natural state. Though the Thunders are usually conceived as plural, Walker's portrait of a singular Thunder spirit suggests an innate part of being that always remains beyond consciousness:

> He [*Inyan*, the Rock] made a shapeless creature and named him *Wakinyan* (Winged one or Thunderstorm). *Wakinyan* is as shapeless as a cloud and terrifying to behold. He has two wings of many joints, which he can spread afar or make very small; he has neither legs nor feet, but has huge talons that can pierce the hardest of things; he has no mouth, but has a huge beak armed with sharp teeth that can rend and tear the toughest of things; he has no throat, but has one voice that is the thunder; and he has no head, but has one eye, and the glance of that eye is the lightning. (1983, 213)

In Walker's mythology, *Wakinyan* maintains a hidden dimension even when he is represented. The idea of his partial invisibility is important to his role as the initiator of wisdom and generation. *Skan* (an invention of Walker's), the *Nagi Tanka* (Great Spirit) and Sky-God, foresaw the necessity of this disguise, when he told *Wakinyan*, "hide yourself from all save only those evil ones whom you would destroy" (Walker 1983, 213).[7] *Skan* then teaches *Wakinyan* to make the clouds, "robes that are shapeless like himself" (213). His true creative nature is further hidden by his consistently "unnatural" behavior: "when he is pleased he seems angry, and when he is furious he seems pleasant. He delights in opposition and contrariness" (214).[8] This is a way of demonstrating that full development is reached only by remaining receptive to "negative" experiences. *Wakinyan* brings forth his young on the top of a high mountain where his lodge has no roof and where he rests on jagged rocks. From this foundation of intensely felt being, *Wakinyan* flies forth to repel the enemies of growth—greed, pride, and the other invasive *wakan sica* (bad spirits) often personified in the oral narratives. The acceptance of *Wakinyan*'s warrior aspect is essential to understanding the Lakota concept of creation.

Neihardt's omission of the soldier weed, the warrior power of Black

---

7. On *Skan* as Walker's invention, see Walker 1937 (73).
8. On the relation between thunder and the *heyoka* clowns, see DeMallie 1984a (6).

Elk's vision, and Black Elk's own reluctance to acknowledge its potential benefit, should not deter us from recognizing the complete vision as a gift from the Lakota spirits.[9] *Wakinyan*'s war power must cleanse the world before he can release potential life into pulsing motion. In Walker's cycle of Lakota mythology the Thunder's rage against pollution precedes his ability to create. *Wakinyan* initiates plant life on the earth after he has purified its surface. Other powers then further the life cycle, but *Wakinyan* creates the *itkasupi* (seeds, eggs, cocoons, and wombs of various kinds). He also makes possible the duration of life in transformed states when he steals rain from the ocean. Walker's *Wakinyan* impels all reproduction, and his powers are most potent at the stage of inception. As in ceremonial communication, *Wakinyan* moves each plant and each person to contain seeds. Impelled by *Wakinyan*, a plant becomes edible in various parts of its body just as mature people evolve many ways to impart motion and direction to children.

Although *Wakinyan* hatches his young in a great nest, his primary role, especially in terms of traditional Lakota society, is male. He protects the people by roaming the world. As he travels, evils become familiar. He knows his targets and how to strike them, and when he passes over or through the people, he knows how to speak to them. The spirit of *Wakinyan* may be heard in the hoofbeats of his *akicita*, the horse, and he is brought into a ceremony in the hail of the rattles and the thunder of the

9. Castro, whose useful scholarship on Neihardt's changes of the stenographic record preceded DeMallie's comprehensive treatment, defends Neihardt for omitting the soldier weed: "The deletion of the war-herb passage underscores the fact that Neihardt was more interested in the teachings of the man, Black Elk, who had had a Great Vision than in the literal content of the vision itself" (1983, 94). The humanism he attributes to Neihardt is implied in Castro's praise for "editorial decisions" that "tended to reduce ambiguity and enhance the clarity and power of . . . Black Elk's essential teaching—the unity and holiness of all life" (94–95). Perhaps Black Elk edited his vision more courageously than Neihardt, because any mature approach to knowing the unity of life must try to understand the place of the soldier weed in that unity. The spirits gave the soldier weed to Black Elk. He in turn gave it to Neihardt. But Neihardt did not recognize the necessity of contemplating the destructive power and withheld the herb from his readers. The non-Lakota attitude is humanistic rather than spiritual. No *wicasa wakan* (sacred man) would place himself before one of the *wakan waste* (good spirits). A vision should be received with some degree of fear before coming to a respectful interpretation. Unfortunately, Neihardt sometimes muffles the Lakota willingness to suffer with pantheistic clichés.

drums. These sounds attract benevolent spirits to assist the people, and by entering a circle where these sounds are made, the spirits show their respect for *Wakinyan*. Because *Wakinyan* impels the process, the other spirits and the people respond by helping to complete it.

Wissler reports how an equine *akicita* of *Wakinyan* inspired various incarnations through the Oglala Horse Society, which possessed medicines to capture wild horses, to make war horses faster, to heal their wounds, and to cure their ills: "A man went up on a high hill to fast. After four days a figure appeared to him. As it approached, it was seen to be a person. This person explained the rules and formulae. Then he became a horse and disappeared among the Thunders" (1912, 96). Soon after, a man captures a black striped buckskin stallion. The black is the color of potentiality, the yellow is the color of growth. The leader of the horse dreamers immediately sees what the horse is and orders it to be released: "At once, there was a great cloud; the horse went into it. Then it rained and thundered, the lightning flashing between the tipis. In the center of the storm, they saw the horse rising to heaven, his halter still trailing behind" (96). Respect for the Thunder horse progresses inevitably to the regeneration of life. Four remarkably swift horses are soon captured. As in Deloria's oral narrative, they breed descendants from which a *wakan* power flows to the people.

Many stories are told of the mystical rapport between men and horses. Bushotter reports several incidents of wounded men being rescued by their horses in the heat of battle. As in the case of other spiritual powers, the appropriate symbolic expression could transform a horse from an ordinary animal to a sentient and sympathetic *wawokiya* (helper): "Some men consider that the horse is mysterious; and they have horse songs. And it is said that when those songs are sung, the horses hear them and come to the place of the song" (E. Deloria ca. 1937, 56: 1). The sound symbols of a song evoked friendship from these spirited animals; the visual symbols, especially of the Thunder as reported by Blish, encouraged the horses to "act properly" in battle: "they include them with the warriors as fighters, and tie rattles or small bells around their necks" (56: 1). But the most dramatic sensory interplay between a spirit's *ton* (direct manifestation) and *tonwan* (embodied manifestation) (Walker 1980, 230), occurred in the rite of *Sunkawakan Wacipi* (the Horse Dance).

The Horse Dance fully unfolds the seed implanted in Black Elk at the age of nine. The Great Vision begins with a visitation from the *Wakinyan* and continues with instruction by them in their various forms. A vision is intended to foretell, in the sense that a seed foretells, what Black Elk will do for his people or more generally how a human being can redemptively transmit courage and vitality to his *takuyepi* (relatives). The word *wakinya* in the Lakota language means "to foretell accurately" and "to initiate, to begin." The reception of a vision begins a process intended to result in full manifestation through ceremony, song, or story. In fact, as DeMallie explains, the Thunder Beings had tormented Black Elk when he delayed the performance of his vision, until he presented the Horse Dance. Neihardt minimized through literary judgment or cultural misunderstanding the initiatory role of the Thunder. The men who take Black Elk to the clouds carry spears that represent the lightning:

> In the notes the men tell Black Elk "Your Grandfather is calling you," referring to the first (western) grandfather; *Black Elk Speaks* has "Your Grandfathers are calling you!", generalizing to all six grandfathers. The cloud house where the grandfathers sit in council is in the west, and it symbolizes the home of the western grandfather. Throughout the stenographic notes, Black Elk varies between referring to the grandfather(s) in the singular and in the plural. It seems that he understood himself to have been called by the western grandfather (for it was to that direction that he went) but that the western grandfather represented all six grandfathers. (DeMallie 1984a, 94)

In Black Elk's vision all the spirits may be considered phases of the spiritual maturation that begins with the Thunder power. DeMallie stresses that the predominance of the Thunder in the stenographic record was not translated into *Black Elk Speaks* with its reduced emphasis on "thunder and lightning, horses, dogs, swallows, butterflies, dragonflies. Each functions as a specific representation of the western powers" (1984a, 99). When Black Elk enters into the first instructive form, the "cloud-tipi," Neihardt does not tell us, as DeMallie does, just which power is exclusively associated with this kind of lodge. Walker reports the tradition of clouds being the garments of the Thunder Beings. Similarly, a Lakota rainbow is symbolic of the *Wakinyan*. The rainbow represents the mediating presence of visible form extending invisible sources of power. Black Elk names Neihardt Flaming Rainbow, "because wherever his words fall, they make the earth greener. And when his words have passed, the memory of them will stand long in the west like a flaming rainbow" (Whitney 1976, 20–21). The rainbow is an especially good symbol of mysterious revelation, the form that mediates between the visible and invisible worlds. Elk dreamers called their hoops "rainbows," because "part of the rainbow is visible in the clouds, and part disappears in the ground. What we see is in the shape of a hoop" (Densmore 1918, 259).

This multihued consciousness represents the maturity that follows a storm. When the black-horse rider gives Black Elk the soldier weed of destruction, Black Elk does not accept it as a precursor of peace. Horrified by its capacity to cause suffering, he eventually escaped the obligation to use it by becoming a Christian in 1904. It is possible, however, that the Thunder Beings did not intend this herb to have a brutalizing effect on the physical world, as Black Elk seems to have feared: " 'There will be a dispute of nations and you will defend your people with this herb' (I was not old enough when I was supposed to use this herb or else I could have used it and killed many enemies. It was too terrible to use and I was glad that I did not get to use it. This herb is in the Black Hills. . . . It looks like a little tree with crinkly leaves, reddish in color. I call this herb a soldier weed)" (DeMallie 1984a, 136).

Neither Black Elk nor Neihardt perceives this power to destroy as the power to scourge and cleanse. The heat of an *inipi* (ceremonial sweat bath) is made especially intense for Sun Dancers in preparation for their captivity in the *hocoka* (Sun Dance circle). Black Elk's power of destruction must be unsentimentally directed at those enemies who have forced the Lakota into "square, gray houses" in which despair has replaced challenge and the growth initiated by the *Wakinyan* has been poisoned. The weed is firmly rooted in the vision despite the Christian-influenced attempt of both Black Elk and Neihardt to bury it. Much of the power of *Black Elk Speaks* is a warrior power of outrage and rejection. If the reader is not aroused to resist the greed and arrogance of Manifest Destiny, the rainbow will remain blurred and faint. Black Elk says he was not old enough when he was supposed to use this herb "or else I could have used it and killed many enemies" (DeMallie 1984a, 136). Perhaps he is saying that he was not ready to realize that the herb of destruction could become words of fierce defense. Shortly after the description of the soldier weed, the result of courageous purification is literally embodied in Black Elk.

The butterfly cocoons are another Thunder symbol omitted by Neihardt, but they are vital to defining the dual aspects of Black Elk's power. The northern Grandfather tells Black Elk, " 'You have given the men of earth the power they have given you, and with courage they are facing the wind' (meaning the wind of life). 'Hundreds shall be sacred; hundreds shall be flames.' He came forward and put butterflies' cocoons onto my arms—a red one on the right wrist and a brown one on the left wrist. (Brown is sacred and red is lightning power.)" (DeMallie 1984a, 139). In order for hundreds to be sacred, the giants and tricksters must be reduced to ashes, though not necessarily by physical means.

Within a circle of consciousness purified by self-discipline and ritual instruction Lakota ceremonies work to complete spiritual growth. The Horse Dance in particular represents the course of this cycle. Fools Crow's Horse Dance fulfilled the expectations of the people by attracting the Thunder Beings. It did not shock them into panic at an unanticipated miracle. The people knew that a Horse Dance was especially pleasing to the western powers. Black Elk's unrevised description of the dance in *The Sixth Grandfather* invokes the west more particularly than does Neihardt's edited version in *Black Elk Speaks*. After the horses begin to dance, the four virgins enter an opening at the west. Because they represent undeveloped potentiality, they enter from the appropriate direction. Black Elk and the virgins then make a circle and exit west through an opening in the horses, followed by the six Grandfathers who also exit to the west. The four horse troops are always led by the black horses, which represent the warrior duties of leading and defending. All the participants face west while the virgin of the west accepts offerings from the sick and heals them. The western virgin temporarily possesses the *Wakinyans'* power of destroying sickness and renewing life.

When the whole village expresses respect and gratitude for the gifts of the Thunder by mounting horses and facing the west, the Thunder Beings respond: "There was a thunderstorm that came up from the west and stood close and watched the dance. This was the Thunder-beings that came to see them. You could see the hail falling, the great sheets of rain descending and the lightning flashing in the clouds and you could hear the thunder roaring" (DeMallie 1984a, 219). This inarticulate approval anticipates the transformation of the Thunder into the dancing horses and the singing men. The Thunders have chosen the horses and the people to be their *akicita* because the people have offered their bodies and voices in prayer. The sending of a vision is initiated by *wakan* powers, but it must be conceived and brought to physical life by the people:

> They will appear—may you behold them!
> They will appear—may you behold them!
> A horse nation will appear.
> A thunder-being nation will appear.
> They will appear, behold!
> They will appear, behold! (J. Neihardt 1979, 166)

The same progression is portrayed in the relationship between the black horse and the bay horse in the vision. Black Elk continually appears upon the bay, which represents the existence of the Thunder power in a mortal being of the earth. The brown or earth-colored animal has a black mane and tail, a corporal sign of *Wakinyans'* creative power, here manifested in an earthly form. While Black Elk is in the spirit world, he heals a sick black horse with an herb given to him by the "west spirit" (whom Neihardt changes into a directionless "Voice").

Just as the participants in a sacred ceremony reciprocally give the spirits life by preparing a circle for their activity, so Black Elk brings the Thunder horses to life ceremonially: "I took the herb and made a circle over the horse and as I did this they all said: 'A-hey, a-hey!' (calling for spirit power)" (DeMallie 1984a, 132). As in the Deloria oral narrative, a Lakota symbol of death and renewal should be noticed in the horse's act of rolling and arising, after which he is ready again to become a potent source of health and recognition. "Every time he snorted there was a flash of lightning and his eyes were as bright as stars. Then the stallion went forth and stopped suddenly, facing the west. He neighed and you could see the dust flying over there as he neighed. In this dust there were a million horses coming. These horses were happy and full of pep" (DeMallie 1984a, 132). Neihardt effectively communicates the role of the black stallion as the source of spiritual consciousness, a source that requires human ritual in order to be heard: "His voice was not loud, but it went all over the universe and filled it. There was nothing that did not hear, and it was more beautiful than anything can be. It was so beautiful that nothing anywhere could keep from dancing" (1979, 41–42).

Neihardt was drawn to Black Elk by a temperamental and mystical empathy, which also attracted Jung and thousands of other readers.[10] Although both Neihardt and Jung wrote extensively of human spiritual development, the symbolic systems with which they were most familiar were not Lakota. Although the vision's religious symbolism may be archetypal, the vision of *Hehaka Sapa* was originally spoken in the Lakota language as an intricate variation on a set of complex conventional symbols. Readers of the autobiography hear the message at two removes. By conscientiously studying and observing *Lakol wicho'an* (traditional Lakota culture) in relation to the text, a reader might look through both Black Elk and Neihardt to a Lakota wisdom tradition more profound than any single instrument or interpreter. Lakota prayers often include the refrain, "*nitunkasila waniyang u kte lo*" (your Grandfather will come to see you). A Lakota begins to pray by remembering the west. Neihardt did not remember the western virtue of *woohitika* (courage) through the full "life-story" or he could not have concluded his book so abjectly: "the nation's hoop is broken" and "the sacred tree is dead" (1979, 270).

At the end of the Horse Dance all the people face inward toward the central tipi, the symbol of sacred mystery dwelling in form. The eldest Grandfather, the spirit of the west and the source of all that lives, calls upon the people to charge the sacred tipi and "who shall coup it first shall have new power" (J. Neihardt 1979, 174). Just as it may be difficult for some people to understand how the Sun Dance pole can be considered an enemy for a warrior to count coup upon, so the treatment of a sacred gift and shelter in this manner may seem strange. But when the threatening face of uncertainty is couped, the people may live in a world of revelatory signs previously obscured by fear of the unknown: "The Grandfathers had sprinkled fresh soil on the nation's hoop that they had made in there with the red and black roads across it, and all around this little circle of the

---

10. H. David Brumble III introduces some atypical skepticism to published commentary on *Black Elk Speaks* by quoting a letter to Black Elk from Neihardt in which he proposes a biography and a history rather than the "strong desire to know the things of the Other World." The letter also proposes "to pay you well for all the time that you would give me" (1981, 29). Nevertheless, Whitney has thoroughly described Neihardt's sincere and highly developed mysticism, which began with a vivid dream at the age of eleven. As is frequently the case with an Indian youth-vision, Neihardt determined the purpose of his life and his vocation as a poet on the basis of this dream (1976, 17).

nation's hoop we saw the prints of tiny pony hoofs as though the spirit horses had been dancing while we danced" (J. Neihardt 1979, 174–75).

These prints are the *wasu* (hail-seeds) of the *Wakinyan*. Neihardt leaves only deep tracks of nostalgia and pity. His conclusion to *Black Elk Speaks* expresses despair for an "irreversible tragedy" that DeMallie identifies as characteristically non-Lakota: "with its unrelenting sense of defeat, *Black Elk Speaks* became an eloquent literary restatement of the theme of the vanishing American" (1984a, 56). The postscript to *Black Elk Speaks* might have a different interpretation than the one Neihardt apparently intended. When Black Elk calls upon the thunder for assistance, he is answered by "a scant chill rain" accompanied by a "low, muttering thunder" (1979, 274). The "muttering" is Neihardt's adjective, but the description of Black Elk standing with tears running down his face in the light rain is an objective image. Neihardt did accompany Black Elk to the summit of Harney Peak, and the light rain and Black Elk's tears did fall. Although the rain lasts for only a moment, the thunder's audibility is a traditional sign of hope. The spirits still answer Lakota prayers and the Thunder Beings still initiate courage by their reassuring sound.

Because the hopefulness or despair of the book's ending has become an interpretive question, it might be remembered that passive surrender is alien to the Lakota tradition and counter to the intent of the Thunder Beings who spoke to Black Elk when he was nine years old. The offspring of the *Wakinyan* grow to maturity on jagged rocks, and it is impossible for them to resist their nature. The sound of a *Cega Tanka Oyate* Big Drum (or Thunder Being) Nation still moves the dance.

PART TWO

Textuality, Cultural Appropriation, and Outright Theft

5

John Neihardt and *Black Elk Speaks*

A Personal Reminiscence

GEORGE W. LINDEN

In the beginning, *Black Elk Speaks* was not a book. It was an oral memory in the mind of an aging man. On May 10 and May 14–28, 1931, Black Elk spoke. There were no wire or tape recorders in 1931. Black Elk spoke in Lakota, his son Ben translated, and Enid Neihardt took shorthand notes. John G. Neihardt, the mystic poet, began writing from the transcript in June 1931. He wrote at a feverish and inspired pace, and by October the book was done. Thus was born *Black Elk Speaks,* which Raymond J. De-Mallie characterized as an "American Indian Rosetta Stone" (DeMallie 1984b, 110), an American Indian Bible, or as Vine Deloria Jr. put it, a "North American Bible of all Tribes" (J. Neihardt 1979, xiii).

I wish to defend the authenticity of this book and the honesty of the man who wrote it. In this passage from *Black Elk Speaks,* one gets a sense of its majesty and power:

> I looked ahead and saw the mountains there with rocks and forests on them, and from the mountains flashed all colors upward to the heavens. Then I was standing on the highest mountain of them all, and round about beneath me was the whole hoop of the world. And while I stood there I saw more than I can tell and I understood more than I saw; for I was seeing in a sacred manner the shapes of all things in the spirit, and the shape of all shapes as they must live together like one being. And I saw that the sacred hoop of my people was one of many hoops that made one circle, wide as daylight and as starlight, and in the center grew one mighty flowering tree to shelter all the children of one mother and one father. And I saw that it was holy. (J. Neihardt 1979, 42–43)

This is philosophy. But it is more. A scholar's overview states: "Amerindians always sensed the toll that human life takes from the environment. Man was not seen as separate from, and superior to, the rest of creation; the world that mattered was this earth, not an imaginary hereafter. Humans lived in a reciprocal relationship with nature, and repayment had to be made for the existence they enjoyed at the expense of other life" (Wright 1993, 34). Neihardt and Black Elk knew this reciprocal relationship and they knew that it was holy.

Some Lakota believe, as Russell Means said, that anything transformed from the oral tradition into writing is, in itself, a falsification into Western consciousness (1980). N. Scott Momaday, a Kiowa, did not believe this first step was a falsification. Speaking of Neihardt, he stated:

> Even though he could not understand the language that Black Elk spoke, we cannot doubt, I think, that he discerned quite readily the rhythms, the inflections and alliterations of the holy man's speech. . . . With the rhythms and pacing well produced, we have a masterpiece of transformation of the oral tradition from one language and culture into another without the loss of the essential spirit of the original narrative. . . . The transformation of speech into writing (and particularly *this* speech into *this* writing) is a matter of great importance, I believe. And Neihardt believed it also. He brought extraordinary care, sympathy and dedication to his task of faithfully reproducing the essence of the speech. (1984, 36–37)

By using the same word that Neihardt did, *transformation* (McCluskey 1972, 238), Momaday avoided the problems posed by *translations*. As a Canadian writer has wryly observed: "The authenticity of these renditions is sometimes questioned, especially when they have literary merit (it being meanly said of translations and wives that the faithful ones aren't pretty, and the pretty ones aren't faithful)" (Wright 1993, 55).

Black Elk Speaks has been called "The Book That Would Not Die." It is an apt label. Although *Black Elk Speaks* did not fall "stillborn from the press," the first edition in 1932 did not sell well and was remaindered. Some years later, Carl Jung discovered *Black Elk Speaks* and commented on the Great Vision. Jung "got it wrong," including the colors of the horses (Jung 1977, 14: 206 n), but that is no surprise. Jung had such an exotic private logic that accuracy was not his forte. The important thing is that Jung urged the work be translated into German. Years later, in 1953, it was published as *Ich Rufe Mein Volk* (I call my people).

Neihardt himself was teaching at the University of Missouri from 1948 on. He held his students spellbound with his renditions of *The Cycle of the West,* and many went on to experience *Black Elk Speaks.* I was one of those rapt students. I was one of Neihardt's "boys," as he put it. Once, when my mother visited him in a hospital after a horrendous car accident, he said: "Yes, Bill is one of my boys."

It was not until the 1960s and 1970s with the rise of the counterculture, ecological sensitivity, concomitant academic and popular interest in American Indians, and Neihardt's 1970 appearances on the *Dick Cavett Show* that the book became a best-seller. It has now been translated into eight languages and possibly more in the future. Popularity, of course, has little to do with literary quality or significance. Still, it is a joyous event when a good book is widely read and deeply appreciated.

Now there is a new stage: academic commentary and criticism. So *Black Elk Speaks* has gone through the phases of the creative collaboration of a determined *wasichu* and Lakota, to the appreciation of a few dedicated students, to wide popularity, to academic commentary and criticism. We are now in the phase of professors writing words about words. It is this latter stage that troubles me, for I am a commentator, not a critic. I do not intend to analyze or explain *Black Elk Speaks.* It is much too rich and more meaningful than anything I can say. You have to experience it yourself. And I hope that you will. I do intend to defend John G. Neihardt and the book he wrote: *Black Elk Speaks.*

If we examine the writings of the commentators and critics of the book, we find four different interpretations of Black Elk.

1. Raymond DeMallie's Black Elk is a tougher and more humorous Black Elk than the one portrayed by Neihardt and appears to be one who retained and returned to his Lakota vision following the writing of the book.

2. Clyde Holler's Black Elk is a pragmatic syncretist who cleverly combines traditional Lakota religion with the faith of the Catholic Church.

3. Michael F. Steltenkamp's Black Elk is a dedicated Catholic who used his Lakota religion as a tool to convert others to the True Faith and as a springboard for his own spiritual progress.

4. Julian Rice's Black Elk is an unreconstructed tribal separatist whose words were warped by the apostolic distortions and Manifest Destiny impositions of John G. Neihardt.

You can choose whichever Black Elk you want. Or you can choose to embrace them all. I want to focus on Julian Rice's book, because I see it as a sustained attack on John G. Neihardt and on the integrity of his book *Black Elk Speaks*.

Rice's animosity toward Neihardt is so great that he lists Black Elk as the author of *Black Elk Speaks, The Sacred Pipe,* and *The Sixth Grandfather* (Rice 1991, 155–56). But Black Elk wrote no books. Black Elk wrote very little except for a few letters, and even they were dictated, perhaps. Like many men of the past, Black Elk spoke. Socrates wrote no dialogues. Buddha wrote no sutras. Even Jesus wrote nothing unless we are to believe John 8:3–11, where he twice wrote something with his finger on the ground. We are not told what he wrote. But by this very act, Jesus undermined most of Western morality. I believe what he wrote was the truth beyond judgment.

Julian Rice is very much concerned with judgment. And his judgment is harsh. After praising *The Sixth Grandfather* (whose editor he later attacks), Rice states the thesis of *his* book, *Black Elk's Story:* "*Black Elk Speaks,* on the other hand, may perhaps be relegated to the ranks of nineteenth century curios, reflecting white misconceptions of Indians" (Rice 1991, 14). To many Lakota, such a statement comes close to blasphemy. It is akin to attacking Saint Paul before a foot-washing Baptist.

There is no question that Rice knows a great deal. He is a master of erudition. He has created a brilliant and sometimes beautifully written book. It has only one problem. It is unbelievable.

Julian Rice attacks Vine Deloria Jr., Raymond DeMallie, and John G. Neihardt. I will not defend Raymond DeMallie and Vine Deloria Jr. They are sensitive, knowledgeable, and articulate men. They can defend themselves. But John G. Neihardt (1881–1975) is dead. I feel it is my duty to say a few words on his behalf.

On what does Rice base his sustained attacks on John G. Neihardt and the authenticity of *Black Elk Speaks?* His arguments are of four types: (1) ad hominems, (2) straw man, (3) assimilation through unsubstantiated analogies, and (4) reversal of cause and effect.

The ad hominem arguments are of two types: (1) that Neihardt was a racist, and (2) that Neihardt was a Platonizing Christian apologist. Rice maintains that Neihardt was "a racist" (Rice 1991, 17) who held a "theory of the master race" (18) "who rode the crest of Manifest Destiny" (31). These assertions are either based on unfounded attributions or can be traced back to Neihardt using the phrase "the Ancient Aryan spirit" in his 1920 work, *The Splendid Wayfaring*. But the word *Aryan* had no such deep negative meaning in 1920 as it has today. It had yet to be distorted by Hitler and further warped by our politically correct times. This is reading a 1990s sensibility into a 1920s assertion.

Then Rice states that "the psychologically Christian Neihardt" (1991, 8), who equates "God" with "the eternal light" (7), "imposed" his "Platonistic sense" (7), a "Platonism that was exclusively Neihardt's" (26) on the Black Elk of *Black Elk Speaks*. How Rice sees this is a puzzle. There is no question that Neihardt's inspiration came from the Greeks. He greatly admired and often quoted Homer, Aeschylus, and Euripides. But Plato is a different fellow. Although Plato was a literary writer, he also developed a complete philosophy. I do not remember John Neihardt ever referring to Plato, though he could, like Freud, quote the Greek dramatists verbatim. As to Neihardt's alleged "Christianity" and his thereby being a "devotional" "apostolic poet" (49), that is answered very simply. John G. Neihardt was a mystic. Mysticism knows no church. Perhaps I may echo a recently retired politician of our day. I knew John G. Neihardt. John G. Neihardt was a friend of mine. He was no apostolic apologist.

Rice's "straw man" argument consists of equating the views of William J. Stolzman, S.J., with those of John G. Neihardt (1991, 36*ff.*). Stolzman maintains that Lakota religion, like Judaism, was merely a preliminary stage to the ultimate truth: Christianity. I have heard of guilt by association. Perhaps this is salvation by association. Stolzman's book was published in 1986. John G. Neihardt had already been dead for eleven years.

As to "assimilated unsubstantiated analogies," Rice spends a great deal of time drawing parallels between *Black Elk Speaks* and the works of Milton and Hawthorne (1991, 36*ff.*). What he says about Milton and Hawthorne is insightful, but it tells us nothing about the Homer-inspired Neihardt. It takes a very clever man to twist the word "emulate" (43, 51) and use it in a pejorative sense as Rice does. One must be careful of being too clever. When Siddhartha asked the Buddha why he had failed to achieve enlightenment, the Buddha replied: "You are too clever, Samana."

The "reversal of cause and effect" arguments all rest on a lengthy analysis of the Christian symbolism in Neihardt's *Song of the Messiah* (Rice 1991, 43*ff.*). But *The Song of the Messiah* is about Wovoka's vision, not Black Elk's vision. Wovoka was a Christianized Paiute whose syncretic prophecy swept the Plains. Furthermore, *Black Elk Speaks* was written in 1931. The *Song of the Messiah* was published in 1935. This is reading history backward.

The rest of Rice's assertions attacking John G. Neihardt and his work *Black Elk Speaks* consist of speculative psychology and are not worthy of refutation.

There is no question that John G. Neihardt was a romantic, which may have affected some of *Black Elk Speaks.* He tones down and even eliminates some of the darker aspects of Black Elk's vision, such as "the killer weed" and some of the destructive aspects of the north. He even "made a mistake" in the vision that has gone unnoticed by his critics (J. Neihardt 1979, 30). But Neihardt was not the falsifier that Rice believes him to be. Raymond DeMallie told me that the stenographic notes are accurate. Fred Robbins and I have examined the handwritten manuscript and compared it with the printed text. It is one of the cleanest manuscripts we have ever seen. And it is one of the most faithful.

So far, you have heard mainly the voice of Julian Rice. Let us hear some voices from the other side: Ella C. Deloria, native Sioux linguist, in a letter to Neihardt, March 18, 1932: "I have finished *Black Elk Speaks.* I want you to know that it makes me happy and sad all at once—sad for the days that are gone, and glad that a white man really lives who can enter into a right understanding of a Dakota's vision and can translate it into so poetic a form" (DeMallie 1984b, 111). Vine Deloria Jr. says of *Black Elk Speaks* and *When the Tree Flowered:* "These Indian books are now regarded as masterpieces of the literature on Indians, the standard by which other efforts to tell the Indian story are judged" (1984, 2–3). Frank Waters: "In developing *Black Elk Speaks,* Neihardt summoned all of his talent for writing poetry and prose. His great book made him justly famous, was eventually translated into eight languages, and endures to enrich us all" (1984, 17–18). Scott Momaday: "It is to Neihardt's credit that he intuitively perceived the underlying oral tradition and . . . merely helped to assist the story to achieve its final polished form. . . . In *Black Elk Speaks,* he exceeds his (written) tradition for a moment and makes that moment live forever thereafter" (1984, 35, 38). Peter Iverson: "[Neihardt] valued the old ways and honored them in both *Black Elk Speaks* and in *When The Tree Flowered,* capturing as no man before or since the flavor of the Sioux idiom" (1984, 106–7). Gretchen M. Bataille: "*Black Elk Speaks* has become a classic in American Indian literature, perhaps unsurpassed in the genre" (1984, 135). The strongest statement, perhaps, comes from the fine anthropologist Raymond J. DeMallie: "No author, either white or Indian, has yet written about the Lakota people in terms that bring their traditional religion and culture to life more convincingly than John G. Neihardt (1984b, 110). And he adds: "Neihardt was an extraordinarily faithful spokesman for Black Elk. Although his psychic empathy for Black Elk might have led him to take great liberties with the material, he did not do so" (120).

Nicholas Black Elk and John G. Neihardt were brother-mystics. This fact is why Black Elk, taking an image from his Great Vision, gave Neihardt the name Flaming Rainbow, and then Black Elk said: "You are a word-sender. The earth is like a garden and over it your words go like rain making it green and after your words have passed the memory of them will stand long in the West like a Flaming Rainbow" (DeMallie 1984b, 118). It was a name that Neihardt wore proudly.

Indeed, if one examines Joseph Epes Brown's *Sacred Pipe,* one finds it to have many more Christian elements than *Black Elk Speaks.* A naïve student reading *Black Elk Speaks* might conclude that Black Elk was not a Christian. But Nicholas Black Elk was a Catholic catechist for many years. He was estimated to have brought "at least 400 conversions through catechetical duties," and Father Westropp said of him: "Ever since his conversion he has been a fervent apostle and he has gone around like a second St. Paul, trying to convert his tribesmen to Catholicity" (Vecsey 1997, 277).

How fortunate Black Elk was to have found an empathic, humanistic poet to help him realize his words! Was it an accident? Was it a coincidence? Was it Jungian synchronicity? Black Elk did not think so. He stated: "Before I ever saw you I wondered about the dream and your brother ghost has put you here to do good to your people. . . . It seems that your ghostly brother has sent you here to do this for me. You are here and have the vision just the way I wanted and then the tree will bloom again and the people will know the true facts. We want this tree to bloom in the world of truth that doesn't judge" (DeMallie 1984b, 118).

Some Grandfathers helped, perhaps.

Some of the most quoted passages from *Black Elk Speaks* are these concluding paragraphs from the last chapter, "The End of the Dream":

> I did not know then how much was ended. When I look back now from this high hill of my old age, I can still see the butchered women and children lying heaped and scattered all along the crooked gulch as plain as when I saw them with eyes still young. And I can see that something else died there in the bloody mud, and was buried in the blizzard. A people's dream died there. It was a beautiful dream.
>
> And I, to whom so great a vision was given in my youth,—you see me now a pitiful old man who has done nothing, for the nation's hoop is broken and scattered. There is no center any longer, and the sacred tree is dead. (J. Neihardt 1979, 270).

Nicholas Black Elk and John G. Neihardt now lie beneath those everlasting snows. But the dream is *not* dead. John G. Neihardt *realized* Black Elk's vision; he made it real in written words, he made it real in the world, and it continues to live. If we believe it, if we follow it, if we live in this world as if all men—the red, the black, the white, the yellow—are brothers, then the flowering tree will bloom, not only in the world of truth that does not judge, but in *this* world. Perhaps.

6

Black Elk and John G. Neihardt

HILDA NEIHARDT AND R. TODD WISE

TODD R. WISE: Could you talk about the significance of why Black Elk adopted you, your sister, and your father?

HILDA NEIHARDT: Yes. In 1931, at the end of an old-time feast, Black Elk participated in a ceremony, and my father, my sister Enid, and I were taken into the Oglala tribe and given names. He gave my father the name "Peta Wigamou-Gke," meaning Flaming Rainbow, and he explained the name in this way: "This world is like a garden, and over the garden go your words like rain, and where they fall they leave everything a little greener." Then he added: "After your words have passed, the memory of them will stand long in the West like a flaming rainbow."

He named my sister "Ta-sa-Ge-a-Luta-Win." Enid was nineteen at the time and was attracted by the handsome young Indian men. Her name means "She Who Walks with Her Holy Red Staff," and Black Elk said that she would be married and have a nice home.

I was named "Unpo Wichachpi Win," which means "Daybreak Star Woman." He said the reason he named me that was because I wanted to learn. I have spent my whole life trying to learn. I haven't arrived yet, but I am still trying.

My father thought it was amazing that Black Elk saw the difference between my sister and me, because we were very different people. The significance of his naming me is that it stayed with me all my life. I care so much for the name and its meaning that I call my home "Daybreak." It is

This interview is an edited version of a talk given by Hilda Neihardt on November 3, 1997, at the University of Sioux Falls, which was made possible by a grant from the South Dakota Humanities Council.

a little hard to say how much the Black Elk experience has meant to me. Black Elk's daughter, Lucy, used to write to me as "Dear Niece Hilda," and she would sign the letters "your Aunt Lucy." The other day I told Esther DeSersa, who is a granddaughter of Black Elk, "You know, you may think this is funny, but I feel related to you." I remember so vividly Black Elk's saying: "There may come a time when you will need something, and we will help you, and there may come a time when we will need something, and you will help us." That has remained with me, because during my life I have had to travel the black road of worldly difficulties, but always seeking the Good Red Road of Spiritual Understanding.

WISE: Why didn't Black Elk share his Great Vision with his children?

NEIHARDT: I don't know why he didn't tell his children, but we must realize how sacred he held such things. You also have to bear in mind that he was living in a very unfriendly world. Our society was then tremendously unfriendly to anything like that, and he felt that he had to keep it secret, lest it might in some way be harmed. He also did not let anyone listen while he told his vision except Standing Bear, who had been his friend from boyhood and who knew him when he had his vision. Standing Bear remembered how sick Black Elk was when he lay for a week as if he were dead. But exactly why he hadn't told his family, I don't know. They knew nothing about it at the time. Perhaps it was the life he had lived, for everything was cut off after Wounded Knee.

My father was very much impressed by Black Elk's vision. In fact, my father declared during its telling that he knew of little in religious literature that was equal to what Black Elk told. It was not easy for my father to get permission to interview Black Elk and the other old men. It is difficult for us now to imagine, for now one can just drive at will to the reservation. But in 1931 he had to apply for permission from the Bureau of Indian Affairs and the secretary of the interior, and it took quite a while for permission to be given. The Board of Indian Commissioners wrote to the agent at Pine Ridge and said: "Mr. Neihardt is not an investigator, an uplifter, or anything of that kind, and while I thoroughly appreciate the fact that it would be unwise to grant wide open permission to strangers to hold meetings in your jurisdiction, I think you need have no fear whatever about helping Mr. Neihardt to get in touch with some of the old fellows up there." Further correspondence was required before Neihardt could go, and it is difficult for us now to realize that in 1931 people were still thinking of the Indians as hostiles, and the authorities were still concerned that a white man would go up there and cause an uprising. This was how they thought, but those Indians had nothing to "uprise" with!

WISE: Were his children taken to boarding school?

NEIHARDT: Oh yes, all of his children were taken to boarding school, where they were not allowed even to speak their native language.

WISE: Who was Flying Hawk?

NEIHARDT: Flying Hawk was the interpreter who went first with my father to see Black Elk. He was at the agency when my father learned from the old fellows gathered there that Black Elk had been in the Ghost Dancing. Flying Hawk offered to go with Neihardt, and on the way over to Black Elk's home he remarked: "You know, I don't think he will talk to you. I went over there two weeks ago with someone else. He is a strange old man, and I don't believe he will talk to you."

Neihardt said: "If he doesn't talk to me, he will be the first Indian person who refused." He had known many Indian people, and they had all been willing to talk to him. As mentioned, there was one person who had gone to see Black Elk and wished to talk to him—a well-known writer. Black Elk had said something to this effect: "I can see that you are a nice person, and I feel that you are good, but I don't want to talk to you about these things." It is noteworthy that my father had gone to the reservation just to find and get to know a holy man who had been in the Ghost Dance. The later interviews were all Black Elk's idea. As for Flying Hawk, it has been suggested that it was not Flying Hawk, but one Emil Afraid of Hawk, who went with my father that first day. I have spoken with the Black Elks about that particular point, and they say it was not Emil Afraid of Hawk, but Flying Hawk, whom they knew to be the interpreter used at Pine Ridge Agency.

After that first meeting in August 1930 as they drove back to Pine Ridge, Flying Hawk said: "Funny thing—it kind of looked like the old fellow was expecting us." My brother, Sigurd, was along, and he said he had noticed the same thing. As they had arrived, Black Elk was standing in front of the pine shade by his cabin, looking down the road. Black Elk knew intuitively many things. For example, I recall when my father and a minister friend had gone to see Black Elk. It was a hot summer day, and as they were leaving, he came out to their cars and said, through his son Ben: "You will have a nice trip today. A little later on it is going to rain, and it will be much cooler. There will come a nice rain about two o'clock." At two o'clock they were some two hundred miles away, and it did begin to rain. Both my father and his friend stopped. The pastor came up to my father's car and said: "You know, I believe it!" Yes, Black Elk was an amazing person.

WISE: Raymond DeMallie has reprinted a correspondence of your father where Black Elk gave him a "beautiful old sacred ornament that he had used a long while in the sun dances in which he has officiated as a priest" [DeMallie 1984a, 28]. In a recent book, Clyde Holler takes this as indirect evidence that Black Elk was a Sun Dance intercessor during the ban. Do you have anything to add to this? Can you offer anything about Black Elk's involvement or noninvolvement in the Sun Dances?

NEIHARDT: It appears that my father wrote a letter saying that Black Elk had used a beautiful old sacred ornament in the Sun Dances. Black Elk did participate in Sun Dances, but I don't know much more about his involvement. In 1944 Black Elk told us in detail about Sun Dances, which material is recorded in the book *When the Tree Flowered*. I might add that *When the Tree Flowered* is just as authentic as *Black Elk Speaks*, because it came from the same person. Because Dr. Wise had asked about the Sun Dance ornament, I recently asked Esther DeSersa, the daughter of Ben, who did the interpreting for Black Elk, if Black Elk had taken part in the Sun Dances. She said, in a most matter-of-fact way: "Oh, yes, he was in Sun Dances." So I am sure that my father would not have written the mentioned letter if he did not have reason to believe that Black Elk had been a participant.

There is a story about Black Elk's introduction to Christianity. As a young man, he was ministering to a sick child in a tipi when a Catholic priest came by. Black Elk was shaking his rattle up and down as part of the ceremony to heal the child. While Black Elk was doing this, the priest came into the tipi, took Black Elk by the neck, pulled him out of the tipi, and stamped on his rattle. He said: "Don't do that heathen thing!" It all seems to me a bit humorous, for a priest moves his golden censer ceremoniously back and forth, much as Black Elk was shaking his rattle made from a gourd or a turtle shell, up and down. The other day I was visiting with Esther and Olivia in Olivia's home near Porcupine, South Dakota. Esther was standing at one end of the room, looking very thoughtful, and—quite "out of the blue"—she remarked: "You know, they say that he was converted, but . . ." Then Olivia broke in with this: ". . . but he was already a holy man."

WISE: It is reported that your father gave his biographer, Lucile Aly, permission to remove his correspondence from the Neihardt archives in Columbia, Missouri. Is this material still available for other scholars?

NEIHARDT: Yes. Lucile Aly did write a biography of my father, and he helped her as much as he could. But her authority was only to go to the archives at the Western Historical Manuscripts Collection at the University of Missouri to inspect documents; they gave her photocopies. So, Dr. Aly had these photocopies, and she gave them to the Neihardt Foundation, and they are kept at the Neihardt State Historic Site in Bancroft, Nebraska. There they have been collated, put in files, and arranged according to date and subject. This material is also available for scholars, as well as the originals, which are at University of Missouri.

WISE: Why did Black Elk speak?

NEIHARDT: He spoke because the vision which he had been given was, he believed, a mandate for him to do something for his people, and he felt he had been unable to do so—that he "had fallen away and done nothing." He told my father when they first met: "If the vision was true and mighty then, it is true and mighty yet. It is for all people, and you were sent to save it." He believed that Neihardt was *sent* to save his vision, and he also felt that his vision was for all people. It is interesting to note the truth of that idea today. His vision is incorporated into the work *Black Elk Speaks*. That book has been translated into numerous languages, the most recent being Hebrew. It is evident that his Great Vision inspires people all around the world.

As we know, there has recently been criticism of *Black Elk Speaks,* although for years there was little or none. The famous Sioux writer Vine Deloria Jr. assured me a number of years ago, when I was concerned about something that had happened, in this fashion: "Hilda, don't worry, because *Black Elk Speaks* will always be the great classic." It seems clear that, had Neihardt not written about him, Black Elk would have remained unknown. The critics would have had nothing to talk about if the holy man had not told his story to Neihardt, and to do so was entirely Black Elk's idea. He chose when and to whom he would tell his vision and his life story.

This kind of confusion is one reason why I am compiling a book which will be the Black Elk family's book. While some students seem to ask everybody else, I want to let the Black Elk family speak. In a pensive mood, Esther had remarked: "Why don't they ask the family?" This book will express the family's experiences and point of view, and the book will be one way for me to do something for them.

Black Elk's counsel to his grandchildren was evidently taken quite seriously by them. I recently had a conversation with Olivia Pourier, the younger daughter of Ben Black Elk, and she told me that her grandfather and her father had often told them: "Get education, because that is the only way you can compete with the white man." Olivia has a little shop and museum which she maintains as part of her home, and she is proud that her children and grandchildren are all "traditional." Esther DeSersa is proud that all seven of her children have some college education.

Olivia and Esther were talking about the Ghost Dance with me recently. As many know, in the 1890s everything had been taken from the Indians. The buffalo had been almost entirely killed—first for their tongues, then for their pelts, and later just for the "fun" of shooting them. Trains had special tours for white sportsmen, who shot the animals out of the trains and fired continuously until their rifle barrels were red-hot. It has been reported that there was a time when one could walk along the Union Pacific Railway for many miles and never step off of buffalo bones.

The Plains Indians depended greatly on the buffalo for everything: clothing, food, shelter. So, with the loss of the buffalo, they were in trouble, and when people are in trouble, they often turn to religion for some hope. The Ghost Dance gave them that hope. It was a mixture, a blending of the Christian religion which they had been taught for years by the missionaries and their own native religious customs and beliefs. The people said that Jesus had come a long time ago to the white people, and they had killed him. "It must be so," they said; "they tell it themselves." They believed that Jesus would come again, this time to the Indian people, and he would be received by them. A critic has blamed Neihardt for putting Christian ideas into his *Song of the Messiah*, which is a book about the Ghost Dance period. Neihardt did not have to introduce those Christian thoughts; there had been Christian influences on the Indian peoples for a hundred years or more, and they were part of the mixture which was the Ghost Dance hope.

Why did Black Elk speak? Well, he spoke because he thought that his vision was something given to him for all people, and he did say "for all people." Today some Indian people understandably seem to be wishing to keep what they created for themselves, but Black Elk believed that it was for all people.

WISE: Why was the Ghost Dance feared by the white people?

NEIHARDT: Well, you see the Indians had been tremendous fighters. As with Crazy Horse, white people were afraid the Indians were going to start fighting again. It was because they misunderstood: when they saw the Indians dancing, they thought it was a war dance. That is all the white people seemed to know: when the drums were beaten, they thought it was preparation for war. Actually, I understand that drums were used more for religious ceremonies than for anything else.

The Ghost Dance began with a man out west, a Paiute Indian named Wovoka who had had a vision in which he was told that Christ was returning, that the world would change, and that all white people would disappear. He thought the earth would roll in waves and be alive again. Train tracks, roads, and fences would disappear. The buffalo and deer would come back, and all the Indian people who had been killed would return. Wovoka's vision showed how they would live under a blue, blue sky on a green, green earth forever. He dreamed that all the Indians needed to do was dance, and it would all happen. The tragic irony of the white man's fear of the Ghost Dance was that the Indians didn't have any weapons with which to fight. Everything had been taken from them. But they danced, even in the snow, and this frightened the white people so much that the Indian agent wired Washington for help because the Indians were dancing. The only thing the white men could understand was the war dance, and it was pitiful, for many of the Indian people were beyond that.

WISE: Could you tell us about the Ghost Dance shirt?

NEIHARDT: Black Elk had a vision about how the Ghost Dance shirts should be made. I remember the one Black Elk obtained for my father, and it seemed to be made out of a flour or feed sack. The shirts were very simple, with fringes cut around the seams and neck, and they were painted with sacred symbols. Wovoka told the people: "If you wear these shirts and dance the dance of the ghosts, our old world will come back and our people who have been killed, and also the buffalo and the deer." The earth would, he said, just roll, and all tracks of the white man would disappear. Some said that white man would disappear, but others said that it would not matter what color a man was. Wovoka and the Ghost Dancers believed that an Indian could not be shot while wearing his Ghost Dance shirt. At the time of the Wounded Knee massacre, while he was at Pine Ridge, Black Elk heard that something was going on at Wounded Knee. He went there and rode in front of the soldiers, holding up his holy stick. In so doing, he made it possible for women and children to escape. Black Elk said that it was not until he forgot for a moment and lost faith in his sacred stick that he was shot, and he showed us where the bullet had gone through his abdomen.

WISE: Was the Sun Dance treated the same way as the Ghost Dance? Did they think it was a war dance? Was that why it was outlawed?

NEIHARDT: They tried to do away with everything Indian, including their religion and their language. By "they" I mean the administration, the education authorities, and the Church. They all tried to do that. The Sun Dance was outlawed because it was an Indian ceremony, for they meant to stamp out everything Indian. I have been told many times that if little children spoke a word in their own language, they were spanked. That is true. The idea was to get rid of all Indianness, and make them be white people. The Indians were not able to do that, and they still are not able. They retained, and wish to retain, their Indianness.

WISE: Black Elk knew of the Christian faith and was a catechist, apparently involved in the conversion of over four hundred persons to Christianity. He knew about the savior concept in the Christian faith. Is there no concept of a savior in Black Elk's vision?

NEIHARDT: No, not particularly of a savior. Although in the Ghost Dance movement they thought there would be—that Jesus was coming back to them. I remember no talk of a savior in Black Elk's vision. The point of it was that one should live in a sacred manner. Indian people strive to live in a sacred manner, and in the old days one could not even enter a village without doing so in a sacred manner. Their religion was a part of their lives. My pastor tells me that is the way it should be in the Christian religion. But Indians lived that way. For me, I don't see serious conflict between basic Christian and the native Indian beliefs. I know there is conflict in doctrine, but in overall concepts, I do not see it. For me, the concepts of the Sacred Hoop are about all one needs to live a good life. Black Elk, I am told, did not see serious conflict between the two religions. One might put it this way: If there is a God—and I do so believe—then you could choose different ways to go to God, much as one could reach Chicago by way of differing roads.

WISE: It seems that some Native Americans don't see any problem with what is called "bi-religiousness" or "bi-theological orientation," that they can be very devout Christians but at the same time believe in traditional beliefs. Martin Brokenleg of Augustana College talks about the ability of Indians to follow faithfully two religious systems and to tolerate contradiction. He says that the Black Elk theology is a model for Native Americans because of this, even for those who are not Lakota. Vine Deloria Jr. has also said that *Black Elk Speaks* is a kind of a Bible for native America. It seems many Native Americans don't see a conflict.

NEIHARDT: Yes, I am told by his granddaughters that Black Elk didn't think there was much of a conflict. But let me recall a conversation that Neihardt and Black Elk had. It was during a break in the telling of the Great Vision, and the two were visiting. My father said: "Black Elk, when you have such a very beautiful religion, why are you a member of a white church?" Black Elk thought for a moment, then replied: "Because my children have to live in this world."

WISE: Raymond DeMallie points out in *The Sixth Grandfather* that the soldier-weed element of the Great Vision was left out of *Black Elk Speaks* [1984a, 97]. He also states that your father "transformed" some of the language or summarized some of Black Elk's original words. Could you talk about that?

NEIHARDT: Raymond DeMallie, he told me, first became interested in Indian people when he read *Black Elk Speaks* as a boy. He is a very enthusiastic student of Indian culture, and he became interested in the transcripts of the interviews as an adult scholar. These transcripts are in the Western Historical Manuscripts Collection at the University of Missouri, and many of my sister's original shorthand tablets, which seemed not to have been transcribed, are also in that collection. DeMallie came to me as trustee of my father's works and asked permission to use the transcriptions of the original interviews and to get someone trained in Gregg shorthand to transcribe the shorthand notes not yet typed. It was difficult for me to agree to his request, because of the protective feeling I had for those documents. It was the sacred nature of them that worried me. Many people urged me to grant permission, and DeMallie—a fine person—said to me that it would be done sometime, and that it would better be done by a friend. At that time I did not know that anyone was unfriendly, but it is apparent now that there are some who are so. With part of the transcription, I helped him; I knew some shorthand, and some matters were known about only by me. He found an expert in Gregg shorthand to transcribe other parts, and he included all of this work in his book.

You asked about the soldier weed which is not included in *Black Elk Speaks*. My father's intention in writing the book was to make a truly entirely Indian book—one entirely out of the Indian consciousness. Although I never spoke to my father about this point, it is possible that he focused mainly on the highly spiritual values which came from Black Elk. In 1932, when the book appeared, reviewers called it a beautiful book, but it did not sell. No one was particularly interested in Indians at that time, and it was remaindered at 45 cents a copy. I wish I could buy a few first editions now at that price! The book was appreciated, however, by the Sioux writer Ella Deloria, aunt of Vine Deloria Jr. In 1932, she wrote to Neihardt, asking "How is it possible for a white man to express the Indian idiom as you do in *Black Elk Speaks*?"

WISE: Julian Rice has written a book on Black Elk's Lakota purpose. In that book he says that your father's orientation to Christianity and to "German romanticism" affected some of the recording of Black Elk's actual words.

NEIHARDT: Professor Rice is one who thinks that Neihardt was too Christian. Of course, he was familiar with the Bible, as are most educated people in our society. By saying "German romanticism" you may be referring to Neihardt's use of the word *Aryan* in the introduction to his *A Cycle of the West*, which deals with the history of our West. As he used it, the term *Aryan* refers to those people who came from Mesopotamia; it has nothing to do with Hitler's notions, and the *Cycle* was completed before Hitler came upon the world scene and used the term *Aryan* in an unfortunate manner. Neihardt wrote about something that is historically true; Aryan people swept across Europe from east to west, and across our country as well. Rice worries about racism, but let me say that John Neihardt was certainly not a racist; in fact, he was a very early nonracist. He cared about Indians as people at a time when it was very unpopular to do so. He used to become quite annoyed when asked to tell about "Indian lore." My mother would calm him by saying, "Oh, John, they mean well," after which he would talk to them about Indian people, not "Indian lore."

The Song of the Messiah is about the Ghost Dance "craze," which was, as I have mentioned, a blending of Christian and native Indian religious notions. Quite appropriately, there is in *The Song of the Messiah* quite a bit that is Christian, and it is unfortunate that a critic seems not to be aware of the blending of religions that formed the Ghost Dance movement. He was no doubt not born early enough to be able to know persons who had taken part in the movement, as was Neihardt. Rice makes a point of Neihardt's reference to "the Word." He seems to believe that Neihardt was so "Christian" that he could not properly tell about Black Elk's native religion. Not so, and it should be known and realized that Neihardt had been close to Indian people for thirty years before he met Black Elk. He lived for years on the edge of the Omaha Reservation, and in his work for an Indian trader he associated with the Omaha people as a friend, visiting them in their lodges, eating their soup, hearing their stories, and cuddling their babies. An Omaha chief, Shonga Ska (White Horse), once stopped a tribal performance, took Neihardt to the center, and said: "This is a fine young man; he has the heart of an Indian. He is a fine young man."

Perhaps some people, unaware of this long association with Indian people, assume that it was just a reporter who went up to the reservation and talked with Black Elk. Of course, the book *was* written by John Neihardt, because Black Elk knew no English and could not write. Black Elk intuitively knew that Neihardt understood, and that is why he was chosen to tell the vision and the story.

WISE: After the work *Black Elk Speaks* came out, Black Elk had a wagon accident that he thought he might not live through. In the Roman Catholic Church there is a sacrament of extreme unction where there is the opportunity to be forgiven of all sins prior to death. There was a letter written at that time that has been described as a quid pro quo or conditional letter. That if you refute some views in *Black Elk Speaks,* then you will be granted forgiveness. Could you comment on that letter that was supposedly written by Black Elk?

NEIHARDT: Well, Black Elk did not know English, in spite of what anyone might say. His granddaughters have told me several times that he knew no English. I don't see how he could have written a letter and known what it said. The church people frightened him almost to death when *Black Elk Speaks* came out. They had him so scared that for a while he denied Neihardt; then, a few years later, he sent a letter to Neihardt as "my dear friend." His letters, of course, were written for him by his son Ben or his daughter, Lucy. He told them in Lakota what he wished to say, and they wrote the letter in English. If he was urged to deny what was in the book in order to be granted forgiveness (for what?) at a time when he was in mortal fear, it does seem that was a shameful thing to do.

I recall an interesting happening in connection with Black Elk's injury sustained in the wagon accident you mentioned. My father had a friend in Branson, Missouri, who was psychically gifted and who could perform at will what he called "astral flights." Sitting in our lighted living room one evening after dinner, my father asked the psychic if he knew "what my good friend Black Elk is doing tonight." Turning the diamond ring he wore around so he could stare at it in the palm of his hand, the psychic achieved the concentration he needed. Then he told us: "Black Elk has been hurt. He was thrown out of a wagon and is in bed. There are several men in the room with him. . . ." When my father asked if he could describe any of the men, he responded that one of them had a long scar down one side of his face. Some weeks later, my father was visiting the Black Elks and asked if there was an evening while Black Elk was bedfast when some of his friends were visiting. They indicated there was, and my father asked if there was anything distinctive about one of the men. The family members talked among themselves for a while, then one of them drew a hand down the side of his face to indicate the presence of a long scar! So we learned in an unusual way about our friend's injury, but I feel sure that Black Elk would not be surprised about it.

WISE: After the work *Black Elk Speaks* was written, did your father go back and read it to Black Elk?

NEIHARDT: No, he did not. But of course it was sent to Black Elk, and those in the family who could read it did so. Ben Black Elk, who had done the interpreting for his father, was happy about the book, and he used it himself and became somewhat of a disciple of his father.

Ben Black Elk traveled to Europe and all over this country, telling about his father and the Great Vision. In the video I am showing here, which was made in 1955 at my father's home in Columbia, Missouri, you can see the friendship which existed for Ben, his wife, and my father.

WISE: A recent author, Michael Steltenkamp, interviewed Lucy Looks Twice, the daughter of Black Elk. He interviewed her during the 1970s. I wonder if you could address the change that took place after she read her father's book. Could you address the discrepancy that is apparent between your own book and Michael Steltenkamp's account regarding Lucy Looks Twice?

NEIHARDT: At the time Steltenkamp talked to Lucy Black Elk, she had been a lifelong member of the Catholic Church, and she knew almost nothing about her own native religious ideas. In a sense, the Black Elk family, as other Indian families, was forced into a religion other than their own, because they were taken as children and sent to Catholic schools. This changed considerably for Lucy upon the death of her husband, Leo Looks Twice. She told me: "When my old man [Leo] died, my church did not do anything for me." She referred, of course, to the Catholic Church. At the suggestion of a friend or relative that she read "the book about your father," Lucy finally did read *Black Elk Speaks*.

Lucy spoke simply about the effect which reading the book had upon her. "It changed my life!" After that, Lucy became something of a pipe carrier, for she took with her the sacred pipe that Black Elk had given to her.

During the time when Steltenkamp was talking to Lucy, her nieces inform me that she was ill, and I know that she had cancer, from which she later died. Her nieces found it hard to believe that Lucy said some of the things reported by Steltenkamp, and they have tried to explain that problem based upon the condition of her health.

Apparently, someone invited Steltenkamp to the family picnic we had in 1975 on Esther Black Elk's land beside Wounded Knee Creek. Christopher Sergel, the playwright who had written a play called *Black Elk Speaks,* was there, and also David Carradine, who wanted to play the part of Black Elk. Because of Carradine's modest behavior, which the family considered much like that of a young Indian man, the Black Elks also wanted David to play the part. While steaks which the photographer and I had purchased in Sioux City were broiling on a campfire, Carradine suddenly appeared before us, swimming in the muddy creek, which was bank-full after a heavy rain. He had unobtrusively walked up the creek, undressed, and swum down to where we were gathered. Everyone was pleasantly surprised at David's rather "macho" effort, Esther later saying that she thought it was "cute." Swimming back up the swollen stream was quite a feat.

A couple of years later, Lucy was visiting at my home, and the academic dean of Stephens College in Columbia, Missouri, invited Lucy to talk at the college. Lucy did, and she displayed the natural dignity which I have noted in Lakota people. After living her entire life on the reservation, Lucy sat in a fine lounge in that exclusive school and told girls from all over our country about her life. Of course, they were interested in hearing about *Black Elk Speaks,* and Lucy told them what I have related before: "When my old man died, my church did not help me any. I told my friends that, and they asked why I did not read the book about my father. So I did read it." Before she could continue, a student raised her hand and asked: "And what did it do for you?" Lucy replied quickly: "It changed my life!"

It was Lucy who first told me that her father stated that he continued to believe mainly in the "pipe religion," and Lucy carried and used his pipe after that. I do not doubt that she, because of many years in the Church, did continue to attend. Her funeral was conducted by a priest, but much of Indian religious matters were included in it. Lucy did become a very earnest proponent of her father's ideas. For example, when she saw the play called *Black Elk Speaks* at the Shakespeare Theatre in Washington, Lucy said: "I heard my father speak tonight."

Lucy told me something interesting that her father told her when he was near death. Esther, Olivia, and Lucy took care of Black Elk when he was old and infirm. One evening, Lucy said, when members of the family were gathered around him, Black Elk told them that he wanted them to know that he did not really believe in anything except the pipe religion. That is the way Lucy told it to me.

WISE: Black Elk was apparently a devout Catholic but was also devout to traditional Lakota belief. I wonder if you could relate this to the Great Vision of Black Elk. Michael Steltenkamp made a comparison of the Great Vision to the "Two Roads" Map. The "Two Roads" Map was a missionary device used to communicate Christianity. On the map there is a road that leads to heaven and a road that leads to hell, I believe. Steltenkamp implies that a blending may have occurred, that Black Elk's Great Vision may have included characteristics from that map. He says at one point that he is tempted to see a "one to one" correspondence between the Great Vision and the "Two Roads" Map. My question is related to the black road of Black Elk's Great Vision. Where the black road and red road cross, that place is said by Black Elk to be sacred. Steltenkamp seems to state that the black road is the same as the Christian understanding of evil. On the other hand, you have stated that the black road is the road of everyday difficulty. Could you address this discrepancy?

NEIHARDT: I am glad to have a chance to address that. First of all, let us remember that Black Elk's vision came to him years before he was "converted" to Christianity, and that the concept of a Sacred Hoop is an old one.

I do not know just when the idea of the "Two Roads" Map originated, but I am guessing that it was preceded by the Sacred Hoop concept.

As Black Elk told us about the Sacred Hoop, it is one of the most beautiful and meaningful concepts I know. In telling it, Black Elk stretched out his arms to form a large circle. "Imagine," he said, "a hoop so large that everything is in it, including the two-leggeds, the four-leggeds, the wings of the air, the fishes of the streams, and all green things that grow. Everything is in this hoop. Beginning in the East, where the days of men begin, and crossing over the Hoop to the West, where the days of men end, lies the black road of worldly difficulties. We must all walk on this road. But, if this were the only road, then this life would not mean much. There is another road, and it begins in the south, where lives the power to grow, and proceeds to the north, the region of white hairs and death. This is the Good Red Road of Spiritual Understanding, and where this road crosses the black road, that place is holy, and there springs a tree which shall fill with blooms and singing birds."

The essence of this concept is true, for does not spiritual understanding make it possible for us two-leggeds to cope with the difficulties which all of us must face as we walk the black road? The crossing place is holy because spiritual values do bring understanding to the difficulties of ordinary life.

Dr. John Schneider of the department of religion at Calvin College, Grand Rapids, Michigan, who is presently the executive director of the Neihardt Center, made a comment to me which I thought shed light upon this subject. His thought: Black Elk's interest, if interest he did have, in the "Two Roads" Map, which consists of two parallel roads, may have been the product of his lifelong belief in the two roads which cross in the Sacred Hoop. In other words, Dr. Schneider would reverse the comment made by Steltenkamp.

As for evil, I can think of no mention of evil or of sin in connection with the Sacred Hoop.

WISE: What impresses me so much about Black Elk is his selflessness. He seems to be so concerned for others. Could you comment on that?

NEIHARDT: I doubt that any truly great person asks for anything just for himself. When Black Elk prayed, which was often, he usually prayed: "Oh, make my People live!" While we stood on Cuny Table in the Badlands, Black Elk prayed, while his son stood on one side and my father, sister, and I on the other: "I myself, Black Elk, and my nephew, Mr. Neihardt. Thus the tree may bloom. Oh, hear me, Grandfathers, and help us, that our generation in the future will live and walk the Good Road with the flowering stick. . . ."

Mother Theresa, who recently left us, probably asked for little for herself. I think that true religion should make one become more like Mother Theresa or Black Elk. Most of us cannot achieve that, but religion should keep us traveling in that direction.

WISE: There seems to be a rebirth of native spirituality. Are there shamans on the reservation, and do they still practice?

NEIHARDT: There are still men who are holy men, and they do practice. I do not know much about that. The term in Lakota for a holy man is *wicasa wakan,* and it is not easy to translate the term *wakan*. It means mysterious, powerful, strange, sacred, holy. Olivia Black Elk said to me not long ago that all her children and grandchildren are doing well and are "traditional." It is quite evident that members of the Black Elk family continue to believe in native spirituality, and of course many white people do as well. There is a great deal of interest, and people are seeing and feeling the genuineness of the Lakota spirituality.

WISE: Could you tell us about the John G. Neihardt Center?

NEIHARDT: The Neihardt Center—now called the John G. Neihardt State Historic Site—is in a small Nebraska town, Bancroft. My father lived there with his mother and sisters, and after he married, our family continued to live there until 1920. It was in Bancroft that Neihardt first came to know the Omaha Indians, and here he wrote his short stories, many of them about the Indian people, and began his major work, *A Cycle of the West*. A number of years after our family left, townspeople became interested in the idea of a memorial to Nebraska's poet laureate, and the idea grew until the Nebraska legislature appropriated a sum to build a building.

The beautiful brick center, designed in the round like the Hoop, was dedicated in 1976, and since that time it has become a popular spot for tourists and scholars. It is managed and operated by the Neihardt Foundation under the aegis of the Nebraska State Historical Society. It is a museum, it houses a growing collection of archives, and it is a cultural center. The Spring Conference held in April has earned widespread respect, and presentations are made by persons of note. The first Sunday in August has been legislatively declared "Neihardt Day," and programs of a more relaxed variety are presented on the grounds on that day. Visitors from around our country and from many countries abroad visit annually.

A special feature is the Sacred Hoop Prayer Garden, which depicts the Hoop as Black Elk described it. A hedge of flowering bushes creates the circle, and two roads—one black and one red—cross where a flowering tree stands. Flowers at each quarter indicate the color which represents it: blue for the west, white for the north, red for the east, and yellow for the south. Originally it was called the "Sioux Prayer Garden," but the name was changed because other tribes also believe in the concept of a Hoop or Circle.

The concept of the Hoop is inclusive, not exclusive.

7

A Retrospective on *Black Elk: Holy Man of the Oglala*

MICHAEL F. STELTENKAMP

Long before the motion picture *Dances with Wolves* captured the imagination of filmgoers, *Black Elk Speaks* and *The Sacred Pipe* conjured up vivid mental pictures of arcane ritual set against the backdrop of Lakota campfires and buffalo-skin tipis. These books gave readers the compelling portrait of Black Elk, a man who became the enduring stereotype of Indians associated with frontier times. As defeated warrior, saddened elder, wilderness ascetic, native ecologist, and religious philosopher, he became synonymous with a clean environment that vanished along with his people.

The holy man won the hearts of readers for clinging to a dream of earlier times when his people roamed free on the open plains. Romanticized this way, he escaped being labeled ethnocentric or racist, but was instead appreciated for maintaining a monocultural perspective that was understandably intolerant of the non-Indian ways that displaced his people's earlier traditions. Revered as someone who was immune to, and unaffected by, contact with anything non-Indian, Black Elk has reigned within native literature as the preeminent spokesman for times past. However, this perception was eventually altered because it became known that his life experience included more than what was previously known.

Black Elk: Holy Man of the Oglala (Steltenkamp 1993) showed that the Lakota elder successfully adapted to changing times, and that his worldview was not as parochial as many had thought. Prior to this biography, the holy man's experience with Buffalo Bill in Europe was simply regarded as a sojourn overseas that had little to no formative impact on him. Similarly, commentators only noted, without question, more universal themes that were congruent with his thought. For instance, Joseph Campbell said that Black Elk represented the native mind untouched by non-Indian religious mythology (1989).[1] However, readers now know that Black Elk was not as monocultural as they once were led to believe.

After reading the Black Elk books, I naïvely assumed that the holy man was representative of "all Indians," and that "all Indians" longed for a resurgence of pre-Christian religious practices within native America. I wanted to learn more about those pre-Christian forms, and in doing so, discovered that there was much about Black Elk and his generation that the earlier books did not address. It was this lacuna that became the basis of his completed biography, and it was this biography that was the fulfillment of his daughter's lifelong dream.

I went in search of Black Elk's secret, sacred information that I thought was accessible only through knowledge and practice of ancient Lakota ways. Contrary to this assumption, I came to learn that the holy man's theological counsel was simple and straightforward. Essentially, he would tell people to pray for insight drawn from a Creator who made all things, and from His Son, Jesus, who pitched his lodge among the two-leggeds. Although Black Elk's words were reverently and kindly uttered, they have become, since his death, a source of, at times, unkind and irreverent debate. The following pages will tell how I discovered Black Elk's world, how it came about that I produced a biography of this special man, and why this biography has stirred debate over what constitutes "true" Indian religious identity.

My Indebtedness to Neihardt and Brown

As a "life story," *Black Elk Speaks* was popularly regarded as the diagnostic biography of native America as a whole. This understanding was widespread (and still is), but it was especially prevalent among many of my generation who found this image of the holy man very appealing. The book set me in search of still-living Indians who could dissipate my agnosticism

1. This lecture of Campbell's was presented in a Public Broadcasting Series that featured talks the scholar gave between 1982 and 1984. As with other readers of the Neihardt classic, Campbell was led to believe that Black Elk was "a man in his nineties" when interviewed by the poet. Black Elk was actually in his mid-sixties.

by unambiguously revealing the Creator who seemed to be on such intimate terms with primordial holy men such as Black Elk. Because it was within their religious landscape that I wanted to camp, I mastered as much literature as I could find that dealt with American Indian life.

Joseph Epes Brown seemed an answer to my prayer when I learned that he was a visiting professor the year I began graduate studies at Indiana University. Just before taking a teaching position on the reservation where Black Elk once lived, I received Brown's blessing on my religious quest when he signed his book: "To my good friend, and student, Mike, who is walking the Good Red Road, and who will help his students catch the Sacred Ball."

Upon leaving Indiana, I held the erroneous notion that anyone who was truly native was not on good terms with the religion exported from Europe. Back then, I subscribed to the still-current thesis that many Indians might have accommodated some externals of Christianity, but within their hearts beat a desire to drum out anything associated with the invasive religion. My thinking changed when I met Black Elk's only surviving child, Lucy Looks Twice, and others who knew the holy man.

Going Beyond the Neihardt-Brown Portrayal

I was told that after Wounded Knee, Black Elk felt aimless, ill, and dissatisfied with what he was doing as a medicine man. He met a Jesuit priest, and was baptized a Catholic on December 6, 1904, on the feast of Saint Nicholas. Black Elk was ever after known to people as someone who "learned what the Bible meant, and that it was good. . . . He never talked about the old ways. All he talked about was the bible and Christ" (Steltenkamp 1993, 54).[2]

As many before me had done, so had I thought that Neihardt and Brown presented the totality of Black Elk's life—in all its nineteenth-

---

2. I am quoting a cousin of Black Elk's, born ten years before the Wounded Knee massacre. Contrary to what the occasional critic has said, I did not rely too heavily on information supplied by Lucy Looks Twice in portraying Black Elk as such a faithful catechist because her remarks were actually representative of all who remembered him. The relative quoted here, almost thirty years older than Lucy, was even more "revisionist" than the holy man's daughter.

century one-dimensionality. However, after interacting with his family and friends, I learned about a man who was respectfully and affectionately remembered as "Nick," the "faithful Catholic catechist." He was not remembered foremost as one who was consumed with nostalgic memories of hunting buffalo, skirmishing cavalry, or practicing rites that predated the Jesuit missionaries.

Eager to learn all that could be known about the man, I plied consultants with a range of questions over the course of several years. Mundane topics included: What was his favorite food? Did he speak much English? Did he consume coffee, soda, or alcoholic beverages? What type of clothing did he wear, and which style did he favor? Did he like riding in an automobile? I also pointedly asked if Black Elk did not like "white people," and if he wanted them to disappear. Was his spirit broken because the old rites were no longer practiced as much as they once were? Would he have wished that Christianity never came among his people? I anticipated receiving affirmative answers that would corroborate the conventional wisdom that still, these many years later, prevails. However, I was as surprised as anyone to learn that the answer to these latter questions was an emphatic "no."

I was disappointed to think that I would not uncover the gnostic mysticism that he was thought to have possessed. However, his daughter and friends said that I already knew about the ancient mysteries that were most important to him. All were insistent that he cherished the doctrine and spirituality of what would today be described as a very typical Catholicism of the period. This information was not the revelation I originally sought.

The Black Elk of Neihardt and Brown was absorbed with the old ways, so it was reasonable to conclude that his melancholy was at least partly attributable to the emergence of Christian practices at the expense of traditional Lakota forms. Curious about his late-life disposition, I regularly raised the topic, and was told that he was far more optimistic than popularly portrayed. Whatever sadness he might have experienced had nothing to do with Christianity, but rather with the growing secularism he saw arise among his people. However, despite testimony from those people who knew him best, the holy man's earlier image is an enduring one that many people are reluctant to alter. I have even heard people say that they stopped reading *Holy Man* because they did not want to let go of the image fashioned by Neihardt and Brown!

My mentor, Joseph Epes Brown, offered the following reason. Refer-ring to Black Elk's years treated in *Holy Man*, he wrote: "I have felt it im-proper that this phase of his life was never presented either by Neihardt or indeed by myself. I suppose somehow it was thought this Christian partic-ipation compromised his 'Indianness,' but I do not see it this way and think it time that the record was set straight" (Steltenkamp 1993, xx). Christianity's place within native America can be a contentious topic, and Brown's position is not shared by everyone. John Neihardt also knew the fuller story but was insistent that Catholicism influenced Black Elk only "here and there in spots" and never in a fundamental way.[3] Although inac-curate, the poet's position is a popular one, and is often stated in even more heated terms.

The Resilience of Black Elk's Prereservation Image

Preserving Black Elk's image as an unreconstructed traditionalist has been creatively argued. One evaluation of Black Elk's identity is that the holy man led two lives. That is, while appearing to be a fervent Catholic, he was, in private, a diehard old-timer (see DeMallie 1984a, 80). Holler and Rice weave this position into their writings, but an Oglala woman's query is more illustrative of the misdirection that has taken place not just among academics, but also within native circles. Concerning Black Elk's praying the rosary, she peremptorily asks: "Who's to say Black Elk wasn't saying Lakota prayers to each bead?" (see Bartholomew 1994, 10).

As with other speculation that now arises long after Black Elk's death, her question is conceivable, but more important, its answer is applicable to other questions of the same variety. That is, those people who knew the holy man would say his Christian practice was transparent. For example, if anything was certain about Black Elk, it was his devotion to praying the rosary. "Who's to say" that this was the case? Everyone who knew him!

I was told by Black Elk's daughter, his old friend John Lone Goose, his granddaughter Regina, and other Manderson residents that: (1) they prayed the rosary with him often; (2) toward the end of his life, he seemed to pray it by himself constantly because he always had one in hand and was

---

3. I received this information from F. W. Thomsen who tape-recorded John Neihardt shortly before the poet died.

heard saying the prayers; and (3) everyone in Manderson knew he said it all the time. His behavior was manifest, and he was known to pray his rosary both silently and aloud. In the last years of his life, there was no social pressure exerted upon the holy man to feign any type of religious behavior. Besides, such pretense would have never occurred to him.

The psychological condition referred to as the "Stockholm syndrome" has also been offered as a reason Black Elk and others of his generation responded positively to evangelization.[4] That is, they were hostage to the alien culture, but through some sleight-of-psychopathology and coercion, they sympathized and identified with their oppressors by adopting the inventory of "foreign," Euro-American cultural ways, such as hairstyles, clothing, religious practices, and so on.

In trying to make sense of that bygone era, this type of analysis can be persuasive, but it in no way reflects the reality of the man people knew as Nick Black Elk. Despite enduring horrific experiences in a convulsive period of history, Black Elk was self-possessed, and was not oppressively constrained by "foreign" persons or institutions. Rather, the holy man stood strong, and was a source of inspiration for others in his role as catechist.

Following the publication of *Holy Man,* Hilda Neihardt published *Black Elk and Flaming Rainbow.* A book largely based on recollections of her father's visit with Black Elk, this volume makes assertions that need the corrective offered here. Apart from misidentifying me as "an author" who "visited Lucy in 1973," Hilda stated that the holy man's daughter became a "pipe carrier" (a designation that gained currency in the 1980s, referring to Indians who associated themselves with "traditional ways"), and that she regretted telling me the story of Black Elk's life as a catechist (H. Neihardt 1995, 13). She further claimed that Lucy forsook her lifelong practice of Catholicism, and that she quit her membership in what Hilda Neihardt tellingly classifies as a "white church." She rhetorically concluded this section of her book with the puzzling question: "Isn't it always important that the truth be known?" (119).

Because *Flaming Rainbow* itself presents a seriously misleading description of Lucy, I was not at all sure as to what truth Hilda Neihardt was

---

4. See West and Martin 1996 as well as Auerbach et al. 1994. Neither of these articles refer to Black Elk or Indians per se, but they refer to the phenomenon that some have informally suggested is applicable to them.

alluding. In addition to this, and contrary to what her book reports, I was not "an author" who only visited Lucy in 1973. Rather, I was a teacher at the Red Cloud Indian School, and my visits with Lucy were numerous from 1973 until her death five years later. Moreover, in a letter written to me just weeks before she died, Lucy said she prayed that our effort would "have success" and that her adult children would straighten out their lives and "return to the Sacraments." She was disappointed that ill health prevented her from attending midnight Mass on Christmas Eve because she had especially looked forward to meeting the visiting African priest who was the celebrant.

When Hilda Neihardt said that Lucy "converted" to pipe-carrierdom upon finally reading *Black Elk Speaks,* I evaluated *Flaming Rainbow* as simply an advertisement for John Neihardt's book. Unfortunately, by contrast, Clyde Holler cited Hilda Neihardt's work as an authoritative contribution (1995, 13). Our perspectives were probably different because I had witnessed Hilda alter Lucy's reality on an earlier occasion (Steltenkamp 1993, 168).

Wanting promotional photographs for the opening of a play based on *Black Elk Speaks,* Hilda Neihardt staged shots of Lucy Looks Twice holding a pipe (not Lucy's, because she did not own one) because this would show (again, erroneously) that the holy man's daughter carried on the religious tradition reported in John Neihardt's classic. Photographs of Lucy praying with a pipe would confirm the adage that "a picture is worth a thousand words." In this instance, however, words were needed to caption the photograph's misrepresentation. Black Elk's elderly daughter had no familiarity with pipe usage, and she needed instruction from others as to how a pipe should be held.

Ironically, whatever appreciation Lucy had for the Lakota pipe tradition was partly attributable to me! We had lengthy conversations about various religious practices, and she was surprised that I knew as much as I did about the pipe (never giving it much attention herself). Because of my reverence for the tradition, Lucy had her son make a pipe for me, and because of our very different interest in Black Elk's story, Hilda Neihardt and I will perhaps always represent polar perspectives.

Because *Holy Man of the Oglala* fleshed out the previously incomplete "life story" of Neihardt's Black Elk, Hilda Neihardt might have been trying to protect the integrity of her father's text by criticizing mine. However, *Holy Man* simply confirmed what DeMallie and others had already addressed, that is, John Neihardt took liberties in portraying Black Elk the way he did.[5] Frank Fools Crow, Black Elk's famous nephew, rendered an even harsher judgment in a biography published before *Holy Man*. There he flatly stated, "That is not my uncle" when *Black Elk Speaks* was read to him by writer Thomas Mails (Mails 1991, 15).

Not to be outdone, Hilda's sister, Alice, might yet find a larger reading audience than any Black Elk author owing to a little-known tradition started by her father that she has continued. Namely, despite Houdini's celebrated debunking of spiritualism, Alice has conducted seances that purportedly enable her to speak with the dead. Just as her father claimed to have special communication with Black Elk during life, so did he claim that their communication was sustained via necromancy after the holy man died. Seances subsequently conducted by Alice have produced revelations that she apparently considered making public by means of yet another Neihardt book.

A man who represented himself as her editor stated that Alice spoke with her father, Lucy, Black Elk, and others from beyond the grave. He showed me some of the new revelations and thought I might be able to authenticate the phraseology attributed to Lucy. My evaluation of the material concluded that, whatever their source, the words and thoughts were not from the person I knew as Black Elk's daughter.

Because Alice Neihardt's manuscript also included communications from her father and Black Elk, it might draw many readers who still seek inspiration from these special persons long dead. However, based on the limited sampling shown me, I do not think they would be very satisfied. If the revelations were, somehow, received from the "Great Beyond," they reveal only that the altered state of consciousness for people in the afterlife is little different from the mundane consciousness of people in this one.

Divorcing Christianity from the Lakota Past

I was not surprised that Black Elk's association with Christianity elicits repudiation from some quarters. Even I had been caught off guard by the

5. The poet himself changed the book's attribution when later editions noted "as told through" instead of "as told to" John Neihardt.

association when first introduced to his fuller story. Still, I was bewildered to see a widely distributed reference work address the topic with little more than polemic. In the egregiously flawed *Encyclopedia of North American Indians,* readers are told that "the role of staunch Catholic was forced upon" Black Elk and that "he played it well to appease his oppressors" (Hoxie 1996, 73).

Unfortunately, this type of ambiguous and misinformed characterization has become commonplace, and is an example of what DeMallie evaluates as "political rhetoric rather than objective assessment" (1984a, 80). A major problem with the approach is that it aims to preserve his legendary stereotype, but it implies that the holy man lacked strength in standing up for what he *really* believed. Consequently, the "corrective" is not at all flattering because it states that Black Elk lived a life of duplicity.

Those people who now separate Black Elk from his Christian participation are latecomers to a fray started long ago and reflected in an incident that occurred shortly after the Wounded Knee occupation of 1973. At that time, a sign was torn off the meeting hall of Saint Agnes Catholic Church (located in Black Elk's reservation village of Manderson). It said that the holy man was the church's first catechist, and that the hall was dedicated to his memory. Manderson residents understood this action to have been perpetrated by members of the American Indian Movement (AIM) from off the reservation. Whoever the responsible party, someone clearly did not want the church to advertize that the holy man was a founding member of its fold (in 1997 a new sign was posted).

It was during this same period that Richard Erdoes, a prolific writer on native religion, joined the best-selling ranks with *Lame Deer: Seeker of Visions.* Anyone who identified with countercultural issues seemed to own a copy of this still-popular text. Where Neihardt and Brown focused just on Black Elk's traditional thought, Erdoes told of Lame Deer's unsatisfying, early-life experience within the Native American Church, and several other denominations. An elder and advocate of practices associated with *yuwipi,* Lame Deer is outspoken in berating Christian presence among his people.

Speaking less poetically than did Neihardt's Black Elk, Lame Deer belittled the senior holy man for living the life of a catechist. He further professed to being a man of the twentieth century whose life did not have the aura of sanctity now associated with his predecessor. Whereas I reported that Black Elk represented all the catechists on one occasion in pledging that they would never commit a mortal sin, Lame Deer openly asserted that a "medicine man shouldn't be a saint" because one should personally experience all that life offers.

His perspective was a welcome relief to seekers of vision who felt excommunicated, at least in spirit, from whatever denomination they might have formerly belonged. Lame Deer's ethic appealed to both Indians and non-Indians, and his thought was ideologically compatible with the existentialism that prevailed before and after Woodstock. If Black Elk's mysticism was too elusive to internalize, Lame Deer's minimalism was not.

Proficient with Lakota religious ways described as traditional, Lame Deer was portrayed as an elder for whom the old rites still worked quite nicely. His life story was of more recent vintage than Black Elk's, and its earthiness appealed to many of the '70s generation whose religious appetite was sated by most anything that was not institutionally mainstream. It foreshadowed by twenty years the equally popular autobiography of another practitioner from the Rosebud Reservation, Wallace Black Elk.

Like the Lame Deer book before it, this life story showed that Neihardt and Brown did not report the entirety of Lakota religious thought. In the *yuwipi* tradition as Lame Deer, Wallace tells of his easy relationship with diverse spirit entities, and of his negative experiences with flesh-and-blood Christians. Reprints of this biography attest to his popularity within New Age circles, and reveal a hunger for accounts that tell of how one might gain access to the world of spirits. Moreover, Wallace's book found an audience quite receptive to hearing how he established rapport with alien beings (what he first called "UFO's" but eventually dubbed "star-nation-people").[6] Together, Wallace and Lame Deer represent a late-

---

6. Wallace portrays Jesuit Father Bernard Fagan as complaining to the reservation superintendent about *yuwipi* practitioners, and states that Father Fagan submitted the names of people who should be punished for such activity. He also claims that the Jesuit eventually sought healing by means of Lakota rituals he formerly persecuted (Wallace reporting that conventional Western medicine had been of no help to the priest) (1990, 27–31). After seeing what Wallace wrote, Father Fagan good-naturedly delighted in telling people about this late-life attention brought to him by Wallace. Although less tolerant persons might have been offended by such a portrayal, Father Fagan always spoke with affection for people such as Wallace, and would smilingly indicate how Wallace's report was a misrepresentation of fact.

twentieth-century ideology that asserts that to be Indian means to be non-Christian. Their thought is the exact opposite of what the revered Black Elk spoke, believed, or felt.

For reasons that are not readily apparent, William Lyon, Wallace's coauthor, suggested that Wallace's religious perspective was comparable to his namesake's. However, long before Lyon popularized Wallace, Lucy was adamant that this contemporary practitioner not be associated with the Black Elk of Lakota tradition. It was only after *Holy Man* was published that a comparison could be made that showed how dissimilar the two men were. By that time, however, Wallace's biography was enjoying one reprint after another. The buying public was as undiscerning as Harper and Row thought it would be when the publisher's sales department cleverly marketed the text with the misleading title "Black Elk."[7]

The Challenge of Reinterpreting the Past

Holy Man of the Oglala was drawn from those people who best remembered Nicholas Black Elk, and is as accurate a reminiscence as could be put together. It is not in the same genre as an award-winning video produced by Indian people a hundred years removed from an event that they claim to authoritatively address. Focusing on the tragedy of Wounded Knee, the video echoes Black Elk's tragic perspective à la Neihardt that a people's "dream" died in the snow on that occasion ("Wiping the Tears of Seven Generations" 1991). Men and women compellingly reflect on that horrible moment of history that saw many Lakota killed in a confrontation with cavalry in 1890.

One segment is of a young man reporting an incident that he says occurred just before the shooting began, and concerns a Catholic priest who administered in communal fashion "the last rites" to Big Foot's people. Moreover, viewers are told that the priest did not get an interpreter to help him, and it is implied that he did not want the people to know what he was

---

7. Because Black Elk died in 1950, there are very few people today who even remember him as anything but a frail old man whose health was not good. Consequently, there is little to no living memory of the man, or awareness of his stature, at Pine Ridge or elsewhere, which is why Lyon can erroneously describe him as someone who was "not particularly renowned among his own people" (Lyon 1996, 34).

doing. Stating that this information is contained in a document penned by a Wounded Knee survivor, the young man further reports that on previous occasions the priest always used an interpreter. When the priest finished administering the sacrament, an officer gave the Seventh Cavalry a command to fire upon the Indian camp.

Although the tragedy of this historical moment is well stated, the inclusion of a "last rites" episode that was never before reported by members of the press who were present, Lakota survivors, the priest, or army personnel indicates how the events of yesteryear can be recast to fit opinion that is current today. Separated for more than a century from what actually happened, the revisionists show: (1) a priest associated with an interpreter when, according to historical fact, the priest was fluent in Lakota; (2) a priest's canonically illicit and theologically groundless administration of a sacrament; (3) the priest's misplacement within the context (he was having a cigarette and conversing with those people he knew among Big Foot's band); and (4) the priest's senseless complicity with a Seventh Cavalry intent on murder. Lakota descendants offer gripping reflections, but significant pieces of misinformation intersperse their otherwise moving commentary. Especially pertinent, and characteristic of most commentaries on Wounded Knee, is the inattention paid to Christian tenets that were embraced by Lakota ancestors who died on the killing field.[8]

Portraying Wounded Knee ancestors as "wisdom keepers" while disparaging the Christian thought they espoused seems contradictory. Nonetheless, those slain are often characterized as martyrs for traditional Lakota religion when, in reality, Big Foot's Ghost Dancers were inspired

---

8. See Utley 1963. Father Francis Craft was wounded after the fighting began, and then crawled around the battlefield "giving first aid and administering last rites to the dying" (215). Adopted by the family of the famous Sicangu chief Spotted Tail, several years before the Wounded Knee incident, Father Craft appears in the literature as little more than a kind of stereotypical, itinerant Irish Catholic priest when, in fact, he was Mohawk on his mother's side, and a convert to Catholicism whose evaluation of Ghost Dancing itself was positive. A member of the Jesuit Order for six years, he departed it to become a priest for the diocese of Omaha. Having worked on the Cheyenne River Reservation, he knew many of Big Foot's people, so the army permitted him to mix with them as negotiations took place. He also requested to be placed with Big Foot's people in the mass burial grave if his wounding proved fatal. I am indebted to Thomas Foley for letting me read his manuscript "Hovering Eagle: The Life and Letters of Father Francis Craft, Sioux Missionary."

by a form of Christian teaching that, albeit nonmainstream and convoluted, won their commitment and devotion. In the course of time, these very ancestors have been invoked to repudiate all Christian presence within the native world. Although this may resonate with the thinking of some, it reflects a mind-set not owned by Black Elk or those people he saw die at Wounded Knee.

Black Elk and the Senior Generation's Acceptance of Christianity

The description of Black Elk as an ardent catechist in *Holy Man* was no surprise to older residents of the Pine Ridge Reservation, though younger people were like their non-Lakota counterparts. This latter group either never heard of him, or was simply not aware of his commitment to Church work. Meanwhile, both Indians and non-Indians (myself included) failed to fully appreciate Black Elk's opening utterances reported in *The Sacred Pipe*.[9]

Brown's intention was to report Lakota religious thought in its pristine, untainted form, and his book indeed became for many the "canonical" nativistic text that authoritatively provided the rubrics for conducting "traditional Lakota rites." However, Black Elk was insistent that whatever he said needed a theological qualification that readers found easy to dismiss in light of the detailed ritual he proceeded to relate: "We have been told by the white men, or at least by those who are Christian, that God sent to men his son, who would restore order and peace upon the earth; and we have been told that Jesus the Christ was crucified, but that he shall come again at the Last Judgment, the end of this world or cycle. *This I understand and know that it is true*" (emphasis added; J. Brown 1974, xix).[10]

---

9. Although it has been regarded by some as a kind of "manual" for performing the "seven rites of the Oglala Sioux," *The Sacred Pipe* should be considered one man's recollection and interpretation of them.

10. Black Elk makes an important distinction that academics sometimes fail to make when he refers to those people with whom the Lakota came into contact (those people who settled and "tamed" the West). Namely, he distinguishes between "white men" who are Christian and those who are not! Some writers often lump soldiers, settlers, government officials, trappers, traders, and all missionaries into the category of "Christians." They should know that the prereservation period was peppered with persons whose religious practice was not foremost in mind.

Such was the profession of faith that Brown, not I, initially reported and that accompanied Black Elk to his grave. Still, given the polemic that so often seeks to dissociate Christian participation from the senior generation, it is understandable that people find it difficult to know exactly what the holy man believed.[11]

Neihardt may have been more interested in Lakota religion and seances than he was in some form of institutional Christianity, and this may (or may not) have influenced his choice of emphases. Regardless of his preference in this regard, my sympathetic interpretation of his effort is that he simply chose to focus on the prereservation period. He likewise chose not to address the formative role of "Church" on Black Elk's life, or the complex social issues that beset the reservation period. Such was Neihardt's authorial prerogative—just as it was Brown's, fifteen years later, to put together an ethnography of traditional Lakota rituals (using Black Elk as a resource). Because neither of these early writers sought to learn how the holy man saw his Catholic practice as a flowering of his vision's sacred tree, their silence on the subject should not be taken to mean his Christian identity did not exist, or that it had been abandoned (Steltenkamp 1993, 108–11).

Like Neihardt and Brown, I carried the desire to hear never-before-told tales of Indian battles, and I wanted to participate in rituals that would give me special access to supernatural secrets. However, my expectations were not met, and I was at first disappointed to learn about the Bible-reading, rosary-praying, mass-attending, communion-consuming

11. Rice states that *The Sacred Pipe* is "overtly Catholic" but then cites acquaintances of Black Elk who say the holy man never spoke about his work as a catechist, and that his silence is proof that he had only "old time religion" on his mind (1991, xi). Such logic is difficult to follow. That is, if Black Elk's *Sacred Pipe* text—recorded three years before he died—is "overtly Catholic," how can one conclude that only traditional Lakota religion preoccupied his thought? As his days came to a close, the holy man was, simply, neither a parochial nativist nor a Catholic ideologue. It is understandable why certain acquaintances of the holy man might have said what they did. Namely, Lakota people commonly do not volunteer information unless asked (and then are circumspect in what they say). Lucy Looks Twice was, for example, willing to be photographed holding a pipe and cohosting a picnic for Hilda Neihardt and her entourage. She was courteous and accommodating to her guests, and did not refer to me as her "*takoja*" ("grandchild") with whom she was putting together a biography of her father. What she and I were doing conflicted with the stereotype that had attracted these people, so there was no need to identify me or tell them why I was present.

catechist whom people remembered as "Nick" Black Elk. Nonetheless, I put aside my preconceptions, and eventually acquired a more intimate sense of the sainted patriarch that neither of the earlier books provided. I never planned to produce a portrait of Black Elk that some would consider iconoclastic. Rather, I simply committed myself to learning what was empirically verifiable.

Although Neihardt reported that Black Elk performed overseas in Buffalo Bill's Wild West Show, he did not detail the full impact of this experience on the young Lakota. This exposure to the large world that existed outside his homeland left a lasting impression on the future holy man who danced for Queen Victoria, fell in love with a French woman, and visited sites that are still popular tourist attractions. Young Black Elk was inspired to witness many Europeans attend religious services at cathedrals and thus, from his perspective, pay due respect to their Creator. His letters home reveal a growing respect for the Christianity embraced by his hosts. Reporting that he was faithful "to the law" (his baptism) by "remembering God," he quoted from the famous passage on "love" (1 Cor. 13), and even expressed a desire to see "where they killed Jesus" (DeMallie 1984a, 10).[12]

When Black Elk arrived home, the "Ghost Dance" religion was spreading rapidly among groups that social analyses generally suggest were in a state of "relative deprivation." In short, blighted conditions made Plains people vulnerable, desperate, and seek hope wherever it could be found. Black Elk was like many others who started dancing, and who placed their hope in a Christian teaching that told of a "*Wanikiye*" (Savior) restoring what had been lost.[13]

The essential story of Christianity was fairly well known prior to the Ghost Dance period. That is, someone said to be the son of God had been

12. DeMallie states that Indian performers were required to "be of the same religious faith" and so were baptized into the Episcopal Church (1984a, 10). He also says that Black Elk informed Neihardt that his "spiritual power disappeared" while in Europe and that when he returned home "his power came back to him." DeMallie further suggests that this perhaps "led him to Christianity." If the holy man made this precise statement to Neihardt and what, exactly, he meant is now impossible to know. Lucy Looks Twice recounted no loss, then return, of spiritual power reported by her father when recalling his time in Europe (8–11).

13. See Mooney 1991, Utley 1963, and Overholt 1986 (122–41); 1989.

killed by non-Indians, but would return at some distant date, usher in a new day by banishing evil, and bring new life to the people. The Ghost Dance added to this doctrine by claiming that God would now send his son to the Lakota who he knew would appreciate such a gift. Upon them God's son had taken pity, for he would bring the dead to life, return the vanished buffalo, and rid the land of cavalry and pioneers.

The new revelation also insisted that special "ghost shirts" be worn because they would deflect bullets. Many people had been shot and killed over the years, so this apparel proffered new hope. Moreover, non-Indians obviously feared that the prophecies would come true because they were calling upon the army to stop the Ghost Dancers. Such was, at least, the thinking of many Lakota whose millennialist dream became the nightmare of Wounded Knee.

Even after Wounded Knee, there still remained a hope that God's son would come to help the people. Because many still harbored a desire for the Savior's return, they began to fill the ranks of Catholic "black robes," Episcopalian "white coats," Presbyterian "short coats," and peyotism's "Road Men." The different denominations gradually recruited native priests, deacons, ministers, and catechists who brought with them a lay following who accepted some version of biblical religion.

Biblical religion became welcome news because it told of a Creator preserving other tribes through floods, famine, and fearsome enemies. This God even gave his son, Jesus, to live among them, and he taught the Lakota tenet *"mitak oyassin"* ("all are relatives"). The Ghost Dance can essentially be regarded as a transitional doctrine that gave way to the different forms of mainstream Christianity.[14]

In light of this history, those people who seek to remove from the Indian world what they sometimes call "white man's religion" are expressing a hostility that was not shared by all of their ancestors. Surprisingly, commentator Vine Deloria Jr., a Lakota whose family has Christian roots in the early reservation period, now states that "Christianity has been the curse

---

14. The religious perspective of "traditionals" older than Black Elk is evident in an interview with the aged Red Feather on July 8, 1930. Eleanor Hinman recorded his memory of Crazy Horse (his brother-in-law), and Red Feather prefaced his remarks by saying: "I will tell you the true facts about Crazy Horse, because I am a Catholic now and it is part of my religion to tell the truth."

of all cultures into which it has intruded" (1995, 22). Such stark appraisals have been associated more with Russell Means, the Lakota activist and actor, than with the heretofore insightful Deloria.

Russell Means and the New Traditionalism

Long before Black Elk died, young Indian people were being raised in a wholly different milieu than the one in which the senior generation's religious outlook was forged. The socialization process of most native people was akin to that of Lakota activist and actor Russell Means. It bore little resemblance to what their ancestors experienced. Nonetheless, he and others of the post–Black Elk generation speak authoritatively about native history, and often project an image of persons raised in a "traditional way."

Appearance-wise, Means looks to be a prereservation traditionalist whose religious convictions reflect ancestral warriors'. However, his autobiography reports that he was raised in California, and then moved to Cleveland where he first attracted media attention (Means 1995). There he was inspired by urban-based, native activists to become "a full-time Indian" (his words) in 1970. Eventually, Means gave up his life as an accountant, adopted a style of dress that seemed authentically Indian, and assumed leadership within the American Indian Movement.

When I was studying with Brown, Means was in the national news protesting Cleveland's use of the name "Indians" for its baseball team. He and other urban Indians (and non-Indians) were adopting nineteenth-century native garb and hairstyles that reservation people later imitated. Appearing this way was a symbolic reclamation of tribal identities that Manifest Destiny had reduced to reservation poverty.[15]

It was during this period that *Black Elk Speaks* became "the bible of the hippie movement" and served as the inspirational touchstone for activist Indians and other vision seekers (like me) who were spiritually rest-

---

15. Indian activism was also fanned by factors that had nothing to do with the Indian world per se. Sporting long hair, embracing one's "roots," consuming "natural" foods, debunking patriotic myths that arose at the expense of others, and redressing grievances were the symptomatic sentiments of the seventies that went hand in hand with causes championed by native-rights activists of the period. It was also argued that the American presence in Vietnam mirrored the past, and this involvement was simply a replay of what "white, Christian civilization" did to Indian America.

less. Likewise, *The Sacred Pipe* was being reprinted after years of relative obscurity. This literary trend was complemented by actor Iron Eyes Cody being pictured on billboards and television commercials as an Indian from the past, tearful that America had become so polluted. These depictions moved AIM members and sympathetic soul mates to question, if not outright condemn, an institutional Christianity that did not exercise good stewardship over the second Eden that was prehistoric America.

Unfamiliar with its theology or the senior generation's experience of it, people like Means championed the exorcism of Christianity from Indian turf. They argued that all Indians were perfectly content until the "white man and his religion" brought ruin. Minus the racial invective, this position gained adherents among New Age non-Indians, environmental activists, and others whose religious thirst had not been quenched by participation within mainstream religions.

People looked to native America in the hope of experiencing "the Sacred," "Supernatural," "God," or whatever the ineffable mystery is variously called by words that cannot fully name or define it. They sought a religious practice that spoke to them in a more personal way than the shopworn clichés of a Bible-reading, churchgoing, or rosary-praying senior generation. Moreover, institutional affiliations were sometimes seen as hypocritical because they were associated with social problems the churches could have ameliorated. Indians and non-Indians alike were trying to reclaim an idealized past in the hope of creating a future that was— if not utopian—at least self-actualizing.

The Convergence of Means, Black Elk, and Me

As these trends unfolded, I came of age looking for my place within an institutional expression of religion whose luster vied with its limitations. Having New Age sentiments before this movement became as popular as it did, and attuned to environmental concerns and social issues, I was like others whose religious quest was open-ended. Mine included participation in sweat lodges and other "traditional" ceremonies when relatively small numbers of Indians, and extremely few non-Indians, were involved in such activity (Steltenkamp 1982). These many years later, my participation has declined, though it is common for many Indians and non-Indians to be active in such rituals throughout the year.

Over time, many Native Americans (and American natives who were not Indian) came to identify with what they positively regarded as a "spirituality" instead of what they negatively associated with "religion."[16] The ecology movement motivated people to want a spirituality that was "more natural," or less institutionalized, than the religions that had evolved within a synthetic (that is, "spiritually corrupt") urban civilization (tribal groups from different continents were even called "natural peoples"). People of goodwill wondered if ritual forms practiced by pre-Christian European or Indian forebears could perhaps restore Earth's many endangered species.

Such was the social climate when Russell Means became an Indian activist, and I went in search of people who might more clearly reveal to me the religious knowledge of elders like Black Elk. Our paths crossed early on when my teaching colleague John Cedarface found the disfigured, lifeless body of Raymond Yellow Thunder in Gordon, Nebraska.[17] It was this homicide that drew Means to Pine Ridge, where I had arrived one year earlier.

When AIM staged the seventy-one-day occupation of Wounded Knee, I was teaching at a reservation high school, and claimed the distinction of being the first non-Indian permitted to enter the cordoned area when residents were allowed to return home.[18] Means continued to take center stage within a number of much publicized protests, and eventually

16. Some people avoid using the term *religion* when referring to their Indian "spirituality," just as they avoid the word *God* in favor of the term *Creator*. Also, when someone in a religious leadership role preaches to, or catechizes, another, they refer to the instructions as sacred "teachings" handed down by the "elders." Because a monotheistic "Creator"-deity is ethnographically elusive within native tradition, and because different "elders" subscribe to a variety of "teachings," this semantic issue might be more a social current that reflects native people simply creating a new vocabulary of discourse that is distinct from what is traditionally idiomatic in Western religious parlance.

17. *The Trial of Billy Jack* was a motion picture that drew upon these events of 1972–1973.

18. Along with a few small churches and businesses, a number of houses were broken into, looted, and used for various purposes by those activists who occupied Wounded Knee. When "residents only" could return to the area, a student of mine asked if I might drive him home. Stopped by National Guardsmen on the village perimeter and told to turn back, I explained who my passenger was, and that I was driving him home. We were then permitted to pass, and only a few residents had returned by the time we arrived.

found fame as a media favorite.[19] I, by contrast, entered into the obscure lives of Black Elk's daughter and friends, and from them learned about the years that previously lay hidden.

Holy Man resulted from my retreat, and it was pretty much universally hailed as "a real step forward in American religious studies."[20] However, the book's modest sales suggest that recollections of Black Elk as a devout catechist do not cast as much appeal as the long-standing impressions generated by Brown and Neihardt. Nonetheless, learning about the holy man's Catholic identity was a forceful-enough experience for me to embrace Black Elk's religion more fervently than I had previously done, and pursue the Jesuit priesthood that is now part of my life.

For many people, however, the story of Black Elk's life as a dutiful Catholic preacher is not as romantic as the image seized upon by *Where White Men Fear to Tread*. In this book, Means invokes Lakota history to countenance his thinking: "In the first half of this century, Black Elk was led down the path blazed by Red Cloud, Crow Dog, Crazy Horse, Sitting Bull, and others of their generation" (Means 1995, 543). He further asserts that "Black Elk's purpose was to preserve our nation's sacred tree of life . . . our people's spiritual survival" (543). Because his references to Christianity are consistently negative, Means is as misinformed as others who did not know that Black Elk's first half of the twentieth century was lived as a Catholic catechist. Most people simply did not know that the holy man's reference to the "sacred tree of life" was a reference to "the Christian life of all people" (Steltenkamp 1993, 109).[21]

It is surprising that this Christian practice, and that of many other "traditionals," creates any controversy at all, because the acceptance of

---

19. Having appeared in several Hollywood movies, Means has stated his desire to remain in the acting profession. A bookstore manager informed me that Means agreed to do a book signing only after being guaranteed a certain number of sales. She said, "He stood like a giant . . . though he wasn't that tall. And he's so charismatic that it seemed traffic just stopped to let him cross the street."

20. *Kirkus Reviews* (June 1993).

21. Means has been in the forefront of the late-twentieth-century's Indian revitalization movement, and his leadership has included behaviors and ideas that some think would have been offensive to Black Elk's generation—especially his disdain for "white people" and "Christianity" (a genre of racist rhetoric and religious bigotry he and others have popularized). Film roles have been steady and public appearances numerous over the years.

Christian teaching by Lakota people is well documented. They not only participated in mainline groups but also formed what might be called native denominations or sects, such as the well-known but theologically ignored Ghost Dance, the Native American Church, the Body of Christ, and others.[22] The ancestors of Means himself were probable participants in one or another of these groups.[23]

Black Elk on the Eve of the Millennium

Black Elk's religious identity will no doubt continue to intrigue readers of Neihardt and Brown. Their definition of the holy man seems so accurate and complete that his depiction as a catechist is easy to regard as an aberration that, before his death, he renounced. The holy man's enduring and revered image will thus remain petrified as an "end of the trail" religious elder who, unwilling to change, felt most at home in a very pre-Christian world. Such is the image that is not easy to supplant with facts that show his life journey followed what he would call the "good red road" revealed by God's son, Jesus.

A catechesis commonly heard is that the senior generation discovered their experiment in biblical religion to be misguided. This understanding thus moves many to join the exodus from Judeo-Christian practice and enter the promised land of esoteric native ritual. Indians and non-Indians alike hope that such ritual needs only a second chance to work its transformative charm.

These sentiments stirred within me years ago when I saw the Indian world as perhaps offering a remedy for my spiritual discomfort. For me, Black Elk was mystically alluring, and like others, I assumed that Lakota rituals made him such an eminent religious figure. However, contrary to expectation, I learned that many people from the holy man's generation were devout in some form of Christian practice. Steeped in, and committed to, a rich religious tradition that predated the coming of the missionaries, holy men such as Black Elk welcomed the new teachings, and were

22. See Stewart 1987 and Steinmetz 1998a.

23. Surprisingly, despite his anti-Christian rhetoric, Means does credit a Catholic nun, Sister Adelaide, for steering him into a treatment center where he could address his long-standing problem with anger (Means 1995, 524).

not the close-minded parochialists that exponents of nativism suggest they were.[24] In telling me what they did, "elders" hoped that my text would preserve their recollections and clarify a religious history that they saw was becoming misinterpreted with the passage of time.

Although the years that separate me from Black Elk's daughter increase, I retain the vivid memory of a woman who did not want her father's commitment to the Church forgotten. Regardless of what Means, I, or other writers say about Black Elk's thought, what is most important is the history she and others reported in *Holy Man of the Oglala*. Therein lies the best witness to religious sentiments that were cherished by Black Elk and many others from his generation. However, I am not surprised that objections to what I reported occasionally surface.

Lucy would sometimes curtail our conversation and change the subject when in the presence of certain persons. She would also say that some people had trustworthy information, and some did not. I was made to realize early on that not everyone celebrated her father's affiliation with the Church, and I think Lucy was pleased that I, and not she, would have to represent her father's identity in forums that were not sympathetic to what *Holy Man* contained. I did not set out to be an apologist for missionary work among native peoples (or anyone, for that matter), but the passage of time has placed me in the position of being, if not an apologist, a defender of truths held dear by Black Elk's family and friends.

Ideological skirmishes that depict the holy man as a dutiful Catholic or hard-core traditionalist will probably continue, and the lens through which I view the different volleys will perhaps forever be considered blurry by some people due to my formal association with the Jesuit priesthood. However, no one will dispute the celestial affirmation that Black Elk's life example received the night of his wake, when he lay with rosary entwined around his hands. On this occasion, the sky was illuminated with stars in

---

24. His life experience being what it was, Black Elk's religious repertoire was broader than most people's. He could sing his grandchildren to sleep using Latin songs from the mass or Lakota songs (which Lucy Looks Twice sang for me). Similarly, he could pray his rosary en route to the top of a hill where he might then sing a vision-acquired song to chase away a thunderstorm. Black Elk could truly think of himself as a Lakota Catholic because his religious vision was appropriately circular—a continuity of the old fueling the new, and the new fleshing out the old, repetitively, as he lived his daily devotions.

"miracle-like" fashion, and among those mourners gathered, there was no reason to debate the holy man's religious identity or where he would spend eternity (Steltenkamp 1993, 128–42). All could agree with Shakespeare who prophetically wrote: "When beggars die, there are no comets seen. The heavens themselves blaze forth the death of princes."[25]

25. *Julius Caesar*, 2.2.30–31.

8

A Postcolonial Reading of Black Elk

DALE STOVER

Although Black Elk is known and generally respected by Lakota people as an articulate spiritual leader of a previous generation, among European-derived peoples he has acquired the status of a mythological figure.[1] European Americans have fixed on Black Elk as a primary image by which they feel linked to the traditional world of the native peoples of North America. For them Black Elk represents quintessential Indianness by his nineteenth-century Lakota origins, his associations with storied events such as the Battle of the Little Bighorn and the massacre at Wounded Knee, and by his status as a visionary, one who was a *wicasa wakan,* a holy man. Black Elk as a traditional visionary becomes the epitome of the cultural "other" for the popular understanding of the European American outsider.

Calling the European American view of Black Elk mythological is a way of acknowledging that this image of Black Elk is tied to the complicated history of colonization during which stereotyped identities were projected onto indigenous peoples that served to justify oppressive poli-

---

1. The anthropologist William K. Powers, in a 1985 academic paper, "When Black Elk Speaks, Everybody Listens," (1990c) sharply criticizes "the Black Elk myth." He claims that elderly medicine men and singers on Pine Ridge Reservation "would wonder why all the fuss about Black Elk" (137). Powers appears hostile, not only toward John Neihardt, Joseph Brown, and subsequent popularizers, but also toward Black Elk himself for what Powers sees as his Christianizing of the Ghost Dance, his blindsiding of Jesuit priests in telling his story to Neihardt, and his unseemly grab for fame and status above fellow catechists and medicine men. However, in his effort to bring the Black Elk myth down to ordinary size, Powers makes unsupported claims, such as that Black Elk's real sacred vision was at age eighteen (138).

cies toward these peoples.[2] The moment European Americans take up the story of Black Elk, simultaneously the whole story comes into play of how immigrant settler peoples from Europe dealt with the indigenous peoples of North America. In the process of dispossessing the native peoples of their lands, European Americans created the myth of civilization versus savagism.[3] This myth portrayed native peoples as rooted in nature and European peoples as carriers of civilization who were dedicated to bringing order and progress to the American wilderness. The grand intention was to share the obvious boons of civilization with the "savages," but the "savages" proved surprisingly and persistently resistant, preferring to remain in their "benighted," natural state. Because this myth lies at the foundation of European American cultural perceptions of native peoples developed over several centuries, its legacy influences the way European Americans read the story of Black Elk. The history of these perceptions is complex, reflecting the continually changing circumstances in the power relations between the indigenous and the immigrant peoples.

European Americans who perceived native peoples as "savages" could discount the native discourse as ignorant and illiterate. Because their own discourse represented internalized beliefs about their civilizational superiority and the inevitable necessity that civilized progress would irrevocably overrun and displace the "savage" realities of native life, they never, or seldom, consciously saw themselves as ignoble intruders.

Since the Second World War, a postcolonial era has begun on a global scale, and the colonizing discourses of previous colonial times have been subjected to genuine critique. From a late-twentieth-century point of view it is readily apparent how earlier European American discourse functioned as a justification for the dispossession and suppression of native peoples, but it is also necessary to recognize that these older patterns of colonizing discourse are still operative in much of contemporary European American understanding of native peoples, pervading the language of government policies, media portrayals, and scholarly writings. Coming

2. Arnold Krupat calls this "domestic imperialism, which, sometimes intentionally, sometimes not, operated on this continent against indigenous peoples everywhere, and which, regardless of intentionalities, continues to operate to this day" (1992, 5).

3. This theme is developed by Roy Harvey Pearce. Robert F. Berkhofer (1978) updates and complements Pearce's work.

to terms morally with this history and its continuing presence is a compli-cated process. The issue is not so simple as correcting a particular error in moral judgment, but involves the reorientation of an entire worldview that includes social mores, gender definitions, religious understandings, scientific claims, and more. All of these issues were, and still are, bound to-gether in the discourse of a European America that, among other, more commendable features, also espoused and espouses colonizing policies and practices.

Although the story of Black Elk initially appears benign to the ordi-nary European American reader who may be drawn to the figure of Black Elk out of some empathic feeling for native tradition, in reality to read the story of Black Elk is to plunge into the "stuff" of European American mythology that still lies just under the surface of everyday cultural dis-course. A postcolonial approach to Black Elk's story invites the reader to be on the lookout for evidence of the still often unrecognized dynamic of colonizing discourse that assumes its continuing competence to interpret Lakota realities. By postcolonial I mean an interpretation that features in-digenous critique of European American discourse of both past and pres-ent so that colonizing perspectives embedded in that discourse are brought to light in the interest of establishing a more mutually respectful and egalitarian discourse.[4]

The Original Telling of Black Elk's Story

The original telling of Black Elk's story was an oral event in which Black Elk spoke in Lakota and his son Benjamin, who was bilingual, translated into English. This original level of telling took place on three occasions. In 1931, Black Elk told the story of his sacred vision and its effect in his life to John Neihardt, while Neihardt's daughter Enid took stenographic notes that she later transcribed into a typed manuscript. In 1944, Black Elk told Neihardt about traditional Lakota stories and teachings, and Neihardt's

4. By postcolonial is meant an approach that brings to awareness the colonial perspec-tives embedded in European American discourse of past and present in order to eliminate them and to engage in respectful egalitarian discourse. Positions on postcolonial theory vary widely; helpful overviews can be found in Childs and Williams 1997, Mongia 1996, and Williams and Crisman 1994.

daughter Hilda typed a record of the conversations as they took place.[5] In the winter of 1947–1948, Black Elk recounted traditional Lakota rituals to Joseph Brown, who presumably made his own notes of Ben Black Elk's translation. Because notes of Black Elk's conversations with Brown have never been made available and are not even known to exist, the original telling to Brown is more inaccessible than is the case with Neihardt.

The 1931 narrative represents the essential telling of Black Elk's story. It differed from the other two narratives because it took place within a deliberately arranged ritual setting that included Black Elk's Lakota adoption of Neihardt and his daughters, Enid and Hilda. It also included, especially in its initial sessions, the presence and participation of respected Lakota elders from the community who were Black Elk's peers.

When Neihardt and Brown created books from the original tellings by Black Elk, these books became the first retellings of Black Elk's story. Both Neihardt and Brown presented their retellings as though they themselves were not there listening and interrogating, so that the stories unfold as though Black Elk is the author and the words are entirely his, an impression reinforced by Neihardt's title, *Black Elk Speaks,* as well as Brown's title, *The Sacred Pipe: Black Elk's Account of the Seven Rites of the Oglala Sioux.* Although Neihardt and Brown were simply following accepted practice of the day, it is important for a reader to appreciate that this retelling involved relocating Lakota oral discourse within the domain of European American written discourse in which the editorial shaping by Neihardt and by Brown necessarily reflected their cultural understanding of what Black Elk meant.

Also, a reader should be aware that the original tellings themselves were bicultural events in which the story of Black Elk was being shaped by the questions that were asked or remained unasked, by differing concepts of outcome, by considerations for the expected readership that would justify and secure publication, and by concern for possible reactions regarding disclosure of sacred matters—all such factors, and more, potentially influenced what was said, heard, and written.

A postcolonial way of reading retellings such as Neihardt's and Brown's is laid out by Greg Sarris in his 1993 book, *Keeping Slug Woman*

---

5. These conversations were later embodied in Neihardt's historical novel, *When the Tree Flowered* (1951).

Alive: A Holistic Approach to American Indian Texts. Sarris emphasizes the oral context that underlies a text like *Black Elk Speaks,* noting "that in oral discourse the context of orality covers the personal territory of those involved in the exchange, and because the territory is so wide, extending throughout two or more personal, and often cultural, worlds, no one party has access to the whole of the exchange" (40). Sarris insists on identifying the voice or story brought to the encounter by the editor-recorder, and he specifies that scholar-critics and ordinary readers must also acknowledge their voices by identifying the story slants they bring to their interpretation of the original oral event. Moreover, Sarris claims that respect for the orality of meaning requires that there be no attempt at closure, at completing knowledge in an authoritative version, but that the story line remain unfixed and open to the future and to the continuation of a many-voiced dialogue (see 130–31). Sarris's advice seems to say that the best way to counter colonial discourse is to insist on full disclosure of the stories of all parties to the interpretation of an oral event and to resist all attempts to collapse the many meanings of an oral telling into the fixity of any single printed version.

Adapting Sarris's approach, I propose that four retellings of Black Elk's story can be identified. The first retelling is by Neihardt and Brown, and the other retellings represent later interpretive phases that reflect shifts in the relationship between European Americans and Native Americans that are marked by changes in European American discourse. I further propose that these retellings can be characterized as follows: the first retelling is by Neihardt and Brown and perceives Black Elk as the vanishing Indian; the second retelling happens in the 1960s, 1970s, and early 1980s and views Black Elk as the archetypal Indian; the third retelling begins in 1984 and lasts until 1992 and casts Black Elk as the Indian intellectual; and the fourth retelling begins in 1992 and identifies Black Elk as the postcolonial Indian.

The First Retelling:
Black Elk as the Vanishing Indian

The most fundamental belief shaping the European American discourse in the era when Neihardt and Brown encountered Black Elk and wrote their respective books retelling his accounts to them was the myth of the vanishing Indian. In *The Vanishing American,* Brian Dippie points to the War of 1812 as the decisive event that "permanently altered Indian-white relations in North America" (1982, 7) and opened the way for looking upon the destiny of native peoples as doomed. Dippie describes how the "savage" in the role of the "vanishing American" easily becomes the "noble savage" whose primary virtue was "innocence of civilized failings" (18–19). In 1826, *The Last of the Mohicans* by James Fenimore Cooper gave classical form to the "noble savage" theme in this European American myth, so that, in Dippie's words, "Chingachgook is fiction's most memorable Vanishing American" (22).

The Ghost Dance of 1890, writes Dippie, can be interpreted in relation to the myth of the "Vanishing American." The Ghost Dance prophecy can be seen as the precise antidote to the vanishing trajectory of the western tribes because it anticipated the restoration of the dead Indian relatives and the return of the buffalo herds, accompanied by the disappearance of the European Americans. "For a moment the rebirth of Indian America had seemed as imminent as a man's next breath, as real as moccasined feet pounding the earth to the thump of drums. Then it was over. The apocalyptic vision of the ghost dance was buried on the battlefield at Wounded Knee. 'A people's dream died there,' an old Sioux holy man remembered sadly. 'It was a beautiful dream' " (1982, 202). The words Dippie places in quotation marks appear in *Black Elk Speaks* as words spoken by Black Elk, but they do not appear in the original typescript. Dippie was unaware that Neihardt had apparently added those words to Black Elk's original statement. It is hardly surprising, however, that Neihardt edited his retelling of Black Elk's story in this way, because the vanishing-Indian myth had dominated the worldview of European American discourse for more than a century and was still stoutly in place in the 1930s and 1940s, and lasted through the 1950s.

Because of their acceptance of the vanishing-Indian myth, both Neihardt and Brown understood their collaboration with Black Elk as an act of preservation. In the same mood inspiring the "salvage anthropology" of Franz Boas and the ethnographic photographing of the presumed last generation of authentically indigenous people by Edward Curtis, Neihardt and Brown intended to capture in a text the authentic, soon-to-be vanished Lakota realities embodied in the life and person of Nicholas

Black Elk. Neither Neihardt nor Brown had any expectation of survival of traditional Lakota culture, and the preservation they had in mind could be called domestication, because their books were not intended primarily for Lakota readers, but for European American readers. Any retelling of traditional native discourse in European American writing involved some sort of domestication, which is why native persons were often reluctant to communicate traditional matters to European Americans. Black Elk, however, was a willing participant with Neihardt and Brown in the domestication process, though a reader should take notice that each of the three men brought differing intentions to this process.

Black Elk's intention may be seen in his comments to Neihardt concerning the story of his sacred vision. "This vision of mine ought to go out, I feel, but somehow I couldn't get anyone to do it. I would think about it and get sad. I wanted the world to know about it. . . . You are here and have the vision just the way I wanted, and then the tree will bloom again and the people will know the true facts" (DeMallie 1984a, 43). It seems that Black Elk wants the European American world to know about his vision, and he perceives Neihardt as the one who can tell it. His comment about the tree blooming again indicates his expectation that Lakota tradition will be renewed through his collaboration with Neihardt. He may have thought that Lakota visions and rituals needed written form in order to assist Lakota adaptability in its relationships to the dominant culture. In any case, it is clear that Black Elk did not share the belief of Neihardt and Brown in the myth of the vanishing Indian, nor is he likely to have thought of himself as a "noble savage."

Although Neihardt and Brown may have had in common the vanishing-Indian myth and a preservationist goal, their intentions differed decidedly. Brown intended his retelling to be scholarly in the mode of ethnography, and his book was published by the University of Oklahoma Press as volume 36 in the "Civilization of the American Indian Series." Brown distanced his scholarly approach from Neihardt's book by describing the latter as a "poetic and sympathetic treatment."[6] He further distanced himself from Neihardt by failing to acknowledge that Neihardt had

6. This comment occurs in Brown's new preface to the 1971 edition of *The Sacred Pipe* (1974, xiii).

arranged for him to meet Black Elk,[7] describing his search for and finding of Black Elk as a fortuitous encounter with the "other" in which Black Elk asked Brown to stay with him "that I might record an account of their ancient religion."[8] The irony here is that Brown's preface to the original edition of *The Sacred Pipe* in 1953 is very romanticized, and the lack of field notes puts in doubt its scientific credibility, whereas Neihardt's supposedly poetic and presumably nonscientific book represents a retelling from a database that is exceptionally rich in ethnographic detail, including the original stenographic notes, a trove of photographs, highly descriptive letters, and oral history.[9]

Neihardt's intention, on the other hand, can be seen in his eschewing of the scholar's critical distance in favor of the poet's intimacy in representing the voice of Black Elk. He clearly saw the employment of his literary skills as the appropriate mode for representing Black Elk's visionary experience in European American discourse. In Lakota tradition a vision had the power to voice itself in oral expression known as *hanbloglaka*, vision-telling,[10] and Neihardt's retelling is structured to give central place to Black Elk's remarkable dream-vision as a nine year old.

Neihardt's intention can be glimpsed in comments written to a friend a few days after completing his meetings with Black Elk in 1931. "This is going to be the first absolutely Indian book thus far written. It is all out of the Indian consciousness" (DeMallie 1984a, 49). A reader should consider whether Neihardt's notion of "Indian consciousness" represents the consciousness of the stereotyped "other," or whether Neihardt has caught some sense of Black Elk's own visionary empowerment and has been able

---

7. Sally McCluskey describes the strain this caused in the relationship between Brown and Neihardt (1992, 239).

8. This comment occurs in the original 1953 preface, which was omitted once the new preface appeared in the 1971 edition (x).

9. Black Elk's descendants shared ongoing family traditions regarding the encounters between the two men at the annual Spring Conference of the Neihardt Center in Bancroft, Nebraska, as recently as April 13, 1996, and at an oral history session of the Rocky Mountain–Great Plains regional meeting of the American Academy of Religion in Omaha, Nebraska, on March 21, 1998. Hilda Neihardt published her firsthand account of the 1931 events in 1995.

10. See DeMallie's comments on *hanbloglaka* and Black Elk's comparing it to Neihardt's epic poetry (1984a, 37, 83–84).

to give it voice. Supporting the latter perspective is another statement by Neihardt, written to his publisher in June 1931. "There was a very peculiar merging of consciousness between me and Black Elk, and his son, who interpreted for me, commented on the fact" (40–41). Perhaps both possibilities are present and influence Neihardt's retelling. The first possibility may come into play because it pervades the discourse of the time in which he writes, and the second possibility may be operative because, unlike his peers, he was deeply influenced by his own dream-visions and mystical experiences (see 41–43).

The Second Retelling:
Black Elk as the Archetypal Indian

The second retelling of Black Elk's story corresponds to a fundamental shift in European American mythology that took place during the 1960s, a time of turbulent change in European American culture. It marked the end of the vanishing-Indian myth, and inaugurated an entirely new era for European American discourse about native peoples. In the early 1950s an aggressive acculturation program featuring termination of tribes and relocation of tribal people to urban centers far from their reservations was instituted in order to hasten the "vanishing" of the vanishing Indian. By the 1960s, however, the shift in the European American perception of native peoples was under way and was most publicly signaled in a speech to Congress by President Lyndon Johnson on March 6, 1968. The speech was titled "The Forgotten American," and in it Johnson called for a new policy of Indian self-determination, requesting Congress to implement legislation to bring it about.

The disappearance of the vanishing-Indian myth was also signified by two other phenomena. The rise of militant activism among native people began in the 1960s and came to national attention through the occupation of Alcatraz Island in 1969, the Trail of Broken Treaties march to Washington in 1972, and the armed standoff at Wounded Knee in 1973. Independent of this activism, there was a resurgence of traditional religious practices, such as the sweat-lodge, vision-quest, and Sun Dance rites among the Lakota. Sometimes the activism and the renewal of traditionalism came together in uneasy, but significant, alliances; both elements gave the lie to the vanishing-Indian myth.

In the new preface to the 1971 edition of *The Sacred Pipe,* Joseph Brown expressed how the changed context of the 1960s led to a new way of perceiving Black Elk's story, in effect becoming a second retelling. Brown acknowledged that previously "it was generally believed, even by the specialists, that it would be only a matter of time—very little time in fact—until the Indians, with their seemingly archaic and anachronistic cultures, would be completely assimilated into a larger American society which was convinced of its superiority and the validity of its goals." However, Brown wrote, "there have occurred many changes which demand that his [Black Elk's] message—and, indeed, similar messages of other traditionally oriented peoples—be placed in new perspective and in a new light" (1974, xv).

Brown's next statement makes a profound admission about the dominant culture's moment of self-doubt. "We are still very far from being aware of the dimensions and ramifications of our ethnocentric illusions. Nevertheless, by the very nature of things we are now forced to undergo a process of intense self-examination; to engage in a serious re-evaluation of the premises and orientations of our society" (1974, xv). Brown seems to suggest that European America, no longer able to believe in the myth of the vanishing Indian, is necessarily facing a moment of truth about its foundational myth, which is the belief in "progress." What Brown did not acknowledge is that if the myth of "progress" were to be put in question, all the complexities of the colonial legacy regarding the original peoples of the continent might have to be faced. Instead of facing this, Brown pointed to what had already been occurring in the 1960s, namely, in moments of crisis European Americans can look "with sincerity to the kinds of models which are represented by the American Indians." Black Elk's mission, wrote Brown, may not have "failed as he thought it had" (xvi). The second retelling presents Black Elk's story as a message for the troubled times of the dominant culture.

Brown's slant on the second retelling suggests that the new European American fascination with native peoples that developed in the 1960s is one way of coping with a historical and cultural identity crisis that was somehow linked to the reality that the indigenous peoples did not vanish as expected. Just as the vanishing-Indian myth was making its exit from the European American belief system, *Black Elk Speaks* soared into public consciousness. Thirty years after the little-noted original publication of

Neihardt's text, the Black Elk mythmaking began to take shape in the popular imagination. Black Elk, formerly an obscure figure, swiftly became European America's archetypal Indian, and Neihardt achieved celebrity status, being interviewed by Dick Cavett on a national telecast in 1971.

Black Elk Speaks is the central text in the second retelling. It is the very same text as before, but it was being read differently, because European American discourse was undergoing a major transition. This new reading that, in effect, became a second retelling through a string of new interpreters and through a popular readership, could be seen as having its genesis in the attention drawn to the archetypal elements in Black Elk's sacred vision by Carl Jung in 1955 (Sayre 1971, 509). A theory of archetypes was one of Jung's central themes, and he sought to find evidence of archetypes in the dreams, visions, arts, and rituals of indigenous cultures to demonstrate that his theory had universal application and was not limited to European-derived cultures.

As the archetypal Indian, Black Elk was far more accessible to European American readers than he was as the "noble savage" of the vanishing-Indian myth. An archetypal Indian was not primarily located in the past or in a strange culture, but was present in the universal structures of human experience. The 1960s and 1970s were a time when experiential reality was emphasized, and it involved embracing new forms of spiritual experience, new desire for what was natural, and new concern for holistic concepts. All of these were available in the rereading, or second retelling, of Black Elk's story.

Two themes dominate the second retelling: emphasis on the extraordinary persona of Black Elk and the literary mastery of John Neihardt. *Black Elk Speaks* became important as literature and was placed into school curricula. The retelling finds form as literary commentary by Robert Sayre in 1971 and Sally McCluskey in 1972. Sayre calls Black Elk "a prophet" and "a new cultural hero," (510) and McCluskey calls him "a mystic" (234). Both Sayre and McCluskey were aware of the notes of the original telling in 1931 and that the book is not a verbatim account of Black Elk's discourse, yet they extravagantly praise Neihardt's literary fashioning of Black Elk's story (514; 231). According to McCluskey, "Neihardt captures the spirit of Black Elk's faith, rather than exploring the intricacies of its letter" (233), and "it reads like poetry" (234).

The second retelling includes exceptional contributions by two well-known native intellectuals, Vine Deloria Jr. and N. Scott Momaday. The 1979 edition of *Black Elk Speaks* included an introduction by Deloria. He recounts the cultural shift of the 1960s, calls *Black Elk Speaks* a "religious classic" and a "North American bible of all tribes," and implies the archetypal significance of the second retelling by noting that, even though the old days of the Lakota camp circle may be past, "the universality of the images and dreams must testify to the emergence of a new sacred hoop, a new circle of intense community among Indians far outdistancing the grandeur of former times" (xii–xiii). Regarding Neihardt's role in shaping this sacred text, Deloria rejects any attempt to interpose scholarly critique between the two men (xiv).

Momaday contributed an essay titled "To Save a Great Vision" to a collection of essays honoring Neihardt, published in 1984 as *A Sender of Words*. Momaday focuses on the transition from Lakota oral tradition to Neihardt's written text. "Black Elk is first and foremost a storyteller" (32) claimed Momaday, and "the telling of the story is a spiritual act" (34). He credits Neihardt with possessing a "poet's sensibility" that was able to track the oral cadence of Black Elk's original telling. "With the rhythms and pacing well reproduced, we have a masterpiece of transformation of the oral tradition from one language and culture to another without the loss of the essential spirit of the original narration" (36–37).

The most substantive of the second retellings is by Paul Olson, whose essay, "Black Elk Speaks as Epic and Ritual Attempt to Reverse History," was published in 1982. Olson signifies the profound shift of worldview under way in the discourse of the time by noting of Neihardt, "No writer whose epistemology is based on naturalistic assumptions could have done the job" (6). He describes the collaboration of Black Elk and Neihardt by portraying Black Elk as the one in charge of the telling, calling him "a religious thinker and master of religious speech" who chooses Neihardt "as his scribe just as an oral-formulaic master may have chosen a literate collaborator at some point in the development of the Homeric epic" (5).

Unlike most second retellings, Olson focuses on the content of the sacred vision and the five ritual enactments of vision episodes as constituting the archetypal (Olson prefers the word *epic*) significance to Black Elk's story. He employs the cyclical symbolism inherent in the vision to claim that Black Elk intended to affect the linear trajectory of European American history by the interrupting and regenerating force of his ritual acts, and that even his narrative giveaway of his sacred vision to Neihardt and of his ritual knowledge to Brown constituted performative ritual acts intended to change contemporary historical realities. Still, Olson has his eye less on Lakota contexts than on seeing Black Elk's approach as relevant to contemporary European American circumstances, because "industrial man has lost his hoop by losing track of his roots, his relation to the natural process, and his former sense of organized, small-group community" (1982, 22). The European American hopefulness characteristic of the second retelling of Black Elk's story is evident in Olson's wish that, "even from the perspective of Western culture, it may have been something more than superstition which led Black Elk to perform his dream in the world and hope that the power of rituals would force history back into the cyclical and constantly regenerating mold of the seasons" (23).

The Third Retelling:
Black Elk as the Indian Intellectual

For some, the 1980s were culturally a time of reaction to the 1960s, and nostalgia for pre-1960 discourse in which the old familiar verities were in place was a powerful social and political force. The recognition had set in that Indians were not only not vanishing, but that regular coexistence must be faced. Contemporary Indian peoples had moved beyond the rhetoric of militancy and were focusing on political and legal battlefronts, arguing for both civil rights and treaty rights, though old forms of economic and political exploitation proved difficult to dislodge. A struggle on both sides of the cultural divide was taking place in which both identities were at stake.

The third retelling of Black Elk's story takes place in this setting of confused cultural conflict. It began clearly in 1984 with the publication of Raymond DeMallie's *Sixth Grandfather* and a pair of articles by Clyde Holler. Its end can be marked symbolically, if not by a clear closure, in 1992 with the observance of the five hundredth year since Columbus's arrival, which was viewed either as discovery or invasion, depending on whose cultural discourse was being acknowledged. Instead of the 1960s discourse arena of popular culture and experiential reality, the setting for the third retelling is the arena of scholarly discourse and the critical dis-

tancing of textual studies. In the second retelling, the old cultural boundaries between the dominant and the indigenous cultures were overthrown
with little forethought, whereas in the third retelling these boundaries
were redefined and duly controlled by European American scholars. In a
way, there was a closer acquaintance between the two opposing culture interests in the 1980s as they worked out their coexistence, which made the
identification of boundaries and scholarly techniques of distancing both
predictable and potentially useful.

The third retelling concentrated on bypassing *Black Elk Speaks* and focusing instead on the notes recording the original telling that Raymond
DeMallie had edited and published in *The Sixth Grandfather.* A reader will
appreciate the scholarly scrutiny of the original telling that highlighted
story elements left out of *Black Elk Speaks* and that identified and assessed
the various discrepancies between those original notes and Neihardt's first
retelling in *Black Elk Speaks.* The third retelling also brings into the story a
close study of the literary and religious interests of Neihardt as well as the
Lakota Catholicism and Lakota oral narratives that characterized Black
Elk's background. With this more detailed context at hand, an astute
reader is provided with a clearer guide to the intentions, expectations, and
discourse styles brought to the original storytelling by the participants.

However, the scholarly mode of the third retelling creates the impression that the stenographic text of the original telling to Neihardt was
equivalent to the oral event itself, as though with this text a reader has direct access to Black Elk's pristine Lakota story. The irony of an ethnographic ambition to bypass Neihardt, the poet, and to grasp the "other"
directly by stepping into the oral realm of traditional Lakota culture
through an English-language text is that the territory of oral narrative is
more like poetry in the many-sidedness of meanings, contextual associations, and relational interactions, whereas the ethnographic ambition is
easily infatuated with the ability of the ethnographer to make distinctions
within the culture of the "other" based on categories governing the
ethnographer's own cultural discourse. The danger is that this ethnographic stance may replicate the colonizing circumstances prevailing in
American cultural history wherein the dominant culture imposed its definitions on the culture of the "other" in order to maintain control over indigenous peoples.

The ethnographic agenda of the third retelling lacks self-awareness of the teller's own cultural consciousness so that the teller's discourse functions without feedback about its inherent distortions. This results in projection of the scholar's own culture-based categories and theories on to the Lakota realities, producing a flattening effect as Lakota meanings are compressed into European American concepts and terminology. This process can be noticed in these scholars' characterizations of Black Elk and his story that appear in the third retelling, because each scholar seems invariably to project his or her own scholarly persona on to Black Elk, so that Black Elk, in one scholar's guise or another, plays the role of an Indian intellectual.

Raymond DeMallie, the archivist of Neihardt's recorded communications with Black Elk, commonly refers to Black Elk's oral narratives as "teachings." This catchall term flattens important distinctions within Lakota terminology so that widely differing Lakota oral narratives are lumped together as "teachings" for European American readers who may view them indiscriminately as simply instances of the cultural meaning of the "other." DeMallie highlights Black Elk's "body of teachings" as his "legacy" to the world (1984a, 74), creating an image of the Indian intellectual as a sort of teacher-archivist carrying around his trove of teachings that he is relieved to unload on Neihardt as "testament and memorial to a way of life now gone forever" (28). Portraying Black Elk as teacher or archivist clearly flattens the Lakota understanding of a *wicasa wakan*.

Julian Rice defines himself as a "literary critic" (1989, 5), and he claims that "the old Lakota culture was so thoroughly metaphorical that the truth of a vision may be like the truth of literature" (xii). Rice implies that Black Elk had a gift for literary expression, asserting that "the stenographic record of the interviews provides not only a closer approximation to what Black Elk actually says but a better literary text" (19). Rice once refers to *The Sacred Pipe* and *Black Elk Speaks* as "Black Elk's major works," though a sentence later he writes that "the most purely Lakota and non-Christian Black Elk texts comprise the body of material collected in *The Sixth Grandfather*" (8). By referring to the records of Black Elk's narratives as "Black Elk texts," Rice conjures up an image of Black Elk as the Indian intellectual in the guise of a literary figure. "Future students of the Black Elk material will find the latter text [stenographic text preserved in *The Sixth Grandfather*] to have the ironies, reversals, and shifts of voice found in most of the Western literature now considered worthy of extended thought and comment" (14). When Rice places "Black Elk's texts" in the context of "Western literature," he implies this is a suitable context for judging Black Elk's identity and stature, but this context would clearly be viewed by traditional Lakota people as a flattening of a *wicasa wakan*'s identity into a European American scholar's notion of human significance.

Clyde Holler's graduate study was in philosophy of religion (1995, xii). He describes Black Elk as "a creative theologian" and as "essentially a religious thinker" (1984a, 25; 1995, 3).[11] In explaining Black Elk's greatness in this regard, Holler introduces European American philosophy-of-religion discourse to pose a dichotomy between literal and symbolic meanings of religious stories or truths. Holler claims that Black Elk was able to make a sophisticated shift from a mythical worldview to a symbolic religious understanding compatible with European American "historical-critical consciousness" (1995, 213–15). As Holler sees it, Black Elk adapted his sacred vision to fit changing systems of symbolic meaning, including especially Catholicism. This fact makes him "so much more than simply a boy who fell sick and dreamed spectacularly of heaven," and it justifies Holler's claim that Black Elk is "the greatest religious thinker yet produced by native North America" (221). This latter phrase is indication that the scholar may have slipped into the realm of projection, because it rests on no comparative analysis and represents a category lying entirely within the realm of European American discourse.[12] Suggesting that the sacred vision of a *wicasa wakan* originated as only a boy's dream of heaven and recasting a visionary's role into that of an Indian intellectual deliberately synthesizing symbol systems is a serious flattening of a *wicasa wakan*'s Lakota identity into the scholar's preferred European American categories.

These scholars' stories of the third retelling reflect both the virtues and the shortcomings characteristic of European American academic dis-

11. I include Holler's 1995 book among the third retellings because it was written, by his account to me, in the 1980s, its belated appearance being due to exigencies of the publication process.

12. The comment of William Powers is apropos here. "The idea of focusing on one medicine man as some kind of paragon of Lakota virtue is strictly a white man's idea" (1990c, 146).

course, which is able to conduct highly focused scrutiny of texts though not always noticing the cultural presuppositions shaping that scrutiny. The third retelling represents the scholar's voice of the dominant culture, and there is a noticeable absence of consultation or collaboration with contemporary Lakota visionaries and elders. This retelling is aimed more toward containing Lakota visionary and ritual realities within the textual boundaries of European American discourse than toward open encounter with the indigenous worldview.

The Fourth Retelling:
Black Elk as the Postcolonial Indian

The fourth retelling is happening now, having begun in 1992 at the five-hundred-year marker of European presence in the Americas. The postcolonial character of the fourth retelling is well represented by the 1993 book by Greg Sarris, the mixed-heritage Pomo scholar whose model I have adapted by looking at the story of Black Elk as a series of tellings. Postcolonial retelling includes both political critique and bicultural dialogue in which the native voice plays a critical role. Assertion of the native voice has brought on "turf war" tensions between European American scholars and native scholars, and there are also differences among native scholars about how best to represent the indigenous worldview of tribal traditions.[13]

European American scholar Arnold Krupat endorses a shift to bicultural retelling in his 1992 book, *Ethnocriticism*. Krupat had subjected Black Elk's story to the dominating categories of European American textual studies in his work during the third retelling (1985), but in *Ethnocriticism* he rejects attempts by European American scholars to impose their own cultural models of knowledge upon native realities; instead, they "must consider other constructions of the categories they would employ, calling its own largely Western assumptions or origins into question," and

---

13. See the account of this "turf war" by Ronald L. Grimes (1996). Elizabeth Cook-Lynn, Crow Creek Sioux and emeritus professor at Eastern Washington University, criticizes contemporary native scholars for "explicit and implicit accommodation to the colonialism of the 'West' that has resulted in . . . an Indian identity which focuses on individualism rather than First Nation ideology" (1996b, 67).

permitting "all who would articulate those alternate constructions to be heard" (27). He recommends "dialogical models" to facilitate "boundary crossings" between European American and indigenous cultural worlds (26).

Postcolonial retelling challenges contemporary European American scholars and readers to give up ownership of the retelling. The Black Elk story may have been read in the past as justifying European American acquisition of Lakota sacred heritage, as though Black Elk handed over his dream-vision to the European American world for safekeeping and universalizing. Postcolonial retelling claims quite the opposite, because it opens a dialogue in which Black Elk confronts European American culture with the truth and forcefulness of his Lakota traditions and calls for mutual understanding at the most profound levels of sacred truth and human meaning. Postcolonial retelling asks a contemporary reader to give up old associations and emotions connected with the figure of Black Elk that may have reflected a one-sided indulgence in European American cultural fantasies and may have included unconscious elements of condescension toward the culturally "other."

Black Elk initiated a postcolonial dialogue by his extraordinary choice to tell his vision story to a European American writer, a decision he made intuitively during his initial visit with Neihardt that included the understanding that Neihardt would publish the vision-telling for the European American world. By this act Black Elk was challenging the dominant culture's view of indigenous religion as primitive and inconsequential, or as misleading and false, or even as evil and diabolic. Colonizing discourse continues to influence contemporary scholarship on religion that hegemonically categorizes religions into such unequal dichotomies as world religions and indigenous religions, historical and prehistorical religions, and literate and preliterate religions, whereas Black Elk's storytelling assumes that all human beings participate together in a common cosmos and that European Americans and their religious traditions do not represent an exception to the common human religious experience. This framing of religious meaning resists and challenges the colonial framing that treats Lakota religion as "other" than civilized religion and hegemonically presumes the superiority of the latter.

The European American ownership that prevailed in previous retellings left the impression that Black Elk's story was religious and not political, because in European American discourse what is religious and what is political are considered separate categories. George Tinker, an Osage scholar, provides European American scholars and readers with a postcolonial understanding of the political implications of religious discourse through his 1993 book, *Missionary Conquest: The Gospel and Native American Cultural Genocide*. Tinker painstakingly demonstrates that the discourse used in missionizing the indigenous peoples was indistinguishable from the colonizing voice of government and economic interests. He describes, for example, the role of the Jesuit priest Pierre-Jean De Smet in arranging tribal participation in the Fort Laramie treaties of 1851 and 1868, for both of which the involvement of the Lakota people was crucial. Tinker shows that De Smet was in complete alliance with the fur companies, the military, and the federal government, and functioned as agent for the pacification of native peoples, that is, for their colonization through destruction of traditional native cultures. "Cultural genocide can be defined as the effective destruction of a people by systematically or systemically (intentionally or unintentionally in order to achieve other goals) destroying, eroding, or undermining the integrity of the culture and system of values that defines a people and gives them life. . . . In North American mission history, cultural genocide almost always involved an attack on the spiritual foundations of a people's unity by denying the existing ceremonial and mythological sense of a community in relationship to the Sacred Other" (6).

Although Tinker does not deal with Black Elk's story directly, his analysis of the colonizing effect of European religious discourse signals the postcolonial recognition that religious discourse is "systemically" implicated in the political, economic, and social dimensions of a culture's voice (1993, 115). Tinker's critique provides a postcolonial framing for a fourth retelling of Black Elk's story that considers the voice of Black Elk as a political voice addressing the dominant culture through the religious discourse of the dominated "other."

Postcolonial retelling of Black Elk's story finds its voice as a telling about kinship. The Lakota view of kinship reaches far beyond the kinship of humans with one another to include animals, plants, winds, rocks, sky, and earth—the whole cosmos. Kinship also embraces the realm of spirit beings, and the intimacy of this kinship is such that there is no ultimate differentiation between spirit beings and animal, plant, and rock beings, nor between all these other-than-human persons and strictly human persons.[14] European American anthropologist Robin Ridington sets the whole discourse of storytelling within the frame of kinship. "Conversation is possible only when storyteller and listener respect and understand one another through shared knowledge and experience. It is possible only when every person can realize a place in every other person's story. It is possible only when the circle of stories includes all the relations of a world that is alive with meaning" (1996, 469).

European American discourse is structured around a cosmology that largely disclaims kinship among human, animal, plant, and spirit entities. Nevertheless, Black Elk held out his vision-telling to European Americans as an act of kinship, thus continuing to acknowledge that the very nature of the cosmos is structured around the fundamental reciprocity of all its component beings. The wholeness of being and time are framed by kinship and its ritual expressions in Black Elk's story so that the Catholics are kin along with the Cheyenne, the Buffalo Nation, and the Thunder Beings, while the hegemonic assumptions of European American discourse are both resisted and invited into dialogue.

14. The phrase "other-than-human persons" is particularly serviceable for expressing the nature of this kinship relation between the human and all the classes of other-than-human kin. The anthropologist A. Irving Hallowell introduced this phrase in his seminal article, "Ojibwa Ontology, Behavior, and World View" (1960).

9

Just What Is Cultural Appropriation, Anyway?

The Ethics of Reading *Black Elk Speaks*

FRANCES W. KAYE

In 1859 Nathaniel Hawthorne finished his last novel, *The Marble Faun*, about an American sculptor in Rome and his circle of friends. Hawthorne, like many nineteenth century American artists and authors—including Mark Twain and Henry James—had traveled extensively and even lived in Italy, and he found the Eternal City the obvious setting for his allegorical novel of good and evil, of the disturbing moral implications of the idea of the "Fortunate Fall." The novel is not a roman à clef but rather an impressionistic portrait of the American artists' community. The sculptor, Kenyon, is Hawthorne's alter ego and sometimes point-of-view character, while the pure and spotless Puritan maiden Hilda is intended as his tribute to his own wife, Sophia, whom he idolized as the angel of his hearth. Although the nineteenth-century ideal of pure womanhood tends to be merely cloying to readers of a century and a half later, Hawthorne intended Hilda's moral power to be real and trenchant. Despite her New England faith, she has become the keeper of one of Rome's folk shrines, a flame to the Virgin, attended by a flock of white doves. As Hyatt Waggoner has noted in a classic article on the novel, "Hawthorne's whole career had prepared him to write *The Marble Faun*," because it is his most comprehensive study of "the complexities of experience in a world of ambiguously mingled good and evil . . ." (1966, 164). Hilda's closest friend

The original version of this chapter was a lecture given for the John G. Neihardt Center at Blair, Nebraska, in April 1996. It was subsequently broadcast on Nebraska Public Radio.

is Miriam, a young Italian artist who has suffered a never quite specified dark trauma in her past and is stalked by some mad spectre of that evil. Donatello, the fourth friend, is an innocent, a man from the countryside whom Hawthorne characterizes as a faun or even, though he never uses the term, a noble savage. When Donatello, who loves Miriam, kills her stalker to protect her, he falls from his state of innocence and into the postlapsarian world of sin and guilt.

Hilda has witnessed the crime and, horrified by what she has seen, eventually seeks peace in the English-language confessional of St. Peter's, the World's Cathedral, as Hawthorne calls it. She justifies her appropriation of the Catholic sacrament by deeming it "universal." " 'Do not these inestimable advantages,' thought Hilda, 'or some of them at least, belong to Christianity itself? Are they not a part of the blessings which the system was meant to bestow upon mankind?' " (Hawthorne 1961, 321).

Explaining herself to Kenyon, although Hilda is quite sure she will not become a convert (indeed she does not), the Puritan girl says: "I have a great deal of faith, and Catholicism seems to have a great deal of good. Why should not I be a Catholic, if I find there what I need, and what I cannot find elsewhere? The more I see of this worship, the more I wonder at the exuberance with which it adapts itself to all the demands of human infirmity" (332).

The priest to whom Hilda has confessed, however, has a somewhat less elastic definition of his faith. When he asks her why this is her first confession, she replies that she is, in Catholic terms, a "heretic." " 'And, that being the case,' demanded the old man, 'on what ground, my daughter, have you sought to avail yourself of these blessed privileges, confined exclusively to members of the one true church . . . ?' "

Hilda explains her appropriation in terms, again, of her universal human need, but the priest still replies, "you claim a privilege to which you have not entitled yourself" (324–25). The priest later tries to convert her, but Hilda will not be converted. Eventually she will marry Kenyon, and both will return to Puritan New England.

You may wonder why one would begin an essay about Black Elk by talking about Hawthorne. I want a neutral ground to define the idea of "cultural appropriation," before I talk about it in terms of native North

American spirituality and Black Elk. Hawthorne's Puritan maiden provides a telling analogue. Hilda is not only a Puritan. She is, as Hawthorne never tires of telling us, pure in every way. Her motives for using the confessional are pure. She wants to be unburdened of the great sin she has witnessed but in which she has had no part. She has a well-developed and genuine appreciation of the beauty of the Catholic faith and its sacraments, and in tending the Virgin's shrine and its doves she has been accepted to play an honored part in the tradition. At the same time, she feels that Catholicism is in some way primitive, if not inferior to her own religion, at least impossible for her to consider in terms of conversion or even in terms of obligation. When the priest asks her what she has to give in return for the relief of confession and his human sympathy, she replies, "fervently," "My grateful remembrance as long as I live!" (327). Thus, Hilda avails herself of the Catholic sacraments at a time her own faith has failed her, claiming them as a universal right of all "mankind," or at least all Christians, but she feels perfectly free to go, cleansed of her troubles, with no obligation to the Church or to her confessor beyond a thank-you. Living in Rome, with all its picturesque and historic associations—including its pockets of squalor and the central crime, grown out of old associations and customs—seems to have given Hilda the feeling that she is entitled to "borrow" its religion. It's a whole new turn on the "when in Rome" idea.

Now Hilda's single transgression does no harm to the Vatican or the Roman Catholic Church, though it does suggest that there may be a particularly "American" willingness to both usurp and deny the religions of old, complex, beautiful, but somehow "corrupt" societies. Let's fast-forward 140 years or so to the present. Mary Brave Bird is a Lakota woman, a strong AIM supporter, a member of the Native American Church, for many years the wife of Leonard Crow Dog, a principal AIM holy man who, with his father, Henry, was one of the people who revived Sun Dancing on the Rosebud Reservation. She has collaborated with Richard Erdoes on two accounts of her life, *Lakota Woman* (as Mary Crow Dog), about the AIM days, and *Ohitika Woman* (as Mary Brave Bird), about her adult life. Mary Brave Bird is not without flaws and certainly not without detractors, and many of the same questions that scholars have raised about who supplied exactly what to the collaboration between John Neihardt and Nicholas Black Elk can be raised about the collaboration between Mary Brave Bird and Richard Erdoes, especially because no transcripts of their conversations are available and some of Erdoes's other collaborations certainly appear to include the commercialization and misuse of Lakota belief and ritual. Nevertheless, Mary Brave Bird raises a number of questions about cultural appropriation that are worth the attention of a reader wondering what uses one can feel comfortable in making of *Black Elk Speaks.*

One of the chapters in *Ohitika Woman* is called "Selling the Medicine," and it begins: "All across the country, among all the tribes, Native Americans are angry because the whites are selling our medicine. What Native Americans are saying is that our religion and ceremonies have become fads, and a fashionable pastime among many whites seeking for something that they hope will give meaning to their empty lives" (Erdoes and Brave Bird 1993, 233). Mary Brave Bird is most concerned by the grossly commercial rip-offs of Indian spirituality by the "New Age Hucksters" who are the descendants of the nineteenth-century patent-medicine entrepreneurs who sold "Kickapoo Snake Oil" and a variety of other products. But it is not just the fakers that Brave Bird condemns. Sincerity, as in Hawthorne's Hilda, is no guard against theft. As Brave Bird explains,

> There is this elderly white woman in Texas who provides a perfect example of white people muscling in on the medicine. Again I won't mention her name. She is actually nice and sincere. She has witnessed a number of our ceremonies and it has gone to her head. She imagines that Crow Dog is her grandfather "who gave her the gift." She runs sweats, she puts people on the hill, and she "teaches the Lakota way." . . . This person actually believes in what she is doing, has her heart in the right place, sends us little gifts; but having witnessed our rituals makes her neither a medicine woman nor an Indian. Well-meaning people can do as much harm as the conniving bullshit artists. (237–38)

What is the matter with what this lady is doing? Or Hawthorne's Hilda? If a few people make confessions and feel better even if they are not Catholics, what difference does it make? If a few white folks want to run sweat lodges and do Sun Dances or pray with a pipe, what's the harm? After all, imitation is the sincerest form of flattery, and if practicing these teachings makes people better human beings with more respect for Indian people and Native American cultures, one would assume that's all to the

good. It is certainly better than outlawing the Sun Dance and sending little Indian children to boarding schools where they are forbidden both
their spirituality and their native language. But this may be a false dichotomy. Again, here is what Mary Brave Bird has to say: "Indian religion
is at the center of my life. It is the spiritual side of myself. It is part of my
heritage. It made me survive. . . . Our religion should be protected from
defilement. . . . Before 1930, we were forbidden to pray in our language.
Our rituals were suppressed. For participating in a sweat lodge ceremony
you could be jailed under the Indian Offenses Act" (1993, 235). Now,
however, Brave Bird feels that the dominant society is trying to put an end
to native religious ceremonies by commercializing them: "[W]hat is happening now is worse than the old effort to stamp out our religion altogether. They tried to kill our faith and triumphantly proclaimed the
'Death of the Great Spirit.' They did not succeed. But they might succeed
now by commercializing it and by giving the world the wrong idea of what
the Indian way of life is about. They are selling our religion, selling the
pipe, the sweat lodge, the fireplace, the peyote. Pretty soon whites will
think of themselves as our teachers, telling us how to perform our rituals
or how to use our sacred medicine" (235–36).

Let's look at the various things Brave Bird is saying in this passage.
"Indian religion is at the center of my life." She is like Hawthorne's priest,
maintaining that the religion is at the center of her life—and also that by
heritage and commitment, she is at the center of the religion. Elsewhere in
the book she talks about the sheer drudgery she endured cooking for the
Sun Dances and cooking for the many visitors she entertained at Crow
Dog's Paradise as the holy man's wife. She has earned her belief by years of
hard physical labor. Although Julian Rice has shown that Erdoes took passages from the writings of turn-of-the-century anthropologists and other
students of Lakota culture and attributed them to the purported subjects
of his other as-told-to autobiographies (1994b), and although Erdoes is
himself implicated in selling the religion, Brave Bird's complaint is a typical one, and her descriptions of her hard work are not likely to be fabrications by Erdoes. Her emphasis on the importance of the actual physical
preparation for ritual echoes the advice Christopher Ronwanien:te Jocks
quotes a Mohawk friend as giving to a New Age group who wanted "to
participate in some kind of American Indian ceremony."

"This is what you do," my friend told them. "First, you prepare the feast. Cook up lots and lots of food. We Mohawks make corn soup, but you can substitute tofu stir-fry if you like. As you're cooking it, think about the people you'll be inviting, about their lives, and about your own. Think about the ingredients too, where they come from, and who helped bring them to you. Then invite everyone you know to come over. Make sure you have enough food. Everybody that comes, you feed them. And you listen to them, pay attention to their advice, their problems. Hold their hands, if that's what they need. If any of them needs to stay over, make a place for them. Then, next month, you do the same thing again. And again, four times, the same way. That's it! You've done an Indian ceremony!"

This friend of mine was not being facetious or making fun of these seekers. . . . Nor was she asserting that somehow hospitality is the essence of ceremony. (Jocks 1996, 415)

The friend's point is that one cannot simply sail into a ceremony without being part of the community, but being of assistance to the community is a meaningful ceremony for an outsider.

Beyond the question of community is the matter of suppression. In his book *Black Elk's Religion,* Clyde Holler states bluntly that cultural genocide was the price native peoples paid for the surcease of physical genocide. Talking about "Grant's Peace Policy" of the 1880s, he says: "The essential program of the reformers was acculturation. They proposed to solve the Indian problem not by eliminating Indians, as the army had done at Sand Creek and elsewhere, but by eliminating Indianness. They regarded it as obvious that if all Indians were fully assimilated, the Indian problem would disappear. Since their proposal was essentially to replace genocide with cultural genocide, repression of the native religion and its priesthood was an obvious strategy" (1995, 113). One should also note that acculturation required not only the "repression of the native religion and its priesthood" but the replacement of a communal ethic with an individualistic one, the replacement of commonly used land with private allotments, and the confiscation of most of the land for the use of white settlers. The 1880s saw not only the proscription of the Sun Dance and all other visible elements of Native American spirituality but also the passage of the Dawes Act, which allotted land to individual persons on most reservations, "freeing" the "surplus" land for settlement by Euro-Americans. Cultural genocide had its material as well as its spiritual element. At least in some sense, the materialism of the dominant culture was placated by the land. Could we say that only when the land itself had been swallowed and digested did the dominant culture return hungrily to gobble up the spirituality that had managed to survive in odd corners of reservations and in the hearts of the people?

Mary Brave Bird suggests that whites will define what is authentically Indian, and one can actually see that happening in books such as Ian Frazier's *Great Plains* (1989). Frazier is a New Yorker who became obsessed with the idea of Crazy Horse and, through Crazy Horse, the Great Plains. When he came to the Plains to write a book about the region, one of the things that disappointed him was the young Indians. Some of them had drinking problems, and he seems to feel that he, sober and successful, is more the true heir of Crazy Horse than are some of the people he meets. Mary Brave Bird is very open about her own drinking, about the car crash that nearly killed her but helped her resolve to quit, and about all the deaths and maimings that result from drinking among people on the reservations as well as urban Indians. If we look back, we can see the way the Dawes Act and the suppression of native religions coincided. To lose one's livelihood, one's land, one's language, and one's religion all in one blow was devastating and demoralizing. That the price of resistance continues to be high should not be surprising. And it hardly behooves the observer from the dominant culture to complain about the dress and manners of the resistance fighters—though one must not, on the other hand, assume that one must be a drunk to be a genuine Indian.

But Brave Bird's main complaint in the long passage quoted above is of the cultural genocide. Ward Churchill, another AIM activist, who now teaches in the American Indian Studies program in the Center for Studies of Ethnicity and Race in America at the University of Colorado at Boulder, has written about the seriousness of cultural—not physical or material—genocide. He brings us back to the ideas of the nineteenth-century reformers who wanted to kill the Indian to save the man. They, of course, believed that Christianity would provide a central meaning to the de-Indianed men they hoped to create, though for most native peoples "assimilation" worked out in practice to mean "marginalization," the loss of land, livelihood, and language—and too often liquor as replacement. Churchill quotes two other researchers, Mark Davis and Robert Zannis, on the nature of culture genocide: "If people suddenly lose their 'prime symbol,' the basis of their culture, their lives lose meaning. They become disoriented, with no hope. As social disorganization often follows such a loss, they are often unable to insure their own survival. . . . The loss and human suffering of those whose culture has been healthy and is suddenly attacked and disintegrated are incalculable" (1989, 24).

Despite the pan-Indian cultural renaissance that has swept North America for the last thirty years, starting perhaps with N. Scott Momaday's *House Made of Dawn,* and the real improvements in legal rights, education, and general self-determination among the native peoples in North America, poverty, despair, and their resultant problems continue to be at home among native peoples. To lose a "prime symbol," that spiritual heritage of which Mary Brave Bird speaks that enables her to survive, to either New Age hucksters or sincere wannabes who would love it to death carries all the tragedy of being shot by the enemy moments before the cease-fire went into effect. People such as Churchill and Brave Bird lament that the dominant society has taken the land, has taken the children, and now is coming back for the only thing left: the spirituality that nineteenth-century Christians for the most part saw as being as blank and godforsaken as they held the dry lands of Pine Ridge and Rosebud and other "reservations." Hawthorne's Hilda, one Puritan in the midst of the teeming world of Rome, could hardly appropriate Roman Catholicism, but a combination of hucksterism and a perfectly sincere loving to death, always against a background of material dispossession and cultural marginalization, does raise a real spectre of cultural appropriation and cultural genocide. "Universal" in this context so often seems to mean, as it did for the Puritan girl in Rome, "what's yours is ours but what's mine is mine."

Does this then mean that non-Indians have to leave Indian material alone? Not according to Mary Brave Bird, whose coauthor is a European who emigrated to this continent as an adult. Nor even according to Ward Churchill, who cites books by various Euro-American writers in his suggestions for various college courses in American Indian studies. But these examples do show us where some of the sensitive issues may lie for nonnatives engaged in studying or teaching—or even reading—texts such as *Black Elk Speaks.* As for me, if I believed that non-Indians have no business with Indian texts, I would not be writing this article.

To understand how *Black Elk Speaks* fits into the arguments about cultural appropriation, we need to look at the actual circumstances surrounding its composition. *Black Elk Speaks* is very much a thirties book—at home both with the "American Scene" images that the Public Works Administration (PWA) and other depression projects were creating and with the restitution of rights to native peoples under the direction of John Collier. True, *Black Elk Speaks* preceded the New Deal and the so-called Indian New Deal by a couple of years, but the ideas were of a piece. The Peace Policy of the reformers of the 1880s had won out. Fifty years later it was clear that the great clashes of the "Indian Wars" were over. During the First World War, native men had joined the U.S. armed forces and fought with great pride and courage—even though they were not yet deemed American citizens. Even before the war the wealthy merchant John Wannamaker had dreamed of a statue in New York Harbor to rival the Statue of Liberty and to depict a native man ceding the land in peace and friendship to the Euro-Americans and arriving Europeans (Barsh 1993). The old imagery of the murdering savages that had led the Seventh Cavalry to turn Hotchkiss guns on the families at Wounded Knee in December 1890 was reverting back to the image of the Noble Savage, the spiritual forebear of the Noble American who was distinguishing himself (always him) from the corrupt European in the same vein but a rather different mode than Hawthorne's Puritans had done. That is not to say that the "Savage" vanished from the popular culture or even from the history books, but only to say that the dominant culture had the land and the power—it could relax on the symbolism.

Thanks to Hartley Burr Alexander, Nebraska's capitol was heavily invested with Native American symbolism, proclaiming to the world Nebraska's heirship of both Native American and Mediterranean-European culture, destined for a hybrid society of grandeur upon the Plains. PWA murals in Texas buildings likewise showed Indians as noble savages, part of the heritage of the Lone Star State. Towns created pageants that showed the land being given to the "pioneers" by some fictitious—or even real—"Indian Chief." Montana insurance executive Frank Linderman began collecting his popular "as-told-to" autobiographies of native people such as Plenty Coups and Pretty Shield. John Collier encouraged a renaissance of Native American arts and ceremonies. Luther Standing Bear published *My People the Sioux* and *Land of the Spotted Eagle*, claiming the importance

of Lakota ways for the education of Sioux children. Mari Sandoz's friend
Evelyn Hinman was collecting information for a book she planned about
Crazy Horse.[1] John Neihardt was collecting material for the *Song of the
Messiah*, which would close out his five-part *Cycle of the West*. The forty-
one years between the killings at Wounded Knee and the visit of Neihardt
to Black Elk was a time when the dominant culture of the United States
consolidated its "conquest" of the Native Americans, consolidated the
myth of the "Vanishing American," and consolidated the idea that Euro-
Americans were the heirs of all that was noble in that "Vanishing American." The heirship idea had been around for a long time, certainly since at
least 1823 and James Fenimore Cooper's first Leatherstocking novel, *The
Pioneers*, but the end of the "Indian Wars" removed the obvious incon-
gruity of government troops taking up arms against the "savages." Although the dominant culture's "war against the Indians" has never
stopped, its venue has changed, and the period between World War I—including the granting of citizenship and voting rights to Native Americans—and the Indian New Deal in 1934 was one of the most significant
periods of that change.

Thus, when John Neihardt met Nicholas Black Elk in August 1930,
conditions in the nation were ripe for Black Elk to return in memory to his
vision and for Neihardt to record and publish it. Even among the syn-
chretic Lakotas, who have a cultural gift for religious innovation through
both diffusion and prophecy, Black Elk seems to have been unusual. He
was a powerful prophet and healer but also an ethnographer, who had
used Buffalo Bill's Wild West Show to explore *wasichu* territory and cul-

---

1. Artists in the various New Deal art projects were to depict the "American Scene,"
and it was to be both recognizable and upbeat. See, for example, O'Sullivan 1989 and
McKinzie 1972, esp. pp. 3–32. For information on the Nebraska State Capitol and its program, see Luebke 1990, esp. pp. 42, 113. For information on Texas post offices, see Carraro 1996. Her talk is part of a larger study that is forthcoming in print. A town pageant,
originally written in 1925, that shows the "donation" theme is mounted by the town of
Thermopolis, Wyoming; see Shalinsky 1986. The best of Frank Linderman's works have
stayed in print fairly consistently; see, for example, *Plenty-Coups, Chief of the Crows* (1957),
which was originally published in 1930 as *American: The Life Story of a Great Indian,
Plenty-Coups, Chief of the Crows*. In the foreword to her biography of Crazy Horse, Mari
Sandoz talks of Hinman's work and of their 1930 trip to collect oral histories relating to
Crazy Horse (1961, ix).

part, they totally neglect the solid and satisfying (if not materially wealthy) life he had built for himself and his family and his belief that by working with Neihardt toward the publication of his story the sacred tree could bloom again (DeMallie 1984a, 55–57). Neihardt saw *Black Elk Speaks* as a tragedy. Although we can also read the transcripts as a comedy in their reestablishment of order, the whole story is probably best understood as history, an ongoing account of the lives of a people who have survived hard times. The mood of the story without Neihardt's interpolations is not unlike the sentence "Life goes on" with which Mary Crow Dog ends *Lakota Woman* (1990, 263).

So, as life goes on, what role does *Black Elk Speaks* play? It continues to be read and taught in dominant-culture schools and colleges throughout the country. I teach it in Plains-literature classes, accompanied in some way by the transcripts of the interviews between John Neihardt and Black Elk in *The Sixth Grandfather.* One of my students told me that her boyfriend's little brother was reading *Black Elk Speaks* in high school, blissfully unaware of Black Elk's years as a Christian catechist. Teachers, scholars, and Native American people seeking enlightenment—as well as casual readers of any age or culture—do tend to take the book at face value, as Neihardt intended it to be taken, as the first "true autobiography" of a Native American, though of course it is not exactly that. Some things are necessarily lost in translation, as must happen between two languages as fundamentally dissimilar as Lakota and English. Neihardt, like Sandoz after him, assumes a rather formal and elevated tone to indicate Lakota speech, which is problematic, because Neihardt knew far less Lakota than Black Elk knew English. The stories were not told in chronological order, but they are so ordered in *Black Elk Speaks,* which shifts the sequence of the book, as Thomas Couser (1988) phrases it, from mythic time to historic time, while the careful excision of Christian references simultaneously places Black Elk in a mythic history, completely cut off from the Christian cattle-raising present in which the interviews were taking place.

DeMallie's publication of *The Sixth Grandfather,* the transcriptions of the actual 1931 interviews of Black Elk plus a ninety-nine-page introduction outlining Black Elk's life after Wounded Knee and the changes between the transcripts and *Black Elk Speaks,* does move us closer to what Black Elk actually said and allows us to see that the beginning and the end of the book, its intellectual framework, are purely Neihardt, but we still remain a considerable distance not only from what Black Elk said in Lakota but also from our knowledge of what Black Elk said because he deemed it important and what Black Elk said in response to Neihardt. The text is wonderfully problematic for literary scholars because it makes apparent all sorts of questions about speaker and audience, about how we construct narrative and how we comprehend it. Simply as a written work, even for readers with no knowledge of, or even interest in, Lakota culture, the relationship that we can only partly divine between any words and "what really happened" is at best tentative and provisional. It seems to me that when the rhetoricians get around to analyzing this text *as* text, they will have less obligation to the meaning of the book than those of us who read it primarily for meaning. Narratives such as the two books by Mary Brave Bird to which I have so often referred above fall under similar scrutiny, with no published transcripts against which to check them and considerable evidence that Richard Erdoes is involved in the packaging and selling of Lakota culture to New Age spiritualists (Rice 1994b). Richard Erdoes becomes a character in Brave Bird's text, also identified as "my co-author" and the person available to lend or advance Brave Bird money from their joint earnings. Clearly, this relationship is even more problematic than the one between Neihardt and Black Elk. In his "Instead of a Forward" to *Ohitika Woman,* Erdoes says of the first book, "I put the manuscript together like a jigsaw puzzle out of a huge mountain of tapes." When an editor replied that he should make the book more mystical—"Make her into a female Don Juan!"—he angrily refused to fake it, and the book waited for more than ten years to be published (1993, xiii). The second book resulted from the success of the first. For this collaboration there is no translation involved, there are tapes instead of transcripts, the interviews went on for about a year for the first book, and the collaborators met because of their joint activism in AIM. The main problem stays the same: Who is speaking, Black Elk or Neihardt? Brave Bird or Erdoes?

Another question that arises more with the text of *Black Elk Speaks* is "Who is Black Elk?" Mary Brave Bird is very much alive and able to speak for herself. Nicholas Black Elk never had enough English to speak effectively for himself to an English-speaking audience, and he died ten years before the book was republished and eventually achieved success. Neihardt therefore took on the responsibility of speaking for Black Elk. According to his daughter Hilda, "During the remainder of his life (after the 1931 interviews), he rarely spoke in public without referring to Black Elk. Through Neihardt's recitations, his adaptation of 'Black Elk's Prayer' became known and loved by many" (DeMallie 1984a, xviii). Black Elk called Neihardt "son" or "nephew," gave Lakota names to him and his daughters, and in recounting his life and vision for Neihardt, intended that they be used for everyone. Neihardt clearly attempted to live up to what he understood to be Black Elk's intentions, but subsequent scholars have suggested that Neihardt may not have understood Black Elk as thoroughly as he believed he did. Michael Steltenkamp, at one pole, claims that Black Elk continued to be a practicing Catholic and that he was simply reciting old "superstitions." As Clyde Holler has pointed out, this requires dismissing a great deal more than *Black Elk Speaks* (1995, 21–22), though Steltenkamp's starting point is Lucy Looks Twice, Black Elk's daughter, who had not read *Black Elk Speaks* when she knew Steltenkamp but was, according to Hilda Neihardt, so moved by the book when she did read it that she herself became a "pipe carrier" and joined Hilda Neihardt in the recitation of Black Elk's prayer (118). Steltenkamp's ingenuousness in not identifying himself as a priest in his own account also tends to undermine the reader's confidence in his willingness to admit the relevance of facts that would undermine his objectivity. Julian Rice is the opposite pole from Steltenkamp, holding that Black Elk never really wavered from his Lakota beliefs, despite his usage of Catholicism, and that Neihardt imposed his own Christian/Aryan/Mediterranean views on Black Elk's story of his vision and his life. Clyde Holler, who maintains a position somewhere between the other two, usefully points out that Steltenkamp's understanding of Black Elk must be interpreted in the context of Wounded Knee Two, distinguishing Nicholas Black Elk from Wallace Black Elk, a Lakota man who, like Neihardt, considered himself the spiritual "nephew" and heir of Nicholas Black Elk (1995, 14–15). Wallace Black Elk was a close colleague of Leonard Crow Dog, a spiritual leader at Wounded Knee and in the Sun Dance revival that coincided with it.

One of the disadvantages in using *Black Elk Speaks* or even the *Sixth Grandfather* transcripts to answer the questions of who Nicholas Black Elk was and thus who may legitimately claim to carry on his tradition is that the relentless concentration on the past severs any connections to that future that is now both our present and our past. The criticism of Neihardt

that is to me the most telling is that he met Black Elk in the pursuit of his
own goal of writing *The Song of the Messiah: A Cycle of the West* as the close
to the frontier epic of North America. The poetic logic of the whole cycle
is that the defeat of the Lakotas becomes a kind of fortunate fall giving rise
to the new nation of the Jedediah Smiths and Hugh Glasses who, in conquering the land and the people, themselves assume the virtues of their
valiant but defeated foes. As I have mentioned in regard to the Nebraska
State Capitol and so forth, this idea that the Indians had fallen so that their
nobility could become the "universal" heritage of the predominantly European peoples of the United States was part of 1930s public iconography.
Thus, Black Elk's assertion that he was telling Neihardt his story so that it
could be preserved for everyone was exactly what Neihardt wanted to
hear. This statement, however, meant that Black Elk's story, too, had to
end at Wounded Knee and that the massacre had to represent the death of
the dream, the death of the nation, the death of the nation's hoop. According to Thomas Couser: "To end the narrative *conclusively* with the
Battle of Wounded Knee is the literary equivalent of killing off the survivors; it is a subtle but insidious form of cultural genocide. The effect is to
encourage white readers to indulge in an uncomplicated pathos at the demise of a noble way of life rather than to compel them to contemplate its
survival in assimilated forms" (1988, 85). That is a fairly devastating conclusion. *Black Elk Speaks* is fervent about Black Elk's vision and the spiritual significance of every part of that vision. It is about preserving the
dream, putting together the broken hoop, making the tree flower once
again—how can it possibly be "a subtle but insidious form of cultural
genocide?"

I clearly remember one semester in a Plains-literature class a young
student from South Dakota who had grown up regarding Indians as lazy
bums who trashed their free BIA housing and drank up their AFDC
checks. She loved *Black Elk Speaks* and wrote passionately about how she
was going to show it to her father so that he would stop his lazy-bum remarks. She definitely "indulge[d] in an uncomplicated pathos." A few
weeks later, we read James Welch's bleak contemporary novel *Winter in
the Blood,* and the same student was very upset. How could I require her to
read a book that just reinforced all the stereotypes she thought she had
shed forever after reading *Black Elk Speaks?* She did not want to be compelled to contemplate the survival of Native American life "in assimilated

forms," and, truth to tell, *Black Elk Speaks* is a powerfully moving book, far more moving than the transcripts are, and a young student really should not have to morally redefine herself more than once in the course of one class. But is the luxury of turning away morally defensible?

It is very difficult to make the case that John Neihardt acted in bad faith with Nicholas Black Elk. He was clearly impressed by the old man and bowled over by the beauty of his vision. He felt that Black Elk's story was a significant contribution to world religion, and he was thrilled to be able to shape the message and make it accessible. According to his daughter, he freely shared the advance he had received from his publisher with Black Elk and the other elders who spoke to him, and he generously and properly sponsored a dance and feast. He kept in touch with the Black Elk family, interviewed Black Elk again in 1944, and wrote a letter of introduction to Black Elk for Joseph Epes Brown. After Black Elk's death, Neihardt and his family retained their connections to Black Elk's children. Although the original edition of *Black Elk Speaks* did not sell well, its existence seems to have helped both Nicholas and Ben Black Elk in their roles with Duhamel's pageant—a sort of Black Hills Tame West Show—and perhaps related appearances. The commercial failure of the first edition of *Black Elk Speaks* and Neihardt's own limited financial capacity during the depression and the war years probably kept him from sharing either as much money or as much time with the Black Elk family as he might have wished.

But that was then and this is now. How can readers read against the insidious form of cultural genocide? Can white readers, like Hawthorne's Puritan maiden, find comfort in Black Elk's vision (as mediated by Neihardt) only for the price of the book (or a library card) and a thank-you? Hawthorne's *Marble Faun* is also about a fortunate fall: the innocent Donatello commits murder on Miriam's behalf. This act results not only in his imprisonment and separation from Miriam but also in his loss of innocence and permanent banishment from the simple arcadian pleasures that had seemed to be his destined lot. Yet, Donatello gains from this a complexity, a knowledge of good and evil, that makes him truly human, no longer the alien faun. The two Americans, Kenyon and Hilda, are, however, the ones who benefit most from Donatello's fall. Hilda is shaken out of her tower into a greater understanding and sympathy for the tragic Miriam. Her purity is allowed to unbend into humanity—enough, in fact, that she is able to come to Kenyon as his wife. The two Americans go back to New England, enriched as well as saddened by what has befallen their friends, but seeing neither possibility nor necessity to intervene on their behalf or to "reform" Rome. Neihardt undoubtedly did not have *Marble Faun* explicitly in mind when he wrote *Black Elk Speaks,* but he was never really very far from its assumptions. His wife, Mona, like Kenyon, had been an expatriate American sculptor in Europe, and his love poems are not entirely foreign to Kenyon's mystic sense of Hilda's purity and power. If Hawthorne's characters felt no sense of obligation to Rome, to the Roman Catholic Church, or to their own friends, certainly the reader of *The Marble Faun* has no obligation to any of them.

But what about *Black Elk Speaks?* Is there an obligation to contemplate, perhaps even approach, the survival of the Lakota people "in assimilated forms"? To put it bluntly, if I am uplifted by reading *Black Elk Speaks* and the culture that it, however imperfectly, represents, am I obligated to working to free Leonard Peltier? Or to improving Nebraska public schools for Native American children? Or to some other political course of action? I think I would have to maintain that the answer is a qualified yes, at least for *wasichus.* Qualified, because the last thing Lakotas or anybody else needs is a whole group of ignorant do-gooders indulging in uncomplicated pathos to come running in anywhere. The folk who called themselves "The Friends of the Indians" did enough well-meaning harm back in the nineteenth century to last for hundreds of years. Besides, what is that ignorant non-Indian to make of all the schisms in the Native American communities? People such as Mary Brave Bird and Ward Churchill are AIM types. Churchill damns Indian fakers, but he has his own detractors who claim he is himself a faker. Elizabeth Cook-Lynn, an eloquent writer, reads *Lakota Woman* as an essentially meaningless text created by a detribalized person who has nothing to say about the community, and, as we have seen, there are reasons to distrust Erdoes's narration (though Cook-Lynn criticizes Rice as well). No, the ignorant non-Indian—or the equally ignorant urban, detribalized Indian—had better play it safe and slow.

If those are the qualifications, what is the "yes" part of the answer? Many of my scholarly colleagues would claim that academic freedom means anyone can read and critique anything without fear or favor, as long as the reader retains a scholarly objectivity. Reluctantly, I reject that argument. For one thing, objectivity, like subjectivity, is itself a scholarly construct, not a human truth. (By this I do not mean that events are unknowable but that their relationship to other events does shift. The Holocaust deniers are not "just as good as anyone else" if we abandon the security of objectivity—but nor are those people who would deny the American Holocaust that affected the Lakotas, among so many others, and proclaim that we have reached "a level playing field.") For another, contemporary North American society is profoundly unequal. Being color-blind in a racist society means being blind to racism as well, and one cannot ameliorate what one refuses to see. Reading a book such as *Black Elk Speaks* does obligate the reader to question why Black Elk had been dispossessed of his traditional powers as a holy man and came to rely on Neihardt to protect his dream.

Even after we pass beyond the question of power differential, there is the question of respect for the material Black Elk describes. Traditional Lakota life was powerfully communal. Black Elk's vision is not just for himself. It must be reenacted for the people in order to have power. Traditional spiritual power was not for the individual but for the group, whether it be to secure food, fertility, health, or success in war. Similarly, the modern traditional life that Mary Brave Bird (or Richard Erdoes) describes is communal. Although the constant pressure to feed everyone who happened to drop into Crow Dog's Paradise was admittedly one of the things that eventually made her marriage to Leonard Crow Dog impossible, Brave Bird never turns her back on her primary commitment to community. "Being involved wears you out," she says. "But I'm still fighting. I try to be sincere, try to hold on to the medicine, try to make my kids understand what it means to be Indian" (1993, 273, 274). The ceremonies cannot ever be divorced from what it means to be Indian, as we saw in the quotation from the Mohawk woman above. In her poem "stupid questions," Shoshone/Chippewa writer nila northSun makes the same point in a series of "stupid questions"—or comments—and her sotto voce answers. At the end of the poem the stupid questioner says

> i'm really sympathetic about the way indians
> were treated, lands taken, treaties broken
> (oh good, does that mean you donate generously
> to the reservation nearest you, that you sponsor
> a scholarship fund? that you donate turkeys for

the elders' thanksgiving baskets so they have something
to eat? that you give canned goods to the social
service program so they can help others? that you
sponsor a child or family at christmas so they can
get a warm coat or toy?)
fuck it
don't waste my breath
put your money where your mouth is
send books, donations, your time and involvement
to the reservation nearest you. . . .

Wasichu readers of *Black Elk Speaks,* like northSun's questioner, take on the responsibility for recognizing the invitation to "uncomplicated pathos" and for counteracting it with a determined effort to contemplate Indian survival "in assimilated forms," including donating time and money. Even the casual and more or less involuntary *wasichu* reader who is assigned the book in some class incurs some slight obligation, if only because *wasichu* education is inherently a privilege based in part on the prosperity gained from the material dispossession of the First Nation's peoples. The University of Nebraska is a "land grant institution." *Whose land was granted?*

Black Elk's Great Vision came to him unbidden. He did not go seeking it. It was revealed to him when he was a child of nine, but it laid a great obligation on him, an obligation to perform the vision and to use its powers for the good of the community. To that vision he remained faithful, in one fashion or another, throughout his life. Anyone of any nation who seeks to benefit from Black Elk's spirituality willingly takes on, I believe, a similar obligation, one that cannot be acquitted by ritual but by giving something back to the Lakota community or at least to one's own local indigenous community or perhaps to the helpless ones in whatever may be one's own community. In traditional Lakota society, with its emphasis on balance, receiving a privilege means incurring a reciprocal responsibility. When Ella Deloria describes the *hunka* ceremony in *Waterlily,* she first tells the reader what an honor it represents for the initiates and then goes on to explain that they have incurred a special responsibility for generosity. Waterlily has "been set apart as one of those who must make hospitality their first concern" (1988, 78). Hawthorne's Hilda finds in Catholic worship and in Rome itself an "exuberance" that "adapts itself to all the demands of human infirmity," and she appropriates it for her own use, thinking to give only a thank-you and, despite a prolonged attempt by the priest to convert her, getting away with little more than the thank-you. Too much has been taken from native peoples for nonnative or even unaffiliated native peoples to take the rituals and run.

Did Neihardt appropriate Black Elk's vision and his "pipe religion"? Of course. Given Neihardt's faith in his own mystic insight, his training in a Mediterranean/Christian ethos and literature that demanded salvation through sacrifice, his lifetime resolve to write an epic of the West in a self-consciously archaic form (heroic couplets), his fascination with Indian traditions, and his sympathy with the appropriative celebration of native materials by such people as John Collier, his future boss, it is hard to see how Neihardt could have done other than appropriate. Does that make *Black Elk Speaks* a corrupt text, to be shunned by all right-minded peoples? Not really. Lakota beadwork is not corrupt because it uses European-manufactured beads nor are Lakota Horse Dances corrupt because the horse was reintroduced to the Americas by the Spaniards. The political renaissance of indigenous peoples around the world that began on the Indian subcontinent in the 1940s has produced a wealth of information on how to "read" materials created in various collaborations of indigenous peoples and colonial writers or governments. Traditional holy men among the Lakotas, such as John Fire Lame Deer or Pete Catches or Sam Moves Camp, and contemporary scholars among the *wasichus*, such as Julian Rice or Clyde Holler, provide a variety of ways for reading both *Black Elk Speaks* and the *Sixth Grandfather* transcripts out of Neihardt's mind-set and Black Elk's external constraints of the early 1930s. These readings back, of course, are "contaminated" by the times of the readings—would Black Elk have supported AIM at Wounded Knee or not?—but such "contamination" is, in fact, part of the gift, because a dynamic religion centered in the community must change as the needs, wants, and powers of the community change.

Should casual or curious or Indian-struck readers continue to read *Black Elk Speaks*? Why not? But it might be nice if it came with a few warnings. The rhetoric of presentation of *Black Elk Speaks* is that John Neihardt—and hence *wasichus* in general—is the spiritual heir of Black Elk, that the vision is for all people. But this happy ecumenism has the downside of disinheriting, at least in part, Black Elk's specific cultural heirs, the Lakota people. As Rice points out, this process is more decisive in *The Song of the Messiah,* for which Neihardt originally solicited the Black Elk interviews as raw material, where the "crucifixion" of Big Foot and his people takes on the explicit metaphor of Christian rebirth through sacrifice, but what is reborn is the Christian dominant culture. But that disinheriting is implicit in *Black Elk Speaks,* too, with the death of the dream and the final image of a pitiful old man whose own son is not his inheritor but rather the paradoxically speechless translator of the vision from Lakota to English— while boarding schools still prohibited Lakota children from speaking Lakota.

To be *wasichu* in America is to be a receiver of stolen property, though poor *wasichus* have themselves been robbed again. If we would decry violence, we must first admit that in American history, as in world history in general, it has worked, over and over again. All landownership in the United States is ultimately based on the principle that might makes right. We live in time, however, and we cannot redo the past, cannot simply give back the land as if it were a CD player taken in last month's burglary. ("Why not?" asks my Seminole friend.) *Wasichus* and all those honorary *wasichus* who have made it to the middle class can, however, be honorable thieves who admit to theft. At the first level, that admission means awareness. One reading *Black Elk Speaks,* no matter what one's cultural heritage, has some obligation to notice that no religion can be given away, that it must be earned, and that in Lakota culture in particular no religion exists without the community. The reader from the dominant culture does not want to become a literary version of the stupid questioner or the lady from Texas that Mary Brave Bird describes, imagining that reading *Black Elk Speaks,* or even studying it reverently along with the *Sixth Grandfather* transcripts, entitles one to be Indian. Be an honest thief. Any *wasichu* reader is the heir to the government that had outlawed the Sun Dance for most of Black Elk's adult life, including the period in 1931 when he talked to John Neihardt. It had denied him, a holy man and healer, the livelihood for which he had trained. It had created for him a dependency relationship in which he had to depend on Neihardt to pass on the vision. Given these cultural contexts, the ethics of reading *Black Elk Speaks* are perpetually charged.

10

Inipi, the Purification Rite (Sweat Lodge), and Black Elk's Account in *The Sacred Pipe*

GREGORY P. FIELDS

Sweat lodges for the rite of purification are nowadays near many Indian homes, and the ancient ceremony is important for many people in the Plains region and other regions of North America—on reservations, in rural and suburban areas, and in cities where a fair number of Indian people reside. A written version of Black Elk's account of the *inipi* or purification rite was published in 1953 in *The Sacred Pipe,* which continues to be an important source of religious understanding for Indian and non-Indian people. Although the book preserves knowledge of the Lakota sacred rites, it also raises problems concerning the meaning of "traditional," and the appropriateness and limitations of written texts for communicating the lived teachings of oral traditions.

The reliability of the text *The Sacred Pipe* as an accurate account of the Lakota sacred rites has been questioned on the grounds that little information is available about how Joseph Epes Brown prepared the text, and no field notes have been available. However, evaluation of Brown's method of producing *The Sacred Pipe* is only one dimension of assessing the text's reliability. Other means of assessment include comparison of Black Elk's account with earlier historical accounts of the sacred rites, with contemporary Lakota people's practice and understanding of the rites, and with meanings expressed in sacred songs integral to the rite. To contribute to the dialogue about the status of the text *The Sacred Pipe,* and about the relationship between text and tradition, I offer a comparative analysis of some prominent features of the contemporary *inipi* rite in relation to Black Elk's account in *The Sacred Pipe.* The emphasis is on two

169

main themes: 1) text in relation to "tradition" and 2) religious syncretism (the mutual influence and combining of elements of different religions) in Black Elk's life and words. My method is philosophical; I seek to articulate some underlying meanings and implications of the *inipi* rite and of Black Elk's contribution to present-day understanding of it. Although problems of method concerning Brown's preparation of the text warrant further investigation, I submit that analysis of Black Elk's account of the *inipi* provides evidence confirming the reliability of *The Sacred Pipe*. However, my conclusions about Black Elk's account of the *inipi* are not intended to represent his account of the Sun Dance and other Lakota sacred rites. This essay is only a step toward assessing the reliability of *The Sacred Pipe*, a task that is important owing to both the tendency of readers to accept the text uncritically and an inclination in critical studies of the Black Elk literature to overlook the value of *The Sacred Pipe*.

Inipi ceremonies are conducted according to a general format established by tradition, but each *inipi* is unique, depending on who is leading the sweat, who is taking part, and the ceremony's purpose. As will be discussed, variations in practice are not inconsistent with Lakota traditionalism. One of the limitations of written language is that the fixed nature of words on paper tends to convey a static quality to that which is described. In my analysis of elements of the *inipi* rite, I do not mean to imply that the sequence and ways of performing the steps of the ceremony are more rigid or invariable than they actually are. My sources for understanding the contemporary practice of the *inipi* rite are others' accounts (oral as well as published in the professional literature) and my participation in sweats at a number of homes with Lakota and other Indian and non-Indian people, in and near Albuquerque, New Mexico, in 1988–1990. I give thanks for the people who helped me learn about the *inipi*, and I ask forgiveness for any mistakes I make here.

Translation and Transformation

Diverse Indian views concerning the rendering of spoken teachings into text are represented by Russell Means's rejection of writing for the expression of native oral tradition, and N. Scott Momaday's view that John G. Neihardt succeeded in conveying in *Black Elk Speaks*—by attention to factors such as Black Elk's rhythm and inflection—"the essential spirit of the original narration" (1984, 36–37). In contrast, Means (who should not, however, be taken to represent the views of all Lakota people on this topic) has said: "[Writing] itself epitomizes the European concept of 'legitimate' thinking; what is written has an importance that is denied the spoken. My culture, the Lakota, has an oral tradition, so I ordinarily reject writing. It is one of the white world's ways of destroying the cultures of non-European people, the imposing of an abstraction over the spoken relationship of a people" (Means 1980, 25). Spoken words expressed in text are inevitably altered by the nature of written language, which lacks the fuller information and nuance conveyed by the speaker's voice and body language, the physical setting in which the words are spoken and heard, the purpose of the words in that context, and the vehicle of the life-breath. Texts are also altered by the perspectives of translators and editors. *The Sacred Pipe* was intended by Black Elk and Brown, according to Black Elk's foreword and Brown's preface, to convey in written English Black Elk's spoken Lakota description and explanation of the seven sacred rites. An interpretive issue is Ben Black Elk's influence on the translation, for it was he who rendered in spoken English his father's Lakota words. Our understanding of *The Sacred Pipe* would benefit from knowing more about the religious life and knowledge of Ben Black Elk, whose mind encompassed both the Lakota and the Christian religious paths, as well as the linguistic and conceptual domains of the English and Lakota languages. Brown makes several interpretive observations from the standpoint of comparative religion, such as explicating the meaning of *Wakan Tanka* in terms of the Christian Godhead and the Hindu concept of *Nirguna Brahman,* the Absolute without qualities (J. Brown 1974, 5 n. 6). Brown's interpretive comments are offered in footnotes and are not incorporated into the text, yet it is possible that his grounding in world religions might have had a universalizing influence on his presentation of Black Elk's description of the sacred rites.

Black Elk himself possessed an expansive vision of humanity and spirituality, informed by his living through nearly a century of major historical changes for the Lakota with the increasing influence of Anglo-Americans and Christianity, and owing to his travel as a young man with Buffalo Bill's Wild West Show to England, where he sought to understand white culture and Christianity. Not least, Black Elk's global vision was informed by his study, practice, and teaching of Catholicism. Raymond A. Bucko writes: "Black Elk himself lived in a period of great changes for the Lakota. He was well-traveled and acted as a Catholic catechist beginning in his mid-thirties. It should thus not be surprising for this individual to incorporate universal elements in his world view for he was immersed both in tradition and innovation, having experiential access to both" (Bucko 1992, 72). Black Elk has been derided by some for exposing the Lakota sacred rites outside their own tradition, thus making the rites, and the knowledge in which they are grounded, subject to misinterpretation and exploitation. Underlying the problem of texts' transformation of meaning is the question of whether traditional religious knowledge should be rendered in print at all. Arguments against production of textual versions of indigenous teachings offer a vital perspective. Yet, these arguments must acknowledge the fact that such texts are a way to help preserve the knowledge and practice of traditional teachings and, further, that it is not uncommon for contemporary Indian people to receive help from books by native knowledge-keepers (*Black Elk Speaks* and *The Sacred Pipe* major among them) in reconnecting with their heritage and revitalizing their traditional religiousness.

The broader issue of proper and improper means of perpetuating traditional knowledge is beyond the scope of this essay. Here, I proceed from this basic standpoint: Although not all traditional knowledge can or should be public domain, textual accounts of some aspects of traditional knowledge can be appropriate and useful, and addressing the limitations of such texts is more fruitful than rejecting the texts entirely. Recognition of problems of misinterpretation and misappropriation of traditional knowledge demands caution and respect in the production and interpretation of written accounts. A fundamental issue is respecting a person's intent in sharing that knowledge. In working with Brown to produce *The Sacred Pipe,* Black Elk expressed his wish to help his people by preserving an account of the sacred rites in light of the passing away of the old ways. Besides wanting to help his people in this way, he declared his hope that others' understanding of their tradition would contribute to a greater peace. He says in the foreword: "I have wished to make this book through no other desire than to help my people in understanding the greatness and truth of our own tradition, and also to help in bringing peace upon the earth, not only among men, but within men and between the whole of creation" (J. Brown 1974, xx). Black Elk's intention, and its result, constitutes a major encouragement for the preservation and revitalization of traditional ways. His words in *The Sacred Pipe* reveal much about the depth and complexity of a great religious tradition and, moreover, about the sacredness of creation and the spiritual nature of human beings within that creation.

Contemporary Lakota holy man Frank Fools Crow is quoted by Thomas E. Mails as saying that Black Elk "has earned a place above all of the other Teton holy men. We all hold him the highest" (Mails 1979, 53). Through *Black Elk Speaks* and his detailed and eloquent account of the Lakota rites in *The Sacred Pipe,* Black Elk is respected as a major figure in world religious philosophy. His account of the rites is, however, one man's expression of a profound religious cosmology and path that can be understood only in lived experience. Readers operating under the presumptions of the text-based Anglo-European intellectual tradition and scripture-based Western religious traditions could mistakenly regard the book *The Sacred Pipe* as canon, a complete and correct expression of the teachings of the Lakota sacred rites. Although variation exists in the details of the *inipi* rite as it is understood and practiced, uniformity in contemporary procedures for the rite, and explanations of the significance of those procedures, indicate that Black Elk's account communicates the *inipi*'s essential elements and their meanings in a way that is coherent with Lakota religious philosophy as understood from a comprehensive view incorporating historical and contemporary articulations.

It could be argued that similarities between Black Elk's account and contemporary practice might be a result of the influence of *The Sacred Pipe* on contemporary practice. Granted, many Lakota people have read *The Sacred Pipe* since its publication in 1953, but even without a formal appraisal of Lakota people's views of the book over the past half century, the fact that Lakota religious teachings and rites are conveyed through spoken language and practice nullifies the claim that texts such as *The Sacred Pipe* could have had more than an ancillary influence. Large numbers of Lakota people—from ancient times to the present day—have learned and taught the philosophy and practice of their religious tradition, and this living tradition provides a weighty context from which to judge Black Elk's account of the rites. *The Sacred Pipe* can induce a reader to think that Black Elk's account provides the standard by which practice of the rites should be judged as correctly performed and understood. Reasons for this include 1) a tendency to regard religious texts as canon, 2) the nature of text itself as "fixing" meanings in written language and thus imputing a "fixed" or invariable quality to that which the language describes, and 3) the fact that a text is accessible to persons outside the tradition, but the whole of a lived religious tradition is not.

As regards Christian elements of *The Sacred Pipe,* Black Elk's foreword expresses his belief in the validity of both Lakota religion and Christianity. Besides wanting to help his people keep their tradition alive and strong, he offers the book so that greater understanding and peace will come to those non-Indian people "who can understand. . . . Then they will realize that we Indians know the One true God, and that we pray to him continually" (J. Brown 1974, xx). Black Elk's words on the similarity of Christianity and Lakota religion in the foreword to *The Sacred Pipe* alert the reader to question whether his account of the sacred rites is Christianized, and if so, to what extent. Many factors bear upon the meaning of Christianity in Black Elk's own spiritual life and in his role as a public figure. Comparison of Black Elk's account of the rite of *inipi* with earlier historical accounts, with contemporary practice, and with meanings expressed in ceremonial songs sung in the *inipi* indicate that though some of Black Elk's explanations of the symbolism within the rite might have a Christian slant, his presentation of the elements of the rite is traditional, as is his dominant interpretation of their meaning. The meaning of "traditional" however, is not limited to historical precedent. The Lakota religious tendency toward flexibility and adaptation gives the concept of "traditional" a meaning including, but not limited to, historical precedent. Characteristic of Lakota religious culture is transformation and innovation. The teachings bequeathed by the ancestors provide a system of symbols and meanings, and the coherence of that system is perpetuated from generation to generation, yet, within that framework, variations occur in practice and interpretation owing to both cultural changes, and the spiritual inclinations of individual practitioners. Contemporary examples of the *inipi*'s changing over time are the prayers offered in the ceremony for modern ailments such as unemployment and alcoholism. A variation contingent on individual inclination and local custom is the orientation of the sweat lodge door to a particular cardinal direction. Christian prayers and meanings are now among the possible elements of a sweat ceremony. The introduction of Christianity to native North America—embraced by some, deplored by others, and about which many were ambivalent—is a major factor in the changes throughout history of native religious practice.

Black Elk was a *wicasa wakan*, a holy man, and *pejuta wicasa*, a medicine man or healer, as well as a Catholic and a teacher of Catholicism. This factor is one of many that are important for understanding his life and the teachings he conveyed. Black Elk was not only a religious practitioner, but also a theologian: one who expresses and analyzes underlying meanings and implications of religious concepts and processes. He understood, practiced, and articulated a tremendous web of knowledge of Lakota religious philosophy, and his account of the seven sacred rites is a remarkable resource for understanding Lakota metaphysics, religion, and ethics. Black Elk's involvement in traditional religion and Christianity is no contradiction; he was neither an iconic spokesman for a dying ancient tradition, nor a Christian who transcended a "primitive" spirituality. A concept that helps clarify Black Elk's relation to Christianity is that of "conversion." In *The Spiritual Legacy of the American Indian*, Joseph Brown presents an alternate model of "conversion." Against an exclusivist notion of conversion (conversion understood as rejection of the old when embracing a new religious path), Brown points to indigenous American relational ontology and a tendency toward open-mindedness and appreciation of different manifestations of the sacred as conditions supporting a syncretic, inclusivist notion of conversion. "If this process of polysynthesis can be accomplished with neither confusion nor dissonance, it is ultimately due to the ability of American Indian peoples to penetrate and comprehend the central and most profound nature of all experience and reality" (1982d, 27). Holler, too, applies an inclusivist notion of conversion to Black Elk, and in presenting Black Elk as a creative theologian—not merely a transmitter of the ancient tradition, but a dynamic force in intercultural religious evolution—Holler recognizes Black Elk as an example that "this process of change has not been in all cases that of traditional religion being acted on by Christianity, but also of genuine encounter and creative, conscious change" (1984b, 47).

The inclusivist notion of conversion and its application to Black Elk's religiousness does not imply that syncretism involving Native American religions and Christianity ought to occur, nor that it ought not occur. It does occur, and it is important in native people's experience, and as a process in the history of world religious traditions. Some Indian people are religious traditionalists, some are Christian, some are both, and some are neither. What we learn from Black Elk's life and the teachings he relayed is important in itself, and those teachings are among the most valuable resources we have for understanding the interaction of Christianity and indigenous religions. Moreover, the meanings in Black Elk's religious syncretism, and ongoing responses to it from scholars and practitioners of religion—Indian and non-Indian—continue to inform our understanding of human religious nature and of that which is sacred.

Inipi: The Rite of Purification

The rite of purification is called *inipi,* which means to renew the life force or breath: *ni* in Lakota. The lodge for purification is called *oinikaga* [*o* is a prefix meaning "the place where" and *kaga* means "to make"]. The lodge is also called *initi: ti* means a house or lodge.

Nineteenth-century Lakota George Sword explains *inipi*'s relation to *ni:* "*Inipi* cause a man's *ni* to put out of his body all that makes him tired, or all that causes disease, or all that causes him to think wrong . . ." (Walker 1980, 83–84). "He may do this to cure himself when he is sick or he may do it to make himself feel strong. He should always do it when he is about to do some important ceremony so that he will be clean inside before the *wakan* beings. When a Lakota says *ni,* or *ini* or *inipi* or *initi,* he does not think about sweat. He thinks about making his *ni* strong so that it will purify him" (100). Sword said on another occasion that *inipi* may also be done "to refresh one, or as a medicine to cure the sick, or as part of any ceremony" (78). "Anyone may do this for refreshment but if it done right it is a ceremony" (81).

The basic format of the *inipi* ceremony is four rounds or "doors," in each of which the door of the lodge is closed, water is poured on the heated rocks as the leader and participants sing and pray, and concluding with the door being opened. *Inipi* can be a rite in itself, or a preparation for another rite; it helps a person become spiritually prepared and to have an open mind and heart before encountering *wakan* or sacred beings. *The Sixth Grandfather* attests to a range of uses of the sweat lodge. Significantly, *inipi* is used in preparation for the *hanbleceya* or "crying for a vision" and again afterward for the lamenter to tell of his vision and receive guidance regarding it from the holy man who sponsors him (DeMallie 1984a, 82–84). Black Elk tells the story of his own *hanbleceya* at the age of eighteen, including the use of the sweat house as part of the ritual (227–32). He tells also of using the sweat lodge in preparation for the Horse Dance and the Elk Ceremony, ceremonies performed as part of his becoming recognized as a medicine man (215, 243). He describes the use of the sweat lodge as part of mourning, and to purify murderers returning to the tribe after banishment (382, 391–94). Historical and contemporary functions of the sweat lodge are documented in Bucko's comprehensive study of the sweat lodge and its role in the constitution of tradition (1992, 1998).

Contemporary uses of the *inipi* are continuous with the traditional purposes of spiritual purification and preparation, as well as serving to revitalize traditional religion. Specific occasions for the ceremony—historical and contemporary—include: after military conflict, to regain spiritual power, for change of heart or intention, for protecting the elders and the young ones, for material help, for blessings, and, significantly, for healing (Bucko 1992, 87). Concerns and prayers for healing and help change with the times, too; it is standard in sweat lodges today that prayers are made in behalf of the homeless, the ones in prison, and the ones in hospitals and nursing homes. Today, persons in recovery from drug or alcohol abuse often use the *inipi* as part of their healing process. People might pray about their own troubles, but it is remembered to pray for others: for individuals, families, people in need. Prayers are made for both the people one knows and those people one has not met, for all are relations. "Relations" and "persons" refer to both human beings and beings other than human persons. Black Elk's description of the construction of the sweat lodge conveys the relationality of the various peoples: "The willows which make the frame of the sweat lodge are set up in such a way that they mark the four quarters of the universe; thus the whole lodge is the universe in an image, and the two-legged, four-legged, and winged peoples, and all things of the world are contained within it . . ." (J. Brown 1974, 32). *Inipi* is a prayer ritual, and healing is a main focus of *inipi* prayers. People go to *inipi* to purify themselves and to pray—to give thanks and to ask for help for themselves and others. *Inipi* helps people get relief from worries or burdens they might be carrying. People go to *inipi* to help get their minds clear and their bodies healed, not only for the intrinsic value of it,

but also because physical and mental healing is part of spiritual purification, which can be characterized as opening the way for spiritual understanding to be better received and acted upon in life.

Healing of physical and emotional suffering is a main use of the contemporary sweat. Black Elk's account does not list among the rite's purposes healing for specific ailments. However, stamina is sought in his
prayer to *Tunkayatakapaka,* the ancient Rock-people: "O Rocks, you
have neither eyes, nor mouth, nor limbs; you do not move, but by receiving your sacred breath [the steam], our people will be long-winded as they
walk the path of life; your breath is the very breath of life" (J. Brown 1974,
37). Purification in the *inipi* is spiritual, in both its process as a religious
ceremony, and in its result of strengthening the *ni*—the person's soul or
life force—by cleaning away mental and physical obstructions to the flow
of that sacred force. People go to *inipi* to get strength—from the spirits;
from prayer-songs; from the medicines of rock, fire, water, and air; from
the community of people sweating together; and from within, as they lead
themselves in enduring the tremendous heat. They also go to *inipi* to suffer for their people, to make a sacrifice in behalf of an individual or group,
for the thriving of the people. Although suffering for the people is not
strongly emphasized in Black Elk's account of *inipi* in *The Sacred Pipe,* this
major aspect of Lakota religion is invoked in contemporary practice of the
ceremony, and is expressed in this *inipi* song:

> Spirits have pity on us!
> Spirits have pity on us!
> I shall live with my relatives
> so I give you these offerings. (Around Him and White Hat 1983, 16)

Black Elk's communication of the principle of sacrificing and suffering for
the people is expressed in the prayer the leader offers when he first pours
water on the rocks: "O Wakan-Tanka, behold me! I am the people. In offering myself to You, I offer all the people as one, that they may live! We
wish to live again! Help us!" (J. Brown 1974, 38). People also go to *inipi*
for physical refreshment and enjoyment and, significantly, for companionship, both spiritual companionship during the ceremony and social companionship in the gatherings before and after, and in the fellowship that
grows among individuals who regularly gather to pray together.

Those participants seated in the lodge find themselves on common social ground due to physical closeness—balanced by the privacy of darkness—and by the shared experience of prayers and songs, the purifying steam, and withstanding the heat. Sitting close together in the darkness—experiencing the sometimes roaring steam when water is poured on the rocks—it does not matter what troubled past each person might carry, nor does it matter what their accomplishments are. The heat tends to burn away anything in the mind other than that which really matters—within individuals and among them. This process is one of the ways the *inipi* functions as a purification: the mind becomes clearer by releasing unnecessary and burdensome thoughts and thought patterns. Clearing the mind is aided by the experience of getting increasingly hotter and abandoning one concern after another, until one wants something as basic as air and water, and wants them badly. One way of realizing the relatedness of the elements of unified creation is to experience that our need for air and water is because we are constituted of these and other basic and sacred elements. Such purification supports spiritual experience: mental clarity permits spiritual insight into the relational unity of creation, and opens the way for feeling and knowing sacredness.

The first door honors the Spirit of the West, from whence comes water. When water is poured on the rocks, water joins earth containing fire, and air is produced: the breath of the Rock-people issues forth. Sage, cedar, or sweetgrass placed on the rocks makes the steam fragrant. (Another means used for combining the herbs and water is to infuse the water with herbs beforehand.) Black Elk says: "It is now very hot in the lodge, but it is good to feel the purifying qualities of the fire, the air, and the water, and to smell the fragrance of the sacred sage. After these powers have worked well into us, the door of the lodge is thrown open" (J. Brown 1974, 38). The open door provides needed cool air, and the ladle used for pouring water is passed around sunwise so that each may drink. Some pour water on their bodies where they suffer from illness or injury. This act is done with remembrance that water is the first medicine that was given to humankind. Black Elk says, "As we do this we think of the place where the sun goes down, and from which comes the water, and the Power of this direction helps us to pray" (38). In some cases individuals forego water, as they do when the *inipi* is a part of their preparation for *hanbleceya*. In general, people in the *inipi* are offered water to drink between rounds. Providing for the needs of the people is integral to Lakota religious culture. As regards the needs of the people in the sweat, I have heard pipe carriers say with conviction: "We are taught not to deny our people anything." The same goes for permitting someone who is having a hard time to leave the lodge; all that person has to do is to say "*mitakuye oyas'in*" ("all my relations"), and the door will be opened for them. (An ideal in the rite of *inipi*, and in ceremony generally, is to be present from beginning to end, for the sake of showing respect to the other persons there—both the human and the spirit persons—and so that one receives the spiritual, mental, emotional, and physical benefits of completing a cycle of sacred activity.)

Ceremonial songs for the purification rite are integral to the contemporary ritual, and historical accounts confirm their use in earlier centuries, as Bucko has documented (1992, 40). In *The Sacred Pipe*, Black Elk speaks of singing and the pouring of water: "Water is now put on the rocks, four times for the Powers of the four directions, and as the steam rises we sing a song, or even just a chant, for this helps us understand the mystery of all things" (J. Brown 1974, 40). What Black Elk means by a "chant" is a song without words, composed of vocables. (A vocable, which may occur in secular as well as sacred song, is a word that has a particular sound but no referent, such as in some Hindu mantras. In various world religions, vocables are used in both silent meditation and prayer, and in chant or prayer-songs.) Lakota ceremonial songs (whether personal songs or songs for the people as a whole), unlike social songs, are considered to be given by spirit powers, independent of the singer's creative influence. Vocables in Lakota ceremonial songs have been described as "sacred syllables which go beyond the mind, beyond language and say the inexpressible." "Therefore, although the philosopher, the musicologist and the anthropologist may have little or nothing to say of these wordless melodies, it should be recognized that these are our highest and most treasured hymns because they go above the intellect and kindle the heart directly" (Around Him and White Hat 1983, 6–7). Black Elk's comment about the power of chant to help us "understand the mystery of all things" conveys the importance of sacred song in the *inipi* rite. George W. Linden's remarks about the aural orientation of Lakota oral tradition, and Black Elk as a member of that tradition, are also descriptive of the sweat lodge, where only darkness is seen, yet it is filled with sound: the sizzle of cedar on the rocks, steam blasting from the contact of water and fire-infused rocks, and the sound of spoken

and chanted prayers, loud singing and drumming, and crying and shout-
ing. "Sound engulfs, surrounds and envelopes us. It unifies and unites according to interior relationships. . . . Images may reflect or refract; sound
resonates. Sound reciprocates. Sound centers. Sound engenders simultaneity, not sequentiality" (Linden 1977a, 20). Sound is important in the
inipi rite not only in being heard, and its vibrations felt, while vigorous
singing and drumming take place in a setting where acoustics are enhanced by the small well-sealed structure, but also in respect of the experience of its production. Black Elk explains the sacredness of the drum: "It
is because the round form of the drum represents the whole universe, and
its steady strong beat is the pulse, the heart, throbbing at the center of the
universe. It is the voice of *Wakan-Tanka,* and this sound stirs us and helps
us to understand the mystery and power of all things" (J. Brown 1974,
69). Along with its symbolism, the experience of drumming and hearing
and feeling the drumbeats experientially enables one to sense the relation
of unity of self and the other beings who make up creation. The rhythm of
the drum—the heartbeat of Mother Earth echoed in the human heartbeat
and in the rhythms of nature—has an entraining effect on the individual
consciousness, potentiating a heightened experience of sacrality, and a
unifying effect on a group, potentiating the experience of relationality.
Similarly, in singing, relationality and the sacred can be experienced in
hearing and feeling the sound current of a song given by Powers beyond
the human—sound that issues from deep within oneself, yet that becomes
indistinguishable among other voices in a palpably enveloping sphere of
sound. The utter darkness of the lodge augments this aural phenomenon.
The leader pours water for each person as he or she prays. Commonly, the
prayer-round proceeds sunwise around the circle, with each person addressing *Tunkasila,* or "Grandfather"—Spirit addressed as an elder relative. Each individual prays in Lakota or her or his native language. The
prayers might be silent, but customarily they are spoken or chanted aloud.
Similar to the way the lodge's darkness affords privacy in a setting that is
physically familiar, at times singing is used to create an auditory cloak, so
that when a person is praying, their words or crying is shielded from everyone's hearing. While affording privacy, the singers' voices are at the same
time an intimate force, demonstrating empathy and encouragement for
the person praying. Prayers and the words shared in the ceremony are considered confidential: they are not to be discussed later. Although prayers

are commonly addressed to *Tunkasila,* participants who follow various forms of Christianity might invoke Jesus Christ, God the Father, or the Holy Spirit. Prayers in Native American Church sweats in the Cross Fire tradition invoke Jesus or Holy Spirit, though this is not the case in Native American Church ceremonies of the Half Moon tradition. Depending on how the leader is running the sweat, participants might pray in turn during each round, or only during designated rounds, or spontaneously as they are moved to do so. Each prayer is concluded by the invocation *mitakuye oyas'in,* "all my relations," which embodies a cosmological, religious, and ethical recognition and reverence for the interdependence and sacredness of all beings in creation. Saying *mitakuye oyas'in* also serves to signal that one is done praying so that the next person may begin.

According to Black Elk, the third round is for the Winged-one of the East, where the sun rises, and from whence comes the light of wisdom. This round feels extra hot, because the heat has built up in both the lodge and in the people's bodies. It is an important round for prayers, and is sometimes called the healing round. Douglas Cardinal says:

> Your whole body is screaming and yelling and you want to get out but you just reach out and pray and sing spiritual songs. There is no way out because of your commitment. The person that runs the lodge brings it as hot as you can stand it and then past that point. You have a choice of burning or praying. When you reach beyond yourself, all of a sudden you have some tremendous strength and your body suddenly becomes one with the earth, air, fire and water. You don't feel pain—you're sort of above it. You're pushed to a point where you sense you are a spiritual being, you see the life force in yourself and other people. (McPherson and Rabb 1993, 68)

The heat has pleasant as well as painful effects. As Black Elk said, "it is good to feel the purifying qualities of the fire, the air, and the water, and to smell the fragrance of the sacred sage" (J. Brown 1974, 38). Sweats are not always extremely hot. Some rounds are briefer or cooler; some leaders' sweats are known to be more mild, and again, at each particular *inipi* ceremony, the Rock-Spirits are understood to afford a degree of heat appropriate to the needs of the people.

When the door is opened for the fourth and final time as everyone cries *mitakuye oyas'in,* people are eager to get out of the lodge into the cool air. Some shout *hokahey!* because they feel good and are glad for the people. Black Elk says of the conclusion of the rite: "This most sacred rite has now been finished, and those who have participated are as men born again, and have done much good not only for themselves, but for the whole nation" (J. Brown 1974, 43). Being reborn from the *inipi* is mentioned in Black Elk's account and in contemporary sweats. Today the lodge is spoken of as the womb of Mother Earth, though Black Elk does not use the term *womb*. Part of the meaning of being reborn is emerging from the lodge with a newly clear mind, then continuing to think about the things one learned in there. Black Elk tells of the *inipi*'s leader saying: "The helper will soon open the door for the last time, and when it is open we shall see the Light. For it is the wish of *Wakan-Tanka* that the Light enters into the darkness, that we may see not only with our two eyes, but with the one eye which is of the heart *[Chante Ishta]*, and with which we see and know all that is true and good. We give thanks to the helper; may his generations be blessed! It is good! It is finished! *Hetchetu alo!*" (J. Brown 1974, 42). With the ceremony concluded, the pipe carrier(s) separates stem from bowl and puts the *chanunpa(s)* (pipes) away. In the meal that follows, the mood is informal but reverent, for all are to show respect at the *inipi* from the moment they first step in front of that Grandfather fire.

Inipi, Tradition, and Text

Misunderstanding and conflict frequently result from equivocations on the term *traditional* as well as from genuine disagreements concerning the meaning of the term. It is important to balance a view of "tradition" conceived as historical precedent, with recognition of the Lakota inclinations of adaptation in response to changing cultural circumstances, and each individual's right to individualized expressions of spirituality. Bucko's work on the *inipi*'s role in the constitution of tradition investigates meanings of the word *tradition, wicoh'an,* in Lakota. One meaning implies "the handing on of a body of material from the past." Another connotes "actions in the present that represent generalized behavior." "Finally, the word 'traditional' is simply used to indicate proper, correct and accurate, implying one or both of the first two criteria. . . . Tradition is, in all cases, synonymous with appropriate and valid" (Bucko 1992, 147). In evaluating the status of *The Sacred Pipe* as a source of traditional knowledge, a major factor is that the Lakota tradition is not text based; it is an oral tradition and a lived tradition. In earlier times, Lakota people did not use texts, for religion or otherwise, but after the introduction of reading and writing they quickly adapted to using them. Black Elk's use of the medium of print to pass on teachings concerning the sacred rites is an instance of cultural adaptation. And despite the danger of text to decontextualize meanings, books are nowadays part of life for Indian and non-Indian people. The oral-culture orientation is, however, strong enough that, as Holler says, "No Lakota would risk ridicule by admitting that he had obtained his sacred knowledge from a book" (Holler 1995, 184). Textual transmission of knowledge is not "traditional" in the sense of conforming with the historical and continuing Lakota practice of conveying teachings through oral language and ritual. However, many Lakota people have read *The Sacred Pipe* since its publication in 1953, and Black Elk's account is, to an extent thus far undetermined, a factor in twentieth-century practice and understanding of the rites.

Incorporation of Christian elements in an *inipi* is not traditional in the sense of according with historical precedent. However, Christian elements have become part of common practice in a subset of the sweat lodges that are carried on today. This complex issue can be illuminated by Black Elk's words and example of religious syncretism, which is not to say that his approach should set any parameters. *The Sacred Pipe* suggests that in Black Elk's expansive religious understanding, the pipe and Christ are both mediators, and that the *chanunpa*'s power as a mediator is not superseded by Christ's, for the Creator who hears the prayers is one and the same. In speaking of the designation "peace pipe," Black Elk laments the lack of peace in the world, and states his hope that some peace may come through his book's showing "that we Indians know the One true God, and that we pray to him continually" (J. Brown 1974, xx). Black Elk was both a transmitter of tradition and an interpreter. Consideration of his Christianity is integral to interpreting his account of the sacred rites. Black Elk states his belief in the equal validity of Christianity and Lakota religion in the foreword to *The Sacred Pipe*, but his account of the rite of *inipi* is not strongly Christianized. Major elements of his account that are consonant with Christianity are his emphasis on acting in accord with the will of *Wakan Tanka* (though he also instructs that prayers be offered to the Powers of the four directions, to Grandmother Earth, the Rock-Spirits and others), and the fact that he casts the Lakota sacred rites as seven, which parallels Catholicism's seven sacraments.

When White Buffalo Cow Woman brought the pipe to the people, she explained its use as a mediator between the people and the Great Spirit. In Black Elk's account of the gift of the sacred pipe, she says: "From this time on, the holy Pipe will stand upon this red Earth and the two-leggeds will take the Pipe and will send their voices to *Wakan-Tanka*" (J. Brown 1974, 7). Black Elk's account of Lakota sacred rites does not instruct that *inipi*, and the pipe ritual that accompanies it and the other rites, are for the fulfillment of a Christian aim. He expresses in the foreword his belief in the validity of both traditions. With that said, he conveys his understanding of the procedures and meanings of the rites, so that people of all nations may appreciate the Lakota tradition, and to help his own people continue to perpetuate and benefit from their own tradition.

The preceding analysis of contemporary practice of the rite of *inipi* in comparison with Black Elk's account provides one species of evidence of the reliability of Black Elk's account of the rite in *The Sacred Pipe*. I have discussed "tradition" in relation to that text and in relation to religious syncretism. In closing, I will submit another form of evidence of the value of *The Sacred Pipe* by approaching it not as a text itself, but as a repository of prayers and ceremonial prayer-songs. This analysis entails understanding ceremonial songs as a nonwritten form of text. The term *text* can be applied not only to written documents but also to oral language in fixed forms, including ceremonial songs and chant. Dennis Tedlock explains this concept in his discussion of the ceremonially chanted Zuni text *chimiky'ana'kowa*, "that which was the beginning." "To *fix a text* without making *visible marks* is to bring *stress* and *pitch* and *pause* into a fixed relationship with *words*. The Zunis call this *ana k'eyato'u*, 'raising it up right up,' and we would call it chant" (1980, 129–30). The principles governing Zuni and Lakota chant are not identical, but Tedlock's idea of ceremonial song as text is applicable to Lakota ceremonial song. Among the contributions of Black Elk's book *The Sacred Pipe*—which was his final written statement—is his communication of many prayers and prayer-songs. Although the words and musical form of sweat lodge songs can be expressed differently by different individuals, there are standard themes in the meanings and musical forms of the songs, similar to the way standard patterns exist in practice of the *inipi* ceremony. No musical notation accompanies the song texts in *The Sacred Pipe*, but Black Elk's words for Lakota ceremonial songs convey a great deal about the religious and philosophical meaning of the Lakota sacred rites.

The songs for *inipi* and other Lakota sacred rites make it possible for the ceremonies to be conducted. The songs perpetuate the life breath of the people: as long as the songs are sung, the ceremonies can continue, and as long as the ceremonies continue, the people will live. The songs carry the life breath of the ancestors, linking present and future generations with the old ones and the ancient teachings. The life breath that carries the songs today keeps alive the strength and wisdom of the ancestors, and makes that strength and wisdom available to the people.

Many people receive help from the *inipi*. People learn in the *inipi* about traditional Lakota teachings, and through their personal experience in the ceremony they may receive teachings about leading their own lives. People can learn how to pray in the *inipi*, through the example and encouragement of others, and through the inspiration each can receive there. People learn many things about being human in the *inipi*, for it is a place to experience both one's strength and one's weakness. People go to the *inipi* to strengthen themselves, and the pipe carriers and other strong ones show their strength so that those participants who need strength can look to them and receive that strength. It is important to be strong, for oneself and for the people, but we are only human. The Lakota way of praying entails humility; in prayers and prayer-songs people admit how weak and pitiful they are, so that the spirits will help them. Going through the sweat can be hard, and in making it through, people face their own weakness. In receiving help from the other persons there—the human and other persons—one recognizes that alone we are not much, all are relatives. Thriving spiritually and on a daily basis requires dealing with fear and hardship. The *inipi* helps people become strong in their minds through their handling difficulties and recognizing blessings. This process recalls Black Elk's speaking of how the sacred water used in *inipi* represents the Thunder Beings who come with fearful noise, but who bring the life-giving rain (J. Brown 1974, 31).

Black Elk expressed an immense vision in making the book *The Sacred*

Pipe with the hope of helping his people perpetuate their tradition, and of helping bring peace among and within human beings, and "between the whole of creation" (J. Brown 1974, xx). His account of the *inipi* communicates the Lakota relational metaphysic that all are related, and its ethical implication of mutual dependence for the well-being of each and all. In the *inipi*, and in Black Elk's account of it, is expression of the relatedness of human beings with one another, with the elements of creation, with the Spirit-peoples, and the relation of all with the Great Mystery.

11

Black Elk and the Spiritual Significance of *Paha Sapa* (the Black Hills)

ALEXANDRA WITKIN–NEW HOLY

> The spiritual regaining of the Black Hills must occur before material restoration. It isn't participating in our ceremonies and life ways but the symbolism and what's involved. If restoration is not successful in our lifetime, our children are prepared to continue the battle.
> —Charlotte Black Elk (Doll 1994, 24)

From the perspective of Lakota theology, the publication and distribution of Black Elk's teachings filtered through dominant society's (that is, Neihardt's) ideology is a secondary concern. Although this secondary concern fuels much academic writing on the teachings of Black Elk, from the Lakota perspective what is more significant is the issue of Black Elk's full re-creation of his vision on earth. The essential element of Black Elk's vision—going to the center of the earth—was "prohibited" by the "white man" because "he" had stolen the Black Hills from the Lakota (see Lazarus 1991 and Gonzalez and Cook-Lynn 1999). Black Elk was unable to return to the center of the earth for many years because of this theft. Through his work and contact with John G. Neihardt, Black Elk was finally able to complete his vision on earth, returning to the center of the earth—Harney Peak in the Black Hills.

The relationship between the Lakota and *Paha Sapa* is inseparable from being Lakota, in part because *Paha Sapa* and the Lakota emerged together near the beginning of creation.[1] In Lakota cosmology, the Black

---

1. Today the Lakota live on the Pine Ridge, Rosebud, Cheyenne River, Standing Rock, Crow Creek, Flandreau, and Lower Brulé Reservations in South and North Dakota as well

Hills, or *Paha Sapa*, were the first place created on the surface of the earth. They are an isolated mountain range located in southwest South Dakota and northeast Wyoming. The Lakota emerged onto the surface of the earth from *Paha Sapa*, and they returned to them during the transformative earth-altering cleansings.[2] *Paha Sapa* formed the nucleus of prereservation resistance to Euro-American imperialism and continued to define the core of traditionalist thought as it evolved in contradistinction to progressive thought during the early reservation period. *Paha Sapa* also lie at the foundation of modern nationalistic revitalization and resistance.[3] Today *Paha Sapa* are an almost universal component in Lakota identity, serving as the common factor among disparate political, social, geographic, economic, and religious positions occupied by contemporary Lakota.[4]

––––––––––

as the Fort Peck reservation in Montana. The Lakota, along with the Nakota and Dakota, are commonly called "Sioux." These three distinct dialect groups, from west to east, are the Great Sioux Nation, or *Oceti Sakowin* (the Seven Council Fireplaces). The Lakota, the largest group of the three, are composed of seven bands: *Oglala, Sincangu* (Brulé), *Hunkpapa, Minikowojou, Itazipco* (Sans Arc), *Oohenunpa* (Two Kettle), and *Sihasapa* (Blackfoot) (C. Black Elk 1986, 191–95; W. Powers 1975, 3–14; McGee 1987, 158).

2. Personal interview with Leland Little Dog, 1994.

3. For a discussion of *Paha Sapa*'s role in Lakota political identity see Witkin–New Holy 1998.

4. This article traces metaphorical and historical aspects of the relationship between the Lakota people and *Paha Sapa*. I theorize that Lakota identity and culture have been, and are, deeply contoured by this human-land relationship. Like all politico-cultural identities, Lakota identity is contested. Among Sioux, Lakota, and Indians in general, who is and is not Lakota eludes any fixed definitions. Certain criteria are applied by tribal governments, other criteria by treaty councils, and yet other criteria are used by differing Lakota and non-Lakota communities. Moreover, there are varying degrees and types of Lakota-ness that have very little to do with band, family, or society affiliation, but are structured around a complex of ascribed and self-identified factors such as blood quantum and political affiliation. In general, other than the IRA tribal government's criteria for deciding tribal enrollment, there are few authoritative guidelines for determining who is or is not Lakota. I do not attempt to alleviate the contestation over definitions of Lakota with the theory of identity I propose in this article. Nor is it the purpose of my research to further a hegemonic concept of Lakota identity, such that one must think or espouse certain precepts in order to be Lakota. Rather, I have traced one crucial and persistent factor in Lakota identity—a deep and indivisible connection to the Black Hills. The expression of this relationship has changed through time, but as long as the relationship is defined indigenously it inscribes those Lakota who embrace it as different from other Indians and non-Indians, in a uniquely

One of the most significant metaphors in Black Elk's teachings is the blooming tree or stick. The Grandfathers (in particular the Grandfather from the south) gave the stick to Black Elk to "make a nation" (DeMallie 1984a, 118). Significantly, this gift was presented in the Black Hills and is deeply connected to them. His only stated goal in recounting his life story and visions to John G. Neihardt was to make the stick bloom, to consolidate the nation, as shown to him in his great vision. Ultimately, the stick is both the people and for the people. They are to rely on it (in conjunction with the pipe) for peace and health (122). The flowering stick is the existence of the people as a nation—the hoop. In the Great Vision, "they put the sacred stick into the center of the hoop and you could hear birds singing all kinds of songs by this flowering stick and the people and animals all rejoiced and hollered. The women were sending up their tremolos. The men said: 'Behold it; from there we shall multiply, for it is the greatest of the greatest sticks.' This stick will take care of the people and at the same time it will multiply" (129). Black Elk understands his role in life to be that of a nurturer of the flowering stick—to use his considerable power for the people, to bring about a nation in prosperity and happiness. Power in Lakota life is not separated into mundane and sacred realms— the political and the spiritual. The spiritual and the political coexist. Hence, the Grandfathers bestowed to Black Elk the power to make a nation.

But, Black Elk consistently faced an unfinished task. After his Great Vision, and for the rest of his life, he confronted a stick that did not bloom—a nation in despair and poverty. From the time that Black Elk first began to use his power, he was aware that the tree was not blooming as he had experienced in his vision. At age eighteen, Black Elk performed his

---

Lakota way. This is not to say that Lakota who do not embrace the relationship, as it is defined at any given moment, are NOT Lakota, only that the relationship remains one consistent marker of Lakota-ness.

Other Indian nations also assert claims to the Black Hills on the basis of their history and culture. Although those claims are outside the scope of this discussion, this essay should not be understood to imply that other tribal claims and relationships to *Paha Sapa* are any less valid then Lakota claims to the Black Hills. In fact, Linea Sundstrom (1996) has theorized that Lakota notions of sacred geography in the Black Hills are related to other Native American Indian nations' oral narratives of the Black Hills, most notably the Cheyenne, Kiowa, and Suhtai traditions.

first public demonstration of his medicine—a necessary component to re-
alizing his power and an event demanded by it. It was during this Horse
Dance that Black Elk caught his first glimpse of the nonflowering stick
(DeMallie 1984a, 223).

He attributes the failure of the stick to bloom, and hence the failure of
the people to prosper, to two sources. The first source is the arrival of the
white people. "This tree never had a chance to bloom because the white
men came. The trunk is the chief of the people. If this tree had seen a
bloom probably I or some of my descendants would be great chiefs" (De-
Mallie 1984a, 130). The second source is Black Elk's own failure to re-
create his vision entirely on earth. In a conversation with Neihardt, Black
Elk said: "The work you were assigned was man thinker. For my part, I am
sorry; I should have done my deed, and because I did not do it I have been
punished. *I should have gone through my vision and performed everything on
earth and then I would have prospered.* At the same time, the tree that was
to bloom just faded away; but the roots will stay alive, and we are here to
make the tree bloom" (emphasis added; 43). Black Elk, prior to his interviews with Neihardt, had failed to perform on earth an essential element of
his vision—the journey to the center of the earth. This journey to the center of the earth, to the Black Hills, was the climax of the Neihardt–Black
Elk encounter and, as I demonstrate, was equally as significant as the interviews themselves and their publication.

Black Elk's teachings, like all Lakota teachings, employ a system of
meaning rich in metaphor and symbol. The Lakota understanding and use
of metaphor and symbol differ from that of the West. Within Lakota culture symbols are widespread—medicine wheels, eagle feathers, and
pipes—and each embodies important cultural values. Language is an important transmitter of symbolic meaning, but it is not the only one. In
general, symbolism is a nonsemiological cognitive system (Sperber 1974,
87). It is also highly visionary, affected by both "the external experience of
daily life and the internal one of dream and reverie" (89). Moreover, "the
Lakota world was especially receptive to vision in symbolic forms because
its thinking was, as a rule, more metaphorical than that of our society"
(Rice 1991, 152). Lakota culture is very much characterized by its relationship with visions and dreams consciously sought, systems constructed
by, and of, symbols.

Symbols, however, do not just "stand for" something. They transcend the notion of representation. For example, an eagle feather not only represents the eagle, but also embodies the entire power of the eagle—the power to communicate prayers to *Wakan Tanka*. Symbols are "spiritual truth embodied, or manifested" (Versluis 1992, 46). According to Clifford Geertz, a cultural anthropologist, symbols do not simply represent preferred values; rather, they *encase* values (1957, 131). "Religious symbols, dramatized in rituals, or related in myths, are felt somehow to sum up, for those for whom they are resonant, what is known about the way the world is, the quality of the emotional life it supports, and the way one ought to behave while in it" (127). Symbols, in other words, both reflect and create the world as it is understood. Jahner notes that the Lakota worldview facilitates presence to oneself, to nature, and to the community (1989, 194). Lakota religious symbols ensure that mode of presence.

Similar values are also present within lived metaphors. Several Lakota scholars have commented on the pervasiveness of metaphor within the culture. Lakota artist and teacher Arthur Amiotte states that metaphor delineates and anthropomorphizes the sacred world, rendering it understandable. The various dimensions of *Wakan Tanka,* for example, are made comprehensible and visible through metaphor (1989, 163).[5] Charlotte Black Elk, great-granddaughter of Nicholas Black Elk, affirms that the metaphorical nature of the Lakota origin story is indicative of Lakota thought in general: "the whole is present in all of its parts and each part represents the whole" (1986, 204).[6] Julian Rice, a non-Lakota specialist in Lakota oral narrative, also recognizes that Lakota cosmology and theology are highly metaphorical (Rice 1991, xii).

By dictionary definition, metaphor is a figure of speech. Language can be particularly embedded with cultural meaning. George Lakoff and Mark

---

5. Missionaries glossed *Wakan Tanka* to mean God in order to correlate Lakota and Christian beliefs to encourage assimilation and conversion. Their gloss simplifies and misrepresents the nature of Lakota belief. Early informants and contemporary commentators usually include in their definition of *Wakan Tanka* the notion of "incomprehensibility." *Wakan Tanka* is both the sum and the parts of all that is unexplainable and mysterious. *Wakan Tanka* creates life, but *Wakan Tanka* is both many and one. See Densmore 1992 (85 n. 2, 120 n. 1); Walker 1980 (68–73); W. Powers 1975 (45–47); and DeMallie and Parks 1987 (28).

6. Charlotte Black's father, Henry Black Elk, is the only son of Ben Black Elk, whose father was Nicholas Black Elk (Doll 1994, 29).

Johnson, pioneers in experientialist linguistics, write of the connections between language and culture: "Since communication is based on the same conceptual system that we use in thinking and acting, language is an important source of evidence for what that system is like" (1980, 3). According to Lakoff and Johnson, all conceptual systems are metaphorical in nature, and the essence of metaphor is "understanding and experiencing one kind of thing in terms of another" (5).

Although metaphor is defined classically as a figure of speech, a Lakota experience of metaphorical meaning calls upon intersubjective cultural meanings and can transcend the realm of speech. Thus, metaphor can be defined as "the synthesis of several units of observation into one commanding image; it is an expression of a complex idea, not by analysis, or by abstract statement, but by a sudden perception of an objective relation" (Read 1952, 23). Both symbol and metaphor, as the Lakota use and understand them, are critical to the Lakota worldview.

One of the most pivotal metaphors in the Lakota worldview is that of kinship. Kinship is the fundamental ordering mechanism of Lakota life. Ella Deloria defines this value: "The ultimate aim of Dakota life, stripped of accessories, was quite simple: One must obey kinship rules, one must be a good relative. No Dakota who has participated in that life will dispute that. In the last analysis every other consideration was secondary—property, personal ambition, glory, good times, life itself. Without that aim and the constant struggle to attain it, the people would no longer be Dakotas in truth. They would no longer even be human" (1944, 16). The primary metaphor in Lakota culture, kinship, is symbolized by *cangleska,* itself a metaphor for several other significant and interrelated values. Temporal and geographic order on the surface world also follows a circular pattern. In these circles, movement occurs from the center (kinship) outward.

Cangleska

The human mind discerns geometric designs, principles of spatial organization, in the environment (Tuan 1977, 34). Place has a geometric quality. For the Lakota, *cangleska* (the circle or hoop) is the predominant geometric design that organizes space. Moreover, it is a central metaphor in the Lakota conceptual system. First and foremost, *cangleska* represents the unity and kinship of all *wakan* (sacred) beings. The overarching theme of Lakota theology is the oneness of the universe (DeMallie and Parks 1987, 27).[7]

The circle is one of the earliest and most prevalent expressions of this oneness. *Cangleska* metaphorically describes the Lakota experience of many things, including the unity of all beings, the universe, and spaces.

The metaphor of the circle appears throughout the teachings of Nicholas Black Elk. His teachings are instrumental in showing the continuity of meaning within Lakota teachings for the symbolic and metaphorical meaning of the circle during a critical phase of Lakota history: the aftermath of the massive cultural disruptions following the genocide of the buffalo by Euro-American sport hunters; the theft of the Black Hills; and the forced confinement of the Lakota to the much diminished land base of a reservation.

In the Great Vision, horse riders from the Four Directions give him a *cangleska*. He interprets this action to mean that the Lakota are to "make a nation and under that we were to prosper" (DeMallie 1984a, 123). He says: "The circle represented the old people that represented the nation. The center of it represented the prosperity of the nation. I was to raise a nation either in prosperity or in difficulty. In presenting the sacred hoop to me [each is a nation], the spirit from the west said: 'Behold this sacred hoop; it is the people you shall have' (meaning that I would own these people)" (123).[8] The circle in this part of the vision is understood by Black Elk to be the *Cangleska Oyate* (the Hoop of the Nation). The *Cangleska Oyate* renews itself through another circle—the *Cangleska Wiwanyang Wacipi* (the Sun Dance circle). "Burning sweet grass in the hands of devout holy men, fervent prayers, copious tears, the shining Sacred Tree, and brightly colored flags for the four directions transform the [Sun Dance] arena into the Mystery Hoop or Circle. The terms are interchangeable, and they are synonymous with the Hoop of the Nation" (Mails 1978, 97). Black Elk interprets the central ceremony of the Lakota, the Sun Dance, in his teachings published in *The Sacred Pipe* to fit the new circumstances of reservation-imposed life (Holler 1995, 187). This interpretation arises

7. However, the universe is not understood as simple or knowable; in fact, the incomprehensibility of the universe is fully accepted (DeMallie and Parks 1987, 28).

8. "Owning the people" is a metaphor that indicates the duties of a chief, who is responsible for the welfare of his people.

from his role of traditional Lakota *wicasa wakan* to interpret ceremony based on individual visions (Jahner 1989, 201; Holler 1995, xxiii). Through the power of his vision, Black Elk helped to renew the value of one *cangleska*—the *Wiwanyang Wacipi* (the Sun Dance)—to heal another, *Cangleska Oyate* (the Hoop of the Nation), within the context of the reservation.

Another circle, *Ki Inyanka Ocanku* (the Race Track), interlinks with *Cangleska Oyate* and *Paha Sapa*. A red clay valley, visible both from the air and on the ground, surrounds *Paha Sapa*. It was formed during the Great Race. Charlotte Black Elk's interpretive translation of the Great Race teaching places the event after a cleansing of the earth when those children of *Maka* (the earth) who no longer heeded her words were destroyed. The four-leggeds blamed the cleansing on the humans, and decided to destroy all two-leggeds. The winged people knowing that Bear, a two-legged, is the symbol of wisdom, allied with the two-leggeds. The four-leggeds, allied with the growing things, agreed to race against the two-leggeds and the wingeds. If the latter won, they would gain "continued life." If the former won, they would wipe out the two-leggeds. The race consisted of four laps around *Paha Sapa*. The bloodied feet of the racers formed *Ki Inyanka Ocanku*. Magpie won the race for the two-leggeds by flying from the back of Buffalo where she had waited and rested until shortly before the finish line. *Maka* decided that *Ki Inyanka Ocanku*, formed as it was by the bloodied footprints of the racers, should stand as a reminder to the two-leggeds of their responsibilities to the rest of creation (C. Black Elk 1992, 44).

In Nicholas Black Elk's account, when Magpie wins the race for the two-leggeds, who now are entitled to eat the four-leggeds, the *Wakinyan* (Thunder Beings) present humans with the first bow and arrow (DeMallie 1984a, 310). The *Wakinyan* give the bow and arrow to *Wakinyan Luta* (Red Thunder), a starving hunter brought by them to observe the race. The bow and arrow gift regenerates and renews the people, starting with the starving hunter, "the Thunder-being told Red Thunder: 'With this weapon the tribe shall expand and be mighty. So you go back to your people and teach them to make these bows. Hereafter you can shoot the buffalo' " (DeMallie 1984a, 310). According to Black Elk, the *Wakinyan* had another message for Red Thunder to relay to the people: "They further told him that at the place where they had the race was the *heart of the earth.* He said, 'Someday your tribe will be in this land.' It was the promised land. 'This land is a being. Remember in the future you are to look for this land.' I think at the present time we found it and it is the Black Hills" (emphasis added; DeMallie 1984a, 310). *Ki Inyanka Ocanku* demarcates both geographically and metaphorically *Paha Sapa,* "The Heart of Everything That Is." It also reminds the Lakota of their responsibility to the rest of creation. The Lakota Nation—*Cangleska Oyate*—interlinks with the *cangleska* of animal nations. The interlinked hoops of the nations are sustained by their links to other hoops, including *Ki Inyanka Ocanku,* and the *Wiwanyang Wacipi* (the Sun Dance).

Hocoka

Lakota theology recognizes *hocoka* (the center) as profoundly sacred. In terms of a Sacred Hoop, the center is manifest in many metaphorical forms, including the pipe, the Sun Dance Pole, the individual, and *Paha Sapa.* "Hocoka is an old word that refers to the inner part of a camp circle, but as used ritually it means a sacred space, the center of the universe, within which a sacred person or supplicant prays, sings, or otherwise communicates with spirits" (W. Powers 1982, 14). To be at a center point is to reaffirm one's identity as Lakota. In one ceremony, the *yuwipi,* "an ordinary frame house is transformed into the hocoka, the camp circle, and all generations of Indians as well as all constituents of the *Oglala* universe are brought together to solidify what is conceived as Indian" (82). Mircea Eliade's work on shamanism, although riddled with evolutionary hierarchies and dualities, conceptualizes the reasons for the highly sacred nature of the axis mundi, or the central axis. According to Eliade, shamanistic societies conceive the universe "as having three levels—sky, earth, underworld—connected by a central axis" (1964, 259). Because the three planes connect only at a central axis, it is there that they can be successively accessed. However, the Lakota do not conceptualize the universe in terms of "three planes" but as integrated. "Black Elk believed in a spirit world parallel to rather than above this world" (Rice 1991, 24). There is a "star world" and metaphysical realms where spirit beings with differing powers exist. But there is not a geometric division between these realms and the one(s) *ikce oyate* (common people) inhabit. Lakota "sacred beings and powers . . . reside in a place believed to be somewhere between the earth and the sky" (W. Powers 1986, 11). Joseph Epes Brown describes the Lakota universe as one consisting of gradations of reality whereby a fluidity and transparency of perceptions in the phenomenal world disallow absolute lines to be drawn between the worlds of animals, humans, and spirits (1989b, 181). Arthur Amiotte characterizes the Lakota universe as consisting of planes with the surface world as an incomplete and mutable reflection of other sacred planes (1989, 163). Spirit beings can and are accessed through a "central axis," that transverses the various, but undifferentiated, planes of the Lakota universe.

Ikce oyate can use a central axis to send offerings and prayers to the spirit beings. Only *wicasa wakan* (holy men) and *winyan wakan* (holy women) can directly contact other realms. After the first cleansing, the *ikce oyate* lost the privilege of "easy communication" with the spirit beings. From that time, the holy men and women exclusively have retained the ability to intercede on behalf of humans with the spirit beings. *Ikce oyate* can and do have direct contact with spirit beings, but it usually takes place only when a holy person petitions the spirit beings (W. Powers 1986, 4; 1982, 20). Such an occurrence usually happens during ceremony (such as the *inipi* (sweat lodge), *Wiwanyang Wacipi, yuwipi,* and *hanblecheyapi*).

Perhaps the *ikce oyate*'s most significant and widely used axis mundi is the sacred pipe. In the "most powerful story in Lakota religious life" (St. Pierre and Long Soldier 1995, 41), *Ptesan Winyan* (the White Buffalo Woman) brought the first *Cannupa Wakan* (Sacred Pipe) to the Lakota people (J. Brown 1974, 3).[9] With the gift of the *Cannupa Wakan,* the Lakota regained the ability to send their voices to *Wakan Tanka* (5). When she gave it to the people, she told them: "All the people, and all the things of the universe, are joined to you who smoke the pipe—all send their voices to *Wakan-Tanka,* the Great Spirit. When you pray with this pipe, you pray for and with everything" (6). At the same time, *Ptesan Winyan* also told the people to protect *Paha Sapa.* According to Royal Bull Bear, Chairman for Life of the Grey Eagle Society, she told the Lakota to move west past the Missouri River to *Paha Sapa,* guard it, and stay for seven generations (Doll 1994, 50).

For Lakota, understanding the universe and their place within it de-

9. See also Left Heron in Walker 1983 (109–17); Dooling 1984 (135–36); and Finger in Walker 1980 (109–12).

rives from actual experiences with the spirit world, the manifestations of *Wakan Tanka.* "There is a cause and effect between the spiritual world and the physical world that provides the faithful with concrete evidence of the sacred" (St. Pierre and Long Soldier 1995, 55). These experiences generally occur through prayer with a personal *cannupa.*[10] For individual Lakota, the primary access to the spirit beings, absent the intercession of a holy person, is through their individual "centers"—their personal pipe. "That smoke from the peace pipe, it goes straight up to the spirit world. But this is a two-way thing. Power flows down to us through that smoke, through the pipe stem. You feel that power as you hold your pipe; it moves from the pipe right into your body. The pipe is not just a thing, it is alive" (Erdoes and J. Lame Deer 1972, 2).

A loaded pipe is held in the left hand, so as to be closer to the person's heart. Prayer with a pipe is foremost from the heart, and secondarily for-mulaic. Today, the Seventh Direction (the center) is interpreted as a person's *cante* (heart). The phrase *Seventh Direction* "is used in reference to the individual spirit of self, the center" (Evans 1995, 325). This direc-tion is also associated with *wanbli gleshka* (the spotted eagle), the messen-ger between a person offering prayers and the spirits who receive those prayers (W. Powers 1986, 180). People pray to the Seven Directions—West, North, East, South, Sky, Earth, and Center—to understand their own pitifulness, their commonality with all creation.

> The first four represent the four quadrants of the universe wherein resides the spirit essence of all life forms (plant, animal, and human). From these directions come meanings and teaching provided by the spirit essence. The sky/upward direction is that which is omnipresence. Earth direction represents mother—grandmother, the source of birth and life of all. The center is the connection and unity of all directions. Each living entity is a center. Therefore continual balance and harmony within the six directions is necessary. All of these directions in unison rep-resent all that is, the sacred hoop. (Evans 1995, 325)

The *Cannupa Wakan* is the *hocoka* of the sacred hoop—the People—the Lakota *Oyate.* It brings, and is, renewal and regrowth. In Black Elk's

10. For accounts of the "Gift of the Sacred Pipe," see J. Brown 1974 (3–9); St. Pierre and Long Soldier 1995 (39–41); Densmore 1992 (63–68); Walker 1983 (109–12); and La Pointe 1976 (23–26).

account of the Sun Dance, *Kablaya,* the man who receives the vision for the first Sun Dance, tells the people, "the sacred pipe is always at the center of the hoop of our nation, and with it the people have walked and will continue to walk in a holy manner" (J. Brown 1974, 69).[11] Before the government imposed a sedentary life on the Lakota, the *Cannupa Wakan* was always placed in a special lodge in the center of the camp circle. Moreover, when the people moved, they carried the *Cannupa Wakan* bundle on a travois positioned in the center of the procession (J. Smith 1967, 23). Today, the *Cannupa Wakan* is kept for the people in their "ceremonial center," Green Grass (Cheyenne River Reservation), by the descendants of the same family who received it from *Ptesan Winyan* (St. Pierre and Long Soldier 1995, 41). Individual pipes, replicas of *Cannupa Wakan,* bring their keepers and others who smoke such a pipe into contact with Lakota *hocoka*—including their own heart. Black Elk teaches that all Lakota centers are one; each is connected meaningfully to the others. When people pray to and with their center, their heart, through ritual use of a *cannupa* (another center), they also become connected to and with *Paha Sapa*: "The Heart of Everything That Is."

The Sun Dance is another circle connecting *Paha Sapa* with the individual. The Sun Dance is quite simply "the greatest ceremony that the Oglalas do" (Walker 1980, 181). In the past, "its celebration was hardly separate from Lakota camp circle society itself, taking place at the center of a ceremonial encampment of the people—the symbolic center was the literal center as well" (Holler 1995, 187). In contemporary times, "the Sun Dance is so strongly associated with traditional Lakota values, to participate in the Sun Dance is to choose to identify one's self as Lakota in the strongest possible terms" (187). The unique nature of the Sun Dance both past and present and the crucial link between the two is attested to by Thomas Mails, biographer of Fools Crow, and author of the most extensive published account of contemporary Sun Dancing:

> When a gifted people are given no place in the present, they dream of the past, they scheme for the future, and for the moment they dance the dances that have sustained their people for generations. They dance resolutely, persistently, passionately, and for a while at least the partici-

11. *Kablaya* is the literary mouthpiece for Black Elk in the account of the Sun Dance in *The Sacred Pipe* (Holler 1995, 141).

pants rise above the earth and the odds. The outside world is still there.
The sun comes up and glares. The ground turns steadily warmer and
warmer, and the heat rises up from it in shimmering and stifling tentacles
to grasp at those who presume to walk and dance upon it. But at the Sun
Dance ground it is neither resisted nor noticed. The Sioux are free and
proud again in mind and body. The thoughts are good thoughts, and a
desire for harmony reigns. The forbidding and the foreboding melt away
for a time, and that is beautiful—at least to those who care about such
things. (1978, 2)

The physical layout of the *Wiwanyang Wacipi* grounds includes a ceremonial circle varying in size from 50 to 150 feet, encircled by a pine-
bough arbor that provides shade for the friends and relatives of the
dancers. Its center is marked by the *can wakan* (Sun Dance tree). Usually
wagacan (cottonwood), the *can wakan* is ceremonially "captured" and
placed at the center of the *Wiwanyang Wacipi* grounds some days, or a
day, before the dancing begins.[12] Selected and placed with considerable
ceremony and ritual, the *can wakan* is the center of the earth, a powerful
axis mundi, connecting the people to *Wakan Tanka*. The preparations for
the placement of the *can wakan* into the earth are done with great ceremony. As Lakota Sun Dancer Arthur Amiotte writes, "this is where the
axis mundi will be placed, the tree of life, that central connection between
the masculine powers of the zenith and the feminine powers of the nadir;
that means, that principle, that pipe, that body, that avenue through which
the sacredness of the world will be connected, and to which man in awe-
some sacrifice will be connected so that he, too, may participate in the
bringing down and bringing up and the sharing of that sacred power of

12. The Sun Dance, as the central ceremony of the Lakota, reflects the core values of
the culture. In prereservation times the Sun Dance "enshrined" war and the buffalo hunt
(Holler 1995, 180). As part of this reflection, the *can wakan* was treated as an enemy. It was
scouted, counted coup upon, captured, and taken back to camp. Today the Sun Dance reflects the core values of community and cultural identity (181). With this shift in emphasis,
the treatment of the *can wakan* also shifted and now bears less association with warfare and
the hunt. In many cases, most of these vestiges have all but completely faded away.

For descriptions and analysis of the *Wiwanyang Wacipi,* including the capture of the
can wakan, see Densmore 1992 (84–151); Mails 1978; Walker 1980 (176–91); Amiotte
1987; Erdoes and J. Lame Deer 1972 (187–202); W. Powers 1975 (95–100); Stolzman
1986b (157–65); and Holler 1995.

the *wakan*" (1987, 79). The *can wakan* reestablishes the center of the hoop, the center of the Sun Dance, as the center of the world where all, through prayer, are connected to *Wakan Tanka*.

As the center of the sacred hoop, the *can wakan* fulfills many roles. *Kablaya*/Black Elk explains the qualities of the *can wakan* in his prayer to it before it is raised. "When you stand at the center of the sacred hoop you will be the people, and you will be as the pipe, stretching from heaven to earth" (J. Brown 1974, 74). As the conduit of prayer, its beneficent power strengthens the people. "The weak will lean upon you, and for all the people you will be support. . . . You will stand where the four sacred paths cross—there you will be the center of the great Powers of the universe" (74). The people are instructed to emulate the *can wakan*. "May we two-leggeds always follow your sacred example, for we see that you are always looking upwards into the heavens" (74). At the center, and together, the people are home, they are united with the past and future generations (Amiotte 1987, 84). More than just the nation, however, is present at the center. *Kablaya* prays to the tree, "with all the peoples of the world, you will stand at the center; for all beings and all things you will bring that which is good" (J. Brown 1974, 74). After the *can wakan* is raised, the people are one, they are (renewed as) a nation. After the *can wakan* is upright, it sings to the people:

maka' hokan'yan	at the center of the earth
wa'kil na'zin po	stand looking around you
oya'te iye'kiya	recognizing the tribe
wa'kil na'zin po	stand looking around you.
	(Densmore 1992, 120)

The process of (re)establishing themselves as a people can be done only in accord with and through *Wakan Tanka*. The *can wakan,* like the *cannupa* and the *Wiwanyang Wacipi,* unites the people, as and at the center, including *Paha Sapa,* through prayer to the power of *Wakan Tanka*.

A crucial focus of Black Elk's Great Vision is the restorative and transformative power of the *hocoka*. In his vision, several culturally significant signs appear at the center of the sacred hoop of the people. DeMallie writes, "The greatness of Black Elk's vision lies not in its uniqueness, but in its very representativeness. . . . Perhaps its most striking feature is the representation of the circle of life as enclosing a central tree, symbolizing regeneration" (1984a, 86). Restorative power emerges in the center—first in the form of a man, then as a buffalo, and finally as an herb. Each of these forms in and of itself is a center of the Great Sioux Nation. They are for Black Elk the source of his power to heal the people.

> As I looked down upon the people, there stood on the north side a man painted red all over his body and he had with him a lance and he walked in to the center of the sacred nation's hoop and lay down and rolled himself on the ground and when he got up he was a buffalo standing right in the center of the nation's hoop. The buffalo rolled and when he got up there was an herb there in his place. The herb plant grew up and bloomed so that I could see what it looked like—what kind of an herb it was from the bloom. After the buffalo's arrival the people looked better and then when the buffalo turned into an herb, the people all got up and seemed to be well. Even the horses got up and stretched themselves and neighed. Then a little breeze came from the north and I could see that the wind was in the form of a spirit and as it went over the people all the dead things came to life. (DeMallie 1984a, 128)

The *cannupa, wanbli gleshka,* and *anpo wichacpi* (the morning star) also fly to, or appear in, the center of the nation's *cangleska* (DeMallie 1984a, 129). Nicholas Black Elk relates that the herb brings knowledge of diseases, the *cannupa* brings peace in everything, *wanbli gleshka* unifies the nation as relatives, and *anpo wichacpi* brings the knowledge that comes from being unified (128). These centering forces will ensure the people's renewal and restoration in the new conditions of the reservation.

Based in Lakota mythology and history, Black Elk's early-twentieth-century teachings restate the centrality of *Paha Sapa* to the continued survival and renewal of the Lakota Nation. Within this theology the *cangleska* is a core metaphor. Living in unity with each other and all other sentient beings—past, present, and future—is the imperative value of Lakota cosmology. In order to move toward this ideal state, individuals and groups must access spiritual beings (including their own) through a variety of *hocoka*. Ultimately, this must include the "Heart of Everything That Is": the penultimate Center—*Paha Sapa*.

Thus, one of the most critical junctures in Black Elk's Great Vision is the point at which he is taken to that same center—the center of the earth. It is at Harney Peak where Black Elk reviews all that he has seen and all that he has been given (DeMallie 1984a, 163). There he sees "what is good for humans and what is not good for humans" (135). By going to the center of the earth, Black Elk comes to know, and then share in, the power of the west: "you shall know the willpower of myself, for they shall take you to the center of the earth" (116). And it is at the center of the earth, Harney Peak, where Black Elk is given the flowering stick by the fourth Grandfather to save the nation. The journey to the center of the earth, a metaphor for the vision itself, is also a metaphor for Black Elk's teachings and responsibilities: "In my vision you have taken me to the peak and there you have shown me the power to make over my nation" (238).

His journey to the center of the earth occupied Black Elk's thoughts throughout the 1931 interviews. On May 25, 1931, while the Neihardts and Black Elk visited in the Badlands, Black Elk offered a prayer for Neihardt's work in recording Black Elk's teachings. Prefacing the prayer he says: "The more I talk about these things the more I think of the old times, and it makes me feel sad, but I hope that we can make the tree bloom for your children and for mine. . . . From here we can see the Black Hills and the high peak to which I was taken to see the whole world and the spirits showed me the good things; and when I think of that it was hopeless it seems before I saw you, but here you came. Somehow the spirits have made you come to revive the tree that never bloomed: (DeMallie 1984a, 44). And then in the prayer: "The flowering stick that you have given to me has not bloomed, and my people are in despair. . . . And to the center of the earth you have set a sacred stick that should bloom, but it failed. But nevertheless, grandfathers, behold it and guide us; you have beheld us. I myself, Black Elk, and my nephew, Mr. Neihardt. Thus the tree may bloom. . . . Help us that our generation in the future will live and walk the good road with the flowering stick to success" (46).

Black Elk had been taught by his ancestors that in order for his power to be realized—for his vision to be realized—he must reenact it for the people. But, by the end of his life, at the time of the Neihardt interviews he had yet to reenact his journey to the center of the earth. Black Elk had never returned to the Black Hills since they were stolen by the United

States in 1877. Hilda Neihardt remembers: "He told my father that he would soon be 'under the grass' and that before he died he wanted to go again to the center of the earth where he had been taken in his vision. Once more Daddy promised him, 'We will go, Black Elk. We will all drive to Harney Peak in the Black Hills together just as soon as your story is finished" (H. Neihardt 1995, 82). When the story was finished all of them did make the journey to Harney Peak. On top of the peak, Black Elk loaded his pipe and prayed:

> Grandfathers . . . you have made me intercessor of my people and you have given a way of living to my people. . . . You have sent me to the center of the earth with your stick to bloom. . . . From the south you have presented me with the sacred hoop of my nation and the tree that was to bloom, but with tears running, I shall say now that the tree has never bloomed.
>
> And here at the center of the earth I am now at the same place that you have taken me and showed me all the good things of the earth that were to be my people's . . . and now my people are in despair and I will thus send a voice again. . . . At this very place, the center of the earth, you have promised to set the tree that was to bloom. But I have fallen away thus causing the tree never to bloom again. . . . May I send a voice once again so that you may hear me and bring my people back into the hoop and at the center there should be the tree that was to bloom and help us and have mercy on us. Hear me, O Great Spirit, that my people will get back into the sacred hoop and that the tree may bloom and that my people will live the ways you have set for them, and if they live, they may see the happy days and the happy land that you have promised. (DeMallie 1984a, 295)

In order for the stick to flower, Black Elk had to tell his story and reenact his vision on earth. Just as it was necessary for Black Elk to return to the Black Hills so that the teachings of the Grandfathers can eventually be realized, it is necessary for the Lakota to return to the "Heart of Everything That Is." Each Lakota must take personal responsibility for the nation, each Lakota must do what is necessary to nurture the flowering of the stick. According to Gerald Clifford (Lakota) of the American Indian Leadership Council, "Our spiritual journey as Lakota people led us back to the Black Hills. Participation in Lakota ceremonies is, in essence, tied to the Black Hills. Every time Lakota people fast and pray or go into sweats and Sun Dances, we're participating in this spiritual journey back to the Black Hills" (Doll 1994, 60). These journeys should not be hampered, as was Black Elk's, by their theft.

PART THREE

Philosophical, Theological, and Religious Studies Perspectives

12

Dakota Philosophy

GEORGE W. LINDEN

At the beginning of *Seven Arrows,* Hyemeyohsts Storm has a passage that I find extremely moving. He states:

> According to the Teachers, there is only one thing that all people possess equally. This is their loneliness. No two people on the face of this earth are alike in any one thing except for their loneliness. This is the cause of our Growing, but it is also the cause of our wars. Love, hate, greed and generosity are all rooted within our loneliness, within our desire to be needed and loved. The only way that we can overcome our loneliness is through Touching. It is only in this way that we can learn to be Total Beings. (1973, 7)

I find in this passage a tremendous sense of isolation, a profound feeling of alienation, an intense yearning for community, and a complete lack of an initial sense of belonging. Or rather, by extension, I find be-longing; a longing for more than human community, a longing for communion, a longing for participation in being itself.

But who is this person whose heartstrings are reverberating? It is not some Cheyenne or Sioux. It is not some Dakota boy responding from the life-world of his cultural ascendancy. It is me. I am a boy born before television had replaced vision, before time had become space, before men walked the moon, before pigeons played Ping-Pong, and before rats learned to react. True, I grew up in the Dakotas. But I grew up as a white

This essay appeared in a slightly different version in *American Studies* 18, no. 2 (1977) and is reprinted with permission.

middle-class Methodist, weaned on books, inhabiting at best an attenuated family, and not a member of a tribe. And it is precisely because this
passage appeals to me, because it touches profoundly on my own experiences, that I cannot trust it to tell me much about the stance of Plains Indians.

Maurice Merleau-Ponty has argued that we must learn to suspend
analysis and return to our initial consciousness of social relationships, our
personal experiences. Only thus can we avoid merely quantitative reflection and approach more closely the lived truth. He states: "[O]bjectivism
forgets another evident fact. We can expand our experience of social relationships and get a proper view of them only by analogy or contrast with
those we have lived. We can do so, in short, only by subjecting the social
relationships we have experienced to an *imaginary variation*. These lived
relationships will no doubt take on a new meaning in comparison with this
imaginary variation (as the fall of a body on an inclined plane is put in a
new light by the ideal concept of free fall), but they will provide it with all
the sociological meaning it can have" (1964, 100). What follows, then, is
an imaginary variation, an attempt to structure a world of genuine participatory perspectivism, a world inhabited, not inhibited, a world not of absences, but presences. And if I can construct such a world, I may be able to
see, and, perhaps even believe, that for a Dakota to be was to belong.

Ontology: To Be Is to Belong
(Space, Time, Cause, and Purpose)

Man is a symbolic animal. He neither acts nor reacts to raw experience as
such. On the contrary, he *re-presents* his experience to himself and others,
and in so doing acts in and through those representations. Hence, though
I grew up in the same geographic location as the Dakota, I did not grow
up in the same space. My space has been Newtonian and post-Newtonian
space. I inhabit the transitional sensorium between a literate and a postliterate culture. What could space have been like to a prechirographic, prety-
pographic, analphabetic Plains person? Space must have been visually vast,
nongeometric, continuous, cognitively delimited, acoustically real, centered, personal, and recurrent.

Abstractly, the Great Plains are a kind of perpetual everywhereness.
The Great Plains, after all, are *great*. City-folk, surrounded by the cacoph-

ony of never-ceasing traffic or wrapped in their air-conditioned cocoons, curse the interminable endlessness of Kansas, Nebraska, and the Dakotas. But to one who grew up here, there is majesty in this vastness. The sea of grass extended visually farther than breaking hearts could break for it; horizons were indeed unlimited. And this sense of spaciousness brought with it a feeling of openness, a sense of the absence of arbitrary external relations and restrictions, a consciousness of a capacity to roam. The Plains warrior also must have seen it so, but with this difference: he saw it concretely. Without maps or Cartesian coordinates, all of his geography was contained in the eyes of the eldest members of the tribe. When the tribe moved, the eldest warriors led the way, for lived space was memorable space. Map space is an aid to or substitute for memory. But memory space is event space. Hence, we find Black Elk providing the most minute topographic detail in every fold of land involved in a battle, but when it comes to distance he resorts to vague words such as "yonder" or "bye-and-bye." The latter is particularly notable because it involves a temporalization of space. In the oral-aural culture of the Plains, a moving culture, distance was expressed in terms of time. Thus, the span between x and y was expressed as so many horse-days' journey, so many walking days, so many suns, or so many moons. We find this way of thinking difficult to imagine because it is the inverse of our literal, linear natural attitude. Modern men are so used to clock time, computer time, timetables, that we are unaware that we automatically break time into sequences of spatial metaphors. As Father Ong has reminded us, we speak of a long time or a short time, though time can be neither long nor short (1967, 43–44).[1] It would be better, perhaps, to speak of a fat time or a thin time, a younger time or an older time.

It is true that the Sioux had pictography. But as Ong reminds us, pictographs serve primarily as memory aids. "They encode little. The information storage remains almost entirely in the heads of those who use such creations which are much more triggers than storage devices" (1967, 35). Furthermore, if we examine what was pictured in this manner, we find ourselves back with memorable events. Neither geography nor history are memory. They are records. But a record "does not belong to us as a mem-

---

1. We might also note that we speak of ancient time as *distant* time. We speak of *split* seconds, and a split-second salvation is a *close call* or a *near miss*.

ory does. It is an external thing" (23). Memory, by its very nature, is something that is held or had. Memory is personal. Hence, memory-space is personal space, but if lived space for the Dakota was visually vast, temporalized, nonlinear, eventful, and memorable, it was also cognitively delimited. Impersonal space is infinitely extendible, but personal space is my space or your space, and your space is not mine. Space for a Dakota was at best tribal space. Hence, it is not surprising that when Red Cloud, Standing Bear, or Black Elk came back with tales of a wider world inhabited by innumerable *Wasichus*—the Lakota word for the whites—they were not believed. Nor is it surprising that when the young Luther Standing Bear awoke on a train in Pennsylvania, he thought he had passed to the other side of the moon. Without the cognitive tools of abstraction, they could not conceive of the extent of this spaceship earth. Space merely extended a little beyond where the people were.

The Dakota were a nomadic people. Consequently, their sense of the extent of space must have surpassed that of agricultural tribes. Nevertheless, their wandering was limited. It was limited by hostile tribes such as the Crow. It was limited by how much they could drag along and how far in any given move. It was limited by the ferocity of the seasons and the adaptations of habit; for example, they wintered in the Black Hills and roamed the Plains in the summers. It was limited by the erratic movement of the food supply. Hence, the inhabited space they traversed was fairly recurrent and thus that much more familiar and memorable.

But perhaps the factor most difficult for us to imagine and most personalizing with respect to space was that it was acoustically real. This is difficult for us to imagine because we are so visually and typographically oriented. Think, for example, of the *silence* of books. It is no accident that we are told to keep quiet in libraries. The space of sight is not the space of sound. Acoustic space is shared. We sit before the orchestra, we sit before the speaker (either stereo or personal), but we sit *within* the sounds they produce. Sound is an interior exteriorized that reverberates in an interior. Acoustic space is voluminous, nonreversible, intensively unified, and not subject to division without loss of quality. The auditor always feels at its center. Space radiates from where he hears. Listen to Black Elk:

> I looked ahead and saw the mountains there with rocks and forests
> on them, and from the mountains flashed all colors upward to the heav-

ens. Then I was standing on the highest mountain of them all, and round about beneath me was the whole hoop of the world. And while I stood there I saw more than I can tell and I understood more than I saw; for I was seeing in a sacred manner the shapes of all things in the spirit, and the shape of all shapes as they must live together like one being. And I saw that the sacred hoop of my people was one of the many hoops that made one circle, wide as daylight and as starlight, and in the center grew one mighty flowering tree to shelter all the children of one mother and one father. And I saw that it was holy. (J. Neihardt 1979, 42–43)

Flaming Rainbow (Neihardt) identifies this mountain as Harney Peak, but then Black Elk remarks in a footnote: "But anywhere is the center of the world."

Books could and should be written about Black Elk's Great Vision. I wish to comment only on a few characteristics. First, his vision had to be *told*. Had he not spoken to a poet,[2] it would have been lost. Second, the vision contains striking visual imagery, not merely because such images are aesthetically exciting, but, as Havelock remarks, because such imagery serves as a recall or storage device (1967, see 188*ff.*). Third, there is emphasis upon the unity of shape. Shape is more concrete than structure, line, or mass. Fourth, there is an emphasis upon centering. Whether it is the sacred spot, the immovable place of the Buddha, the sacral circle of St. Peters, or that navel of the universe, Washington, D.C., the idea of all things being radiated from a sacral point, an omphalos, is characteristic of verbo-motor cultures. Thus, though Black Elk is speaking in ocular equivalents, he is thinking in aural terms. He is in tune with all things and at their midst. The mode of unity of Black Elk's vision is aural.

Vision arrests. Vision is spectation; sound is participation. Sound engulfs, surrounds, and envelops us. It unifies and unites according to interior relationships. It reveals presence with an immediate fullness that vision cannot. Images may reflect or refract; sound resonates. Sound re-

---

2. This suggests that we might learn more by sending the orally-aurally arrested, namely poets, to record verbo-motor cultures rather than sending those people dominated by the quantified quotients of consciousness. Indeed, Levi-Strauss argues a favorable position for the poet when he states that "art lies half-way between scientific knowledge and mystical or magical thought" (see 1966, 22*ff.*).

ciprocates.[3] Sound centers. Sound engenders simultaneity, not sequentiality. "Sound situates man in the middle of actuality and in simultaneity,
whereas vision situates man in front of things and in sequentiality" (Ong
1967, 128). Vision, as Merleau-Ponty has remarked, is not merely a distance sense, it is a dividing, a dissecting sense. But sound, and hence
acoustic space, is organic and, ultimately, indivisible. Vision displays sur-
faces; sound reveals interiors. Because the space of the Dakota was tribal
space, unifying space, it was also a space, which by its very nature was socializing. The Dakota inhabited a space where he belonged.

This tribal, personal life-world was destroyed by the engine of
progress, that father of all timetables, that sanctifier of the pocket watch
and ultimate applied Cartesianism, the iron horse.[4] How strange that the
range should become a grid. Look, for example, at western towns with
their neat numbered streets intersecting named avenues with perfect symmetry. Follow the Union-Pacific across Nebraska, and you will find even
the towns ordered according to the alphabet. How could a man who grew
in the presence of shape make any sense of dividing the land into sections,
quarters, and sixty-acre plots? As Black Elk remarked, the *Wasichus* are so
crazy they even fence the grass.

If Sioux space was different from ours, the same thing must have been
true of their concept of time. Not only was there a shift in the sensorium
between an oral-aural culture and an alphabetic one, but also, as we saw,
space became temporalized. *Mutatis mutandis:* it would seem to follow
that time was not spatialized. For the Dakota, time must have been non-
spatial, memorable, recurrent, fluid, durational, eventful, and clustered.
The other senses—taste, smell, touch—do not move with time but dwell
in it. And they become increasingly attenuated with time's passage. Sight
seeks to arrest time. Sound is inherently temporal. Sound is progressive in
or through time. From the point of view of typographic man, verbo-
motor man's sense of time is especially frustrating. Verbo-motor man's
sense of time appears vague, amorphous, and chaotic. But that is the way

3. One recalls Chief Joseph's sexist but perhaps perceptive remark: "When you can get
the last word with an echo, you may have the last word with your wife."

4. Actually, the term *Iron Horse* is a *Wasichu* word resulting from seeing too many
movies. The Lakota word was *Maza Canku,* or Iron Road, very close to our "railroad."

it appears *to us*.[5] The more spatialized consciousness becomes, the more specialized it becomes. Thus, we must pity the most precise among us, the historians who struggle to determine exact dates for Indian events. But there is no such thing as precise time or "being on time" in an oral-aural nonclockwork culture. Time consists of happenings, doings, goings-on. Such events form clusters that are, from our point of view, disorderly, but that from the Dakota point of view are eminently memorable.

It would appear that the Dakota "organized" time in the following ways: as durational flow, by natural recurrent events, by natural nonrecurrent events, by recurrent human events, and by human nonrecurrent events. Time thus organized is instantiated, that is, clustered around the standing instance. Hence, we find a predominance of the nonliteral, the mythic, the parabolic, and the symbolic. These tales do not need explanation, they *are* explanation. It is much more important that they be suggestive and resonant, true goings-on themselves, than that they be literal pinpoints of history. Because the cruelty of vision is abolished, time is warmly remembered.

I do not wish to spend too much time elaborating this point. Actually, only abstract time can be "spent." Happening-time is either endured or lived. Let me give an instance. Time and time again, we find Black Elk using vague and imprecise transitional phrases. His favorites are "and then," "bye and bye," and "afterwhile."[6] All of these phrases express, though they may not denote, the direction of durational flow. As for natural recurrent events, each month has its own specific experienced name. Thus, March is the Moon of the Snowblind; May, the Moon when the Ponies Shed; November, the Moon of Falling Leaves; and so on. A natural nonrecurrent event would be a striking, memorable, vivid event. Thus,

5. This is particularly true when we are sentimental. That hunger for home, nostalgia, has since the Greeks meant a nostalgia for space (see Eisley 1969, 18). Because the Plains culture arose and disappeared in less than two hundred years, we may be here confronting a nostalgia for time (see Lurie 1968, 28*ff*.).

6. This sense of flow and the evanescence of all life was expressed with great depth by Crowfoot: "What is life? It is the flash of a firefly in the night. It is the breath of a buffalo in winter time. It is the little shadow which runs across the grass and loses itself in the sunset" (McLuhan 1972, 12).

Momaday dates the events of the Kiowa by the rain of falling stars (1973).[7] Examples of recurrent human events could be "during my first buffalo hunt," "during the second Sun Dance with the Cheyenne," "during the fourth raid on the Crow," or "during the last Ghost Dance." Certainly, a nonrecurrent human event was the wiping out of Long Hair, the death of Crazy Horse, or the massacre at Wounded Knee.

Because time was neither abstract nor quantified, it was not subjectivized but was objectively concrete, that is, clustered. Time moved according to the work; work was not forced to accord with quantified time plans. Luther Standing Bear describes the shaping of tipi poles: "When all the trees had been brought to camp, one would be leaned against a standing tree for a brace. A block of wood was fastened to the butcher knife to be used as a drawshave. Before the Indian had steel knives he used a sharp stone to do this work. As most of the poles were cut to about the required size, it was not very hard work to finish them. The Indian had no boss standing over him, and he took his own time" (1975, 18). Furthermore, though there were certain times of increased tension, such as the buffalo killing, fighting the enemy, or fleeing the blue coats, normal time was without intensive urgency. Nobody was in a hurry. Compare this fact to our sense of mechanized time: "In the early spring, when we moved away from our winter quarters, our band of Indians looked better than any circus parade. Each family had its place in line. Nobody was in a hurry to get ahead of those in advance—as the white man in his automobile tries to do in this day and age" (23). Because normal time was not hasty time, the white man saw the Indian as unmotivated and lazy, which assumption was a mistake. Dakota time was not lazy time. It was leisure time. Such time converts labor into work and work into serious play.

Exactness is a virtue only when events are pregnant. Otherwise, the world is a flow of happenings. But memorable happenings are also personal. Hence, Dakota time was, at best, tribal time. The Dakota lived in a time where he belonged.

Now happenings and events are not Cartesian or Humean. They are neither clear and distinct nor simple. Happenings imply movement and change; they flow out of one another and into one another; they are cu-

---

7. The time of falling stars was November 13, 1833.

mulative, mutually penetrating, conditionally constitutive, and evanescent. Any one can be the transverse summation of the others. It depends on how you slice them. Consequently, we should not be amazed to discover that the Dakota sense of cause was much more Eastern than Western. It was not that the Dakota were not interested in proximate efficient causes. They simply did not have the tools to look for them. It takes an enormous fund of knowledge and a high degree of abstraction to ask whether x is the cause of y. In fact, it is doubtful that logic can even arise without dead print. Hence, cause as we know it was de-emphasized among the Dakota and, again, personalized. Instead of asking "what is the cause of x?" the Dakota was much more likely to ask "what likes to happen with x?" In this mode of thinking, *how* and *why* replace *what*. Relations are once more internal. Those things happen together that belong together.

As for teleology, it is a commonplace that purpose dominates consciousness in an oral-aural culture. Speech, after all, is not merely the presence of power, but its exhibition. Thus, all things are seen to have powers for good or ill. All things have meanings to be unraveled. All things are symbolic for they are living and semianimate, they are not reduced to their bare thing-hood. A world of made is not a world of grown. Hence, we find the sense of purposiveness expressed in the sense of unity, relatedness, movement, and growth.

Perhaps Luther Standing Bear best expresses the sense of centering, the sense of being grounded in the unity of being: "The man who sat on the ground in his tipi meditating on life and its meaning, accepting the kinship of all creatures and acknowledging unity with the universe of things was infusing into his being the true essence of civilization" (McLuhan 1972, 99). Unity and relatedness are not just there. Unity and relatedness are directional, and their direction is that of human growth. "[T]he old Dakota was wise. He knew that man's heart, away from nature, becomes hard; he knew that lack of respect for growing, living things soon led to lack of respect for humans, too. So he kept his youth close to its softening influence" (Standing Bear 1978, 197). But this growth is not merely human, but is also growth in brotherhood. Standing Bear adds that the Dakota became so close to their animal victims and friends that "in true brotherhood they spoke a common tongue" (193). And this acknowledgment of brotherhood engendered an awareness of respect, individuality, and purpose. Listen to Okute (Shooter):

From my boyhood I have observed leaves, trees, and grass, and I have never found two alike. They may have a general likeness, but on examination I have found that they differ slightly. . . . All living creatures and all plants are a benefit to something. Certain animals fulfill their purpose by definite acts. The crows, buzzards and flies are somewhat similar in their use, and even the snakes have a purpose in being. (19)

Persistence in existence was not mere continuance. To be was to be for the best.

Being was *being-for*, and being-for engenders a sense of movement, purpose, and numinous value, what Otto called "the sense of the holy." Flying Hawk, an Oglala, states, "If the Great Spirit wanted men to stay in one place he would make the world stand still; but He made it to always change, so birds and animals can move and always have green grass and ripe berries, sunlight to work and play, and night to sleep; always changing; everything for good; nothing for nothing (McLuhan 1972, 64). And Ohiyesa reflects on the holy quality of motion and rest: "Everything as it moves, now and then, here and there, makes stops. . . . So the god has stopped. The sun, which is so bright and beautiful, is one place where he has stopped. The moon, the stars, the winds, he has been with. The trees, the animals are all where he has stopped, and the Indian thinks of these places and sends his prayers there to reach the place where the god has stopped and win help and a blessing" (37).[8] In Heidegger's language, the Dakota was *Gelassenheit* to Being. He was not next to being. He was with it. And what he was with was presence; what he was with was power. The greatest of the Oglalas, Sitting Bull, expressed it best: "Every seed is awakened and so has all animal life. It is through this mysterious power that we too have our being and we therefore yield to our neighbors, even our ani-

---

8. Compare this with the following passage from Henri Bergson: "A great current of creative energy gushes forth through matter, to obtain from it what it can. At most points it is stopped; these stops are transmuted, in our eyes, into the appearances of so many living species, that is, of organisms in which our perception, being essentially analytical and synthetic, distinguishes a multitude of elements combining to fulfill a multitude of functions; but the process of organization was only the stop itself, a simple act analogous to the impress of a foot which instantaneously causes thousands of grains of sand to contrive to form a pattern" (1970, 1152–53). Because the Dakota were not Bergsonians, it can only be that Bergson thought like a Dakota.

mal neighbors, the same right as ourselves, to inhabit this land" (90). In such a world, learning is not cerebration, but celebration, for man participates in being; he is a brother of all beings; he is a caretaker of being. In such a personalized, purposive world, it is not possible not to belong. The Dakota inhabited a world where he belonged.

Institutions: To Be Is to Be Responsible (Language, Society, Art, and Religion)

Reflection upon Dakota ontology in terms of space, time, cause, and purpose has revealed a way of relating to being that engendered a sense of belonging, a sense of objective relatedness and felt identity. If these qualities are true of the ontological representation, then we should expect them to be embodied in more concrete modes of behavior, such as in institutions. An institution may be described as behavior objectified and constructed to ensure cultural continuity. Let us turn, then, to a brief examination of Dakota language, social relations, art, and religion.

We inhabit and are shaped by a mass language. Not only do uncounted millions speak English, but the deaf also speak it through type. Furthermore, this mass language has been expanded—not only by typography but also by electronic technology. The whispering voice (telephone) covers the world. Television extends us to the planets, and radio listens to the echoes of the galaxies. Although we may know *of* everyone, we may never truly know anyone in an intimate sense. Our language is dispersed and ceasing to be disparate. As the electronic web intensifies, local differences and nuances disappear. Such was not the case for the Dakota. He lived within a highly restricted tribal language. Restriction engenders unity.

It is true that there was intertribal communication. But this communication consisted of either standard signals or sign language. The standard signals were few. Sign language was gesture. Now gesture, like voice, is an interior exteriorized as progression through time. The meaning of an upraised hand resides in the movement to an upright position. Yet, gesture encodes less than voice. Furthermore, gesture must be highly formulaic and typic. Gesture is movement visually or imaginatively or both apprehended. It lacks the true interior quality of speech. Because its use among the Plains Indians was to diminish the gap of disparate tongues, gesture demanded set patterns of movement of formulas to clarify meanings and provide proper context. Because of these limitations, the sign language of the Plains could not have extended the Dakota's sense of language to anything beyond narrow practical purposes. Nor could it have engendered much sense of unity. Walter Ong, writing of gesture, states, "gesture is 'interfering.' It demands the cessation of a great many physical activities which can be carried on easily while one is talking. Further, it is not so directly interiorizing as sound by the fact that it is visually apprehended. Gesture has surface, although it does not consist simply of surface. Finally, it is not so socializing as sound, nor so reciprocating, nor so versatile. The intertribal sign language of the plains Indians of the United States did not unite the Indians so intimately as did the spoken languages of the individual tribes" (1967, 147–48). If the sign language of the Sioux provided him with a sense of relatedness, belonging, and felt identity, it must have been minimal. Just the opposite must have been true of his tribal language, for his tribal language was limited both quantitatively and qualitatively. Furthermore, it was spoken.

The Sioux language is a member of the linguistic group Siouan. But "Siouan" covers a wide range of languages and is not an adjectival form of the word *Sioux*. The two are not to be confused (Nurge 1970, xii). Perhaps we should refer to the language as Dakota. Even this term is less than precise. The Dakota were divided into seven bands, and these bands were further grouped into three divisions: the Santee or Eastern Dakota, the Yankton or Middle Dakota, and the Tetons or Western Dakota. Each division had its own dialect. Hence, the Santee spoke Dakota, the Yankton spoke Nakota, and the Teton spoke Lakota. The Tetons (Dwellers-on-the-Plains) were by far the largest group, their number exceeding that of all the other bands combined. Furthermore, they were the most historically dramatic and are the best known, consisting of the Hunkpapa, Minneconjou, Sihasapa, Oohenonpa, Brulé, Sansarcs, and Oglala bands. Because the Tetons were the largest group, the most dramatic and the best known, I shall refer to the language as Lakota. What do all these divisions mean? They mean that if you were a Plains warrior, perhaps less than twenty thousand people in the whole world spoke your own tongue, and many of them spoke with a different dialect. Because there were no modern media and because the language was unwritten, it meant that you could always ask somebody, but you could never look anything up. Such quantitative restriction would foster a strong sense of tribal identity and group loyalty. It would also foster hostility to those people who did not speak your tongue. In short, Lakota was chauvinistic. Hence, you would refer to yourself as "Dakota" (the United People), while others, the Ojibwa or Crow, would call you "Sioux" (Enemies). You would call your neighbors "Sheyela" (Speakers-of-Difficult-Language), and they would call themselves "Cheyenne" (Human Beings). You knew your brothers. They spoke your language. A quantitatively restricted language, a language of few speakers, is an intimate language.

This progressive and intensive intimacy was carried out even in the behavior of naming. Hence, a Plains warrior often had three names. He had the name given to him, the name he achieved, and his personal name. Few, if any, knew the latter, and those few could use it seldom. Hence, Luther Standing Bear had the name given to him by his father when he was born: "Ota Kte" or "Plenty Kill" because his father had killed many enemies. Later, when Luther Standing Bear had displayed his courage in hunting, battle, and a vision quest, his name was changed from Plenty Kill to Standing Bear. If Luther Standing Bear had a personal, private name, we do not know it. He did not write it down. In any case, one often had a given name, a social name, and a personal name. The latter might be analogous to the phenomenon familiar to members of a subgroup in our mass culture: the nickname.[9] Such naming practice designated acknowledged achieved status, and conferred personal identity. The Lakota had names that belonged to him.

Beyond this, one might say that the Lakota was concrete, nondogmatic, motion oriented, durational, and action and person directed. It was an eventful language. Lakota lacked many generic concepts, hence it was concrete. One could not ask, "What color is this?" but one could ask, "Is this blue?" It was nondogmatic, that is, personal and qualified. Print language, spread out in impersonal page space, becomes dogmatically assertive. Hence, we say "This is an automobile" or "Custer is approaching." There is no specification of the stance of the speaker—he "stands" nowhere—nor any indication of his attitude. With both Black Elk and Luther Standing Bear and others, one finds constant use of personal qual-

9. Now that we inhabit a postliterate situation, a renewed orality, it would be interesting to know whether the use of nicknames is on the increase or decrease.

ification, such as "I think" or "It appears to me," and of attitudinal perspective, as in "perhaps," "maybe," and so forth. Hence, they are much more likely to say, "I think this is an automobile, maybe" or "It appears to me that Yellow Hair is approaching, perhaps."

Such a nondogmatic language was also motion, action, and person oriented. Hence, one would not say, "He puts on his clothes," but rather, "He is moving into clothing." A person's way of moving in the world, his gait or the way he rode, were as important a part in his description as his nose. Hence, if one were an awkward or ungainly walker, one might say, "He moves newly." The durational aspect of the language I have already noted with Black Elk's constant usage of "afterwhile," "bye and bye," and "yonder." Claude Levi-Strauss puts it this way: "The Dakota language possesses no word to designate time, but it can express in a number of ways modes of being in duration. For Dakota thought, in fact, time constitutes a duration in which measurement does not intervene: it is a limitless 'free good' " (1969, 172).[10] From the point of view of the literate person, such language appears vague and imprecise. But this is simply because we suffer from the illusion that if we have the precise word, the exact word, we will have the exact meaning. And that meaning, usually, is the literal meaning. But the Lakota, like the Chinese, had no letters. hence they were unable to worship the literal. Speaking of a chirographic language, Chinese, Ong expresses some of the phrases used for the least important, the literal meaning of characters:

> In Chinese, where literal meaning is ordinarily not conceived of, since the writing system provides no *literae* or letters on which the concept literal can be built, the roughly equivalent concepts are "according to the surface of the word," "according to each word in each utterance," "according to the dead character." These are hardly laudatory expressions. Here too in a chirographic but analphabetic culture, the first or most accessible meaning appears in at least vaguely depreciatory light. The rich suggestiveness of Chinese characters favors a sense of the fuller meaning lying much deeper than the literal. (1967, 47)

For the Lakota, also, it was much more important to be symbolic than literal, to be suggestive, poetic, and profound than to be clear and precise.

---

10. Levi-Strauss (1966) attributes this information to Malan and McCone (1960).

Like the Chinese, he could not be so unkind as to explain everything to another. Such usage fosters a high degree of participation on the part of the auditor. It even alters the function of silence. Silence in a literal language is simply a gap. Silence in poetic language is pregnant, a way of funding the nuances of meanings. Hence, both the spoken and the unspoken language of the Lakota was such that it engendered participation, relatedness, belonging, and a felt sense of identity. The Lakota used a language that belonged to him and to which he belonged.

The Dakota still lives on in the American imagination, either "standing eagle-armed on hills in the sunrise" or as a synthetic savage attacking a wagon train. Such images cannot be merely the results of inept paintings in poor motels or of stereotyped motion pictures. These media do not create beliefs, they reflect them. Even Longfellow would not have been popular had he not been accepted. To reflect upon the Dakota, then, is to call in question the whole concept of *Wasichu* individuality. To reflect upon the Dakota in his concrete cultural circumstance is to throw in relief a common mythic basis.

This mythic belief may be singularly American, but it is dual in nature, grounded upon, first, the myth of the unspoiled country lacking in original sin, the Garden of Eden, the Golden West or, more recently, the New Frontier, and second, the Promethean myth of the isolated, transcending, absolutely autonomous individual whose justification is a negative form of freedom and whose destiny is conquest and control.

From the myth of unspoiled Eden, the white man concluded the Indian was a laconic noble savage; from the Promethean myth, he inferred that he, himself, had unlimited power and that the Indian was a savage devil destined for extermination. Both images derived from these myths rest on a common philosophic base: the assumption that autonomy of the individual means the *absence* of relations. Freedom conceived negatively becomes freedom *from*, freedom from obligation, freedom from restraint, freedom from responsibility. Hence, the pioneer viewed himself and the Indians as loners, outside culture and against nature. This view of the isolated individual was a functional rationalization for the frontiersman. He saw himself as independent, culture transcending, self-generating, self-sustaining, and self-justified, and he saw others through that image.

These myths were partially appropriate to the Plains warrior. It is true that the Sioux was autonomous. If he, or his family or his band, did not wish to move with the tribe, no one could order him to do so. It is true that he was not accountable to any other individual, but he was responsible; he was responsible to the people. For the white settler, accountability was an external relation of person to person; for the Plains Indian, accountability was an internal relation of person to group. Hence, it was not true that the Dakota acted without obligation, restraint, or responsibility, for all action went beyond the self and was grounded in the whole. In fact, one could claim that, for the Dakota, to be was to be responsible. Why? Because his lived philosophy was one of acknowledged relativity and objective relatedness. He was an individual who was a member of a tribe, and being a member, he never acted against, apart from, or *as* the whole without good reason. Freedom for him was not negative. Freedom for him was not absence but presence. Freedom for him was positive; it meant freedom *for*, freedom for the realization of greater relationships. Thus, growing and individuality for him meant corporate individuality. Individuality meant growing in enhanced relatedness.

What is at stake here is not merely the concept of individuality, but concrete community. Contrast Black Elk's views when the nation's hoop had been broken with those views of Eagle Voice when the hoop had been whole, holy, and one: "The nation's hoop was broken, and there was no center any longer for the flowering tree. The people were in despair. . . . The life of the people was in the hoop, and what are many little lives if the life of those lives be gone? . . . I looked back on the past and recalled my people's old ways, but they were not living that way any more. They were traveling the black road, everybody for himself and with little rules of his own, as in my vision. I was in despair, and I even thought that if the Wasichus had a better way, then maybe my people should live that way" (J. Neihardt 1979, 214–15). And so he went to New York City and found that the *Wasichu* way was not *the* way. "I did not see anything to help my people. I could see that the Wasichus did not care for each other the way our people did before the nation's hoop was broken. They would take everything from each other if they could, and so there were some who had more of everything than they could use, while crowds of people had nothing at all and maybe were starving. They had forgotten that the earth was their mother. This could not be better than the old ways of my people" (217). No wonder Black Elk was in despair. Community had disintegrated. Man was no longer solidary, but solitary. Man no longer thrived in tribal presence, he was alienated in isolated, negative relations. Eagle

Voice is, perhaps, fictional, but here fiction founds truth. Listen to the way it was before the breaking:

> If you broke a law, it was like breaking the sacred hoop a little; and that was a very bad thing, for the hoop was the life of the people all together . . . [if you did a bad thing you were thrown out before all the people] and it was better to die than to see shame on every face . . . [but if I am brave and generous] even the *wichasha yatapika* [leaders] begin to talk about me in their meetings, and at last they say, "This young Eagle Voice ought to be one of us." So they have a big feast and a ceremony at the center of the hoop, with all the people sitting around. And before they take me to be one of them, the people are asked to say any evil thing they may know about me. But all the people cry out together, "*hi-yay, hi-yay*" and not even a jealous one can say anything bad at all. So they make me a man whom all praise, and before all the people they teach me what I must do, and they say I do not belong to myself any more, but to the people. (J. Neihardt 1970, 29–31)

The ceremony described here was simply in order to be a leader or keeper of the rules, but one could become a counselor or even a chief. But being a chief had to be earned and confirmed. And Eagle Voice adds that this was "hardest of all" because a chief "must be '*wachin tonka*' (great minded) standing above himself, as he stands above others" (31). Luther Standing Bear, a true chief, wrote this description: "But the Indian chief, without any education, was at least honest. (Contrasted to the wasichu politician.) When anything was sent to his band, they got it. His family did not come first. He received no salary. In case of war, he was always found at the front, but when it came to receiving gifts, his place was in the rear. There was no hand-shaking, smiling, and 'glad handing' which meant nothing. The chief was dignified and sincere" (1975, 59). Thus, the chief was not first among equals, but was sometimes first and sometimes last depending on the situation of the people. He had the authority of status, not the status of authority. Even Crazy Horse, when presented the pipe of peace in council, said, "Ask my people what they wish to do."

What we see here is an ontology of relatedness translated or embodied as social responsibility. What was communion in metaphysics is community in society, a form of autonomy *with* responsibility for not all autonomy nor all responsibility were the same. Such matters depended on the individual's place within and relationship to the whole. Dorothy Lee expresses it this way: "Wherein lies the responsibility of the Dakota? Primarily, I believe it derives from being—being a member of a family, or of a specific camp circle; being Dakota, being human, and being part of the universe. Not all parts of the universal whole carry the same responsibility. It is the responsibility of the four-leggeds to furnish food for the two-leggeds, for example; this was determined in the beginning, before beings were differentiated into four-leggeds and two-leggeds. As I understand it, it is the responsibility of man alone to actualize the universe; it is his unique role" (1959, 68). Because no one else has expressed this embodiment so eloquently or so adequately, let me quote Lee once more: "The Dakota were responsible for all things, because they were at one with all things. In one way, this meant that all behavior had to be responsible, since its effect always went beyond the individual. In another way, it meant that an individual had to, was responsible to, increase, intensify, spread, recognize, experience this relationship. To grow in manliness, in humanness, in holiness, meant to plunge purposively deeper into the relatedness of all things" (61).[11] This translation of ontological relatedness into the social sphere changes what we normally mean by the word *choice*. Choice, for us, normally means a free decision of alternatives, the assumption of a relationship or a burden. But in this perspective, choice becomes coextensive with awareness. Choice is acknowledgement. One does not choose to relate. One is already related. Hence, one chooses which relations to acknowledge and, on the basis of that decision, which ways to actualize that acknowledgment. The good for the self thus became coextensive with the good for the tribe.

This way of relating also changes the meaning of "responsibility." Responsibility, for us, normally means being held accountable by the other. But in a shame culture, as distinguished from a guilt culture, there is no single given other to whom one is responsible. Responsibility here comes closer to the Chinese virtue of *chun-tzu;* it does not mean accountable, but something like spiritual availability or, perhaps, reciprocity, for responsibility is responding, *re-spondere,* speaking-back-to. To be responsible is to be responsive. And it means to be responsible to a web of relationships al-

11. Lurie also emphasizes this sense of group-identity membership and decision (1968, 43).

ready objectively existing. Dorothy Lee states this strongly: "Responsibility and accountability had nothing in common for them. Ideally, everyone was responsible for all members of the band, and eventually for all people, all things. . . . Yet no Dakota was accountable to any one or for any one. Was he his brother's keeper? Yes, in so far as he was responsible for his welfare; no, in so far as being accountable for him. He would never speak of him, decide for him, answer prying questions about him. And he was not accountable for himself, either. No one asked him questions about himself; he gave information or withheld it, at his own choice" (1959, 65). From our vantage point of negative freedom, this is a difficult concept to grasp. From the Dakota point of view, where the ideal was the real, responsibility simply meant growth. To realize greater relationships was to grow in being. To be responsive was to grow into greater wholeness and thus enhance the hoop of the people.

The basic education of the Dakota child was learning to grow in enhanced relatedness. The method was positive ideals and the divorcing of the material consequences from acts or achievement. Responsibility began early and was appropriate to the age of the child. Hence, Luther Standing Bear, at the age of three, was given the privilege of bridling his father's horse and finding the village whetstone. Such tasks must have been difficult for a young child, but his father never ordered him, never checked on him, and trusted him to carry them out. From time to time, he would say to him, "When you are older, you may do this" or "When you are a man you will do this." Higher ideals were constantly set beyond his state of development. One knew one's place, but one also knew the direction in which he was expected and privileged to grow. Children were neither bribed nor coerced. They learned to recognize what was demanded by the situation, to acknowledge those demands, and to do them. Such an option was never posed as a restriction on the child's right to play, but as an opportunity to become what all children desire to become: adult.

Perhaps the most effective and profound of the methods used to train the Dakota child was the divorce of material consequences from acts of achievement. When Luther Standing Bear, after several failures, shot his first bird, his father immediately notified the town crier who went through the camp announcing that Plenty Kill had killed his first bird, "and that Standing Bear, his father, was giving away a horse in consequence. . . . On this occasion the horse was given to a man who was very poor" (1975,

10).[12] Again, when he returned with his first deer meat, his father had the crier notify everyone in the village that his son had brought home his first meat. The father then gave away another horse to another poor old man. Standing Bear says that this act was the beginning of his religious training. It was certainly his social training. He was accorded all verbal praise, praise shared by every member of the band, and then gifts were given to the needy. This behavior is how one was taught to acknowledge wider related-ness, and it is how one was guided to become a man whom all praise, a man who did not belong to himself anymore, but belonged to the people.

Art and religion were intertwined for the Dakota. Most songs were chants, most stories were myths, most dancing was sacral. Even the func-tions of art and religion were parallel and highly analogous. The problem of art was how to restore harmony. The problem of religion was how to present and maintain the numinous. Both were socially grounded and cos-mic in function. Common to both was the sacred center, the omphalos, and the basic shape was the circle. Richard Erdoes describes the cosmic, social, and personal meaning of the circle: "The Great Mystery's symbol was the circle. It stood for the Sun and the Earth, the Tepee and the Sa-cred Hoop of the Nation. As long as the circle was unbroken, the tribes would flourish. The sacred powers always worked in circles. The eagle, a holy messenger of the 'ones above,' describes a wheel in its flight. The wind moves in round whirls. The sun comes and goes in a circle. If a man is not aware that he, too, has within himself this sacred center, that he is part of the mystic circle together with all other living creatures, then he is not really a man" (1972, 95–96). Even those things that appeared to be linear were not. The four-stage ascension in Black Elk's vision is really a movement for completion and a preparation for return. An examination of ritual also shows a four-phase movement to closure. All good things for the Dakota happened or were done in fours. But these things were not the four corners. They were the four quarters.

The circle is the visual and aural symbol of what Hegel called "good

12. Speaking of the concept of individualism in education today, Rosalie and Murray Wax state: "But these alienated and educated young Sioux might be lamenting the fact that their accomplishment signified little because it was truly individualistic. That their parents and relatives had not helped them though school seemed to be a cause for shame (1968, 168).

infinity" as distinguished from linear endlessness. And the task of most art and all religion was to translate the eternal into the phenomenal realm. One's parents could only teach one to acknowledge the ever widening spread of phenomenal relationships. Art and religion could introduce one to the eternal. Relatedness and responsibility permeated being. Consequently, even in the most intimate of all Dakota rituals, the vision quest, one's responsibility was to come in touch with and actualize what already was. It was not one's responsibility to create. Creation became translation. And the power to create, to see the unseen, to hear the unheard, and to heal came from the circle, a manifestation of the Great Spirit itself. Black Elk eloquently describes the power of the sacred as manifest in *natura naturata:*

> Everything the Power of the World does is done in a circle. The sky is round, and I have heard that the earth is round like a ball, and so are all the stars. The wind, in its greatest power, whirls. Birds make their nests in circles, for theirs is the same religion as ours. The sun comes forth and goes down again in a circle. The moon does the same, and both are round. Even the seasons form a great circle in their changing, and always come back to where they were. The life of a man is a circle from childhood to childhood, and so it is in everything where power moves. Our tepees were round like the nests of birds, and these were always set in a circle, the nation's hoop, a nest of many nests, where the Great Spirit meant for us to hatch our children.
>
> But the Wasichus have put us in these square boxes. Our power is gone and we are dying, for the power is not in us any more. (J. Neihardt 1979, 195–96)

The circle was manifest not only in the tipi and the hoop of the people, but also in the sacred shield.

Painting, among the Dakota, and quill and bead work, too, had three functions: to invoke power, to record events, and to decorate harmoniously. One might paint one's shield to invoke the power of his vision, to record past deeds of bravery, or simply for decoration. One might also paint on the outside of one's tipi for the same purposes. Another purpose was also fulfilled in tipi painting. Like the totem poles of the Northwest, tipi painting functioned as history and as advertising. It announced to all viewers, here lives a brave man, one must take notice. The body, also, was painted on such occasions as going on the warpath. Clothing was painted for decoration or, again, for special protection or rituals. The Dakota did not make a painting and then hide it in a museum. Painting was for the public. Painting was a means of unification. Painting was for the people.

The act of painting was divided according to sex. There were two styles: one used by men and one used by women. Men painted in a vivid, animated, nonperspectival style. Their paintings were generally naturalistic representations (lacking the third dimension) of hunting scenes, battles, or other memorable events. These paintings were rendered on skins, clothes, shields, and tipis. The painting of women was restricted to abstract designs either of geometric balance or of flowers. Neither sex worked in the style of the other. "This appears to be due to the fact that their naturalistic arts are often connected with magic and religious practices, which belong in the realm of men" (Douglas and D'Harncourt 1941, 145–46). Porcupine quill embroidery was the province of women. Quill decoration is a Native American craft, found nowhere else in the world. Feather work, such as in the war bonnet, had the function of invoking power and expressing status.

It may seem strange to talk about the architecture of a nomadic people, but the Dakota had architecture. He had the tipi, the sweat lodge, and the Sun Dance lodge. All three were circular, functional, and symbolic. The number of poles and size of a tipi, varied according to the wealth and status of the owner. The tipi, by its very nature, fostered sociality and sharing. There is no privacy in a tipi. One could obtain privacy only by putting a blanket over one's head, a practice used by courting lovers, whereupon the rest of the village pretended that they had ceased to exist. In the summer, the tipi was even more social because the lower sides were rolled up for air-conditioning. The most important tipi faced the East because it was the direction of enlightenment and the morning star. The circle of tipis was open to the east; the sweat lodge also faced east. It was small, circular, and had a circular pit in the center for the placing of heated stones.

The most complex form of Dakota architecture, the Sun Dance lodge, was also the most sacred. The center pole of the lodge was the ritualistically consecrated "whispering brother," the cottonwood. This pole was surrounded by twenty-eight poles. The numbers four and seven were sacred for the Dakota. As Black Elk said, when you add four sevens you get twenty-eight. Furthermore, he added that the "moon lives twenty-eight days, and this is our month" and informed Joseph Epes Brown, "You should also know that the buffalo has twenty-eight ribs, and that in our war bonnets we usually use twenty-eight feathers" (J. Brown 1974, 80). When one realizes that the Sun Dance was the most sacred of all Dakota rituals, and that it was a sacrifice not merely for the good of the people, but also for the good of their buffalo brothers—to ensure that the sacred species would survive and multiply—one can see the profound meanings in this numerology. Black Elk is even more specific in his description of the cosmic significance of the Sun Dance lodge: "I should explain to you that in setting up the sun dance lodge, we are really making the universe in a likeness; for, you see, each of the posts around the lodge represents some particular object of creation, so that the whole circle is the entire creation, and the one tree at the center, upon which the twenty-eight poles rest, is *Wakan-Tanka*, who is the center of everything. Everything comes from Him, and sooner or later everything returns to Him" (80). The architecture of the Dakota engendered a sense of relatedness, belonging, and felt identity.

Most dancing was done in a circle accompanied by the drum, also round. Most was done by the men alone, although women did participate in the ultimate dance of desperation, the Ghost Dance.[13] Singing and chanting were formulaic and exhibited a high degree of parallelism, repetition, and symmetry. The same was true of narrative stories, most of which were mythical and symbolic. Thus, one finds little narrative suspense in Dakota stories, for the epic dominates, and as in singing, the whole usually comes first. The rest is articulation of that whole.

Dakota religion was not based on nausea, fear, or a desperate yearning for another world. It was a religion of awe and acknowledged presence. Prayer was not primarily propitiatory, but sacramental. Its main function was to express gratitude and hope, hope for the good of people. Sacrifice and ritual had the same communal goal, the unity and good of the people. This religion was of felt identity, of wonder. Its function was to conjure presence, to present, maintain, and provide access to the holy. At the same time, it united the people, providing them with a sense of wholeness.

---

13. The Ghost Dance was introduced to the Dakota via Wovoka (Jack Wilson, a Paiute). Jack Wilson had traveled to the northeast coast and had come into contact there with the Shakers. There may be a women's liberation angle here.

Hence, it was also therapeutic, for the word *therapy* means "to make whole." Even the most painful sacrifice, the Sun Dance, was not done to exhibit bravery on the part of the dancer, but to provide benefits to the people. Beyond the individual lay society; beyond society lay the cosmos. Hence, even the most individual of all religious acts, the vision quest, was a quest for awareness of wider relatedness. Although the experience was personal, its meaning was communal. Thus, Black Elk's heirophantic realization was a *mysterium tremendum* that happened to him, but it was also a vision for the people, and he felt himself to be a failure for not having translated the eternal adequately into the phenomenal realm. And so he laments:

> I did not know then how much was ended. When I look back now from this high hill of my old age, I can still see the butchered women and children lying heaped and scattered all along the crooked gulch as plain as when I saw them with eyes still young. And I can see that something else died there in the bloody mud, and was buried in the blizzard. A people's dream died there. It was a beautiful dream.
>
> And I, to whom so great a vision was given in my youth,—you see me now a pitiful old man who has done nothing, for the nation's hoop is broken and scattered. There is no center any longer, and the sacred tree is dead. (J. Neihardt 1979, 270)

Even lamentation was social. When the one who lamented prayed, and especially when he prayed with the sacred pipe, he prayed for and with everything. No wonder the Dakota had a sense of objective relatedness, belonging, and felt identity.

Behavior: To Be Is to Share
(Fortitude, Fidelity, Bravery, and Generosity)

We have seen that the ontological stance of the Dakota was embodied in their institutions, thus engendering a sense of objective relatedness, belonging, and felt identity wherein the individual was autonomous and responsible. He saw it as his responsibility to exemplify the ideal, to actualize it, to translate the eternal into the phenomenal realm. The task remains to examine what the ideals of behavior were that the Dakota perceived himself destined to embody. The normative values that he believed to be necessary—not merely regulative, but constitutive of his behavior—were four: fortitude, fidelity, bravery, and generosity. They will be discussed in order of increasing value.

The Dakota were great orators. Council meetings were often as much an opportunity to display verbal pyrotechnics in the fullness of time as an opportunity to come to a decision about what was right for the people. Yet, the Dakota learned something as important as oratory very young. He learned to shut up. A squalling baby was no desirable asset if you are fleeing danger or huddled in the close dark surrounded by enemies. Hence, when the baby would cry, the Dakota mother would pinch its nostrils until it learned to be silent. Silence, that out of which sound comes and that into which it returns, was the first lesson learned with firm love. Fortitude began in the tipi or travois.

The early training in silence and patience would serve the boy well when he later went on his vision quest. This training was equally important for the girl. The Dakota believed that a desirable woman was one who exhibited poise, reserve, and dignity. Girls were taught not to laugh. Laughter can be a danger in a world where silence has strategic value. One learned early to adjust the expressions of one's feelings not to what one wanted, but to the objective demands of the given situation. It is not that the Dakota were laconic stoics. They were simply realists.

Plains weather is extreme. In winter the blizzards are brutal; the snow is deep, and the air is crackling cold. Always there is the wind. In summer the heat rises visibly from the Plains in writhing strands. In the spring there are hot tornadic winds. Only in fall are there the cool, reassuring breezes to create true Indian summer. To live in a world such as this demands that one cultivate patience, endurance, and fortitude. Furthermore, the life of the hunter is different from that of the settled round of the farmer. Sometimes the deer would be scarce, the buffalo would not be tempted to run, and the people were starving. Even the sacrifice of a finger joint to the world powers might not help. Again, patience, endurance, and fortitude were necessary. They were necessary not only for the individual, but also for the good of the people.

The most important event in the young boy's life was his vision quest. It put him in direct touch with the absolute, which provided him his adult name and his destiny. After instruction and purification, he had to walk forth alone clad only in a breechcloth, protected only by a few symbolic feathers and a sacred pipe, sit down in a sacred circle in the great solitude, and in utter humility and complete self-abnegation pray and await his destiny. He never kneeled in stuttering supplication; he never groveled; he faced the Great Mystery as a man and alone. If he received a vision, he returned to have it interpreted, and it then shaped his future. If Thunder Beings came in his vision, he had to become a *heyoka*, a contrariwise or backward man who lived as a tribal clown. If his spirit broke and he fled in fear or if he refused to go on the vision quest at all, he joined the women. No one condemned him.

Perhaps the situation that called for the greatest endurance and fortitude was the Sun Dance. It was an exhausting four-day ritual invested with intense holiness. The men who volunteered to be the dancers had their breasts and sometimes their backs pierced by bones that were then attached to the central sacred pole. On occasion they were additionally burdened by buffalo skulls. What might appear to us as torture was to the Dakota a highly sacred sacrifice. Suffering alters the focus of the mind. And although one might dance for some personal reason, such as to have a relative cured, the ultimate reason for the dance was the good of the people, the continuance of the buffalo, and the identity of all. The dancers wore rabbit skins, for the rabbit represented humility "because he is quiet and soft and not self-asserting—a quality which we must all possess when we go to the center of the world." Black Elk continues his description:

> When we go to the center of the hoop we shall all cry, for we should know that anything born into this world which you see about you must suffer and bear difficulties. We are now going to suffer at the center of the hoop, and by doing this may we take upon ourselves much of the suffering of our people. . . . [T]he flesh represents ignorance, and, thus, as we dance and break the thong loose, it is as if we were being freed from the bonds of the flesh. It is much the same as when you break a young colt. . . . We too are young colts when we start to dance, but soon we become broken and submit to the Great Spirit. (J. Brown 1974, 85)[14]

Eagle Voice also interprets this ritual. "In the sacred dance the proud heart dies with pain and thirst, hunger and weariness, that the power of Wakon

---

14. Compare this with the first Noble Truth of the Buddha: *Sabe Sankara Dukka*, know that to be is to suffer.

Tonka may come in and live there for the good of all the people. . . . It is a happy time; but it is also a time to suffer and endure, for pain is wise to teach and without courage there is nothing good" (J. Neihardt 1970, 115, 114). The Dakota endured. When it came to the wider *Wasichu* world, he did not prevail.

Oral-aural cultures foster a high degree of interdependence and strong loyalty. The Dakota were no different. Killing those people outside the group was sanctioned. Killing within the group was absolutely condemned. Regardless of his motives or justification, a kills-at-home was banished from the tribe. Only under truly exceptional circumstances was he ever accepted back among the people, and then his name was changed. Murder, for all practical purposes, was practically unknown. One was faithful to the people. Fidelity meant that one also trusted the word of another. When scouts returned with news of the enemy or of buffalo, no one questioned their word nor checked their information. Their word was their bond. Promises were meant to be kept; otherwise, promises were not made. A forked tongue was destructive of the people, for it made trust untenable. Luther Standing Bear's father advised him repeatedly that a man who lies is not liked by anybody, and so he learned to tell the truth, and it made him feel better. He describes his father running a country store in violation of "good American business practice": "Father did not need to look through a lot of books to determine what Running Horse owed him. When the other five dollars were paid, Father just crossed out all the lines. There were no receipts given. If Running Horse, or any other Indian, wanted credit in those days, they got it. They did not need to bring any security. Their word was as good as gold; they were still honest and uneducated" (1975, 102). The lessons Luther Standing Bear learned when he worked for Wannamaker's were not the ones taught by his father.

Besides fidelity to individual others and fidelity to the people, one had to be faithful to his personal vision. This destiny, once had, was never to be betrayed. To do so would have been worse than being inhuman; one would have been non-Dakota. Such intense fidelity was also exhibited in male bonding. A brother-friend did not have the same parents, but he was closer to you than your consanguineous brothers. You were as one person. If that meant you had to risk your life or even lose it for him, you did. Crazy Horse brought great honor on himself by turning alone against a band of Crow and rescuing a Sioux on foot. No matter how successful a war party, the leader was disgraced if he lost so much as a single man. Fidelity in everyday matters brought honesty and trust. Fidelity in war was an absolute necessity.

War, for the Dakota, was a great adventure. Eastman likens it to our current game of football. The Dakota did not fight like the white man did. They did not fight to conquer and subdue another tribe or to exterminate them. Killing did not mean much, and killing the white man meant even less. There was little bravery in such an act. Counting coup—touching an enemy with a stick—brought much greater honor. Touching him alive, or touching him with a hand, taking his gun from him while he was alive, was an even greater deed. Being wounded, especially in front, showed great courage, but the utmost of valor was to rescue an on-foot comrade who was surrounded by the enemy. Admiration of courage did not apply to one's warrior-brothers alone. Hence, when Standing Bear and others had a brave Pawnee surrounded, and he, refusing to move, wounded all five of his Dakota foes, they did not kill him or take him prisoner; they withdrew from the field.

Although bravery in concert was as good as it was necessary, individual bravery was even better, perhaps, in part, because it was not necessary. Going on a raiding party and stealing horses from the enemy brought great honor. Going on one's own and returning with booty brought even greater prestige. Going alone, on foot and unarmed, was the ultimate demonstration of courage and skill. Again, we are back to the concept of facing things alone. When, at the age of eleven, Luther Standing Bear volunteered to go to the *Wasichu* school at Carlysle, he did so not because he had the faintest idea what a white education would be or do for him, but because he was convinced that he would be killed. He believed that if he died a brave death in *Wasichu* country, it would bring great honor on him and please his father very much. The Dakota did not fear death. He feared the bad death—the death of betrayal, the death of cowardice, the death of decrepitude and nonaccomplishment. When the good death came, he sang.

The courage initiated in the vision quest was carried throughout life. Facing the Great Ultimate without running away, without fear and trembling, but tall and proud, confirmed one in his life's course and conferred his true name. One's name could also be changed by great acts of valor and bravery, especially in warfare. They were the names one earned. Bravery brought status. But even bravery was not enough to make one a chief. One could be a great warrior, hunter, and trusted brother, but to be a man whom all looked up to, something of even greater value than valor was necessary: generosity.

Generosity was the highest of Dakota virtues, a virtue so high that, perhaps, no man ever achieved it adequately, the ultimate expression of human-heartedness and the good of the nation, the ground for the life and succor of the Life of the lives of the people. Paraphrasing Confucius, one might imagine Black Elk to have said: "All my doctrine is strung on one sinew: generosity."

Embedded in our ordinary language are a multitude of unkind cuts against the Indian. But the most unkind of all is this: you are an Indian giver. The Dakota gave. They gave freely and without strings. And they gave for good. This truth does not mean that the Dakota was seeking to create for himself some guaranteed, birth-proof safety suit of social self-lessness. He was no saint, no noble savage. He knew the trauma of birth, the frustrations of life, the decrepitude of age, and the phobia of a disgraceful death. He knew that among him there were people who were venal as among others. But he also knew that to share was to survive. He had a different view of property. Sitting Bull remarked that the white man acquires things to keep them, but the Oglala gather things to give them away.

Territory and property are not the same thing. Territory is the habitation of the nation. It must be remembered, fought for, and cherished for the good of the nation and for the good of the four-leggeds and the wingeds of the air as well. Property implies a *who;* property belongs to somebody, property is a principle of division. But if space is one, indivisible, centered, recurrent, auditory, memorable, personal, and continuous, how could land ever possibly be *private* property? The land, the great rolling Plains, belonged to everybody or nobody. The Great Spirit ultimately "owned" everything and had created everything to be shared. Not only the land but also all beings belonged to him and all things. Man was but a caretaker of being, and eventually all would be returned to its proper owner, even one's own body. Therefore, as a temporary trustee of being, it was proper to share. Being was not having. To be was to share.

Generosity had many functions for the Dakota. Generosity was a technique of education, a means of achieving status, an economic necessity, and an expression of grieving. In the case of Luther Standing Bear, we saw that the divorce of material consequences from acts of achievement was a primary method of education. In the buffalo hunt, it was a great honor to be chosen as one of the lead killers, for this act not only acknowledged one's prowess in the kill but also meant that one's kills would go to the neediest in the village. Richard Erdoes describes it well:

> The Plains people were forever mindful of the poor, and especially those who could no longer care for themselves. Nobody was allowed to go without food or shelter. Often the crier would admonish the members of the warrior society: "Young men, you hunt well, we know. You never fail. Today you will feed the helpless. Old people who have no sons. Little ones who have no fathers. Women whose husbands are dead. What you kill today will be for them!" . . . Undistinguished and stingy men, bad fighters or hunters, were not invited to join the warrior's society. "Such men just live," said a brave old warrior. It was really the worst one could say about anybody. (1972, 32, 55)

Because every young boy yearned to be a member of the warrior's society, the lesson of the virtue of generosity and responsibility for the welfare of others was ingrained early.

Bravery was important in being a hunter or warrior. But bravery alone would never provide access to council or to the status of chief. For that event, as important as bravery was, one needed respect, and respect came from sharing with the people—not bribing, but sacrificing for the neediest of the nation. Because freedom meant growing in responsibility, once one became a counselor or a chief, he was responsible to be even more generous. Luther Standing Bear describes his becoming a chief:

> In different places they started to sing songs of praise for me. Frank Goings, the chief of the Indian Police and interpreter at the agency, had brought over the Boys' Band from the boarding school, with all their instruments. In between the Indian songs, the band would play. I then started giving away the things I brought along.
>
> I kept this up until I had given away everything I owned, and my wife and I walked away with practically nothing. We figured that we gave away that day about a thousand dollars' worth of goods ourselves, not

counting all the presents that had been donated to be distributed. (1975, 275–76)

Spiritual wealth and material wealth were not the same thing. A man was often wealthy in proportion to what he could afford to give away.

Beyond status, sharing was also an economic and political necessity and a method of grieving. The welfare of the whole depended on the welfare of each. A nomadic people cannot afford weak and disabled stragglers. Furthermore, at times of great productivity, such as after a successful hunt, all hands were needed for the butchering, drying of the meat, and treatment of the skins. Sharing with the less fortunate was an economic necessity. It was also a death ceremony. When Standing Bear's father died, he gave away all possessions, and he and his relatives lived off the land for two months to express their grief. When they returned to camp, they were given numerous gifts by others, and normal life was resumed.

Perhaps even more important than the fact of giving was the way of giving. Giving meant nothing if what was given was not of value to the giver, regardless of its value to the recipient. Furthermore, one did not give in order to gain recognition or to attain ephemeral gratitude. Though a shame culture, the Dakota did not give as do the Japanese whose concept of *on,* or indebtedness, drives them to give unto others before someone gives unto them. In fact, giving, if done properly, was done in such a way that the recipient was never saddled with a sense of internal regret. Generosity, that burden in some cultures most difficult to bear, was intended as simply sharing, as simply doing what was right, as simply doing what was proper for the people. Or, in some cases, it simply meant doing what the other desired. George Catlin tells of a Cheyenne with beautiful leggings. He tried several times to purchase the leggings to no avail. As his boat was pulling out from shore and heading down the river, the Cheyenne rode alongside and finally threw a package on board. Catlin unwrapped the package and found the leggings he could not purchase. By the time the unwrapping was done, the Cheyenne had disappeared. "To give without embarrassing or humiliating the receiver was as important as the gift itself" (Erdoes 1972, 83). The Cheyenne knew how to give. He would have been a good Dakota.

This essay has been an attempt to describe a people's world, a world of genuine participation, a world inhabited, not inhibited, a world not of absences but of presences. Categories are useless. But for those readers who like tags on things, one could say that Dakota philosophy was a combination of Platonic valuation and Bergsonian duration. This conceptualization may tell us something of the Dakota. Perhaps it will also tell us something about ourselves.

13

The Great Vision of Black Elk as Literary Ritual

R. TODD WISE

There are as many vantage points on the Great Vision of Black Elk as there are readers who have encountered it. In this essay I will discuss the hermeneutical implications of approaching Black Elk's vision as literature. The first part of the essay attempts to address some of the concerns regarding reader comprehension, and ultimately argues that Black Elk's vision can be grasped by persons with a rudimentary familiarity with Lakota culture. I will frame these remarks within the tensions found between the historical-critical method and a participatory hermeneutic. It was Black Elk's belief that his vision was not only for his people, but would also be relevant for persons outside his own Lakota context. The first sections of this essay address the implications of this transfer to literary culture in general through the exegetical considerations outlined by Eugen Drewermann (1990).[1] The final sections summarize some of the major ways in which the Great Vision has been interpreted by the academic community since the publication of *Black Elk Speaks*. These sections assess the contribution of traditional Lakota and Christian elements, arguing for a constructionist approach. The article as a whole attempts to support Black Elk's assumption that the outsider to Lakota culture could grasp the significance of the Great Vision through the medium of a text.[2]

Recent scholarship has clarified the meeting of John Neihardt with Nicholas Black Elk as a ritualized event (Holler 1984a). Black Elk made

1. For the term *literary culture,* I am borrowing from Sande Cohen (1988).

2. The testimonio-like format of *Black Elk Speaks* raises questions as to a selectivity in Black Elk's disclosure with Neihardt. Although all may not have been said, Black Elk assumed that what he did share could be grasped by others outside his Lakota context.

extensive ritual preparations by erecting a ceremonial tipi decorated with sacred symbols and by planting a circle of pine trees around his cabin. Neihardt's visit included a feast, dancing, kill talks, prayers, special clothing, and the smoking of the sacred pipe, all normal features of Lakota ritual. The event also included Black Elk's giving to Neihardt a morning-star pendant used in the most sacred of traditional Lakota rituals, the Sun Dance. Of chief significance in the encounter was the adoption of both Neihardt and his daughters into the Black Elk family, with Nicholas Black Elk becoming a spiritual father to all three. DeMallie states that each name corresponded to an aspect of Black Elk's Great Vision (DeMallie 1984a, 36). The new name given to John Neihardt, Flaming Rainbow *(Peyta-Wigmou-Ge)*, corresponded with the rainbow door of the Grandfathers in his Great Vision.[3] A further significant aspect of the ritual occurred at the close of the interviews when Black Elk presented the sacred pipe smoked during the meeting as a symbol of the passing of the Great Vision's power on to Neihardt (H. Neihardt 1995, 85).

Although there are many ways to approach the "intentions" or motivations of Black Elk's consent to the now famous meeting with John Neihardt, it is clear that Black Elk's central objective was the sharing of his Great Vision. Hilda Neihardt records in her journals during the meeting that Black Elk showed a minimal interest in historical facts about his life, but "when he talks about his vision he is marvelous!" (DeMallie 1984a, 40). Sources confirm that Black Elk conceived the entire affair as a historical extension or concretization of his vision. The ritual of renaming Neihardt as Flaming Rainbow was performed so that his vision could "'go out'—like the flames from the rainbow—so that people would understand its meaning" (37). As a result the Neihardts were incorporated into the living drama of Black Elk's Great Vision. Although there are many concerns in approaching *Black Elk Speaks*—Neihardt, for example, showed an appreciation for historical details—the central message of Black Elk's teaching to Neihardt was to convey the vision and its significance to others.

3. In an interview with Hilda Neihardt, Ben recalls how the naming of Neihardt was related to his poetic talents as a "word sender" (1995, 126). Enid was given the name *Ta-Sa-Ge-a-Luta-Win*, which Ben Black Elk translated as She Who Walks with Her Holy Red Staff. Hilda was named *Unpo Wichachpi Win*, or Daybreak Star Woman.

Black Elk's message produced several important dilemmas for his progeny. The sharing of sacred knowledge with an outsider was unprecedented and audacious, but not foreign to his character. Black Elk was a proved pioneer as shown through his travels with the Buffalo Bill Wild West Show, his work as a *wicasa wakan,* his bravery in battle, his participation in the Ghost Dance, and his conversion and involvement as a catechist in the Catholic Church. There is no question that the sharing of his vision was another bold experiment for him. Neihardt recorded that Black Elk "knew nothing" of literary culture—he could not read English, yet he attempted the transfer. Not only was he passing his intimate religious awareness to a cultural outsider to whom he had strong affinity, but he was also conveying it through the medium of a literary text to many unknown persons who received none of the special attention given to Neihardt. Lakota shamans had never attempted to initiate individuals into secret and sacred knowledge through the medium of literature. Perhaps it was as much of a question for him as it is for us today. Would this work?

The Literary Vision Quest

From our vantage point as readers and receivers, there are numerous sources that establish an assumption that it is difficult for mainstream literary culture to comprehend visionary experiences, placing the reader at a genuine disadvantage. Shamanic studies have charted a consistent prejudice by social science researchers to pathologize visions. Walsh has recently compared the various diagnoses of epilepsy, hysteria, and schizophrenia to shamanic experience (1997, 101*ff.*). Merkur also noted an inherent racism or cultural prejudice from the dominant Western scholarly community in its psychiatric stereotyping of whole cultural groups who valorize visionary communication (1992, 26). Even the charitable term *creative illness* finds current objection for the unique work of the shaman, because the conception of illness tends to "sicken" a profound wisdom (26).[4] Although many current discussions distinguish between the "exemplary" and the "pathological" attraction and orientation of visions, there is

---

4. Black Elk's complaint of illness could be seen as a work or effort, not without its physical costs.

enough said to indicate a hermeneutical problem with visionary experience in general.

There is a further indication that many mistake the literary form of vision for some other genre. Because Black Elk chose to speak not only through Neihardt but also to literary culture, his vision has become ciphers on a page. The reader is consequently faced with three major obstacles, which will be discussed in the body of this essay. He or she must first attempt to wrestle with an entrenched prejudice against visionary experience, must forego the physical ritual induction given to Neihardt, and, in most cases, must approach the vision as an outsider to the culture in which it was birthed. Although it is doubtful that Black Elk was fully aware of these obstacles, it is certain that he thought the attempt worth trying. Although the international impact of *Black Elk Speaks* establishes that literary culture has incorporated Black Elk's words as worthy of attention, it remains a question as to how much of the Great Vision is understood by the average reader.

The problem with understanding visionary experience and distinguishing the visionary genre is not a new one for Western literature. Biblical scholars have long noted the importance of determining literary form, distinguishing, for example, between a moral code and a song. We find some of the same dilemmas regarding Black Elk's vision in the exegesis of the Bible. An apt example is the entire book of Revelation, which is a visionary experience. Although scholarship has recognized that the visionary symbol deserves special consideration as a unique genre, it has not done so without disagreement. The hermeneutical wars that have been fought over interpreting certain passages in a "literal" or "symbolic" fashion illustrate some of the problems (that is, the pre, post, amillennial positions on Rev. 20:1–6). For scholars who interpret the vision of Revelation as a symbolic text, the isolated picking and choosing of certain portions as literal seems arbitrary. For example, though Ladd and Hoyt argue for a literal thousand-year reign of Christ, they maintain a symbolic interpretation of other numbers such as seven and twelve (Cohn 1970; Mounce 1977). Neither would say that a harlot "literally" "sits on seven hills" in Rev. 17:9.

It is consequently important to determine how the Great Vision will be read. The symbolic/literal debate indicates a need to distinguish the transcendent, partially irrational, and sometimes unknown referent of a symbol from the closed, specifically known identity of a sign. The former involves participation in depth, levels, and dimension, and the latter refers to an exact single-leveled meaning (that is, the cross of Christianity versus the limited meaning of a stop sign).[5] Not only does the reader have to contend with how Black Elk's vision is to be read as literal sign or metaphoric symbol or both, but he also has to contend with how it is to be seen or envisioned. Ricoeur observed the disparity between a "semiotics of language" and a "semiotics of image," stating that it is "a mistake to believe that everything semiotic is linguistic. At the same time, however, it is also an error to believe that the image does not arise from the semiotic order" (1978, 293–94, 311). Elsewhere, Gaston Bachelard has spoken of the rivalry of "word and image" in human epistemology (1964, xix*ff.*) Is the Great Vision symbolic or literal? Should the Great Vision be read without being envisioned?

Of course, we are free to read a text any way we like, but this does not mean that our approach is adequate to understanding the message of its communicator. To begin, we need to establish that the Great Vision was a vision, requiring unique hermeneutical attention. Because Black Elk states that he had a vision, we should take him at his word. DeMallie has broken the vision segments into eleven sections, which I will use here for illustration. As each segment is read, the reader might pause and momentarily image the section in the mind's eye to consider the difference between a linguistic and an imaginary form of comprehension. DeMallie records the following breaks in the vision text: 1) The two men take Black Elk up into the clouds; 2) Black Elk is shown the horses of the four directions; 3) the

---

5. Jung writes, "Every view which interprets the symbolic expression as analogue of an abbreviated designation for a known thing is semiotic. A view which interprets the symbolic expression as the best possible formulation of a relatively unknown thing, which for that reason cannot be more clearly or characteristically expressed, is symbolic" (Jung 1971, 6: 474). In one sense anything can be looked at as symbolic or literal. Charles Pierce has stressed that it is the subjective attitude that determines if an object is symbolic and not the object in itself (Heisig 1987). We are to contend with not only the "intended" meaning of a communicator, but the inexplicit multilevels of communication itself. Writers such as James Hillman (1979) argue for symbolic levels to all communication, acknowledging levels and a symbolic "underworld" to every perception. For Jürgen Habermas, the speaking and acting subject is not "master of his own house" but already surrenders to a preexistent network of *sensus communis,* indicating a "paleosymbolic" level to all communication and understanding (1985, 299*ff.*).

bay horse leads Black Elk to the cloud tipi of the six Grandfathers; 4) Black Elk walks the black sacred road from west to east and vanquishes the spirit in the water; 5) Black Elk walks the red sacred road from south to north; 6) Black Elk receives the healing herb of the north, and the sacred tree is established at the center of the nation's hoop; 7) Black Elk kills the dog in the flames and receives the healing herb of the West; 8) Black Elk is taken to the center of the earth and receives the daybreak-star herb; 9) Black Elk receives the soldier weed of destruction; 10) Black Elk returns to the six Grandfathers; and 11) the spotted eagle guides Black Elk home.

Not discounting the possibility that many persons can both read and see, it can be plausibly argued that a purely linguistic hermeneutic significantly alters the nuanced perspective and attraction of a vision, typically transferred in an oral and ritually conscious tradition. A vision in the eye of the seer is not the same as passively viewing a television or movie screen. In order to see the vision of another, it is necessary to use a disciplined imagination.[6] Moreover, the images that Black Elk is offering are to be grasped spontaneously by the viewer as his own breathing production. The unfolding of the vision script requires a participation in a dynamic symbolic space as an aspect of symbolic comprehension.[7] In short, we are asked to enter the vision mapped out by Black Elk's descriptions and explore the process that he described through our own imaginistic creations in our own local context.

The honest, natural, and immediate critique of such a visionary experiment is related to spontaneous alterations of our own imagination. "Seeing" may not mean viewing or understanding what Black Elk was communicating. For example, the crossed roads are described as enclosed in a circle of life with a tree at the center point. Although DeMallie de-

---

6. Esoteric Buddhism has always known the unique and difficult task of imaging the mandala, which is a meditative image (cf. Yuasa 1987, 124–56). We also know of the difficult preparations and ordeal of the vision quest in Lakota religious practices (cf. Stolzman 1996b, 9–12).

7. This is not unlike a game that is played on an open field. The entire rules and boundaries are nonmaterial in a sense. A child's pretending or a ball game is played within a conceptual framework that is mostly unseen outwardly. Although there may be some props such as lines or a referee, most of the game structure is envisioned through the mind's eye of the participants. Symbolic comprehension through a vision has certain analogies to the play and pretend of a game.

scribed the black road as symbolizing "warfare and destruction," Hilda Neihardt stated in a personal interview in 1997 that it reflects the hard "everyday difficulty" of everyday life, and Steltenkamp found the black road to represent "a way of evil" in a Christian sense (DeMallie 1984a, 86; Steltenkamp 1993, 96). Such differences affect the entire symmetry of the vision's central structural symbol. The distinction between "everyday difficulty" and "a way of evil" is particularly outstanding. The central concern among differing interpretations is the "truthful" referent or object that Black Elk was communicating. Although the concern for finding the "real" Black Elk or "the" "objective" explanation for his vision would be treated in many circles as an old Enlightenment idea, passé from a modern/postmodern point of view, it is my contention that Black Elk's unique message can be grasped even by an outsider to his Lakota community. In other words, I do not think that differences in perspective have to mean confusion for the reader.

Understanding Black Elk

Current writers describe "objectivity" itself in fluid, complex, and multileveled ways. For example, the disparate philosophical writings of Gadamer and Derrida illustrate significant points of view toward the "truth." While Gadamer has argued for a "truth" that can be found in our struggles with textual hermeneutics, Derrida has argued for "codes" and "signs" that are purely makeshift transcendent constructions or "debris" that immediately separate the reader from any truthful referent.[8] Consequently, a playfulness enters the contemporary approach to an object of textual study. Understanding *(Verstehen)* retains an intersubjectivity, but in a way that involves a play between deconstructing or mocking our interpretations, while promoting the construction of new ones. Such an ac-

8. Applying structural linguistic insights to the field of psychoanalysis, Jacques Lacan (1968) pointed out ways in which self-constructions and self-representations are a language and text. Lacan showed the relevancy of linguistic analysis by demonstrating how language allows the personality to posit itself. Language creates a "textual self," an "I," that replaces lived experience. This textual or linguistic "I" is a re-presentation of the actual self. This difference between the textual and the experiential self creates an unconscious order of experience. This distance or "gap" between the textual "I" and the lived personality is the unbridgeable experience that is referred to as the unconscious in psychoanalytic study.

tivity takes place at any level of analysis. Although there are perhaps many ways to describe this basic hermeneutical tension, it is one that is sharply encouraged when approaching the very difficult task of understanding another.

A multileveled playful entry into Black Elk's vision would also be multivoiced through the appreciation of other perspectives and ways of seeing. Such an approach serves to protect the subject matter against a narrow deciphering for the one "right" answer, as well as holds the symbolic/literal debate within a larger dialogue of possibility. Eugen Drewermann has recently argued for a twofold approach to textual study that accepts the complexity of multileveled symbolic participation (1990). His depth psychological exegesis distinguishes a basic hermeneutical difference between the historical-critical *(historisch)* approach and an unhistorical *(unhistorischen)* hermeneutic.[9] The "unhistorical" approach refers to the timeless internal meaning and participation with a symbol. By "timeless" Drewermann does not mean Platonic essences, which are nonhistorical, but asserts that symbolic texts share a common meaning in every historical situation, making them meaningful at all times in time. The actual historical application of symbolic meaning involves a connection with archetypal patterns rooted in our own local time and space.

The dynamic relationship between the live archetypes of symbolic comprehension and the historical facts that outline the evolution of a text entails a respect for both points of view. Drewermann states that the unhistorical approach to a symbolic text does not replace the historical-critical method, but presupposes it. Clifford Geertz described this same

---

9. The history-of-religions approach follows a similar division with the historical, which includes all levels of symbolic experience, and historicism, which is an areligious modern "decomposition product of Christianity" (Rennie 1996, 103). Drewermann and Eliade are not concerned with meaningless external accidental data. They share a critique of the one-sided emphasis on reason in the historical-critical method. Also, Drewermann uses a distinction of outward *(aeusserlich)* and inward *(innerlich)*, to distinguish "historical" and "unhistorical." Drewermann borrows from depth psychology to transform historical inquiry, and emphasizes Kierkegaard's "simultaneity" or "contemporaneity" *(Gleichzeitigkeit)*. The attention is taken away from a privileged "objective" understanding given to the original speaker (Black Elk) and placed on the shared present perspective of current readers/hearers (Drewermann 1990, 59). The concern is not only with the subjectivity of history, but also with the unique personal history of each reader and how this contributes to understanding. I discuss Drewermann more fully in my dissertation (1995b).

relationship when he stressed that the "universal" aspects of a symbol are always "local," demonstrating that our reflections and intuitions regarding universal and "timeless" themes are possible only through an appreciation of the very specific local context (1982). All relevant historical information serves to amplify our application and involvement with the symbolic. In other words, if we do not become familiar with the descriptions that Black Elk or Lakota people give for their own symbols, as well as the interpretations we give for these same symbols from our own historical context, we risk losing the "real" historical orientation of Black Elk's message. Our hermeneutical task is to maintain a dialogue between the meanings of our own "local" visionings and the approximate historical reconstructions of Black Elk's time.

Drewermann cautions against treating a symbolic text as a mere archaeological object or shard. Although presupposing a continued dialogue with historical sources, Drewermann claims that symbolic apprehension demands a level of participation utterly different from the historical-critical method. Expressing a thinking pattern dominant between 1880 and 1920, the historical-critical method has tended to see history as "objective" facts that isolate the "subject" from the hermeneutical process (Drewermann 1990, 19). As a rational linear cognitive endeavor, the historical analysis of the symbolic image encourages forms of detachment and a conscious distance between then and now (Schramm 1992). In contrast, there is an immense literature that suggests that a vision cannot be understood through "objective distance." Rather than frame our approach to Black Elk's vision in a nonparticipatory "objective" polemic (that is, symbolic/literal debate), we can rephrase our dilemma as a difference between a historical-critical and an "unhistorical" participatory approach.

An acceptance of both the historical-critical and a participatory hermeneutic seems to be of particular importance with Black Elk's visionary text. Perhaps we may begin with only a rudimentary impression of what Black Elk has seen, reading Neihardt's rendition with no other sources and no other knowledge of Lakota culture. In Drewermann's framework this would be an acceptable first approach.[10] Drewermann has

---

10. Symbols can evoke an understanding and attraction in any context. Following Levi-Strauss, Turner recognized the binary nature of all symbols in that symbols carry contradictory or opposing forces or forms. Because symbols carry opposing meanings, they in-

argued that it is the feeling *(Gefühl)* element that is most crucial in the comprehension of a symbol, referring us to levels beyond a rational linear awareness. The German word for symbol *(Sinnbild)* expresses a tension between known and irrationally known. While *Sinn* refers to a conscious meaning, *Bild* (picture) involves forms of participation that are sometimes vague, or unconscious. Pictorial symbols orient the participant to an awareness beyond linguistic expression.[11] Because of the emotional attraction or fascination with symbolic images, Black Elk's vision can in some respects do the work of bringing persons to the "same place," in historically parallel or convergent settings, without extensive historical reading.[12]

---

volve a dialogue between structure and antistructure. For example, the cross in Christian circles represents life and death. Certain rituals address murderous or sexualized impulses, while at the same time offering taboos. The Oedipus conflict displays both an impulse to love the mother and a warning against it. For Turner, the symbols consequently serve to evoke raw impulses or desires, show tensions between these impulses and societal norms, and to help "canalize" this raw energy into appropriate social forms (1992).

11. Ferdinand de Saussure had trouble with this distinction as shown in his reactions against Wilhelm von Humboldt (Jameson 1981, 108–9). Humboldt bifurcated thinking into the linguistic and prelinguistic. The prelinguistic level implied a level of thinking that was outside language, a "nonconceptual and non-self conscious" state akin to the sensory awareness of an infant or animal. Saussure rejected any protolinguistic analysis. However, numerous approaches from outside a linguistic structuralist perspective confirm Humboldt's early observations. Biogenetic structuralists describe symbolic comprehension as involving brain structures not connected with language (cf. d'Aquili 1983). Ethnologists have used Niko Tinbergen's hypothesis of innate releasing mechanisms to describe "lock and key" patterns of innate perception that are not learned by speech and can be used to interpret symbolic responsiveness (cf. Stevens 1983, 56). Acterberg (1985) has documented the physical reactions to symbolic imagery described as "eidetikers." Heart rate, blood pressure, fight/flight mechanisms, endorphins and enkephalins, skin temperature, and other spontaneous biochemical reactions are associated with the symbolic image. Elsewhere, mind-body scholars have discussed the ongoing nonverbal comprehension of the body and space in symbolic comprehension, advancing beyond Merleau-Ponty's discussion of spatial body and habit body (cf. Yuasa 1987). Eliade has noted the up and down axis of the body and the directional orientation of the shoulders as essential features of symbolic comprehension (Eliade 1978).

12. But, on second glance, it will not be easy to let the symbols do their work if we do not examine our prejudices, because our prejudices affect the historical application of the vision. An unexamined superficial integration can lead to hasty "collective" associations that may simply perpetuate cultural arrogance or "colonialism." We risk perpetuating our unexamined prejudices and our "imperialism" when we do not remain in a playful dialogue with the "truth" or historical relevance of the Great Vision. The increased awareness of historical

But symbolic comprehension is no easy task. Black Elk's own ritual preparations and instruction to Neihardt suggest his acknowledgment of the special kind of attention that is needed. For the apprehension of the symbols in his Great Vision Black Elk referred to a "clarity of understanding." While describing the symbolic image of the first Grandfather of his Great Vision to John Neihardt, Black Elk offered the following instruction to Neihardt when referring to the Grandfather's gift of power: "If you think about it, you can see it is true" (J. Neihardt 1979, 5). For Black Elk, and his Lakota culture in general, belief and knowledge were equated; understanding was experiential and playful. The point of the vision symbol was not found through general philosophical truths, but through the power that was to fill the seer or student. While describing the message of the Grandfather in his Great Vision, Black Elk recognized the possible distance and abstraction for Neihardt. His instruction to "think" and "see" illustrates his desire to pass to Neihardt the lived "clarity of understanding."

Clarity may involve more than an appreciation of image and sight, but will likely include the embodied and spatial factors of symbolic comprehension. Black Elk's "clarity" is not Descartes's "clear and distinct" ideas (cogito), which separate mind from body, subject from object, or person from his lived world. Historically we know from Black Elk's own life and from Lakota culture that a vision was frequently required to be acted out in ritual or dance form. The gesture and reaction of the actor or ritual participant communicated a fuller understanding of the symbolic referent in an embodied manner. There would be important affective codes conveyed through a body hermeneutic.[13] Although there is a substantiated bias in Western scholarship against an appreciation of an embodied and spatial epistemology, current authors speak of a "hazy" or dark consciousness of the body that contributes significantly to symbolic apprehension.[14] "So-

---

context amplifies, clarifies, and expands our involvement with the picture we have already formed. Although crucial to the process, historical precision and accuracy cannot be used in place of a participatory grasp of Black Elk's vision.

13. There have been attempts to enact Black Elk's message through a self-reflexive drama (cf. Laeuchli 1996).

14. Symbolic studies have stressed the importance of bodily reactions and the grasp of resistances. Yuasa (1987) draws a distinction of "bright" and "dark" consciousness, where "dark" consciousness involves forms of perception connected with an "acting intuition" as-

matic knowing" and reactions to "silence" are considered crucial hermeneutical features to symbol and ritual (Laeuchli 1992). We become inspired at many levels of awareness.

Spontaneous feeling and the habits of the body may also show possible defensiveness or resistance. We may experience a sense of fear or hesitation. Philosophical writers maintain that genuine understanding requires a self-reflexive dialogue with our own prejudices. Gadamer (1994) and Heidegger have shown that our prejudices are "thrown" prior to our awareness as essential structures of understanding. A full engagement with Black Elk's vision would entail an awareness of our limitations and biases. Because we cannot pretend to dispose of biases for a more "objective" understanding, we embrace any immediate or spontaneous reactions as an expression of boundaries to be explored. Staying in dialogue with the anxiety or uncertainty of these boundaries leads to further forms of awareness.

When we read of possible biases on the part of Neihardt, such as his interest in seeing Black Elk as a tragic figure in the wake of a Western Christian expansion, we actually come closer to what Black Elk has to say. Likewise, when we discover our own prejudices, both positive and negative, we can distinguish Black Elk's position for our situation. Self-reflexivity and the examinations of defensiveness, resistance, and anxiety can reach affective aspects. How do I respond? What is my reaction and orientation? That I have come in contact with a genuine feeling, impression, or prejudice is in fact a step forward in my contact with what Black Elk has to communicate. Above all it is the effort to participate, empathize, and understand that is important. Our attempts to grasp Black Elk's message are never a mere romantic illusion, but are our contact, limited and inadequate as it may be.[15] The illusion begins when we do not

---

sociated with the body and spatial orientation. Yuasa states that psychological resistances are related to this form of spontaneous perception.

15. A historical-critical illusion might be the positing of objective "origins," which distance the reader from the hermeneutical event itself. The Nietzschean sense of "genealogical" history serves to express the relation of history to symbol/myth as found in the history of religions. Rather than a "linear" model of historiography that proceeds from a historical "origin," a genealogical historiographer traces an interpretive event "backward" in time from the hermeneutical event (1956, 156*ff.*).

continue to seek understanding, close ourselves to other perspectives, lie, or opt for a metahistorical survey to objectify and circumvent self-involvement.

The Literary Ritual

In his study of the reading practices of the early Puritans, Ebersole has recognized a ritual action to reading itself (1995, 35). Although the devotional religious reading habits of seventeenth-century Puritans are certainly distinct, there are analogies for literature reading in general. The habits of reading, our posture, our focus and trance, and somatically invoked reactions indicate a ritual quality to serious reading.[16] The quasi-ritual status given to reading is not without significance for literary study. There is a sense that we may consider the continued interest in Black Elk's message as a communal effort of literary culture as a whole to grasp his Great Vision. Our dialogue with others in the written community creates a certain interdependence and interpretative tradition. In one sense, the literary ritual has its own unique point of view, distinct from nonliterary perspectives.[17]

Several writers have contributed to a fuller literary sense of Black Elk's vision. There have been three major emphases to consider, which include seeing the vision as: 1) a Lakota nonuniversalistic message, 2) a Christian message, and 3) a Christian-Lakota message with universal implications. Although Julian Rice pays little attention to the Great Vision directly, he represents the first position by describing a nonuniversalistic Black Elk who ultimately speaks in order to protect his uniquely Lakota purpose.

16. Turner (1992) recognizes a "preliminal," "liminal," and "postliminal" phase to ritual. He assigned the status of "liminoid" to many modern-day quasi-ritual activities. A recent example might be computer use.

17. Reading and writing are certainly treated with the exactness of a ritual. Turner (1992) finds that liminal activity creates a *communitas* or profound communal bond. He also notes differences of emic (insider) and etic (outsider) perspectives in ritual. Zuesse (1979) records micro, meso, macro levels of analysis. Winquist (1983) has recently discussed (theological) literature and reflection as a "genre of symbolic action." Literary reading and writing can be conceived as a liminal-ritual activity for culture in which a "trace of the body" is found through the "body of the text" in the silence and gaps of textual writing. The "imperialism of speech" halts before a larger metaphorical understanding.

Rice acknowledges the metaphorical nature of the Great Vision (Rice 1991, 152), and of a "metaphorical character" to Lakota consciousness. He notes how Black Elk repeatedly ritualized his Great Vision throughout his life in a "historical unfolding," signifying a paradigmatic guide to which Black Elk returned over and over. What is significant for our purposes is Rice's tendency to attribute no "universal" message to Black Elk's vision, other than through the editorial liberties of Neihardt. Rice portrayed Neihardt as a "transcendentalist" and a believer in Manifest Destiny and Western expansion (21). Neihardt's own writings regarding the Ghost Dance and the Messiah movement as a transition to Christianity illustrate for Rice an ethnocidal aspect to what Rice notes as embellishments of the purposes and intentions of the Great Vision. Rice clearly states that it is Neihardt who added the universal application to fit his portrayal of a tragic Black Elk and a dying Lakota culture (15–35).

The helpful aspects of Rice's polemic are the contemporary concern for textual violence against indigenous people, more specifically the Lakota. For Rice, the contents of the Great Vision are property of a Lakota context. Rice encourages deep suspicions of comparative or "collective" interpretations to the Great Vision in an effort to preserve Black Elk's Lakota voice. Although Rice tends to see "ecumenism" and "Christian Platonism" in many of the literary interpretations of Black Elk, we can appreciate his reminder of Black Elk's specific context, which on many levels was hostile to traditionalism. The "ban" on the Sun Dance from 1883 to 1933, which continued in a de facto form to the 1950s, is a stark reminder of a hostility toward traditional Lakota religious culture. It is entirely possible that Neihardt could have been an extension of dominant culture violence. Rice mentions the figure of Sharp Nose, whom Black Elk knew and spoke of, and who lied about the sacred to protect his people (Rice 1991, 148). Rice believes that like Sharp Nose, Black Elk spoke to protect his people, and that it is possible that his reports to Neihardt involved deception.

Holler has recently stated that is possible to see Rice's own descriptions of Lakota culture as romanticist in that Rice tends to argue for a pristine traditional culture (Holler 1995, 28). Although Rice's observations undoubtedly point to an important hermeneutical consideration, that Black Elk spoke under oppressive conditions, his tendency to portray all of Black Elk's Lakota context as in disharmony with Christianity and mainstream culture is a bit of a stretch. Rice finds "ecumenism" not only in Neihardt, but also in such recent authors as Vine Deloria Jr. and Raymond DeMallie for incorporating a "universalism" to Black Elk's message, which Rice stresses was foreign to Black Elk and his culture (Rice 1991, 18). Hilda Neihardt has recently stated to the contrary that it was Black Elk's "expressed wish" that the vision would be saved as something that applied "to all people" (1995, 120). Rice counters any universalist claims of Black Elk himself with a sociofunctionalist explanation of Black Elk's Christianity, stating that Black Elk involved himself in Christianity "for a warrior's reasons" (Rice 1991, xi).

There are two further reasons for considering Rice's polemic against a universalist interpretation. DeMallie has identified numerous aspects of the Great Vision as conventional Lakota symbols. The horseback riders that are painted with lightning streaks and race across the sky are shown as conventional embodiments of Thunder Beings. The color of the horses and their associations with the four directions is also from Lakota culture. In addition, DeMallie notices several points of agreement in Black Elk's vision with other visions from other Lakota natives. He argues that the greatness of Black Elk's vision lies not so much in its uniqueness, but in its "representativeness" of Lakota culture. Destruction and renewal, the powers of earth and sky and of land and water, the four directions, the contact of the living with the dead, are all considered Lakota. The central tree surrounded by the circle of life signified the Sun Dance pole and ritual. DeMallie states that a hasty comparison of common archetypes with other religious cultures misses the fact that such universalistic applications were foreign to Lakota culture (86).

Beyond the representative and conventional nature of the Great Vision, Rice's views add additional consideration for what is not spoken by Black Elk. Black Elk himself never offered a final interpretation for his Great Vision. We have his witness, but not his interpretation. There are plenty of gaps and openings, and much that is not said. Merleau-Ponty has shown that silence is in fact "alive with words," and so we begin to flesh out latent questions raised by what Black Elk has not said. Rice's views direct us to an "oppositional text" that may be hidden from our immediate hermeneutical awareness (cf. Foucault 1977). As we move through Black Elk's vision, Rice reminds us of other possible linkages that may not be obvious to all readers. By illuminating a potential bias in stressing the woes of a traditional Lakota culture with a universalist message foreign to Lakota cultures, Rice allows us to see a possible hidden dimension to Black Elk's message.

Tipping the scale in another direction within the literary community is the Jesuit Michael F. Steltenkamp, who worked on the Pine Ridge Reservation in the 1970s. Steltenkamp opposes the view that Black Elk was an old man despairing with nostalgia for bygone days. Like Rice, he sees Black Elk as an advocate for his people. Steltenkamp, however, differs sharply with Rice in that he evaluates Black Elk as a progressive Catholic leader who is concerned about the spiritual void developing in the Lakota community. He conceives Black Elk, through the disclosure of the Great Vision, as trying to reach out through spiritual means in the service of a solid commitment to Christianity. Black Elk was a respected Catholic catechist at the time of the Neihardt interviews, and by some calculations contributed to more than four hundred conversions to Christianity. Steltenkamp critiques Rice's perspective as "armchair ethnology" and portrays Black Elk as a Christian warrior.

For our purposes the Steltenkamp perspective adds a different reading to the Great Vision. Offering his own oppositional text within a position of silence, Steltenkamp points to the widely used "Two Roads Map" that was a picture catechism used by the early missionaries. Black Elk himself was intimately familiar with the map and used it often as a teaching device in his work as a catechist. The maps picture Christian salvation history through a two-roads format, "a golden road leading to heaven and a black one ending in hell" (Steltenkamp 1993, 94). Steltenkamp described these maps as demonstrating in "picture form the basic world view of traditional Christian theology" (95). To Rice's consternation, Steltenkamp finds numerous parallels of Black Elk's vision to the very Christian Two Roads Map. They include "thunder beings, a daybreak star, flying men, tree imagery, circled villages, a black road, a red road, friendly wings, an evil blue man living in flames, a place where people moaned and mourned, emphasis on the people's history, and gaudily portrayed, self-indulgent individuals" (95).

DeMallie also acknowledges Christian influences, some of which are indirectly related to Black Elk's participation in the Ghost Dance religion. DeMallie documents a pantribal universalistic tone and a stress on Christian redemption, and adds that the "reinterpretation" of the six Grandfathers as six-in-one illustrates a Christian influence. DeMallie credits Black Elk himself with interpreting the sacred hoop "as symbolizing all the continents of the world and embracing peoples of all colors" (1984a, 89). DeMallie finds the promise of salvation for all peoples within the harmony of the sacred circle as Christian. Steltenkamp attributes further Christian nuances to Black Elk's vision with his direct comparison of the Two Roads Map to the roads imagery of the Great Vision. Steltenkamp acknowledges Black Elk's role as an intercessor for his people, quoting Black Elk as attempting to bring his people "out of the black road to the red road" (1993, 96).[18] Rather than follow DeMallie's interpretation of the roads imagery as conventional Lakota symbols, Steltenkamp detects an actual blending of Black Elk's imagery with the Two Roads Map. He states that he is tempted "to find a complete one-to-one correspondence between the two" (98). Steltenkamp argued that it is likely that Black Elk's original vision was "a foreshadowing of what was later amplified via Ghost Dance themes and the Two Roads Map" (99). The blending that Steltenkamp sees in the Great Vision is portrayed as a continuum of Black Elk's own religious development, from Lakota medicine man to Catholic catechist.

The weight of Steltenkamp's comparative hypothesis is "ultimately" supported by Black Elk's daughter, Lucy Looks Twice. Steltenkamp's record of his interviews with Lucy Looks Twice includes discussing her recollection of her father's conversion, her belief that her father did not speak out of sadness during the Neihardt interviews, and her memory that her father wanted to be most remembered as a praying Christian man. Steltenkamp records Lucy as stating that the tree of her father's Great Vision, the tree that may someday bloom, represented her father's hope for the Catholic faith in the Lakota community (1993, 109). The tree of the Sun Dance is here replaced with the "tree" or cross of Christianity. Through these remarks, Steltenkamp tends to reduce Black Elk's spontaneous vision to a mere recapitulation of the Two Roads Map in the service

18. He curiously leaves out the next remarks of Black Elk to clarify his purpose of getting his "people back into the hoop again" (DeMallie 1984a, 294). Steltenkamp's association of the black road with the "way of evil" is not really substantiated by anything Black Elk has said. His argument should be accepted as a conjecture.

of Black Elk's commitments as a Christian teacher. Steltenkamp cautions
that "those who have chosen instead to hunt for something more sublime
will, as before, never catch it" (173).

Holler has critiqued Steltenkamp's use of the Looks Twice interviews
as not taking into sufficient account her own context (Holler 1995, 14).
The interviews took place in 1973 in the aftermath of the AIM occupation
of Wounded Knee. Black Elk and his testimony carried social and political
implications, both then and now, in Lakota culture that warrant a cautious
contextual reading. Holler chides Steltenkamp for not addressing Lucy
Looks Twice's own contextual biases, because her stress on a Christian
Black Elk may have been meant to distance him and her from a militant
traditionalism. Recent publication of Hilda Neihardt's recollection of the
interviews supports Holler's remarks. During a visit at the annual Neihardt Day in Bancroft, Nebraska, in 1977 Lucy confided in Hilda Neihardt about Black Elk's death. Before passing away Black Elk told Lucy
that "The only thing I really believe is the pipe religion." Hilda surmises
that the statements Looks Twice had made to Steltenkamp had probably
troubled her because Lucy had not even read *Black Elk Speaks* until after
her meeting with Steltenkamp. Although Steltenkamp's portrayal of Lucy
shows a fervent and loyal Catholic, Hilda records that Lucy became a pipe
carrier in her later years (1995, 119). Upon the death of her husband Leo
Looks Twice, Lucy reported to Hilda that her Catholic religion "didn't
help me." It was after Steltenkamp's interviews that Lucy read her father's
work, stating it "changed my life." Because Steltenkamp's own conclusions rested "ultimately" on Looks Twice's recollections during the 1973
context, her 1977 testimony throws into question Steltenkamp's entire
conjecture.

Steltenkamp's position regarding the Great Vision does, however,
contribute for its consideration of a "blending" and of the influence of
Christianity. Although special consideration must be given to the reliance
of memory in an oral culture and to the special role of *wicasa wakan* in
Lakota culture, it is widely held that early "memory" is a constructive
process and not faithfully reproductive or eidetic (Bartlett 1932).[19] Cur-

19. Steinmetz recorded eleven basic versions of the White Buffalo Calf Woman, and
noted that each tribe and each holy man had their own versions to sacred stories. Elsewhere,
C. G. Jung has pointed out the problems with perceiving symbolic imagery as purely re-

rent scholarship on memory recognizes that biases contribute to the alteration of memory (Bruhn and Last 1982). Steltenkamp's argument for a
blending in the Great Vision fits with what is known about memory and its
tendency to find the greatest relevance in the present. In light of the holistic orientational significance of the symbol for the present existential situation, it may be best to speak of a maturing and adaption of original
imagery to the changing historical situation. Black Elk states, "It was as I
grew older that the meanings came clearer and clearer out of the pictures
and the words [of the Great Vision]; and even now I know that more was
shown to me than I can tell" (J. Neihardt 1979, 49). That the meaning of
the Great Vision became clearer with time is a testament to the continuing
relevance of his vision for his changing context. A specific example is with
the destructive soldier weed of his Great Vision. Black Elk told Neihardt
that he was to wipe out his enemies, including women and children, when
he reached the age of thirty-seven. Black Elk refused to honor this aspect
of his vision, in order to elevate a deeper significance.[20]

Holler has critiqued either/or presentations of Black Elk as a Catholic
or a traditionalist. Casting doubt on both Rice's one-sided traditionalist
view and Steltenkamp's "Two Roads" ecumenism, Holler expresses concern for those critics who imply that Black Elk was insincere. Holler holds
that Black Elk's involvement in Christianity and traditional Lakota religion should be taken as sincere and not as attempts for a sophisticated deception. Rather than approaching Black Elk's "dual participation" in the
form of separate and distinct propositional truths, in order to find either a
Lakota or a Christian Black Elk, Holler points to Black Elk's creative participation with sacred power. "Black Elk seems to have seen two basically
compatible beliefs, or two modalities of what was primary, the sacred"

---

gressive and reductive to a former time in his critique of Freud's perspective. From his notion of "transcendent function" Jung describes ways in which imagery projects its "essential" structures into the present and future. For Jung, imagery is mimesis and poesis (cf.
1956, 5: par. 25; 1953, 7: par. 122). Memory, in other words, is related to contemporary
relevance.

20. Neihardt himself excluded the soldier-weed section of the Great Vision in *Black
Elk Speaks*. The reader can find this portion in DeMallie 1984a (135–37). DeMallie holds
that Neihardt, like Black Elk, excluded this aspect because the warlike destruction did not
square with the inclusive universalistic aspects of the Great Vision.

(Holler 1995, 220).[21] The witness of his Great Vision was his best description of his relationship to the sacred. Similar to some of Drewermann's remarks about a distinction between the historical critical and an unhistorical hermeneutic discussed earlier in this article, Holler states that it is the historical-critical consciousness, with its tendency to objectify a process, that creates the "either/or" cognitive dissonance for literary culture.

Although literary culture identifies at least two oppositional texts related to his traditionalism and Catholicism, Black Elk expressed a coherent relationship to the sacred through the disclosure of his Great Vision.[22] I have argued for a constructivist understanding. Although Black Elk experienced the Great Vision initially as a nine-year-old boy, the vision he shared with Neihardt had gone through years of clarification and testing. Black Elk was "clearer" about his vision as time progressed, and consciously stressed aspects of the Ghost Dance and Christianity in his Great Vision as they converged in his understanding. Not only did his vision shape historical events, but, to some extent, history also clarified his original visionary perception. Consequently, the Great Vision represents a creative unified expression of the sacred, colored by his maturation in a traditional Lakota and Christian context.

I have argued that an outsider to the Lakota culture can gain an un-

21. Several authors have commented on the problematic nature of the term *sacred* (Rennie 1996). The usefulness of the term is to highlight the religious aspect of symbolic apprehension. The history of religion uses the term not as an a priori category of the mind, or to obscure a subject matter, but as an existential awareness of transcendent "truth." Eliade has described this as a "transconscious" awareness, illustrating the most comprehensive approach to the "real." Eliade's *Sacred and Profane* was a response and further extension and development of Otto's analysis of the "holy" (*das Heilige*) as a *mysterium tremendum et fascinans* (Eliade 1961).

22. Black Elk's message seems to confront the pagan/Christian distinctions entrenched in the history of Western religion. Laeuchli records the intense ambiguity and politics of Christian councils, particularly in the early Church. An example is with creedal formulas that forbade "pagan" art forms. This statement existed side by side in Church centers with the strict creedal statements against them. He refers to this situation as a "transmythologization," which illuminates a larger, more complex relationship of pagan and Christian. Black Elk's witness could be approached as a Living Word or Logos that transcends pagan/Christian conceptions (1980).

derstanding of Black Elk's Great Vision. The approach I have stressed is symbolic within a historical-critical and participatory hermeneutic. Although literary culture expresses its own ritual through scholarly dialogue and the reading of texts, I have proposed alternative approaches to counter the bias of historical-critical methods found in the reading community. The disparate reactions to John Neihardt's record of Black Elk's vision have illustrated ways in which literary culture explores hidden textual oppositions, revealing forms of engagement with the Great Vision. Against a closed, final, or authoritative interpretation that forces the reader into an "objective" either/or position, I have shown ways in which readers can participate by historically amplifying and clarifying the levels and dimensions of the Great Vision in the present context.

Black Elk's silence on a final interpretation is instructive because symbol and myth refer ultimately to that which is unspeakable.[23] Our basic hermeneutical task is to relate Black Elk's experience with the sacred, shown in his Great Vision, to our own experience with the sacred today. Such a task is beyond rationality, consciousness, and words, because our whole being must express what is most profoundly meaningful. Perhaps a multiperspectival, polyphonic approach to visionary experience may assist the contemporary understanding of Black Elk's legacy better than the point of view of any one "absolute subject" or interpretation (Clifford 1988, 23). Our ability to catch some of the dynamic Black Elk offered depends, according to contemporary writers, on our own ability to playfully respect and participate with many levels. A Socratic multivocal dialogue could serve to enhance the continuing relevance of Black Elk's Great Vision for our own context.

---

23. DeMallie states the vision means "that the powers of the Lakota universe exist and have the ability to aid mankind in all endeavors, to protect people from disease and from their enemies and to bring joy and contentment." It was said and sent out through Neihardt to "make the tree blossom" through "bringing Indians and non-Indians together in the harmony of a common circle" (1984a, 53).

14

The New Missiology and Black Elk's Individuation

PAUL B. STEINMETZ, S.J.

In recent years scholars have engaged in an extensive discussion of the relationship between the traditional and Christian religions in Black Elk's life (Holler 1984b, 1995; DeMallie 1984a; Rice 1991; Steinmetz 1998; Steltenkamp 1993).[1] The purpose of this chapter is to show that Black Elk is best understood as a person who followed the path of individuation to-

---

1. William Powers attempts to discredit both *Black Elk Speaks* and *The Sacred Pipe* as authentic documents: "One of the most critical disciplines [anthropology] has ironically almost totally ignored the possibility that much of what Black Elk had to say was manufactured by a white man" (1990c, 146). It is true that we must trust Ben Black Elk as a faithful interpreter and John Neihardt and Joseph Brown as faithful transcribers. There is no evidence that they were not. As regards *Black Elk Speaks*, the method guaranteed accuracy. Regarding *The Sacred Pipe*, questioning Brown's method for its accuracy is being judgmental, doubting his professionalism without evidence. There is no evidence that Brown had any hidden agenda, and certainly there was no reason for him to add Christian elements to Black Elk's account because the Indian and non-Indian worlds were not expecting a Christianized version of Lakota tradition. Powers further argues "that much of what passes as Lakota religion today is the product of the white man's imagination and soon the Lakota religion, if it follows the path of *Black Elk Speaks* shall simply be absorbed by other religions or philosophies" (136). Powers seems to make the assumption that telling Lakota religion to the non-Indian necessarily distorts it, but both Neihardt and Brown gave a new dimension to Lakota religion by placing it in the landscape of comparative religion, which will not lead to an absorption in the other religions but rather to a new understanding and a new mission. This hope is what Black Elk had in mind when he told Brown: "I have wished to make this book through no other desire than to help my people in understanding the greatness and truth of our own tradition, and also to help in bringing peace upon the earth, not only among men, but within men and between the whole of creation" (J. Brown 1974, xx).

262

ward wholeness by assimilating unconscious elements of his traditional religion into his Christian consciousness. In achieving this assimilation, he perceived his Christian practice as an expression of his traditional religion. His intuition of today's missiology enabled him to do so. In order to achieve this objective, I will use today's principles of missiology, Jung's depth psychology, and my own model of religious identity.

It is important that in any discussion of Black Elk the radical changes that have taken place in the Catholic Church since Vatican II be considered. Black Elk was a man ahead of his times and had an intuition of today's missiology that went considerably beyond the principles of inculturation endorsed by the missionaries of his day.[2] Joseph Wong states that: "Vatican II, with its openness and positive outlook, marked a watershed in the Church's understanding of her relationship with other religions. It has been generally acknowledged that Karl Rahner was the chief contributor to the teaching of Vatican II on this matter. The substance, if not the highly disputed term, of his theory of 'anonymous Christians' has been endorsed by the Council in its various documents" (1994, 610).

Rahner's concept of the anonymous Christian is based on the fact that Christ is the end of creation to Whom everything in the world is orientated (1994, 5: 185, 11: 219). Rahner argues that there are "supernatural grace-filled elements [derived from Christ] in non-Christian religions" (5: 121). And if we fail to recognize them, "perhaps we may only have looked too superficially and with too little love" (130). "It would be wrong to regard the pagan as someone who has not been touched in any way by God's grace and truth . . . [when] he has already been given revelation in a true sense even before he has been affected by missionary preaching from without" (131). "The declaration [of the Second Vatican Council] recognizes what is 'true' and 'holy' in the different religions and that the concrete forms and doctrines of these religions are to be regarded with straightforward seriousness" (18: 289).

This means that non-Christian religions retain their validity independent of Christianity until a real opportunity for conversion is presented, so that one is convinced of the validity of Christianity (1994, 5: 118). For

2. However, Ross Enochs presents an amply documented case that the missionaries of Black Elk's time had a much greater sympathetic appreciation of Lakota religion than previously thought.

Rahner, "the success of missionary preaching depends on the anonymous presence of Christ" in its hearers (10: 171). The same point, however, can be made regarding Lakota religion. Non-Lakota respond to it because there is an anonymous presence of this religion in their psyche. The Christian is an anonymous Lakota.

Even after conversion, however, non-Christian religions retain validity because of the mutual fulfillment between the two religious traditions. Although non-Christian religions reach their fulfillment in Christianity (1994, 5: 134, 10: 40), Christianity also reaches its fulfillment in non-Christian religions, as the Church absorbs non-Christian religions into itself, creating "a new incarnational presence of Christ himself in the world" (18: 289).[3]

Carl Jung's depth psychology, which explains the individuation process, also helps us understand Black Elk's religious life. I will let Jung himself explain the role of archetypes in the unconscious. "[The archetypes] are images and at the same time emotions. One can speak of an archetype only when these two aspects coincide. When there is only an image, it is merely a word-picture, like a corpuscle with no electric charge. It is then of little consequence, just a word and nothing more. But if the image is charged with numinosity, that is, with psychic energy, then it becomes dynamic and will produce consequences" (18: 257).

Jung explains the nature of the personal unconscious. "The [personal unconscious] comprises not only the repressed material but also the other psychic components which do not attain the threshold of consciousness. The principle of repression does not suffice to explain why these components remain on the other side of the threshold of consciousness; for if that explanation were sufficient, the removal of repression ought to confer upon the person concerned a prodigious memory which would henceforth forget nothing" (7: 278).

The personal unconscious and the collective unconscious are intimately related, and Jung calls the process of assimilation of unconscious elements into consciousness by which one achieves an undivided wholeness "individuation." "Individuation means becoming a single homogenous being, and, in so far as 'individuality' embraces our innermost, last,

---

3. I discuss Rahner's theology more fully in *The Sacred Pipe: An Archetypal Theology* (1998b, 49–73).

and incomparable uniqueness, it also implies becoming one's own self. We can therefore translate individuation as 'coming to selfhood' or 'self-realization' " (7: 182).

Jung describes the process of individuation. "As a rule these processes have the peculiarity of being subliminal, i.e. unconscious, in the first place and of reaching consciousness only gradually. The moment of irruption can, however, be very sudden, so that consciousness is instantaneously flooded with . . . quite unsuspected contents. That is how it looks to the layman and even to the person concerned, but the experienced observer knows that the irruption has been preparing for many years, often for half a lifetime" (7: 184–85).

Jung develops the means of achieving individuation and one's need for it. "If we can successfully develop that function which I have called transcendent, the disharmony ceases and we can then enjoy the favorable side of the unconscious. The unconscious then gives us all the encouragement and help that a bountiful nature can bestow upon man. It holds possibilities which are locked away from the conscious mind, for it has at its disposal all subliminal psychic contents, all those things which have been forgotten or overlooked, as well as the wisdom and experience of uncounted centuries which are laid down in its archetypal organ" (7: 126).

An understanding of the principles of today's missiology and depth psychology offers a dramatically new approach to understanding Black Elk's commitment to two religious traditions.

I will also use my model of religious identity. I first proposed the idea that Lakota religion was an Old Testament reaching its fulfillment in Christianity (1970). Later I developed two positions that I called Ecumenist I, the recognition of common religious forms in the Lakota and Christian religions, and Ecumenist II, Lakota religion reaching its fulfillment in Christ (1998a, 191–93, 177–79). My observation is that many, if not most, of the medicine men and serious thinkers during the 1960s and 1970s were in the Ecumenist II position. I have given evidence of this elsewhere (189–91).

I came to realize, however, that my Ecumenist II position failed to recognize the mutual fulfillment that was necessarily concurrent in this position—the Sacred Pipe finding its fulfillment in Christ and Christ finding His fulfillment in the Sacred Pipe.

The Sacred Pipe finds its fulfillment in Christ because it has an orientation to Christ as a Divine Incarnation. In becoming man Christ becomes the fulfillment of all creation because the Incarnation of Christ, as Rahner states above, "constitutes a hypostatic union with matter." Consequently, Christ can be seen as an unfolding of the tradition of the Sacred Pipe, a conclusion not reached by anthropology but by theology.

Second, Christ finding His fulfillment in the Sacred Pipe is true because, as Rahner developed above, the Incarnation is not complete until Christ assumes the religious traditions of humankind, including that of the Sacred Pipe. The Sacred Pipe is an extension of the Incarnation. Although Christ is historically unique from the standpoint of Christian faith, He is not exclusive. Belief in Christ does not exclude belief in the Sacred Pipe. Consequently, the Sacred Pipe has a validity in itself and does not lose that validity even when it becomes a prefiguration of Christ. Christ needs the Sacred Pipe for His fulfillment. That there is the need for a mutual fulfillment eliminates any notion of one tradition being "superior" to the other. Consequently, I believe that Holler is now in agreement with me in saying that "I could accept Steinmetz's description of Black Elk's conversion as 'giving the Lakota tradition a Christian meaning' if it were mutually balanced with the observation that Black Elk also gave Christianity a traditional Lakota meaning—and perhaps a Ghost Dancer's as well" (Holler 1995, 34). My Ecumenist II position now has this balance.

It is interesting that Steve Charleston, a Choctaw who was consecrated as the sixth bishop of the Episcopal Diocese of Alaska in 1991, is developing a "Native People's" Christian theology upon this very position. He writes:

> The place I stand is in the original covenant God gave to Native America. I believe with all my heart that God's revelation to Native People is second to none. God speaks to generations of Native People over centuries of our spiritual development. We need to pay attention to that voice, to be respectful of the covenant, and to be unafraid to lift up the new [Christian] covenant as the fulfillment of the ancient promise made to the Native People of North America. [That means seeing Jesus] as a living Christ that arises from the Native covenant and speaks with the authenticity of Native America. (1996, 69)

Charleston develops the value of using this model.

> First it would give us a new vocabulary in dealing with what we have been describing as a Native spirituality. We might start treating them [the books of the Native America's Old Testament] more seriously and critically, since they would be describing the foundational theology for a contemporary Christian theology. . . . Native American women and men could finally speak for themselves . . . as reputable scholars of an Old Testament tradition. . . . Instead of Western writers hacking away at a Native spirituality, we would begin to see the emergence of more theologians from within the Native community itself. . . . [They] would not necessarily be Christian, but they would be treated with respect by the Christian community, just as Jewish scholars are respected. (1996, 72)

Considering the Lakota tradition as expressed by Black Elk in *Black Elk Speaks* and *The Sacred Pipe* as an Old Testament would lead to valuable research in new academic circles. This whole new area would depend not only upon the relationship between the two traditions that Black Elk had in his mind but also on a new understanding that scholars would bring to the subject, which would give a new dimension to the academic discussions currently taking place.

In order to understand Black Elk's place in the Ecumenist II position, in which Lakota religion is an "Old Testament" to Christianity, it is necessary to have a true understanding of conversion. A conversion involving sincere commitment does not imply substitution of one religion for another but is compatible with the incorporation of one religious tradition into another. This definition is the understanding that Black Elk had because he gave the traditional religion a Christian meaning while accepting the fact that Christianity would be understood in Lakota religious symbols, which is precisely what he did with two important images. He gave both the Ghost Dance Messiah and the Sacred Pipe a Christian meaning, identifying them with Christ. Christ, in turn, received a new meaning being expressed in Lakota religious symbols. Rahner might say that Black Elk's Ghost Dance vision made his conversion possible because it was the presence of the unknown Christ in the Ghost Dance Messiah (and in the Sacred Pipe) that made Christianity acceptable. Black Elk was a man ahead of his times in accepting as a Catholic the Ghost Dance Messiah as a valid expression of Christ, a position contrary to what the missionaries taught. But this belief did not weaken his sincere commitment to Christianity. Black Elk was both a sincere traditionalist and a sincere Christian.

Black Elk was a sincere traditionalist. Even after his conversion to Christianity, he never lost his faith in traditional Lakota religion. His overpowering visions could never be eradicated from his psyche, especially on the unconscious level. The passing on of Lakota tradition to John Neihardt and Joseph Brown is a clear indication of sincere belief, which he never rejected. He talked to Fools Crow who told Thomas Mails: "I stayed with him [Black Elk] quite often, and sometimes for long periods of time. We also made a few trips together, and over the years talked about many things. I learned a great deal about *Wakan-Tanka,* prophecy and medicine from him" (Mails 1979, 53). We also know that, according to Ben Marrowbone, a contemporary, Black Elk told the catechists that God prepared the Lakota through the Sacred Pipe to accept Christ (Steltenkamp 1993, 104–5). And in *The Sacred Pipe* he clearly expresses the desire for a revival of traditional religion for those Lakota for whom this religion would be a help in overcoming the secularization of Lakota life that he saw taking place.

Black Elk, however, was also a sincere Christian. We can be grateful for this final chapter in Black Elk's life (which his son Ben told me should be written) to Michael Steltenkamp. He interviewed Lucy Looks Twice, the last remaining member of Black Elk's family, and other Lakota contemporaries of Black Elk.

Looks Twice gives an account of her father's conversion. Father Lindebner came into a tent to give Holy Communion and the last rites to a sick boy whom he had baptized. Black Elk was there performing a ceremony to cure the boy. Lindebner took whatever Black Elk had prepared on the ground and threw them into the stove and the drum and rattle outside the tent. He told Black Elk, "Satan, get out." After Lindebner gave the boy his sacraments, he came out of the tent and saw Black Elk looking downhearted as though he had lost all his powers. He told Black Elk to get into the buggy and took him to Holy Rosary Mission. After two weeks of instruction he baptized Black Elk on the feast of Saint Nicholas, from which he received his Christian name (Steltenkamp 1993, 33–34).

Holler questions the historicity of the story, saying that it might be a "twice told tale" (1995, 15). However, whether this type of conversion experience actually took place is not important. It may have been a retold story of another event. What is important is that the story has mythological value. It is a very apt symbol of Black Elk's giving up his *yuwipi* practice (a healing ceremony in which the medicine man prays through the spirits) for his untiring work as a catechist. This story was Looks Twice's way of expressing her belief that her father had a profound conversion that led to a sincere commitment. Certainly, she knew more about her father and his true feelings than anyone reading about Black Elk today.

Black Elk's sincere commitment was also expressed during a retreat that he made. "During Holy Week, 1922, Father Placidus F. Sialm gave the first of an annual series of retreats for Oglala catechists at the mission. He told one anecdote from that retreat over and over throughout his life; it signified for him, perhaps, a turning point in the Lakota's acceptance of the church. In Father Sialm's words: On the third day of that retreat, Nick Black Elk came to me with this very worthy resolution: 'We catechists resolve never to commit a mortal sin' " (DeMallie 1984a, 24–25).

But there are more details of Black Elk's sincere commitment. Looks Twice tells us that when Black Elk "converted, knowing Christ was very important to him, and receiving communion was what he really held sacred" (Steltenkamp 1993, 35). His involvement in the Catholic Sioux Congress was considerable. "Being a catechist, his duties included organizational details, preaching, and instructing new converts. This ever-active participation in society work, and congresses molded Lucy's religious formation" (47). As Steltenkamp points out, "More was involved with this type of religious commitment, as Lucy's memories of her father show a man who took this responsibility so seriously that for many years it was a way of life the family as a whole accepted as their own" (48–49). "Since my father was one of the first catechists, the Blackrobes might come for him at any time to go on a trip. So right away he had to work—and he worked. They used to come for him very often, and he was really willing to accept any kind of trip they were supposed to make—even in the coldest weather. He would go with Father Lindebner or Westropp or Father Henry Alder, and people would come to them, attend Mass, and even have their young ones baptized. There would be converts, and he would teach them" (50–51).

Black Elk was also a prominent member of the St. Joseph Society, which entailed considerable responsibilities (DeMallie 1984a, 15–16). According to Father Henry Westropp, Black Elk was a "fervent apostle" who learned to read, knew his religion thoroughly, and won many converts (Steltenkamp 1993, 65). From all this testimony it is very obvious that Black Elk was a sincerely committed Christian actively involved in establishing the Church not only on the Pine Ridge Reservation but on other ones as well. DeMallie is correct in saying that Black Elk's baptism, probably in the Episcopal Church, in 1887 was not a personal conversion but simply "a stipulation of the contract with Buffalo Bill . . . that all the Indians selected to join the show 'shall be of the same religious faith' " (DeMallie 1984a, 10). "[But] Black Elk's conversion [to the Catholic Church] was unquestionably genuine" (14). If Black Elk would have become a Christian for pragmatic reasons, he would not have performed his catechist's duties with such intense energy and dedication.

There have been some remarks intended to discredit Black Elk's sincere commitment to Catholicism. Charles Hanson Jr., a young man visiting at Pine Ridge about 1948, claims that Ben Black Elk told him that "many of their conversations then were about the old religion, and that Black Elk now felt he had made a mistake in rejecting it for Christianity. Perhaps, after all, the Lakota religion would have been better for his people" (DeMallie 1984a, 72). This claim is contradicted by Black Elk's actions as an old man. Father Zimmerman wrote that "old age, blindness and the seven miles between him and the nearest Catholic church prevent him [Black Elk] from often hearing mass, so at times I promise to say mass at his home. Then he sends out word and gathers in the entire neighborhood, and as in his old time catechist days leads them in hymns and prayers" (Duratschek 1947, 207–8, quoted in DeMallie 1984a, 61). It is very possible that Ben told the young man what he wanted to hear. Certainly, one remark of a young man does not outweigh the extensive testimony given above.

Hilda Neihardt makes a similar attempt to discredit Black Elk's sincere commitment to Christianity, saying that "Before he passed away, Lucy revealed, Black Elk told them, 'The only thing I really believe is the pipe religion' " (1995, 119). She also reports remarks that indicate that Lucy was disappointed in Christianity. " 'When my old man died,' Lucy remarked, 'my religion *did not help me any*. When I told my friends this, they said, "Why don't you read the book about your father?" And so for the first time, I did read *Black Elk Speaks*.' Before Lucy could continue, a student raised her hand and asked, 'And what did the reading do for you?' 'It changed my life!' was Lucy's response" (117).

These are strange remarks from a person who, according to Steltenkamp in a private conversation, vested him at his diaconate ordination at the local powwow grounds in 1976, invited him to celebrate mass at her cabin in 1977, and wrote him shortly before her death in 1978 expressing the hope that her children would "return to the Church." There is no indication that Lucy Looks Twice gave up her Catholic faith as Hilda Neihardt would have us believe. Hilda claiming that Lucy told her that her father's only real belief was the pipe religion is also contradicted by the extensive testimony she gave Steltenkamp.

Hilda Neihardt even fails to acknowledge Black Elk's Catholic life. She comments that on a videotape made by Charles Sigsbee, television director at the University of Missouri, her father "described the book [*Black Elk Speaks*] as 'the complete story of the developing life of a holy man from his youth to his old age' " (1995, 115). She, with her father, was obviously unaware or forgot that Black Elk had lived as a Catholic for forty-six years, many of them as a catechist, and died as a Catholic. We will see below that Black Elk's story can hardly be complete without presenting his life as a Catholic.

An important issue, however, is how did Black Elk express his sincere commitment to his traditional religion after he became a Catholic catechist? Fools Crow comments that "the renowned Black Elk has earned a place above all of the other Teton holy men. We all hold him the highest" (Mails 1979, 53). Although some might think this implies Black Elk's participation in traditional ceremonies, there is no direct evidence that he did so. He gave Neihardt a morning-star pendant described as a "beautiful old sacred ornament that he had used a long while in the sun dances in which he has officiated as a priest" (DeMallie 1984a, 28). DeMallie says Black Elk made his public announcement of being a holy man when he first performed the Horse Dance in 1881 (7), and Holler states that this role made him eligible to conduct the Sun Dance (1995, 18). Consequently, Black Elk's involvement with Sun Dances might have occurred only between 1881 and 1904, the year of his baptism.

DeMallie interprets the holy man's work for the Duhamel Sioux Indian Pageant as evangelistic: "Black Elk's motivation in publicly performing these sacred rituals appears to have been to teach white audiences that the old-time Lakota religion was a true religion, not devil worship as the missionaries claimed. . . . This was the logical extension of Black Elk's wish to make his vision 'go out,' to share the traditional ways with white men" (DeMallie 1984a, 66).

Seeing his participation as the extension of his interviews with Neihardt seems to be a valid interpretation of his motivation. But to say he wanted to discredit the Jesuits is speculation. And, wanting to extend his interviews with Neihardt certainly was not his only reason and probably not his primary one. It is interesting that the claim is made that Black Elk became a catechist for financial gain (receiving, according to Looks Twice, only ten dollars and to DeMallie, only five dollars a month), while a much larger financial gain is overlooked for his motivation in participating in the Duhamel pageant. DeMallie admits that the Indians "were provided with wood, water, food, and, at the end of the season, a percentage of the pageant profits" (DeMallie 1984a, 63). Because Black Elk was never shy about appearing in public, the pageant was attractive. It gave him some excitement, the adulation of tourists, and a welcome relief from a sweltering summer on the reservation. And the pageant was performed as a tourist attraction. To cite this participation as an example "of using every means possible to promote Lakota tradition," as Rice does (1991, 4), is unwarranted.

There is another reason to indicate that Black Elk did not participate in traditional ceremonies after his conversion. Fools Crow told Mails that "another religious dance whose song was a prayer was the Horse Dance. I was one of the riders in the last true and sacred Horse Dance, which was also held that day at Whiteclay [Nebraska] in 1931" (Mails 1979, 79). Fools Crow mentions the names of three other riders but not Black Elk. If Black Elk had been there, Fools Crow would have mentioned his name. Because Black Elk enacted the Horse Dance as a public acknowledgment of his Great Vision in 1881 (DeMallie 1984a, 6–7), it would be very strange for him not to be present in the one performed in 1931 if he had been actively engaged in traditional ceremonies. From the above evidence it would seem that Black Elk's sincere commitment to traditional religion was on the level of belief.

The objection can be made that if he had a sincere commitment to his traditional religion, we should expect involvement on a ritual level. The explanation lies, in addition to his constraints as a catechist, in two facts: first, Black Elk's traditional religion remained to a very large extent in his

unconscious until the Neihardt interviews; and second, his Christian practice became an expression of his Lakota religion, making participation in
traditional ceremonies unnecessary.

First, his traditional religion did not have sufficient psychic energy to
remain in consciousness, that is, it was subliminal. His extremely busy life
as a catechist between his conversion in 1904 and his interview with Neihardt in 1932 did not give him the time or the proper conditions for his
traditional religion to remain in consciousness. By the time Black Elk met
Neihardt, "his eyesight continued to deteriorate and his health began to
fail" (DeMallie 1984a, 26). His strenuous years as a full-time catechist
were over. Black Elk had many hours to himself to become introspective,
which made it conducive for the traditional religion to surface in his
consciousness.

In Jungian terms, there was also partial repression of traditional religion in his earlier life. Although repression may involve rejection or denial,
it does not necessarily do so. Rather, in Black Elk's life it was the result of
it not being the proper time for him to make the inner journey of individuation toward wholeness. The integration of the two religious traditions
found in *The Sacred Pipe* would come later, near the end of his life.

DeMallie's remarks on the first meeting between Black Elk and Neihardt are pertinent here. "It was as if something long bound up inside the
old man had broken free at last, an impulse to save that entire system of
knowledge that his vision represented and that for more than twenty-five
years he had denied" (DeMallie 1984a, 28). As is evident from the intensity with which Black Elk responded to Neihardt at their first meeting,
Neihardt had definitely stirred Black Elk's unconscious and the repressed
material that Black Elk would relate to him. "The rapport that grew almost immediately" is a sign of this resurgence (27). And the intensity of
the interviews with so much material being given in such a short amount
of time could only have been an "irruption" of material from his unconscious. DeMallie's remark that something broke loose that for more than
twenty-five years he had denied (or, more accurately, repressed) makes a
great deal of sense viewed from the insights of depth psychology. It will be
shown below, however, that Black Elk did live up to his vision through his
Christian practice and did not have to carry a burden through life.

Despite Black Elk's many years as a Catholic catechist, he was now
ready to tell the world about his traditional religion. And more important,

he was ready to deal with it in his own psyche. Black Elk's later life must be considered as a process of individuation, the integration of unconscious traditional material into his Christian consciousness. It is during the period between the Neihardt and Brown interviews that Black Elk's psyche was seeking wholeness, which is why, according to DeMallie, "in his old age . . . Black Elk turned his attention increasingly to Lakota tradition. Apparently this began with Neihardt's first visit in 1930" (1984a, 71). His intuition of the new missiology made this possible.

It would be a journey, however, he would never complete because even near the end of his life the traditional material coming from his personal unconscious, as expressed in *The Sacred Pipe*, was only partly integrated into his Christian consciousness. It is remarkable, however, how much Black Elk did achieve on his own without the theological help of the missionaries. Unfortunately, there was no exchange of ideas such as took place in the meetings between the missionaries and the medicine men lasting for six years in the 1970s on the Rosebud Reservation in South Dakota (Stolzman 1986b).

The second fact that explains Black Elk's lack of participation in traditional religion on a ritual level is that his Christian practice became an expression of this religion, making it unnecessary for him personally to take part in traditional ceremonies. We can see just how true this statement is by examining how Black Elk lived up to his Great Vision both as a young boy and as a Ghost Dancer.

Black Elk saw his Christianity as an unfolding of his Great Vision as a young boy in using a catechetical tool known as the Two Roads Map. According to Steltenkamp, "Black Elk used the Two Roads Map during his life as a catechist, and many references within his vision correspond directly to the old picture catechism. Some of the surprising parallels include thunder beings, a daybreak star, flying men, tree imagery, circled villages, a black road, a red road, friendly wings, an evil blue man living in flames, a place where people moaned and mourned, emphasis on the people's history, and gaudily portrayed, self indulgent individuals. Other, more detailed segments of Black Elk's vision are either explicitly or implicitly present on the Two Roads Map" (1993, 94–95).

In teaching the Catholic faith through the Two Roads Map, Black Elk would experience it as a fulfillment of his vision as a boy because the images of his Great Vision were now part of his Christian journey toward heaven. These images were also archetypal and were not primarily rational identifications but sources of psychic energy released from his personal and collective unconscious depths. The images were expressions of the transcendent function bridging the gap between his unconscious and his conscious psyches.

Black Elk also lived up to his Ghost Dance vision. He told Neihardt a detail that did not find its way into *Black Elk Speaks*. It is a detail that is of the utmost importance in understanding this vision. His statement from the field material follows in full:

> As I landed there, I saw twelve men coming toward me and they stood before me and said: "Our Father, the two-legged chief, you shall see." Then I went to the center of the circle with these men and there again I saw the tree in full bloom. Against the tree I saw a man standing with outstretched arms. As we stood close to him these twelve men said: "Behold him!" The man with outstretched arms looked at me and I didn't know whether he was a white or an Indian. He did not resemble Christ. He looked like an Indian, but I was not sure of it. He had long hair which was hanging down loose. On the left side of his head was an eagle feather. His body was painted red. (At that time I had never had anything to do with white men's religion and I had never seen any picture of Christ.)
>
> This man said to me: "My life is such that all earthly beings that grow belong to me. My Father has said this. You must say this." I stood there gazing at him and tried to recognize him. I could not make him out. He was a nice-looking man. As I looked at him, his body began to transform. His body changed into all colors and it was very beautiful. All around him there was light. Then he disappeared all at once. It seemed as though there were wounds in the palms of his hands. . . . It seems to me on thinking it over that I have seen the son of the Great Spirit himself. (DeMallie 1984a, 263, 266)

DeMallie comments that the statement that Black Elk had not seen a picture of Christ "is not strictly true, in that Black Elk was clearly familiar with Christianity while he was in Europe. Black Elk probably meant to indicate that at this time he had not yet accepted it." DeMallie also comments that "the account he gives here rings of the imagery of the Transfiguration" (1984a, 263 n). Although DeMallie suggests that Black Elk identified the

Ghost Dance Messiah as the Christ of his Catholic faith, neither he nor anyone else has developed the significant conclusions of this recognition.

The full meaning of the vision was not apparent to Black Elk at the time because "He did not resemble Christ." Although Wovoka had given the Ghost Dance Messiah a Christian meaning, Black Elk at first failed to recognize the Messiah as Christ. It was necessary for Black Elk to arrive at this perception on his own. The signs were there in the Messiah's body becoming transformed and the apparent wounds in the palms of his hands. But it would take time for Black Elk to recognize the Messiah's true identity. Black Elk tells Neihardt: "It seems to me on thinking it over that I have seen the son of the Great Spirit himself." He would need to accept Christ as he did in his conversion to Catholicism and not just learn about Christ as he did in Europe in the Buffalo Bill show in order to understand his Ghost Dance vision. He would need to identify the Ghost Dance Messiah as the Christ whom he knew personally and not as a Christ he knew through hearsay. In making this identification the Ghost Dance Messiah becomes the Christ of his Catholic faith and this Christ is seen as an unfolding of the Ghost Dance Messiah.

Black Elk's faith in the Ghost Dance Messiah was shattered in the Wounded Knee massacre. DeMallie states that "the ghost dance proved a cruel disappointment to the Lakota people, but to none more than Black Elk. Rather than salvation, it brought death to as many as three hundred Lakotas at Wounded Knee, who were mowed down by gunfire in an unthinking, horrible slaughter" (1984a, 11). He knew the Ghost Dance Messiah as understood by his fellow dancers could not save his people.

Holler claims that "in fact nothing in Black Elk's interviews with Neihardt suggests that he repudiated the fundamental thrust of the Ghost Dance" (1995, 218). But he did not have to do so because he discovered a new unfolding of it in Christianity. Black Elk's later reflection would save him from despair because he knew the Ghost Dance Messiah was Christ, and his work as a catechist bringing the Lakota to accept Christ was the fulfillment of his vision.

On an unconscious level the Ghost Dance Messiah was an archetypal image. As such it could release energy even during those times in which he may not have been consciously aware of this identification. The energy did not come from his conscious identification but from his unconscious depths. The source of the energy was not merely the personal unconscious

of subliminal and repressed material but far more the collective unconscious of the archetypes (including that of the Messiah). Thus, it was the
energy of his Ghost Dance vision that flowed into his life as a catechist and
was a major source of the intensity in his work. On the unconscious level
there was never a division. Black Elk continued to believe in the Ghost
Dance Messiah, but he was now the Christ of his personal faith as a catechist. This identification was only an intuition that to a large extent remained in the unconscious. This intuition was only the beginning of the
individuation process that would take many years.

Black Elk would also see Christ as an unfolding of the Sacred Pipe.
Ben Marrowbone, Black Elk's contemporary, relates:

> The catechists would get together, have meetings, encourage each
> other. . . . At one such gathering, Nick Black Elk stood up and said: . . .
> "We have a pipe here. We use that. God gave us that pipe from heaven
> through a woman. . . .
> "That pipe—it's a road to take—a road of honesty—a road to
> heaven. It teaches how to lead a good life, like the Ten Commandments.
> They understood what that woman was saying, and that worship was my
> formation—my foundation. But my foundation is deepening.
> "God made me to know him, love him, serve him. To make sure I do
> this, God sent us his Son. The old way is good. God prepared us before
> the missionary came. Our ancestors used the pipe to know God. That's a
> foundation! But from the old country came Christ from heaven—a won-
> derful thing—the Son of God. And the Indian cares about this." (Stel-
> tenkamp 1993, 104–5)

These remarks deserve reflection. Black Elk equates the morality of
the Sacred Pipe with the Ten Commandments. He says that the Sacred
Pipe is his foundation, but that this foundation is deepening from the new
religion that he embraced. Then Black Elk gives us a precise understanding of present-day missiology. We hear in Black Elk an echo of Rahner:
"The old way is good. God prepared us before the missionary came"
through the traditional religion. The Sacred Pipe is a foundation upon
which Christianity is built, that is, a prefiguration of Christ. Black Elk was
not necessarily encouraging the catechists to pray with the Sacred Pipe

(because there is no evidence of them doing so), but he was certainly telling them to understand Christianity as an unfolding of this tradition.[4]

This understanding that Black Elk expressed to the catechist would continue to develop in his mind until it reached a culmination in *The Sacred Pipe*. Commenting on this book, DeMallie says that "these teachings seem to represent the end point in Black Elk's synthesis of Lakota and Christian beliefs, for in them he structures Lakota rituals in parallel fashion to the Catholic sacraments. Perhaps this was Black Elk's final attempt to bridge the two religious traditions that his life had so intimately embodied" (1984a, 71).

Holler develops this synthesis. He calls attention to Black Elk's remark to Joseph Brown that just as Christ is coming at the end of the world, so the White Buffalo Calf Woman comes with the Sacred Pipe. Holler correctly understands this as an identification of the pipe with Christ (1984b, 42).

Holler also points out that Black Elk's explanation of the Sun Dance brings out the same synthesis. He abandons the traditional purpose of individual vows "made in time of anxiety, usually on the warpath" (see Densmore 1918, 88–91), for instead taking on the suffering of the people that they may live, a purpose that shows a Christian influence. The Sun Dance symbols also acquire a Christian meaning; for example, an armlet of rabbit skin represents humility "because he is quiet, soft and not self-asserting," while he removes references to war and interprets the color *black* as representing ignorance and sin. Black Elk, thus, frees the Sun Dance from its association with the hunter-warrior complex and gives it a new interpretation "in terms relevant to the radically changed conditions of reservation life." This is done in terms "commensurate with Christianity" (Holler 1984b, 44–46).

---

4. Lucy Looks Twice said that Black Elk "didn't have a pipe until after he was retired from his missionary work" (Steltenkamp 1993, 107). Black Elk's granddaughter Olivia stated that when Black Elk was stronger, he prayed on the hill with his Sacred Pipe (Archambault 1998, 60). However, this could still refer to the time after his retirement. It is quite possible that Black Elk prayed with the Sacred Pipe as a ritual expression of the individuation process in the same manner that Carl Jung built the Bollingen Tower as an expression of his (Jung 1965, 225).

Julian Rice is unable to accept the influence of Christianity on Lakota religion. He also misunderstands the conversion process and the relationship between the two religious traditions. In commenting on *The Sacred Pipe*, Rice states that Black Elk "has not Christianized so much as modernized the ceremony, making it acceptable to partially assimilated Lakota and feasible in the white man's world. All this is a conscious strategy on Black Elk's part, consistent with protecting the people's spiritual life and self respect in changing conditions. . . . Black Elk became a Catholic to find metaphors that would infuse the Lakota religion with life and assure it continuance. In the process he developed sincere respect for Christianity but never to the point that he believed Christianity to be deeper than a Lakota foundation" (1991, 6).

My analysis of the Ghost Dance Messiah and *The Sacred Pipe* shows that the traditional religion was significantly Christianized as well as modernized. Rice also says the Christianization of traditional religion was a conscious strategy on Black Elk's part implying insincerity in his Christian commitment, a position contradicted by the abundant evidence above. This was not a strategy but rather an attempt of a man sincerely committed to two traditions to understand his religious identity. Black Elk did not become a Catholic to "find metaphors that would infuse the Lakota religion with life" but, rather, discovered them after his conversion in giving his traditional religion a Christian meaning. In doing this Rice states that Black Elk "had developed a sincere respect for Christianity but never to the point that he believed Christianity to be deeper than a Lakota foundation." But Black Elk told the catechists that his Lakota foundation was "deepening through Christianity." Rice claims that in *The Sacred Pipe*, Black Elk's interpretation of black as ignorance is incongruous. One could ask, incongruous to whom? It would be to a non-Christian Lakota but certainly not to a Christian Lakota, who according to Holler (as we shall see below) was reading back into his tradition the insights that occurred to him after years of being a catechist. Although the essential values of traditional religion remain valid, its Christianization will make significant changes in the understanding of it. The color *black* has changed and acquired a new meaning. Rice has difficulty accepting Black Elk as a Lakota Christian, but that is exactly what Black Elk was.

As stated above, Black Elk saw traditional Lakota religion as an Old

Testament reaching its fulfillment in Christ. It is remarkable that Black Elk himself used this model in his remarks to the catechists. Holler accurately expresses its meaning:

> [I]t is typical of Black Elk's way of thinking and speaking to read back into his great vision an insight that could only have occurred to him after his years as a catechist. The same "reading back" characterizes Black Elk's entire account of the seven rites of the Lakota. Second, there is no hint of substitution in Black Elk's statement. Christ does not replace the pipe, both have co-equal validity. Third, and most obviously, Black Elk is saying to the Sioux, in what was his last written statement, that Indians should "pray with the pipe," that is not abandon traditional religious practices for Christianity. (1984b, 42)

Black Elk wanted "praying with the pipe" and other traditional practices to be continued. He did not want them abandoned for those people for whom they were helpful. This traditional religion, however, would have a Christian meaning because of his "reading back" into it the insights of a catechist. Both Christ and the Sacred Pipe would have coequal validity in the sense of a mutual fulfillment. Although Black Elk did not want those Lakota who would be helped to "abandon traditional religious practices for Christianity," neither did he want them to abandon Christianity for traditional ones.

When Black Elk identified the Ghost Dance Messiah and the Sacred Pipe with Christ, he saw them as expressions of the same sacred. But he also did more. He did not say the Ghost Dance Messiah is "our Christ," as Eagle Feather said that the "Pipe is our Christ" (Mails 1978, 88). This statement would have made the Ghost Dance Messiah and Christ merely equal expressions of the same sacred. When Black Elk saw the Messiah's body radiant and apparent wounds in the palms of his hands, the Ghost Dance Messiah became the personal Christ whom Black Elk knew as a catechist, and Christ became an unfolding of the Ghost Dance Messiah. And there was a mutual fulfillment. He is no longer a white man's savior but is on the level of religious imagination a Native American, a perception that more and more Native Americans are seeking (Peelman 1995, 97–132). In understanding the Ghost Dance Messiah as Christ, Black Elk was in the Ecumenist II position.

The symbol that was at the center of Black Elk's religious experience was the tree in the center of the sacred hoop that must be made to bloom again. The Ghost Dance reminded him of this symbol in his Great Vision as a young boy.

> They had a sacred pole in the center. It was a circle in which they were dancing and I could clearly see that this was my sacred hoop and in the center they had an exact duplicate of my tree that never blooms and it came to my mind that perhaps with this power the tree would bloom and the people would get into the sacred hoop again. It seemed that I could recall all my vision in it. The more I thought about it, the stronger it got in my mind. Furthermore, the sacred articles that had been presented were scarlet relics and their faces were painted red. Furthermore, they had that pipe and the eagle feathers. It was all from my vision. So I sat there and felt sad. Then happiness overcame me all at once and it got ahold of me right there. I was to be intercessor for my people and yet I was not doing my duty. Perhaps it was this Messiah that had pointed me out and he might have sent this to remind me to get to work again to bring my people back into the hoop and the old religion. (DeMallie 1984a, 258)

But, the Ghost Dance Messiah had become Christ in Black Elk's religious imagination. He saw Christ as the unfolding of the Messiah. As to be expected, he did not explicitly elaborate on this belief to Neihardt who was not receptive to Christian ideas when talking about this experience. In order for the tree to bloom the people must be brought back to the traditional religion, but a traditional religion now understood in the light of Christ as *The Sacred Pipe* indicates. Black Elk saw the traditional religion as an Old Testament reaching its fulfillment in Christ. His Christian practice became an expression of his traditional religion. The tree blooming in the center of the sacred hoop would be a Lakota Christian religion.

15

Black Elk and the Jesuits

ROSS ENOCHS

When John Neihardt published *Black Elk Speaks* in 1932, a controversy arose regarding Black Elk's religious beliefs. This book was a beautiful account of the life of a Lakota Sioux visionary. The book, however, raised a controversy on Pine Ridge Reservation, South Dakota, where Black Elk lived, because he was a prominent lay leader of the Catholic Church there. In 1887 the Jesuits established the Holy Rosary Mission on Pine Ridge Reservation, and they have been an active force on the reservation since then. The Jesuit priests on Pine Ridge were upset that Neihardt both portrayed Black Elk as a devotee of Native American religion and failed to say that Black Elk was a Catholic for the last forty-five years of his life. Yet, some people had questions about the depth or the nature of Black Elk's conversion to Catholicism; some believed that Black Elk retained his belief in the traditional Lakota religion while also claiming to be a Catholic. This paper will show that this view of Black Elk's religion is inadequate. Black Elk and the Jesuits, as this study will show, believed that the Lakota religion had truth in it that came from God; however, they also felt that some aspects of the Lakota tradition were not good and should not be practiced. To accept Catholicism Black Elk did not have to reject his basic ideas about the nature of rituals and God. But Black Elk did put aside some of the traditional Lakota rituals and ethics for the same reasons that almost all Lakotas abandoned them: some of their traditional rituals failed to produce adequate results, some of their ethical standards were not well adapted to the modern lifestyle, and their religion was closely tied to their hunting economy, which no longer existed.

One of the reasons the Catholic missions were so successful was that Catholicism was structurally similar to Native American religion in some ways (J. Moore 1982). The Lakotas' views of rituals, helper spirits, the dead, justification, salvation, and reconciliation were similar to Catholic beliefs, and the Jesuits used these similarities to draw the Lakotas to the Catholic Church. A ritual for both of these traditions was a series of human actions that invoked the presence of God's grace or power, made this power present in the community, and bound the community's members to each other and to the sacred. For Catholics and Lakotas, rituals ordered the sacred power, made it usable, and channeled it to certain specific purposes that God intended. Through ritual, Lakotas and Catholics believed that they cooperated with God, and both God and human beings acted in these rituals. Both Catholics and Lakotas also believed that each person had a helper spirit or guardian angel who would give assistance to that person and to whom that person could pray. Therefore, when Catholics advised Black Elk to pray to his guardian angels, this was a practice that essentially he was already doing. Additionally, both Catholics and Lakotas believed that the prayers or ceremonies that the living performed had some impact on the destiny of the dead. Lakotas and Catholics also stressed that works and faith were both necessary for salvation. For Catholics and Lakotas salvation was not only a matter of having the correct beliefs but also a matter of practicing these beliefs in the world. Also related to their conception of works was their conception of reconciliation. The Lakotas gave gifts to atone for misdeeds (Chittenden 1905, 1: 190), and similarly, Catholics did penance to help make up for the effects of the sins they committed. Finally, for both Catholics and Lakotas, sacrifice was a central aspect of their religions. The Lakotas performed their own sacrifice in the Sun Dance in which they offered their flesh and blood as sacrifices for the benefit of the community. Therefore, the sacrifice of Christ was not unreasonable to them. In terms of the structure of these religions, many similarities existed, and the Jesuits actually used the similarities of the two religions to lead the Lakotas to Catholicism (J. Moore 1982). When Black Elk converted to Catholicism, many of the basic Catholic conceptions of rituals, spirits, the dead, justification, reconciliation, and sacrifice were not so foreign that they were difficult for him to accept.

Black Elk and the Jesuits who evangelized him believed that there was continuity between the Lakota tradition and Catholicism. One of the ways that the Jesuits indicated this continuity was by retaining the word the

Lakotas used for God, *Wakantanka,* which could be translated as the "Great Spirit." The Jesuits who evangelized the Lakotas preached in the Lakota language and used the word *Wakantanka* interchangeably with God. So instead of telling the Lakotas to reject their old religion, the Jesuits told them to continue praying to *Wakantanka,* and thus many Lakotas came to believe that *Wakantanka* was the same as the God of the Christians. This belief was in fact exactly the intention of the missionaries who believed that the Lakotas had a notion of the one true God through natural law before the coming of the missionaries. Though the Lakotas may not have been true monotheists, the Jesuits thought that they were, and therefore were able to identify *Wakantanka* with the Christian God. According to the Catholic doctrine of natural law, any people, including non-Christians, have the ability to perceive the truth about the existence of God and the practice of good morals through studying nature and examining their consciences. God has written in nature and has inscribed on human consciences the truth, and this truth can be perceived and practiced by all people. When the Jesuits came to evangelize the Lakotas, they looked for and found many natural virtues in the Lakota culture and religion. The missionaries believed that any good in the Lakota religion or culture came from the one source of goodness, which is God.

The Catholic natural-law approach to the traditional Lakota religion was evident in the writings of many of the Jesuits in the Sioux missions. For example, Eugene Buechel, one of the Jesuits who worked on the Pine Ridge Reservation, published two books in the Lakota language, *Wowapi Wakan, Wicowoyake Yuptecelapi: Bible History in the Language of the Teton Sioux Indians* (1924) and *Lakota Wocekiye na Olowan Wowapi: Sioux Indian Prayer and Hymn Book* (with the Jesuit Fathers of St. Francis Mission, 1927), in which he translated the term *God* into the Lakota as *Wakantanka.* The Jesuits distributed these two books widely among the Lakotas. Additionally, in their sermons in Lakota and in their published articles, the Jesuits at Holy Rosary Mission used the term *Wakantanka* interchangeably with *God* to indicate to the Lakotas that continuity existed between their traditional religion and the Catholic faith (Enochs 1996, 95–100). For example, a Jesuit at Pine Ridge, Leo Cunningham, said that at the Holy Rosary Mission boarding school, "367 Sioux Indian boys and girls are being taught to know and love *Wakan Tanka,* the Great Spirit" (1928, 60). Similarly, in 1941, John Scott, another Jesuit at Holy Rosary, wrote the following: "Thanks to the untiring efforts of the Blackrobe, the faith of the Sioux in *Wakan Tanka,* the Great Spirit, was not crushed under the wheels of invading *Wasichu* [white people]" (1941, 167). Rather than trying to obliterate the Lakotas' faith, the Jesuits, in Scott's opinion, preserved the Lakotas' faith in the Great Spirit. Additionally, in 1944, Joseph Zimmerman, a Jesuit of Holy Rosary Mission and friend of Black Elk, commented that among the Lakotas "there is almost universal acceptance of the God of Christianity as the Great Spirit, *Wakan Tanka,* in whom the race has always believed" (1944, 16–17). Thus, the Jesuits encouraged the Lakotas in their belief that the God to whom they had always prayed was the Christian God. If the Jesuits thought that the Lakota religion was simply devil worship, as some scholars asserted, they certainly would not have used the term *Wakantanka* as a translation for *God* in the prayer books.

Further evidence that the Catholic missionaries did not believe that the Lakota religion was "evil" was their attitudes toward the Lakota legends. Quite often in Catholic magazines that covered the missions before 1940, missionaries published many different Native American legends to educate and interest their readers. Furthermore, Zimmerman clearly stated his opinion of the Lakota legends when he referred to "the beautiful mythology of the Lakota, or Western Sioux" (1927, 180–81). When Father Sialm, S.J., attended a gathering where a Lakota man told the Lakota legends, Sialm referred to the stories as "wonderful tales" and had no complaints about them (1931, 54). Another Jesuit missionary to the Lakotas, Eugene Buechel recorded wholly in the Lakota language one hundred Lakota legends, which were published posthumously and called *Lakota Tales and Texts* (1978). Even though these legends were an essential part of the Lakota religion, Buechel wanted to preserve them. If the Jesuits thought these stories were evil, they never would have recorded them and never would have reprinted them in their mission journals.

The Jesuits esteemed many aspects of Lakota religion and believed that the Lakotas' generosity and charity were additional examples of their perception of the natural law. Father Charles Weisenhorn, S.J., of Holy Rosary, commented on their charity: "No people is more generous than the Indian and gladly does he put all he has at the disposal of his guest, no matter at what hour of the day or night the latter may show up" (1920b, 157). Similarly, Zimmerman, a friend of Black Elk, also praised the Lakotas for their practice of the natural virtue of charity: "No one holds on to food or other necessities when others are in need, but everything is shared willingly and gladly. There is a genuine feeling of neighborly responsibility among our Indians here and elsewhere. But this is not altogether new. The old Sioux way of living was based upon mutual help rather than upon selfish individualism. Generosity was esteemed as a great virtue and was ostentatiously practiced" (1940, 11–12). The Jesuits especially appreciated and relied on the Lakotas' hospitality because many of the Jesuits spent a good deal of time living with the Lakotas in their houses. Because Pine Ridge was so large, many of the Jesuits traveled the reservation by horse and buggy on trips that often lasted a month. They visited the different Lakota Catholics, lived in their houses, ate with them, traveled with them, prayed for their sick, mourned with them, and celebrated the sacraments with them. The Jesuits had respect for many of the Lakotas' ethical beliefs and sought to preserve their ethics of charity.

Black Elk, however, abandoned some of the traditional ethics of his religion after becoming Catholic. One of the ethical differences between Catholicism and the traditional Lakota religion is that the Lakota religion did not instruct the Lakotas to love their enemies and do good to those people who hated them. Because the Lakotas were a "tribal" group, they were concerned for the welfare of others in their group and not in the welfare of rival bands. For the Lakotas, as with many Native Americans, revenge against enemies was seen as a virtue. If a Lakota man wanted to prove his manhood, a customary practice would be for him to kill members of an enemy band or steal horses or women from them. Black Elk even told a traditional story in *Black Elk Speaks* that condoned such practices. In the story of "High Horse's Courting," Black Elk spoke of High Horse, a Lakota man who was wooing a woman whose father would not allow him to marry his daughter. To prove his worth, High Horse traveled to a Crow Native American band, killed two men, and stole horses. After bringing these horses to the father of the woman he loved, the father pronounced him a worthy son-in-law (J. Neihardt 1979, 76). In contrast, most Christian fathers do not believe that someone who kills people to steal their horses would make an ideal son-in-law. Christianity also does not advocate the killing of people to prove one's manhood or bravery. The story of High Horse's courting is quite a contrast to the story of the Good Samaritan. When Black Elk became a Catholic, he converted from a tribal religion to a universal religion, and the Jesuits introduced him to the concept of universal love and the love of enemies. When Black Elk became a Catholic, he gave up the traditional tribal ethics of bravery and revenge.

Additional aspects of Lakota culture also fell out of practice, not because the Jesuits forced the Lakotas to give up these things, but rather because the Lakotas abandoned them. One of the most important reasons for Black Elk to leave behind many of his traditional religious practices was that they did not work. If a curing ceremony or a shaman was ineffective too many times, the Lakotas no longer believed in that ceremony or the shaman who performed it. In contrast to Christianity, Native American religion focused on the efficacy of its rituals to produce the intended material results: curing the sick, bringing the buffalo, or causing rain. When they no longer believed that the rituals were effective and when they were not as dependent for their survival on these rituals, Native Americans began to abandon their rituals. Most traditional Native American religions, including the Lakota religion, taught that sickness was a result of individual sin, community sin, or witchcraft. By expelling the evil influence or atoning for the sin, the Lakotas believed that the shamanic ceremonies healed the ill person. Because healing was a central aspect of all Native American religion, the religion changed dramatically when Native Americans rejected the idea that sin caused sickness and started to adopt modern medicine. Black Elk was a healer and was also an honest person. He knew that his ceremonies were ineffective at curing whooping cough, small pox, and influenza. The Lakotas also realized this, and when they had appendicitis, they went to the hospital if they could. After Black Elk converted to Catholicism he no longer performed the *yuwipi* curing ceremonies; this was one major aspect of his religion that he abandoned (Enochs 1996, 106).

The Sun Dance was another example of a Lakota practice that fell out of use. One of the central purposes of the Sun Dance was to bring the buffalo to the Lakotas. After the United States Army and other white hunters killed most of the buffalo, the Sun Dance was no longer effective in this respect, and it became irrelevant to most of the Lakotas shortly after they were confined to reservations. Because the Lakota economy was so closely linked to its religion, the demise of the buffalo caused the Sun Dance to lose some of its significance. Though the Sun Dance had religious significance other than simply bringing the buffalo, the Sun Dance diminished in importance when the buffalo no longer returned. Furthermore, in traditional Sun Dances, the entire Sioux community sponsored the dance. After confinement to the reservations, only relatively small groups performed the Sun Dance. Some groups charge fees to the participants in the ceremonies, and some of these dances have become commercialized. Recently, women and white people sometimes dance in these ceremonies, which also has changed the character of the event. Moreover, the Sun Dance was so named because the participants stared at the sun. Modern Sun Dancers do not stare because it is damaging to the eyes. In the traditional ceremony, Sun Dancers would often have several pieces of their skin cut off as offerings to God. Modern Sun Dancers also do not endure nearly as much physical suffering as the Sun Dancers of old did to prove their commitment to God. Though some small groups of Lakotas still perform the Sun Dance, the modern Sun Dances are now radically different from those dances of the past.

Another aspect of Native American religion that fell out of practice was the Ghost Dance religion. The Ghost Dance was a new religion that emerged in the 1870s and spread around the Plains until the 1890s after which it disappeared. The Ghost Dance promised that Jesus would return to the earth, a cataclysm would kill all the white people, the buffalo would return, the world would be reborn, and the dead Native Americans would rise and reunite with the living. There were even several predictions that this apocalypse would happen around the year 1890. Because the religion was based on an apocalypse happening in a certain period of time, the Lakotas, including Black Elk, lost faith in this religion when the prophesies did not come true. One of the claims of the Ghost Dance devotees was that bullets would bounce off the shirts that the Ghost Dancers wore. After the horrible massacre at Wounded Knee in which the Seventh Cavalry slaughtered about three hundred Sioux, including many Ghost Dancers, Black Elk and the other Lakotas realized that the shirts did not protect those Ghost Dancers. After Wounded Knee, the Lakotas, including Black Elk, abandoned the Ghost Dance and became more skeptical of visions that promised magical powers and an end of suffering.

Another example of a religious ritual that Lakotas can really no longer perform as they once did was the giveaway ceremony. In this ceremony a Lakota person gave away most or all of his or her possessions. Traditionally, the Lakotas performed giveaway ceremonies at dances, rites of passage, adoption ceremonies, funerals, and other significant events. In the old days the Lakotas had a more communally oriented society, and the community took care of the person who gave away his or her possessions. Also, the person who gave away his or her possessions would have the chance to get others' possessions when they had giveaway ceremonies. In modern times this ceremony is impractical if it is practiced in the traditional way. If some in the community take more than they give or do not give at all, the balance of taking and giving is disrupted. Furthermore, modern property laws make it difficult to dispose of property or give away a house in the way that the Lakotas traditionally did. The more communal nature of the traditional Lakota society and the support of the entire community made possible rituals of charitable extravagance. Though the Lakotas perform versions of the traditional practice today, they are significantly different from the traditional practices. Before confinement on reservations, the Lakotas did not own individual tracts of land, and the modern experience of reservation life has changed their view of property. Also, since the U.S. government confined the Lakotas to reservations, they did not have the same access to their sacred places as they did in the past, which also changed their modes of worship.

One of the central forms of Lakota worship was the performance of the visions that people experienced, and this idea was essentially the focus of *Black Elk Speaks*. In this book Black Elk recounted a vision that he had when he was nine years old. He explained that the vision had to be enacted so that the power of the vision could be brought to the world and thus benefit the people (J. Neihardt 1979, 204). Finally, when he was seventeen years old, he told an elder of his vision, and the elder said to him: "You must do your duty and perform this vision for your people upon earth" (161). The Lakotas considered the visions an expression of true reality, and to act out these visions brought them in contact with the sacred powers. Because there were so many characters displayed in his vision, he needed the entire community to cooperate to enact the vision. However, this community cooperation and the community interest in enacting visions ended a decade or so after the Sioux were confined on their reservations. The Lakota religion was designed to bring the revelations of the spiritual world to the temporal world through the members of the com-

munity portraying the roles of the characters in the visions and thus becoming identified with these characters. When the Lakotas stopped performing these divine dramas, their religion changed profoundly.

After Black Elk converted to Catholicism in 1904, he became a prominent catechist on Pine Ridge Reservation and lived as a Catholic until he
died in 1950. But even before his conversion, he was interested in Christianity. In a letter he dictated when he was in Europe in 1889, he quoted
the New Testament and expressed a desire to see "where they killed Jesus"
(DeMallie 1984a, 10). When he returned to Pine Ridge, however, he continued his practice as a medicine man, and also was a Ghost Dancer. Black
Elk married Kate War Bonnet, and she had their children baptized in the
Catholic Church in 1895 (13). In 1904, Black Elk decided to join the
Catholic Church, and Father Joseph Lindebner, S.J., of Holy Rosary Mission baptized him. Following a common missionary practice, Lindebner
named Black Elk after Saint Nicholas, on whose feast day he received
baptism.

Shortly after his baptism, Black Elk became a catechist who instructed
other lay people in Catholic doctrine. As a catechist, Black Elk was a great
help to the Jesuits, and they recognized him as a model Catholic. Black
Elk was also a zealous missionary who traveled long distances to spread the
Catholic faith, and the Jesuits supported his missionary work. In 1908,
Black Elk traveled to Wyoming to evangelize the Arapahos. On May 31,
1908, the *Sinasapa Wocekiye Taeyanpaha: Catholic Sioux Herald* published Black Elk's letter describing his trip:

> We [Black Elk and Joe Red Willow, a Lakota catechist on Pine
> Ridge] are invited by a majority of people, and we had a really big meet-
> ing with the Arapahos and what they want to know about is the St.
> Joseph and St. Mary's Societies [Catholic men's and women's organiza-
> tions]. . . . And they asked me to say a few words to the members there,
> so I told them about the St. Joseph and the St. Mary's organization. First
> how to conduct a meeting, and then I told them about the order of the
> meeting: that you've got to have a president, vice-president, secretary,
> treasurer, a critic, and a doorkeeper. And they were all so enthused that
> they are going to start their own St. Joseph and St. Mary Society there.
> And then they asked me how to pray, so this is what I said to them. When
> you say the Our Father, remember that there is one Father and one Son.
> This is what you've got to believe. And after my talk, they were so inter-

ested so they want us to go back to the land of the Arapahos again, in the
near future. . . . They had a big election of officers [of the St. Mary's and
St. Joseph's Societies] while we were there. . . . The next Catholic Congress is in Rosebud. These officials are planning to come there and to get
more ideas while the meeting is going on. (Steltenkamp n.d., 259–60)

Additionally, the letters between the Jesuits of Pine Ridge and the director
of the Bureau of Catholic Indian Missions (BCIM) indicated that Black
Elk was quite a traveler and was willing to undertake these missionary
expeditions; in November 1908, the BCIM also financed Black Elk's
monthlong expedition to help convert the Winnebagos (Westropp Nov.
8, 1908; Ketcham Dec. 12, 1908). Moreover, Black Elk demonstrated his
willingness to work as a missionary in a letter to the director of the BCIM
on September 7, 1909: "The Assiniboins in Canada want the prayer [the
Catholic faith]. They want to see me very much. The other thing is this: I
want to take care that many children in North and South Dakota join the
Society for the Preservation of the Faith [a Catholic organization]. Therefore I want to go round for 2 or 3 months" (N. Black Elk 1909).

Father Westropp, a Jesuit at Holy Rosary Mission, believed that Black
Elk accomplished a great deal among the Lakotas and the other nations he
visited, and he often complimented Black Elk for his work: "I would say
that Nick [Black Elk] is a very faithful fellow and when he travels he always
has the spread of the faith in view, even if he goes in business" (c. 1909).
Westropp also credited Black Elk with many conversions: "One of the
most fervent of [the catechists] is a *quondam* [onetime] ghost dancer and
chief of the medicine men. His name is Black Elk. Ever since his conversion he has been a fervent apostle and he has gone around like a second St.
Paul, trying to convert his tribesmen to Catholicism. He has made many
converts" (c. 1910, 12). Long before any discussion arose concerning
Black Elk's fidelity to the Catholic faith, the Jesuits praised Black Elk as a
model Catholic. Black Elk often traveled with Westropp, and in 1910,
they traveled together to the Sisseton Reservation in South Dakota to
evangelize the Sioux people there (DeMallie 1984a, 21). Moreover, in
1913, Westropp arranged for Black Elk and Ivan Star-Comes-Out to help
start a mission to the Sioux on the Yankton Reservation, located in South
Dakota and Nebraska, because no priest could be found to do this (Sialm
c. 1932, 84). Through his years as a catechist, Black Elk traveled hundreds

of miles to spread the Catholic faith, visited several different reservations, attended numerous congresses, dictated more than a dozen letters to a Sioux Catholic newspaper, and served as a missionary to several Native American nations.

To prepare the Lakota catechists to evangelize, the Jesuits provided them with rigorous training and took them on retreats. Beginning in 1922, ten to twenty catechists underwent Ignatius's Spiritual Exercises each year when they went on their three-day retreats. The Jesuit retreat instructor, Sialm, reported that "the method of the examination of conscience especially pleased them, and they demanded that I should give it in writing so that they would not forget it afterwards" (1922b, 305). In 1923, Sialm recorded Black Elk's reactions to the exercises: "On the third day of that retreat, Nick Black Elk came to me with this very worthy resolution: 'We catechists resolve never to commit a mortal sin.' . . . Nick Black Elk wished to invite all the Sioux catechists to the coming retreat" (1923, 78). Black Elk went on the annual retreat eight times (N. Black Elk 1934a). The retreats were also an example of the similarities between the Catholic and Lakota religions. In traditional Lakota religion, young men went on a vision quest, a type of retreat involving intense prayer, called the *hamble iciyope* or *hanble ceyapi*, "crying for a vision." The Jesuits even used this traditional Lakota term, *hamble iciyope*, to describe Catholic retreats. By doing so, they pointed out the similarities between the two religions and drew on the Lakotas' traditions to help them understand the significance of the retreat (Digmann diary, Dec. 5–7, 1895).

To set the record straight about his dedication to the Church and to show that he was a faithful Catholic catechist, Black Elk wrote a letter in 1934 affirming his Catholic faith. He dictated this letter to his daughter, Lucy Looks Twice, and she and Father Zimmerman both signed as witnesses. In this letter, dated January 26, Black Elk said:

> In the last thirty years I am different from what the white man [Neihardt] wrote about me. I am a Christian. I was baptized thirty years ago by the Black-gown [Catholic] priest called Little Father *(Ate-ptecela)*. After that time all call me Nick Black Elk. Most of the Sioux Indians know me. I am now converted to the true Faith in God the Father, the Son and the Holy Ghost. I say in my own Sioux Lakota language: *Ate-*

unyanpi: —Our Father who art in heaven, hallowed be thy name . . . as Christ taught us to say. I say the Apostle's Creed and I believe every word of it. I believe in seven holy Sacraments of the Catholic Church. I myself received now six of them; Baptism, Confirmation, Penance, Holy Communion, Holy Marriage, and Extreme Unction. I was for several years a regular companion of several missionaries going out campaigning for Christ among my people. I was nearly twenty years the helper of priests and acted as a Catechist in several camps. So I knew my Catholic Religion better than many white people. For eight years I made the regular Retreat given by the priest for Catechists and I learned much of the faith in those days. I can give reasons for my faith. I know Whom I have believed and my faith is not vain. My family is all baptized. All my children and grand-children belong to the Black-gown church and I am glad of that and I wish that all should stay in that holy way. . . . I now know that the prayer of the Catholic Church is better than the Sun-dance or the Ghost-dance. Old Indians danced that kind for their own glory. They cut themselves so that the blood flowed. But Christ was nailed to the Cross for sin and he took away our sins. The old Indian prayers did not make people better. The medicine men looked for their own glory and for presents. Christ taught us to be humble and to stop sin. Now I hate sin. I want to be straight as the Black-gown church teaches us to be straight to save my soul for heaven. (N. Black Elk 1934a)

Just as the Jesuits, Black Elk accused the medicine men of being greedy and expecting presents for their spiritual services. He also condemned the Sun Dancers and Ghost Dancers for their pride, but still he did not reject the other aspects of the Lakota religion.

In another letter he wrote in September 1934, Black Elk complained that Neihardt did not send him half the proceeds from the sales of *Black Elk Speaks* as he promised. In that letter, Black Elk said that he asked Neihardt to include in his book that he was a Catholic: "I also asked [John Neihardt] to put at the end of this story that I was not a pagan but have been converted into the Catholic Church in which I work as a Catechist for more than 25 years. I've quit all these pagan works" (N. Black Elk 1934b). Nevertheless, Black Elk did not reject all of the traditional beliefs of his religion. In *The Sacred Pipe*, Black Elk affirmed his faith in Christianity, but he also said that he believed that the White Buffalo Cow

Woman brought the sacred pipe to the Lakotas and would return
(J. Brown 1974, xix–xx). He did not feel that his Catholic faith was inconsistent with his belief in these stories.

Although Catholic missionaries at times attempted to eliminate certain specific Native American beliefs and rites, the Jesuit missionaries accepted many aspects of Lakota culture and participated in several Lakota
rituals and customs throughout their time among the Lakotas. Furthermore, the Jesuits sought to preserve those aspects of Lakota culture that
they believed were consistent with Catholic values, and attempted to abol-
ish those practices or beliefs that they thought were in conflict with the
Catholic faith. In short, the Jesuits practiced missionary adaptation: the
process of adapting to an indigenous culture and using the symbols and
language of that culture to explain Christianity in terms that the natives
understood.

Wherever the Jesuits went, they tried to be flexible and adapt to the indigenous culture. In the Native American missions, in many cases, they
conformed to the Native American traditions of burial, and allowed Lakotas to be "buried" according to their traditional customs on scaffolding
aboveground (Digmann 1924, 26). Rather than insisting on following
European burial customs that were inessential to Catholic rituals, the Jesuits believed that the Lakotas' requests to be suspended on scaffolding
after death should be honored. In addition to their flexibility about modes
of burial, the Jesuits tolerated the Lakota custom of wailing over the
graves of the dead or singing death songs (Chronicles of the Sisters of St.
Francis 1903, 18).

Many of the Jesuits, however, from the 1890s to the 1920s, tended to
discourage Lakota Catholics from taking part in Lakota dances. One of
the reasons for this caution was the influence of the Ghost Dance religion
that gathered a following on the Lakota reservations in the years 1889 and
1890. The Jesuits wanted to eradicate dances such as the Ghost Dance and
the dances associated with the *yuwipi* healing ceremony because they saw
them as being contrary to the Catholic faith. By the 1920s the Jesuits at
Holy Rosary and St. Francis became more tolerant of the dances and believed that Lakota Catholics could view the dances and participate in them
(Enochs 1996, 131–37). The Jesuits also attended the dances at this time.
In 1934, Leo Cunningham, S.J., said that on their Fourth of July celebration, the Lakotas of Holy Rosary Mission held "various Indian dances" on

the mission grounds (134). By their willingness to allow the dances to take place on the mission grounds, the Jesuits indicated that they accepted the dances. Furthermore, several of the Catholic Lakota elders who were at Holy Rosary and St. Francis in the 1930s said that the Jesuits at this time objected to neither the Lakota dances nor the Lakota Catholics' participation in them (135). Also, in 1936, in the *Sina Sapa Wocekiye Taeyanpaha: The Catholic Sioux Herald*, an article appeared that set down guidelines for the St. Joseph's Society, a lay organization of Catholic Lakotas: "A member of the St. Joseph Society may go to Indian dances, but must govern his conduct properly" (DeMallie 1984a, 16).

From 1939 to 1941, when he taught at the Holy Rosary Mission School, John Scott, an American Jesuit, often went to the Lakota dances. He commented that the Jesuits did not mind at all if Catholics took part in these dances (1992). In 1941, Scott attended a Sun Dance, which did not involve piercing the chest. He praised the dance and indicated that the Jesuits tolerated the Lakota Catholics' participation in the Sun Dance because the Lakotas removed the aspects that the Jesuits found objectionable and transformed this dance so that it was consistent with Catholic morals (1941). Some scholars of religion believe that Black Elk's participation in Native American pageants and dances near the end of his life indicated that he still believed in the traditional Lakota religion, but this claim is not an adequate indication of his religious faith. Many of the Jesuits in the 1930s and '40s, when Black Elk took part in some dances, were happy to see Lakotas participating in such dances and saw the dances as cultural rather than religious events.

Another example of the Jesuits' desire to preserve aspects of Lakota culture was the Catholic Sioux Congresses that they helped establish. Beginning in 1890, the Catholic Sioux Congresses that were annual gatherings of one to four thousand Sioux Catholics from reservations in North and South Dakota (Enochs 1996, 53–72). The Lakota or Dakota Sioux Catholics on the reservations organized and managed these events, and these events served as a way of reestablishing the national unity of the Sioux. Traditionally, the Sioux were a large nation composed of several different bands. During June, several of the different Sioux bands gathered and held councils and Sun Dances together. However, the reservation system imposed on the Sioux broke down the national unity of the Sioux by placing them on distinct reservations that were widely separated. Therefore, the annual Catholic Sioux Congresses returned to the Sioux these annual gatherings and helped bolster their unity. The congresses, like the traditional councils, took place in June, and the Sioux traveled by horse and buggy (or later in trucks) often more than one hundred miles to come to the congresses. When they arrived at the site, they camped out in tipis or tents and stayed for usually four days. The site was organized and ordered on the basis of the traditional Sioux customs for their annual gatherings. Traditionally, when the Sioux bands gathered together for their national councils, they had the huge task of managing all the different people, and they developed customs that governed the organization of these large gatherings. These customs determined the arrangement of the tipis, the pasturing of the hundreds of horses that came, and the distribution of food and water. When the Sioux camped out at the Catholic Congresses, they had many of the same organizational tasks, and so they simply integrated their traditional customs into the congresses (Luther 1924b, 351).

Even the architecture on the grounds of the congress was similar to their traditional structures. At the Sun Dances, the Sioux would erect a circular scaffolding covered with pine boughs. At the center of the circle, they erected a center pole, from the top of which they would hang cords. During this dramatic sacrificial dance they pierced themselves through the chests, placed pieces of wood or bone under the skin of their chests, and attached the cords from the center pole to those pieces of wood or bone. At the Catholic Sioux Congresses, they still erected the same type of scaffolding and center pole. However, under the center pole they put an altar for mass (Enochs 1996, 59), and thus replaced the Sun Dance sacrifice with the Eucharist. Therefore, the Jesuits and Lakotas used the architecture and symbols of the Lakotas to help them understand and accept the sacrifice of Christ.

Before the 1940s, the congresses were also one of the places where the Lakota catechists, including Black Elk, would preach in their native language. The Jesuits recognized that the Lakotas were formidable orators, and they felt this talent should be used to help spread the gospel. Traditionally, the Lakotas were a culture that stressed oration, and at their councils they held forth for hours. The Jesuits lauded the abilities of the Lakotas and encouraged the Catholic Lakota catechists to preach to the people in the Lakota language (Enochs 1996, 61). In sum, the Catholic

Congresses that Black Elk attended sought to preserve the Lakota language, bolster their faith, encourage the Lakotas to develop lay leaders who organized and spoke at the event, unify the Sioux as a nation, and preserve some of the Lakota customs of the traditional annual councils.

One of the other signs that the Jesuits on the Pine Ridge Reservation accepted some aspects of Lakota tradition was their participation in the Lakota adoption ceremonies. The Lakota adoption ceremony, *hunka lowampi*, was a religious ritual in which a Lakota person decided to adopt another person because he or she had great respect for that person. In this ceremony, the Lakotas called upon the sacred powers to bind the two people together as relatives. The Lakotas adopted several Jesuits into their families, and the Jesuits were proud of participating in these ceremonies. The Lakotas adopted Albert Riester (the Jesuit superior of Holy Rosary Mission from 1926 to 1932), Father Henry Westropp (a Jesuit who traveled with Black Elk on missionary journeys), Joseph Zimmerman, S.J. (another Jesuit who was close to Black Elk), and several others (Riester 1930–1931, 7; Enochs 1996, 145–46). Because Black Elk saw that the Jesuits participated in adoption ceremonies, he realized that it was perfectly acceptable for Catholics to participate in some Lakota ceremonies, even ceremonies that were religious, as long as they were not contrary to Catholic teaching. The Jesuits' willingness to participate in these ceremonies showed their desire to adapt to indigenous culture, to become part of the Lakota extended families, and to preserve what they could of these cultures.

The Jesuits tolerated many other Lakota customs and made some explicit statements that described their policy of preserving Lakota customs. For example, Placidus Sialm, S.J., Black Elk's retreat director, described his participation in a baptismal feast that the Lakotas combined with the traditional Lakota name-giving ceremony:

> Mary had the feast announced beforehand, just as the Indians used to do in the old days. The Sioux always held a naming ceremony a few days after a child's birth. A messenger was sent around the camp to announce the celebration. Friends and kinsman would gather around the tepee to congratulate the proud parents, who would in turn feast them and give away presents. Catholic Indians like Mary Kills Two like to keep up the old custom in a Christian way. . . . This feast is also a sample of

how old customs have been transformed and transfigured into Christian
customs, with still a strong flavor of their Indian character. . . . Christianity has helped the Sioux to preserve many of their fine old customs and by
its touch has made them finer. It has deepened and strengthened their
natural virtues. (1937, 67–68)

Mary Kills Two preserved the structure of the traditional ceremony: the
announcement, the prayers, the songs, the speeches, and the name-giving
ceremony in which the child was "adopted" into the band. The combination of the baptismal feast and the name-giving ceremony is especially interesting because the adoption symbolism of the name-giving ceremony
was in some ways similar to baptism in which one is adopted into the
Christian community and adopted by God (Stolzman 1986b, 21–32). By
combining the name-giving ceremony and baptismal feast, Mary Kills
Two on her own initiative adapted her traditions to make them consistent
with Catholic practice. Sialm's comments showed that the Jesuits accepted
such innovations.

Joseph Zimmerman, S.J., shared Sialm's appreciation of Lakota culture. An experienced missionary, Zimmerman was with the Lakotas from
1922 until he died in 1954. Zimmerman also made a clear statement of
the Jesuits' pastoral theology: "The Church has always emphasized that
the missionary should adapt himself to the ways of thinking of his converts, should take what is good and noble in their way of life and preserve
it not destroy it" (Scott 1963, 5–6). Similarly, William Moore, S.J., who
was a scholastic at St. Francis Mission at the time, also stated that the Jesuits at St. Francis did not try to eradicate the Lakota customs: "The missionaries of St. Francis Mission on the Rosebud reservation, South
Dakota, try to adapt their work to the Indian spirit. They are concerned
about instilling the life of grace into the souls of their people, not about
imposing alien customs upon a race which clings to its traditional ways"
(1939, 118). The approach of Moore, Zimmerman, and Sialm was consistent with that of Pope Pius XII who stressed in *Summi Pontificatus* (1939)
that the good aspects of indigenous culture should be preserved to help
enrich the world (Carlin 1981, 11). At the Holy Rosary Mission, the pastoral ministry of the Jesuits advocated the preservation of Lakota art, medicine, food, games, language, and some of their traditional rituals and
ethics (Enochs 1996, 101–50). Furthermore, they believed that some

continuity existed between the traditional Lakota religion and Christianity. The Jesuits saw that some of the Lakotas' indigenous customs and religious beliefs contained rays of truth that could be built on and perfected by Christianity.

Black Elk lived on a reservation where the Jesuit priests tried to adapt in many ways to the Lakota culture. Jesuits took part in Lakota adoption ceremonies and attended Lakota dances. The Lakotas prayed to *Wakantanka* in Catholic churches. The elders told Lakota legends with the encouragement of the Jesuits (Enochs 1996, 94). The people gathered annually in Sioux national congresses that the Sioux organized according to their traditional customs. Even the architecture at these gatherings resembled the Sun Dances of old. Lakota catechists preached in the Lakota language and maintained positions of respect and leadership in the communities. All of this was encouraged by the Catholic Church. The Jesuits whom Black Elk knew well, like Zimmerman, encouraged the preservation of many Lakota traditions and spoke the Lakota dialect. Thus, Black Elk did not have to be a "traditionalist" to tell Lakota legends, participate in certain Lakota ceremonies such as the *hunka,* take part in traditional dances, and worship *Wakantanka.* He could do all these things and remain a Catholic. The basic structure of Catholicism and the Lakota religion was similar in some respects, which facilitated Black Elk's conversion. The similarities also allowed Black Elk to see that the Lakota religion was in continuity with Catholicism. In the Catholic and Lakota religions, the conceptions of reconciliation, the dead, rituals, justification, and sacrifice all were similar. Therefore, Black Elk did not see his conversion as a complete change of worldview. As a Catholic, Black Elk took part in Ignatian retreats that resembled the vision quests of old in some ways. He prayed to guardian angels just as he prayed to the helper spirits of his traditional religion. Black Elk saw the Catholic faith as refining his traditional beliefs, validating some of those beliefs and practices, and building on some of the virtues (such as charity) of his traditional religion. Even though he retained his belief in some Lakota legends, still he did not advocate returning to other central aspects of the Lakota religion such as the *yuwipi.*

When Neihardt wrote *Black Elk Speaks,* he saw the religion and culture of the Native Americans dissolving in the face of modernity, and he wrote a romantic epic to try to recapture the sense of majesty of the Lakota Nation. Today the Lakotas no longer hunt buffalo. They wear modern clothing and have televisions. Few are interested in the traditional Lakota religion, and many are Christian. Through Black Elk, some people and scholars are trying to recapture the romance of a lost era, and some still try to portray Black Elk as a "traditionalist" Lakota. However, this cannot be true because the traditional Lakota religion changed so dramatically by the 1890s that it ceased to exist as their traditional religion. The Lakota religion involved the Lakota community gathering to celebrate or gathering to enact visions. After confinement to the reservations, the Sioux Nation and even the Lakota communities did not celebrate their religion as a whole. Rather, a few individuals gathered and performed versions of traditional rituals adapted to modern times. The traditional Lakota religion was a community religion that was also inextricably linked with a nomadic hunting lifestyle that the Lakotas by 1890 no longer practiced. It also focused on shamanic healing practices that had become largely obsolete with the advent of modern medicine. When people try to argue that Black Elk or any other Native American in the twentieth century was a "traditionalist," they overlook the fact that the traditional Native American religion was closely tied to their economies of hunting or farming, to their conceptions of space, to their communities, to their warfare, and to their sacred places. All of these things have changed so dramatically that the term *traditionalist* Native American is a misnomer. Native Americans who are interested in their traditional religions do not practice anything like their traditional religion, and Black Elk was the same. After converting to Catholicism, Black Elk no longer went out on war parties to prove his bravery, the prime virtue of the Native American man. After his conversion, he did not steal horses from rival groups of Native Americans to prove his bravery or to use as a bride price. He did not seek many wives, which was a common practice for Lakotas. He also no longer hunted buffaloes, and thus the Sun Dance no longer held its traditional meaning. He no longer practiced the shamanic healing ceremonies. Though he may have been generous with his possessions, he did not perform the giveaway ceremony as he would have prior to being confined to a reservation. All of these things were aspects of traditional Lakota religion that he gave up because of the realities of modern living. In the modern world none of the Sioux can be said to practice their traditional religion, because they no longer practice the central Lakota rituals or rely upon these rituals in the way that they did in the past. The traditional Sun Dance, the giveaway, the healing rituals, the community performance of visions, their observance of menstrual taboos, and their warrior ethics were all central aspects of Lakota religion that Black Elk and the other Lakotas abandoned as they entered modern society.

PART FOUR

Reading about Black Elk

16

Sources and Suggestions for Further Study of Black Elk and Lakota Culture

RAYMOND A. BUCKO, S.J.

To understand Black Elk and his impact on contemporary Lakota and non-Lakota culture, it is important to take a variety of paths, realizing that each has limitations. Black Elk himself spoke in Lakota. John Neihardt, a poet, and Joseph Brown, a historian of religion, collaborated with Black Elk to create two core texts in English. Still others have written representations and interpretations of his words and their essential meaning. Because Black Elk has died, we cannot simply ask him exactly what he meant, nor can we ask what early commentators or the early Lakota meant for they, too, have passed away. Thus, we need to use a variety of sources to understand the worldview from which Black Elk came, as well as the commentaries of those people who sought to learn about Black Elk and Lakota culture in general.

Black Elk was and remains part of a vibrant living culture that has always had its own self-understandings and that has taken a growing role in representing and interpreting itself to the outside world. The essence of Lakota culture resides in the life of the people, not in the records of cul-

Special thanks to Mary Lee Shanahan, who helped the author and editor resolve bibliographic questions. Michael Steltenkamp, Todd Wise, Paul Steinmetz, George W. Linden, Greg Fields, and Clyde Holler contributed valuable suggestions for this bibliography. I take full responsibility, however, for the final selection of works. Special thanks also to Brother Simon, who allowed me access to the Heritage Center Library at Holy Rosary Mission and to Inga Barnello, Ann Waterbury, and a very patient group of student workers at Le Moyne College, who helped me track down some material.

305

tural observers. The documents provided in this bibliography can help illustrate earlier and contemporary Lakota culture, but they remain representations of it, recorded by travelers, military personnel, missionaries, and a variety of scholars, who generally wrote for a non-Lakota audience.

This bibliography is neither exhaustive nor critical. I have chosen works that provide a variety of opinions from as many disciplines and interests as possible. I do not judge which works are more accurate or more appropriate than others. There are a variety of debates about the interpretation of Lakota culture in terms of content as well as method that will become clearer as you read broadly. Some debates are abandoned or resolved, and new concerns are picked up over the years. Also, Lakota concerns and debates are not necessarily the same as outside observers'.

The "Allies" (a translation of the word *Lakota*) consist of three divisions, distinct in dialect and geographical range. The Santee, who call themselves Dakota, are the easternmost group; the Yankton, who also refer to themselves as Dakota, are in the center; and the Teton, who call themselves Lakota, are westernmost (DeMallie 1986, 20). This bibliography is primarily focused on the Lakota, but I have included some important material from the other two groups, as they are closely related to the Lakota both culturally and linguistically.

When examining this material, keep a few principles in mind:

1. Be aware that observers themselves are the products of their time and culture. Often the new introductions to older works that have been reprinted will help alert you to the biases of the observer, even though individuals writing introductions themselves have limitations and biases. It is helpful to understand the history and philosophy of the times in which particular works are written. Try to read a variety of a single author's works and to understand the cultural context from which the particular author comes.

2. All cultures change. Culture is best imaged as a verb rather than a noun. Contemporary American society has a dual standard. It expects its own culture to change continually yet, at the same time, bemoans change in other societies, particularly Indian societies. In the nineteenth century, Europeans held that all peoples should be compelled to change their lifeways and "progress." Today, romantic Europeans and Americans often contend that non-Europeans should remain "as they were." The tragedy of Indian-white relations is not that Indian groups changed (such groups

were and continue to be highly adaptive and innovative) but that outsiders compelled changes without consultation or consent.

3. Cultures are internally heterogeneous. Not all individuals in a culture see the world the same way or agree among themselves about what is culturally proper. The Lakota had various points of view at contact with Europeans, and most likely before this. Historically, the Europeans exacerbated the splits among this people. Any dynamic society will construct itself out of disagreement as well as agreement. Primal harmony, though clearly an ideal, probably never existed.

4. No single individual can represent an entire culture. Cultural knowledge belongs to individuals and to groups that are divided by age, gender, and other social categories. Thus, to understand any culture, it is important to read widely and to listen to as many individuals and observe as many groups as possible.

5. Lakota society is as contemporary as any other. In the nineteenth century, Europeans defined native people as primitive (first, primary) and aboriginal (from the beginning). They thought that, by studying the Indian present, they could understand their own past. Often, such observers considered that the past, in which they thought Indians were living, was degraded and backward, because they believed that their own culture represented the pinnacle of progress. Today, as with the thought of Rousseau, this primal fixation places non-European people in an exalted position. In fact, Lakota culture is as contemporary as any other. Lakota people have made different cultural choices. Lakotas today have an interest in Black Elk as well as other spiritual and political leaders (and one need not separate these functions). While the Lakota themselves look to their past for strength and inspiration, they also look to the present and future.

6. Cultural groups assert a primacy of interpretative voice. From their first contact, European Americans have been interested in native peoples as have natives been interested in European Americans: Black Elk himself "did research" in Europe. Some Lakota contend that their ancestors concealed their true culture from outsiders and that this untouched knowledge still exists, but clearly an overwhelming amount of material has been documented and preserved by European and American scholars, at times at the request of native peoples. This corpus of written material is a potential resource for Lakota people, but it also represents alienated knowledge. While Europeans were busy preserving this knowledge, they were equally

busy convincing the original possessors of this knowledge that it was no longer of value. Thus, as the Lakota continue, revive, or re-create their religious and social behavior, much of which was suppressed by the churches as well as by the government, this material understandably creates ambivalence.

7. The material in this bibliography is "about" Lakota history and culture. I remind my students whenever we embark on a study of native America that we study the recorded impressions of other peoples at different times and places and from different perspectives. Each work, whether generated by a Lakota or an outside scholar, presents (and in some ways creates) an image. The image helps us to understand the cultural reality of Lakota people but should not be confused with the reality itself. Some images (and the information that constitutes them) are more accurate than others. Much scholarly debate is precisely on this point. A good entrée into the idea of how the image of Native Americans has been and continues to be constructed is the classic work by Robert Berkhofer Jr. (1978; see also Bordewich 1996; Clifton 1990; P. Deloria 1998; Dippie 1982; Pearce 1988). A more recent anthology of essays on this topic is also available (Bird 1996), and Thomas Biolsi has written on this topic in the context of Lakota anthropology (1997).

8. Finally, no matter how well described a group is, the reality is more dynamic and beautiful than any representation can be. To study the Lakota is not to know the Lakota nor does it give one the authority to be Lakota. Reading is not a substitute for experience and actual historic connection. Insight into a culture can give one an enhanced worldview, but one cannot simply read oneself into a culture.

The study of Lakota spirituality and Indian religion in general has become a particularly controversial subject within native communities and in academic circles (Grimes 1996; Hernàndez-Ávila 1996; Ridington 1996). Native people have seen land, material possessions, language, livelihood, and free choice quickly alienated by encroaching European populations. Today, many Lakota hold that their religion is the last thing they have left. At the same time, Lakota religion is highly democratic in that individuals act as religious leaders according to individual inspiration through dreams and visions, as well as community assent when individuals, often relatives, participate in specific ceremonies and support the spiritual leader. When non-Lakota set themselves up as experts in a culture not inherently their own, and when both traveling medicine men and non-Lakota learn and then enact Lakota ceremonies off of the reservations and out of reach of community control, the Lakota rightfully protest the exploitation of their religion.

Some Lakota also see their religion as universal with prayers and rituals beneficial for and accessible to all peoples. Many Lakota say that the four colors in ceremonies represent all the nations or races in the world and that all should be included and welcomed to participate. For the most part, any sincere person is welcome to pray with Lakota, and Lakota do not hold that they own spirituality. The Lakota do, however, retain the right to interpret and perform their own ceremonies. Some hold for a strict isolation from the outside world, others for total inclusiveness, and still others walk between the two extremes. To begin understanding this controversy, start with a helpful series of articles by Avis Little Eagle (1991a; 1991b; 1991c; 1991d; 1991e; 1991f; 1992a; 1992b) as well as editorials by Tim Giago Jr. (1992; 1993) and a commentary by Ward Churchill (1994). Anthropologist Alice Kehoe has also commented on this phenomenon (1990).

There exists an Internet web page with a statement by one group of Lakota concerning their rights to their own spirituality (a statement that not everyone would totally agree with in every element). This statement can be found at: *http://web.lemoyne.edu/~bucko/war.html,* and is reprinted in Churchill (1994).

An ongoing dialogue concerning this statement written by both Indian and non-Indian people can be found at: *http://web.lemoyne.edu/~bucko/war_resp.html.*

Works "by" Black Elk

Although Nicholas Black Elk himself wrote several letters and entries in missionary newspapers that have been preserved (see DeMallie 1984c), he was not the author of the works most commonly associated with his name. Two authors wrote works based on separate interviews with Black Elk: John G. Neihardt, *Black Elk Speaks* (1932); and Joseph E. Brown, *The Sacred Pipe* (1953). A second work by Neihardt, *When the Tree Flowered,* incorporates elements of Black Elk's narrative (1951). The original transcripts of the narratives that Neihardt collected and used in his own work have also been published (DeMallie 1984a). There are no transcripts available for Brown's work.

Neihardt's other works include both poetry and literary analysis (1900; 1907; 1908; 1909; 1910; 1911; 1912; 1913; 1914; 1915; 1919; 1920a; 1920b; 1925a; 1925b; 1926; 1928; 1935; 1941; 1945; 1953; 1965; 1971a; 1971b; 1972a; 1972b; 1978; 1988). Joseph Brown also wrote a variety of items on the Lakota and native peoples in general (1964; 1976; 1978; 1979; 1980; 1982a; 1982b; 1982c; 1982d; 1983a; 1983b; 1984; 1989a; 1989b; 1992; 1996). A familiarity with these materials will assist the reader in understanding the perspective that each author brought to his work on Black Elk, as well as how collaboration with Black Elk has transformed their subsequent thought.

Materials "about" Black Elk

Works about Black Elk include those written by anthropologists Michael Steltenkamp (1993; for information on Lakota religious practice see 1982 and his n.d.), William Powers (1990c), Alice Kehoe (1989a), and Raymond DeMallie (1984b; 1984c; 1995). Julian Rice, a professor of English, has also written about Black Elk (1985; 1989; 1991; 1998) as have philosopher Clyde Holler (1984a; 1984b; 1995) and Daniel Dombrowski (1987). Kiowa author N. Scott Momaday has written about Black Elk's vision (1984). There are also works of literary analysis and criticism that include those works by philosopher George W. Linden (1984; see also 1977a; 1977b; 1994), George W. Linden and Fred Robbins (1984), as well as scholars Robert Berner (1984), Anne Downey (1994), Roger Dunmore (1997), Arnold Krupat (1985b), Sally McCluskey (1972), William Nichols (1983), Paul Olson (1982), Reece Pendleton (1995), Robert Sayre (1971), James Spresser (1985), Albert Stone (1982a), Todd Wise (1995), and Hertha Wong (1992b). John Neihardt's daughter Hilda wrote a reminiscence on her encounters with Black Elk based both on her own recollections and the diary of her sister, Enid (1995). Lakota Ed McGaa has produced audio and visual material in which he repeats elements from the Black Elk corpus, as well as comments on Black Elk and his teachings (n.d.-a; n.d.-b; n.d.-c). Works focusing on Black Elk from other fields include pedagogy (Couser 1996; see also 1988) and religious studies (Almqvist and Lambert 1985). Recent work on Black Elk includes Arnold (1999), S. Howard (1999), and Lakota author Archambault (1998).

Works focused on John Neihardt that also deal with his writings on Black Elk include those by Lucile Aly (1977; 1984), Gretchen Bataille (1984), W. E. Black (1969), Bobby Bridger (1984), Dee Brown (1984), Michael Castro (1983), Julius House (1920), Peter Iverson (1984), Alvin Josephy Jr. (1984), Frederick Manfred (1984), Carl Starkloff, S.J. (1984), Helen Stauffer (1981), Frank Waters (1984), and Blair Whitney (1976).

Lakota History

To understand contemporary Lakota, it is essential to understand their history. Recent work on Lakota history includes a biography of Sitting Bull (Utley 1993), a history of the Oglala (Price 1996), a general history of the Lakota (Allen 1997), as well as a history told from a Lakota woman's perspective (Bettelyoun 1997). Two recent biographies of Red Cloud have also appeared (Larson 1997; Paul 1997). Other historical works include those works by John Ewers (1938), George Hyde (1937; 1956; 1961), H. Scudder Mekeel (1943), James Olson (1965), and Doane Robinson (1956). One of the most important sources of participant narratives by Lakotas who took part in many historic events is the work of Stanley Vestal (1934; 1948; 1957; 1984). Richard Hardorff has collected a series of narratives on the Battle of the Little Big Horn, an engagement in which Black Elk himself participated (1997; see also 1991; 1993; 1995; 1998). For a more contemporary history, anthropologist Tom Biolsi has written about the New Deal on the Pine Ridge and Rosebud Reservations (1992; see also 1995).

In addition to oral traditions, Lakota and other Plains peoples kept Winter Counts, mnemonic records of their history that represent each year by a pictograph of a significant event that occurred during that year. There is an extensive literature on these counts (Feraca 1994; Finster 1968; Grange 1963; Howard 1955b, 1960b, 1976; Karol 1969; Mallery 1886, 1893; W. Powers 1994; and Praus 1962. Amos Bad Heart Bull sketched a pictographic history of the Oglala (Blish 1967). Joseph White Bull recorded his deeds in image and text (1998).

The Ghost Dance and Wounded Knee

Black Elk makes specific mention of his involvement with the Ghost Dance, a phenomenon of religious revitalization that swept large parts of native North America. The classic work on the Ghost Dance contains considerable Lakota material and was written by James Mooney, who interviewed many of the participants (1896; reprinted in 1991). David Miller wrote a more recent account, which also relies on participant narratives (1985). Alice Kehoe has produced a contemporary ethnohistory of the Ghost Dance (1989b), as has Raymond DeMallie (1982). William Powers has published a collection of Ghost Dance songs in Lakota and English (1990a). Robert Utley wrote a comprehensive history of the events leading up to the tragedy at Wounded Knee (1963). Other writers about Wounded Knee include the Lakota George Sword (1892), Rex Smith (1975), Renee Sansom Flood (1995), Elaine Goodale Eastman (1945), and Jensen, Paul, and Carter (1991). The most accessible account about Wounded Knee and other tragic incidents in Indian-white relations was written by Dee Brown (1972). William and Marla Powers have compiled a bibliography on Wounded Knee material (1994; see also Osterreich 1991). Conger Beasley Jr. has written an account intertwining descriptions of the original tragedy with the contemporary Big Foot Memorial Ride (1995).

Approaches to Lakota Culture by Native Scholars

To gain a broad picture of Lakota culture, one should read a variety of materials, keeping in mind that different people will have different and sometimes conflicting perspectives. Pay close attention to when the material was written, what audience the author was addressing, and what the background of the writer was.

From early on, the Lakota have represented themselves diplomatically, economically, and culturally first through oral presentation and then through the written word. Marie McLaughlin (1842–?), a mixed-blood Dakota, recorded a series of Lakota stories (1916). Anthropologist Franz Boas worked extensively with native experts who acted as anthropologists in their own right. One of his most notable colleagues was linguist and ethnologist Ella Deloria (1889–1971), who wrote extensively on Lakota language and culture (1929; ca. 1937; 1944; 1954; 1961; 1972; 1974; 1988). This anthropological tradition is carried on today by Lakota Beatrice Medicine from the Standing Rock Reservation (1969a; 1969b; 1976; 1978; 1981; 1987).

One of the most important authors on contemporary political, religious, and legal issues is Vine Deloria Jr., a Lakota from the Standing Rock Reservation (1969; 1970a; 1970b; 1972; 1974a; 1974b; 1975; 1976; 1978; 1979a; 1979b; 1980; 1982; 1984b; 1992; 1995; 1997; 1999). His son Philip Deloria, a historian, has written on native identity (1998). A recent anthology assesses Deloria's impact on anthropology (Biolsi and Zimmerman 1997).

With regard to religious experience, Arval Looking Horse has written about the Sacred Pipe (1987). Lakota artist and scholar Arthur Amiotte has also written about his own religious experiences and understanding of Lakota spirituality (1976; 1982a; 1982b; 1987; 1989). Joseph Iron Eye Dudley has also written about the Lakota experience (1992). Virginia Driving Hawk Sneve has written on Lakota culture, the Episcopal Church among the Lakota, and folktales (1974; 1977; 1993; 1995; 1997). In an article on preaching in a Lakota context, Martin Brokenleg provides helpful background for understanding both Lakota religious perspectives and the phenomenon of dual participation (1998).

One of the earliest writers is Charles Eastman (1858–1939), a Santee who became a doctor, worked at Pine Ridge during the Wounded Knee massacre, and moved freely between Indian and white worlds (1894; 1898; 1902; 1904; 1907 (reprinted as 1991b); 1910; 1911 (reprinted as 1980); 1913; 1914; 1915; 1916 (reprinted as 1977); 1918 (reprinted as 1991a). His prolific writings include works about history, religion, and mythology. He collaborated on several works with his wife, Elaine Goodale Eastman (1909, reprinted as 1990; 1919; 1930). Elaine Goodale Eastman also wrote about her own experiences (1978).

The Yankton-Nakota Zitkala-Sa (Red Bird, 1876–1938), whose American name was Gertrude Simmons Bonnin, recorded a series of stories as well as her own reflections on Indian and American life (Zitkala-Sa 1901, reprinted as 1985b; 1921, reprinted as 1985a). Lakota author Luther Standing Bear (1868–1939) wrote a series of works that focus on his own life and cultural experiences (1975; 1978; 1988a; 1988b). Contemporary Lakota educator Allen C. Ross has produced two largely auto-biographical texts, which include reflections on Lakota religion (1989; 1992). Delphine Red Shirt has written about her experiences of growing up on and off the Pine Ridge Reservation in the 1960s and '70s (1997).

There are several Lakota people who teach Lakota religion to non-Lakota, stressing their belief that these beliefs (referred to as "ways") are for all peoples. The most published of these teachings is Ed McGaa, Eagle Man (1990; 1992; 1995; 1998). He also maintains his own web site: (*http://members.aol.com/eagleman4/index.html*). Floyd Hand has also written on his experiences (1998).

"As-told-to" Narratives

Black Elk Speaks lies in the genre of "as-told-to narrative" in that the narrator, Black Elk, is not the actual author. This form of literary conveyance has continued into the present. Thomas Mails, artist, author, and minister, is the main chronicler of Frank Fools Crow's life (1979; 1991). He has also written and illustrated works on the Lakota and other Plains groups (1972; 1973; 1988) as well as a work on the Sun Dance that contains extensive interviews with Fools Crow and Eagle Feather (Bill Schweigman) as well as excerpts from early authors on the Lakota (1978). There are many illustrations and photographs of the Sun Dance ceremony itself. Today, photographing ceremonies is forbidden.

A second prolific author of "as-told-to" narratives is Richard Erdoes, an Austrian-born writer who has chronicled the life of John Fire Lame Deer (Erdoes and Lame Deer 1972; see also Erdoes 1973), and his son, Archie Fire Lame Deer (Erdoes and Archie Lame Deer 1992). Erdoes has also compiled two narratives by Mary Brave Bird (formerly Mary Crow Dog), once wife of medicine man Leonard Crow Dog (Erdoes and Mary Crow Dog 1990; Erdoes and Mary Brave Bird 1993), and the Crow Dog family, medicine men from the Rosebud Reservation (Erdoes and Leonard Crow Dog 1995). Erdoes has also written on other Plains Indians, as well as the Lakota (1972; 1976; 1990).

In addition to these works, Mark St. Pierre assisted Madonna Swan (1991) and compiled a second book of narratives (St. Pierre and Long Soldier 1995), William Lyon assisted Wallace Black Elk (not a relative of Nicholas Black Elk) on his autobiography (Black Elk and Lyon 1990),

Carolyn Reyer has collected narratives and original writing with native scholars Beatrice Medicine and Debra Lynn White Plume (1991), and Robert Holden taped and transcribed the words of Pete Catches Sr. and Peter V. Catches (Catches, Catches, and Holden 1997; see also Jeltz 1991).

Nineteenth-Century Anthropological Approaches

There was much written about the Lakota during the nineteenth and beginning of the twentieth centuries, when it was falsely assumed Indian culture would soon disappear. There was an interest in learning about societies that were very different from those societies of European origin. In addition, the government and churches sought to understand Indian peoples so that they might guide their policies and better "ease their transition" into Christianity and American society.

Much of the work of nineteenth-century and early-twentieth-century anthropologists was salvage anthropology, an attempt to reconstruct the life of tribes before contact with Europeans (Hinsley 1981; Bieder 1986). This work was accomplished through memory ethnography: the use of informants' memories to reconstruct an often idealized and systematized past. Thus, there was more focus on the remembered past than on then contemporary native life as Indians struggled with new political, cultural, and economic realities.

The late nineteenth century and early twentieth century were marked by the belief that cultures all evolve from the primitive through the barbaric into a civilized form. Thus, anthropologists believed that native people would eventually "progress" through these stages. The government and churches thought it their duty to move "primitive" people toward civilization through education and transformation of their economic systems. These ideas of social evolution were abandoned, by and large, in the mid-twentieth century.

The most extended fieldwork at the turn of the century was carried on by Dr. James R. Walker. Walker was a physician at the Pine Ridge Reservation, dedicated to working from within the culture to help alleviate the ever increasing health problems of the Oglala. He was enlisted by Clark Wissler of the American Museum of Natural History to gather data on the Lakota. Although Walker did not publish extensively when alive (1905;

1906; 1914; 1917), he collected a rich variety of firsthand accounts of Lakota life and religious beliefs that were published posthumously (1980; 1982; 1983).

Another important publisher of Lakota materials at the turn of the century was James Owen Dorsey of the Bureau of American Ethnology (1884; 1885; 1889a; 1889b; 1889c; 1891a; 1891b; 1892; 1894; 1897). One of his principal collaborators was the Lakota George Bushotter (De-Mallie 1978a). In addition to working with James Walker, Clark Wissler wrote several pieces on Lakota culture (1904; 1907a; 1907b; 1912). George Dorsey wrote an early article on the Sacred Pipe of the Lakota (1906). Another important early ethnographer of the Lakota was Alice Fletcher (1882; 1883; 1884a; 1884b; 1891; 1896).

Twentieth-Century Anthropological Approaches

The early-twentieth-century ethnographers remained concerned with the remembered past (a concern that perdures today) but also focused on the "assimilation" and acculturation of native groups (Herskovits 1958; Redfield, Linton, and Herskovits 1941). This is the era of assimilation studies. The assumption was that native people would eventually lose their distinct cultures and identities. As it became clearer that native culture, although radically transformed in many ways, would not disappear, the focus of anthropological study changed in the middle twentieth century to an examination of cultural persistence: how native groups have remained distinct and retained cultural, religious, and economic patterns from the past. Thus, contemporary anthropology focuses on both the historical past and the transformed past brought into the present by various native groups. Anthropologists continue to be interested in the phenomena of cultural persistence and the reinvention and reinvigoration of culture (Hobsbawm and Ranger 1986; see also Handler and Linnekin 1984).

An important early-twentieth-century source for both music and cultural information is ethnomusicologist Frances Densmore (1916; 1918, reprinted as 1992; 1920a; 1920b). There are also works on then contemporary religious practice written by Robert Ruby, a physician stationed on Pine Ridge (1955; 1966). Ruby discusses *yuwipi*, a healing ritual utilized by the Lakota that Black Elk does not mention in his narratives. Louis Kemnitzer has also written extensively on this topic (1969a; 1969b; 1970;

1975; 1976; 1978). Other information on *yuwipi* can be found in Eugene Fugel (1966) and Hurt and Howard (1960). William Powers has devoted an entire narrative ethnography to this topic (1982). Stephen Feraca, who began fieldwork with the Oglala in 1954, has written on Lakota religion and ritual practice as well as other concerns (1957; 1961; 1962; 1963, reprinted 1998; 1990).

Anthropologist James Howard researched a wide variety of topics on the Lakota as well as the Dakota both in the United States and in Canada, focusing on historical and contemporary practice (1950; 1951; 1954a; 1954b; 1955a; 1960a; 1960c; 1961; 1962; 1966; 1968; 1972; 1980; 1984). Elizabeth Grobsmith has written on language as well as social reciprocity and religion (1974; 1976; 1979a; 1979b; 1981a; 1981b).

Works concerned with Lakota cultural transformations in the acculturationist school include those by Macgregor (1946), Goldfrank (1943), Vernon Malan (1956; see also 1958; 1962; Malan and Jesser 1959; Malan and Powers 1960; Malan and Schusky 1962), Haviland Scudder Mekeel (1932a; 1932b; 1936), and an anthology of articles compiled by Ethel Nurge (1970). The interest in assimilation waned as anthropologists abandoned the notion of cultural evolution and native culture proved more resilient than outsider observers had anticipated.

Later-twentieth-century anthropologists remain interested in portraits of cultural pasts as well as cultural persistence. Anthropologist William Powers wrote and later published his doctoral dissertation on contemporary Lakota religion (1975). Some knowledge of the anthropological theory of structuralism is helpful in reading this work. He has published extensively on Lakota culture as well as music and dance (1970; 1979; 1980a; 1980b; 1981a; 1981b; 1982; 1985; 1986; 1987a; 1987b; 1990a; 1990b; 1994). His wife, anthropologist Marla Powers, has also focused her research on the Lakota (1980; 1986; 1988; 1990a; 1990b; 1991). They have also collaborated on projects (1984; 1986; 1994).

Ethnohistorian Raymond DeMallie has published significant material on the contemporary Lakota (1978b; 1979; 1987; 1988) although the bulk of his research and writing focuses on the Lakota past (1971; 1976a; 1976b; 1977; 1978a; 1982; 1983; 1986; 1987; see also DeMallie and Lavenda 1977). History of religions student Paul Steinmetz wrote on heterogeneity in Lakota religious practice (1998a). There is also a very useful volume of articles largely originating from a 1982 conference titled "American Indian Religion in the Dakotas: Historical and Contemporary Perspectives" (DeMallie and Parks 1987). Raymond Bucko has written on the constitution of tradition using the sweat lodge as an example (1998; see also 1992). Writers on the use of Sacred Pipes among the Lakota include John Smith (1967; 1970) and Patricia Kaiser (1984). The most recent example of medical doctor turned ethnographer is Thomas Lewis, whose work focuses primarily on cross-cultural psychology (1968; 1970; 1972; 1974a; 1974b; 1975a; 1975b; 1980a; 1980b; 1980c; 1981; 1982a; 1982b; 1987; 1990).

Contemporary Lakota secular and sacred music has been commented on by a variety of authors, including Frances Densmore (1916; 1918, reprinted as 1992; 1920a), Franz Boas (1925), William Powers (1970; 1980a; 1980b; 1990a; 1990b), Harry Paige (1970), Ben Black Bear Sr. with Ron Theisz (1976), Ron Theisz (1996), and John Around Him and Albert White Hat (1983). Ron Theisz has also collected contemporary oral narratives (1975).

Royal Hassrick produced a comprehensive and approachable ethnography of the Lakota at the time of contact (1964). For a general introduction to contemporary Lakota life there is a ethnography on the Rosebud Reservation in the 1970s (Black Elk settled on the Pine Ridge Reservation to the west of Rosebud) (Grobsmith 1981b) and a more contemporary ethnography from the early 1990s focusing on ethnic identity on the Pine Ridge Reservation (Kurkiala 1997). Ernest Schusky has written a historical ethnography of the Lakota of Lower Brule (1977). Early observers and writers on the Eastern Dakota, culturally and linguistically related to the Lakota, include the trader Peter Pond (1908), the missionary brothers Samuel and Gideon Pond (S. Pond 1908, reprinted as 1986; G. Pond 1854; 1857; 1889), and Alanson Skinner (1919). Later writers using the genres of history and anthropology include Robert Lowie (1913), Gary Clayton Anderson (1984), Ruth Landes (1968), Janet Spector (1993; 1994) and Roy Meyer (1967).

Literary Approaches to Lakota Culture

The main writers who look at Native American literature using the perspectives of literary criticism as well as cultural analysis are Arnold Krupat

(1985a; 1987; 1989; 1992; 1993; 1996), Hertha Wong (1992a), Greg Sarris (1993), and H. David Brumble (1981; 1988). Douglas Parks and Raymond DeMallie approach the same interpretive problems from an anthropological perspective (1992). Lynn Obrian (1973) and Mick McAllister (1997) have also written about Plains Indian autobiographies. Julian Rice incorporates both ethnographic and literary approaches in looking specifically at Lakota narrative and mythological texts (1984; 1989; 1991; 1992a; 1992b; 1993; 1994a; 1994b; 1998). Elaine Jahner has written on Lakota oral narrative as well as mythology (1977; 1983a; 1983b; 1987; 1989).

Philosophic and History-of-Religions Approaches

The Jesuits have been involved with the Lakota since their first meetings with Father De Smet in the mid-1800s (see Enochs 1996). The twentieth century has produced several Jesuit scholars who have written on the Lakota, all of them having extensive experience living among the people. Paul Steinmetz, S.J., did his academic work in the history of religions in Sweden under Åke Hultkranz and writes on Lakota religious pluralism as well as the relationship between Christianity and Lakota religion (1970; 1984a; 1984b; 1990; 1998a; 1998b). Father William Stolzman, a former Jesuit, worked both on the Rosebud and the Pine Ridge Reservations and hosted a dialogue between the Catholic priests and Lakota medicine men on the Rosebud (1986b). He also wrote a narrative on proper conduct during Lakota ceremonies (1986a). Michael Steltenkamp, S.J., taught on the Pine Ridge Reservation as well as doing research there (n.d.; 1982; 1993; 1997).

Thomas Parkhill has written a general work on the study of Native American religions with some references to Black Elk (1997), and Lee Irwin also refers to Black Elk in his work on Plains Indian visions (1994).

Photographic Approaches

The Lakota have been subjects of photographic as well as ethnographic representations. Edward Curtis made the Lakota part of his photographic as well as textual portrait of North American Indians (1970). There are two collections of early reservation photographs by John Anderson (Hamilton and Tyree 1971; Dyck 1971). Jensen, Paul, and Carter's work on Wounded Knee includes an extensive photographic record (1991). Don Doll, S.J., has also worked to bring into publication historic photographs by Anderson and the Jesuit missionary Eugene Buechel, S.J., as well as his own contemporary work (Doll and Alinder 1976; see also Buechel 1974 and Paige 1987). Doll has also published a book containing portraits and narratives of contemporary Lakota and Dakota peoples that gives a remarkable portrait of internal diversity while showing strong tribal solidarity and cohesion through his own photographic work and the first-person narratives of those people whom he depicts (1994; 1996).

Contemporary Social Issues

Although most outside interest in Lakota peoples lies in their religion, authors have also written on other areas of Lakota life. Anthropologists Murray and Rosalie Wax and Robert Dumont have written on education on the Pine Ridge Reservation (Wax, Wax, and Dumont 1989), and Erik Erikson (1939) provides a psychological portrait of this population. Peter Matthiessen has written about Leonard Peltier, an Indian activist who was on Pine Ridge (1983). Roxanne Ortiz has written about contemporary political and legal issues (1977; 1980), and Edward Lazarus has written a comprehensive work on the history and legal issues concerning the Black Hills (1991). Ron Goodman has written about Lakota star knowledge in general as well as its relationship to Lakota claims on the Black Hills (1992). Writers on the protest at Wounded Knee in 1973 include Robert Burnette and John Koster (1974), Rolland Dewing (1995), Jay Furlong (1980), Stanley Lyman (1991), Edward Milligan (1973), Terry Schultz (1973; 1974), and Bill Zimmerman (1975).

Lakota Language

The earliest published materials in the Lakota language were produced by missionaries. As the Lakota learned to write their language, they began recording business accounts as well as personal correspondence in Lakota. The most comprehensive Lakota dictionary was produced by Eugene Buechel, S.J. (1970). It draws on earlier works written for the Dakota language, a dialect closely resembling Lakota, by two brothers who were missionaries, Gideon and Samuel Pond, and later missionary Stephen Return

Riggs (1852; 1890, reprinted as 1992; 1893). The missionary John Williamson also produced a Dakota-language dictionary (1902, reprinted as 1992). Although Father Buechel's dictionary has the largest collection of words, the majority of the dictionary translates only from Lakota to English, and some of the words have fallen out of contemporary usage (they are not indicated as such in the dictionary). Father Buechel also wrote a grammar modeled after a classic Greek or Latin grammar (1939). Paul Manhart, S.J., also edited a series of stories Father Buechel collected in their original Lakota forms (Buechel 1978) and has also published English translations of these stories (Buechel and Manhart 1998). Father Buechel also collected Lakota botanical terms, as well as uses for each species (Rogers 1980). There are interesting recollections of Father Buechel in Dudley (1992). The anthropologist Franz Boas, working with Ella Deloria, wrote on Lakota grammar (Boas 1937; Boas and Deloria 1941).

A series of texts and tapes produced by two linguists are aimed at learning contemporary spoken Lakota (Rood and Taylor 1976a; 1976b; 1976c). The Sinte Gleska College Center produced an earlier course aimed at gaining conversational competence that also uses both tapes and text (Hairy Shirt et al. 1973). Edward and Ivan Starr have also produced Lakota language materials (E. Starr 1994; I. Starr 1997). A series of stories written in Lakota and English in the 1940s by Ann Clark has recently been republished (1994a; 1994b; 1995a; 1995b; 1995c; 1996a; 1996b).

Other Resources

An effective way to increase your range of understanding of Lakota culture through written records is to read bibliographies. They will help you trace down the sources used by each author you read, which will also aid you in determining the author's particular perspective. At the same time, keep an eye out for new publications and reprintings of rare materials. The University of Nebraska publishes a large amount of Plains Indian material, including Lakota material. Lakota Books specializes in reprinted material and also publishes some original works. Other presses, such as the University of Oklahoma and Syracuse University Press, also publish some Lakota material.

Indian Country Today, formerly the *Lakota Times,* prints many articles and editorials focused on the Lakota. In addition, there are many sources on the Internet. You can use various search engines to locate these sites. There are a variety of pages dedicated specifically to the Lakota such as one kept by the author of this bibliography: *http://web.lemoyne.edu/~bucko/lakota.html*. The author also keeps a bibliography of Lakota and related materials on the Internet (this list is without annotations): *http://web.lemoyne.edu/~bucko/biblio.html*.

Published bibliographical works on the Lakota and related groups include those by Hoover (1979), Hoover and Marken (1980), and DeMallie (1970).

Although the Internet is an interesting and easily accessible tool for research, keep in mind that not everything you want is out there, nor is everything that is out there reliable. As with published material, you need to use the material critically. Simply typing something and posting it on the Net does not make it authentic.

Finally, keep in mind that written sources are a way to begin to understand a culture and are not the culture itself. Culture is dynamic. The written word may capture the dynamism of culture, but it also freezes it in a particular moment. Culture is not simply a collection of dances, ceremonies, and rules for behavior. Culture is made primarily of groups of historically connected people who continually preserve, innovate, and negotiate the lessons handed to them by previous generations while handing them on to the next generation. Reading as widely as possible can expose that dynamism and help you begin to appreciate it. Studying another culture is a process that helps bring to consciousness your own culture. When we begin to understand and respect the way others have viewed the world in the past, we can better appreciate cultural diversity in the present, both in the cultures of others as well as our own, and we may even learn how to live together better in the future.

Works Cited

Acterberg, Jeanne. 1985. *Imagery in Healing: Shamanism and Modern Medicine.* Boston: New Science Library.

Albanese, Catherine L. 1990. *Nature Religion in America: From the Algonkian Indians to the New Age.* Chicago: Univ. of Chicago Press.

Allen, Charles. 1997. *From Fort Laramie to Wounded Knee: The West That Was.* Lincoln: Univ. of Nebraska Press.

Almqvist, Kurt, and Stephen Lambert. 1985. "The Three Circles of Existence: Cosmology of Black Elk." *Studies in Comparative Religion* 17, no. 1/2: 24–29.

Aly, Lucile F. 1977. *John G. Neihardt: A Critical Biography.* Amsterdam: Rodopi.

———. 1984. "Trappers and Indians: Neihardt's Short Stories." In *A Sender of Words: Essays in Memory of John G. Neihardt,* edited by Vine Deloria Jr., 72–84. Salt Lake City: Howe Brothers.

Amiotte, Arthur. 1976. "Eagles Fly Over." *Parabola* 1, no. 3: 28–41.

———. 1982a. Foreword to *The Gift of the Sacred Pipe,* edited by J. E. Brown. Norman: Univ. of Oklahoma Press.

———. 1982b. "Our Other Selves: The Lakota Dream Experience." *Parabola* 7, no. 2: 26–32.

———. 1987. "The Lakota Sun Dance: Historical and Contemporary Perspectives." In *Sioux Indian Religion,* edited by Raymond J. DeMallie and Douglas R. Parks, 75–89. Norman: Univ. of Oklahoma Press.

———. 1989. "Our Other Selves." In *I Become Part of It: Sacred Dimensions in American Life,* edited by D. M. Dooling and Paul Jordan-Smith, 161–72. New York: Parabola Books.

Anderson, Gary Clayton. 1984. *Kinsmen of Another Kind: Dakota-White Relations in the Upper Mississippi Valley.* Lincoln: Univ. of Nebraska Press.

Archambault, Marie Therese, O.S.F. 1998. *A Retreat with Black Elk: Living in the Sacred Hoop.* Cincinnati: St. Anthony Messenger Press.

Arnold, Philip P. 1999. "Black Elk and Book Culture." *Journal of the American Academy of Religion* 67, no. 1 (Mar.): 85–111.

Around Him, John, and Albert White Hat. 1983. *Lakota Ceremonial Songs.* Rosebud, S.D.: Sinte Gleska College.

Auerbach, Stephen M., Donald J. Kiesler, Thomas Strentz, and James A. Schmidt, et al. 1994. "Interpersonal Impacts and Adjustment to the Stress of Simulated Captivity: An Empirical Test of the Stockholm Syndrome." *Journal of Social and Clinical Psychology* 13, no. 2 (summer): 207–21.

Bachelard, Gaston. 1964. *The Poetics of Space.* Boston: Beacon Press.

Barnet, Miguel. 1968. *The Autobiography of a Runaway Slave.* Edited by Esteban Montejo and translated by Jocasta Innes. New York: Pantheon Books.

Barsh, Russell. 1993. "An American Heart of Darkness: The 1913 Expedition for American Indian Citizenship." *Great Plains Quarterly* 13 (spring): 91–116.

Bartholomew, Marianna. 1994. "The Search for Black Elk." *Our Sunday Visitor* (29 May).

Bartlett, F. C. 1932. *Remembering: A Study in Experimental and Social Psychology.* Cambridge: Cambridge Univ. Press.

Bataille, Gretchen M. 1984. "Black Elk: New World Prophet." In *A Sender of Words: Essays in Memory of John G. Neihardt,* edited by Vine Deloria Jr., 135–42. Salt Lake City: Howe Brothers.

Beasley, Conger, Jr. 1995. *We Are a People in This World: The Lakota Sioux and the Massacre at Wounded Knee.* Fayetteville: Univ. of Arkansas Press.

Benjamin, Walter. 1968. *Illuminations.* Edited by Hannah Arendt and translated by Harry Zohn. New York: Schocken Books.

Bergson, Henri. 1970. *Les deux sources de la morale et de la religion.* Paris: Presses Universitaires de France.

Bergstraesser, Arnold. 1949. *Goethe's Image of Man and Society.* Chicago: Henry Regnery.

Berkhofer, Robert F., Jr. 1976. *Salvation and the Savage: An Analysis of Protestant Missions and American Indian Response, 1787–1862.* 1965. New York: Athenaeum.

———. 1978. *The White Man's Indian: Images of the American Indian from Columbus to the Present.* New York: Random House, Vintage.

Berner, Robert L. 1984. "Trying to Be Round: Three American Indian Novels." *World Literature Today* 58, no. 3 (summer): 341–44.

Bettelyoun, Susan Bordeaux. 1997. *With My Own Eyes: A Lakota Woman Tells Her People's History.* Edited by J. Waggoner. Lincoln: Univ. of Nebraska Press.

Beverley, John. 1993. *Against Literature.* Minneapolis: Univ. of Minnesota Press.

Bieder, Robert. 1986. *Science Encounters the Indian, 1820–1880: The Early Years of American Ethnology.* Norman: Univ. of Oklahoma Press.

Biolsi, Thomas. 1992. *Organizing the Lakota: The Political Economy of the New*

Deal on the Pine Ridge and Rosebud Reservations. Tucson: Univ. of Arizona Press.

———. 1995. "The Birth of the Reservation: Making the Modern Individual among the Lakota." *American Ethnologist* 22, no. 1: 28–53.

———. 1997. "The Anthropological Construction of 'Indian.' " In *Indians and Anthropologists: Vine Deloria, Jr. and the Critique of Anthropology,* edited by Thomas Biolsi and Larry J. Zimmerman, 133–59. Tucson: Univ. of Arizona Press.

Biolsi, Thomas, and Larry J. Zimmerman, eds. 1997. *Indians and Anthropologists: Vine Deloria, Jr. and the Critique of Anthropology.* Tucson: Univ. of Arizona Press.

Bird, R. Elizabeth, ed. 1996. *Dressing in Feathers: The Construction of the Indian in American Public Culture.* Boulder, Colo.: Westview Press.

Black, W. E. 1969. "Ethic and Metaphysic: A Study of John G. Neihardt." *Western American Literature* 2, no. 3: 205–12.

Black Bear, Ben, Sr., and Ron Theisz. 1976. *Songs and Dances of the Lakota.* Rosebud, S.D.: Sinte Gleska College.

Black Elk, Charlotte. 1986. "Prepared Statement." U.S. Congress. Senate. Committee on Indian Affairs. *Sioux Nation Black Hills Act: Hearings on S. 1453.* 99th Cong., 2d sess., 185–214.

———. 1992. "Children of the Four Relations Around the Heart of Everything That Is." In *Lakota Star Knowledge: Studies in Lakota Stellar Theology,* edited by Ronald Goodman, 44–45. Rosebud, S.D.: Sinte Gleska Univ.

Black Elk, Nicholas. 1909. Marquette Univ. Archives. Holy Rosary Mission Collection, series 1, box 63, folder 3.

———. 1934a. Marquette Univ. Archives. Holy Rosary Mission Collection, series 1/1, box 1, folder 5. Pine Ridge, Jan. 26.

———. 1934b. Marquette Univ. Archives. Holy Rosary Mission Collection, series 1/1, box 1, folder 5. Sept. 20.

Black Elk, Wallace H., and William R. Lyons. 1990. *Black Elk: The Sacred Ways of a Lakota.* New York: Harper and Row.

Blish, Helen H., ed. 1967. *A Pictographic History of the Oglala Sioux.* Drawings by Amos Bad Heart Bull. Lincoln: Univ. of Nebraska Press.

Boas, Franz. 1925. "Teton Sioux Music." *Journal of American Folklore* 38, no. 147: 319–24.

———. 1937. "Some Traits of the Dakota Language." *Language* 13, no. 2: 137–41.

Boas, Franz, and Ella Deloria. 1941. "Dakota Grammar." *Memoirs, National Academy of Science* 23, no. 2: 1–183.

Bordewich, Fergus W. 1996. *Killing the White Man's Indian*. New York: Doubleday.

Bridger, Bobby. 1984. "The Enduring Presence of John Neihardt." In *A Sender of Words: Essays in Memory of John G. Neihardt,* edited by Vine Deloria Jr., 46–58. Salt Lake City: Howe Brothers.

Brokenleg, Martin. 1998. "A Native American Perspective: That the People May Live." In *Preaching Justice: Ethnic and Cultural Perspectives,* edited by Christine Marie Smith, 26–42. Cleveland: United Church Press.

Brown, Dee. 1972. *Bury My Heart at Wounded Knee*. New York: Bantam Books.

———. 1984. "The Power of John Neihardt." In *A Sender of Words: Essays in Memory of John G. Neihardt,* edited by Vine Deloria Jr., 5–11. Salt Lake City: Howe Brothers.

Brown, Joseph E., ed. 1953. *The Sacred Pipe: Black Elk's Account of the Seven Rites of the Oglala Sioux*. Norman: Univ. of Oklahoma Press.

———. 1964. *The Spiritual Legacy of the American Indian*. Vol. 135, *Pendle Hill Pamphlet*. Lebanon, Pa.: Sowers Printing.

———, ed. 1971. *The Sacred Pipe: Black Elk's Account of the Seven Rites of the Oglala Sioux*. 1953. Harmondsworth, Eng.: Penguin.

———, ed. 1974. *The Sacred Pipe: Black Elk's Account of the Seven Rites of the Oglala Sioux*. 1953. Norman: Univ. of Oklahoma Press.

———. 1976. "The Roots of Renewal." In *Seeing with a Native Eye,* edited by W. Capps, 25–34. New York: Harper and Row.

———. 1978. "Sun Dance: Sacrifice—Renewal—Identity." *Parabola* 3, no. 2: 12–15.

———. 1979. "The Wisdom of the Contrary." *Parabola* 4, no. 1: 54–65.

———. 1980. "The Spiritual Legacy of the American Indian." *Studies in Comparative Religion* 14, nos. 1–2: 18–33.

———. 1982a. "Becoming Part of It: Native American Sacred Values as Models for Our Own." *Parabola* 7, no. 3: 6–12.

———. 1982b. "Book Review: People of the Sacred Mountain." *Parabola* 7, no. 1: 99–101.

———. 1982c. "Knowledge and the Sacred." *Parabola* 7, no. 4: 100–102.

———. 1982d. *The Spiritual Legacy of the American Indian*. New York: Crossroad.

———. 1983a. "The Bison and the Moth: Lakota Correspondences." *Parabola* 8, no. 2: 6–13.

———. 1983b. "The Unlikely Associates: A Study in Oglala Sioux Magic and Metaphysics." *Studies in Comparative Religion* 15: 92–100.

———. 1984. "Book Review: Lakota Myths—J. R. Walker." *Parabola* 9, no. 2: 99–100.

———. 1989a. "The Pipe of Reconciliation (a Native American Symbol of Relationship)." *Parabola* 14, no. 4: 82–83.

———. 1989b. "The Bison and the Moth." In *I Become Part of It: Sacred Dimensions in American Life,* edited by D. M. Dooling and Paul Jordan-Smith, 177–87. New York: Parabola Books.

———. 1992. *Animals of the Soul: Sacred Animals of the Oglala Sioux.* Rockport, Mass.: Element.

———. 1996. "The Sacred Center (the Peace Pipe)." *Parabola* 21, no. 3: 40–41.

Bruhn, A. R., and J. Last. 1982. "Earliest Childhood Memories: Four Theoretical Perspectives." *Journal of Personality Assessment* 46, no. 2: 119–27.

Brumble, H. David. 1981. *An Annotated Bibliography of American Indian and Eskimo Autobiographies.* Lincoln: Univ. of Nebraska Press.

———. 1988. *American Indian Autobiography.* Berkeley and Los Angeles: Univ. of California Press.

Bucko, Raymond A., S.J. 1992. "Inipi: Historical Transformation and Contemporary Significance of the Sweat Lodge in Lakota Religious Practice." Ph.D. diss., Univ. of Chicago.

———. 1998. *The Lakota Ritual of the Sweat Lodge: History and Contemporary Practice.* Lincoln: Univ. of Nebraska Press.

Buechel, Eugene. 1924. *Wowapi Wakan, Wicowoyake Yuptecelapi: Bible History in the Language of the Teton Sioux Indians.* Edited by Paul Manhart. New York: Benziger Brothers.

———. 1939. *A Grammar of Lakota: The Language of the Teton Sioux Indians.* St. Louis: John R. Swift.

———. 1970. *Lakota-English Dictionary.* Edited by Paul Manhart. Pine Ridge, S.D.: Holy Rosary Mission.

———. 1974. *Eugene Buechel, S.J.: Rosebud and Pine Ridge Photographs, 1922–1942.* El Cajon, Calif.: Grossmont College Development Foundation.

———. 1978. *Lakota Tales and Texts.* Edited by P. Manhart. Pine Ridge, S.D.: Red Cloud Indian School.

Buechel, Eugene, and Jesuit Fathers of St. Francis Mission. 1927. *Lakota Wocekiye na Olowan Wowapi: Sioux Indian Prayer and Hymn Book.* St. Louis: Central Bureau of the Catholic Central Verein of America.

Buechel, Eugene, and Paul Manhart. 1998. *Lakota Tales and Texts in Translation.* Vols. 1 and 2. Chamberlain, S.D.: Tipi Press.

Burnette, Robert, and John Koster. 1974. *The Road to Wounded Knee.* New York: Bantam Books.

Campbell, Joseph. 1989. "When People Lived Legends: American Indian Myths." William Free Productions and Mythology.

Carlin, Claudia, ed. 1981. *The Papal Encyclicals.* Wilmington: McGrath.

Carraro, Francine. 1996. "An Art Historian Reassesses the New Deal Murals." *Gallery Talk* (14 Feb. 1996), Great Plains Art Gallery, Lincoln, Nebr.

Castro, Michael. 1983. *Interpreting the Indian: Twentieth-Century Poets and the Native American.* Albuquerque: Univ. of New Mexico Press.

Catches, Peter, Sr., Peter V. Catches, and Robert I. Holden. 1997. *Oceti Wakan (Sacred Fireplace).* Pine Ridge, S.D.: Oceti Wakan.

Charleston, Steve. 1996. "The Old Testament of Native America." In *Native and Christian: Indigenous Voices on Religious Identity in the United States and Canada,* edited by James Treat, 68–80. New York: Routledge.

Childs, Peter, and Patrick Williams. 1997. *An Introduction to Post-Colonial Theory.* New York: Prentice-Hall.

Chittenden, Hiram Martin. 1905. *Life, Letters and Travels of Pierre-Jean De Smet.* New York: Francis P. Harper.

Chronicles of the Sisters of St. Francis: 1888–1940. 1903. Unpublished manuscript in Marquette Univ. Archives.

Churchill, Ward. 1989. "A Little Matter of Genocide: Native American Spirituality and New Age Hucksterism." *Bloomsbury Review* (Sept./Oct.): 23–24.

———. 1994. "Declaration of War Against Exploiters of Lakota Spirituality." In *Indians Are Us?* edited by Ward Churchill, 273–77. Monroe, Maine: Common Courage Press.

———. 1996. "Spiritual Hucksterism." In *From a Native Son,* edited by Ward Churchill, 355–61. Boston: South End Press.

Churchill, Ward, and M. Annette Jaimes. 1988. "American Indian Studies: A Positive Alternative." *Bloomsbury Review* 8, no. 5 (Sept./Oct.): 27.

Clark, Ann. 1994a. *The Pine Ridge Porcupine—Wazi Ahanhan Pahin K'un He.* 1941. Reprint, Kendall Park, N.J.: Lakota Books.

———. 1994b. *The Slim Butte Raccoon—Paha Zizipela Wiciteglega Kin.* 1942. Reprint, Kendall Park, N.J.: Lakota Books.

———. 1995a. *The Grass Mountain Mouse—He Pejiit Unkala Kin.* 1954. Reprint, Kendall Park, N.J.: Lakota Books.

———. 1995b. *The Hen of Wahpeton—Unjincila Wahpetun Etanhan Kin He.* 1954. Reprint, Kendall Park, N.J.: Lakota Books.

———. 1995c. *Singing Sioux Cowboy—Lakota Pteole Hoksila Lowansa.* 1947. Reprint, Kendall Park, N.J.: Lakota Books.

———. 1996a. *Bringer of the Mystery Dog—Sunka Wan Wakan Agli Kin He.* 1943. Reprint, Kendall Park, N.J.: Lakota Books.

———. 1996b. *There Still Are Buffalo—Nahanci Pte Yunakpi.* 1942. Reprint, Kendall Park, N.J.: Lakota Books.

Clifford, James. 1988. "On Ethnographic Authority." In *The Predicament of Culture,* 21–54. Cambridge and London: Harvard Univ. Press.

Clifton, James A., ed. 1990. *The Invented Indian*. New Brunswick, N.J.: Transaction Publishers.

Cohen, Sande. 1988. *Historical Culture: On the Recoding of an Academic Discipline*. Berkeley and Los Angeles: Univ. of California Press.

Cohn, Norman. 1970. *The Pursuit of the Millennium*. New York: Oxford Univ. Press.

Cook-Lynn, Elizabeth. 1996a. *Why I Can't Read Wallace Stegner and Other Essays: A Tribal Voice*. Madison: Univ. of Wisconsin Press.

———. 1996b. "American Indian Intellectualism and the New Indian Story." *American Indian Quarterly* 20, no. 1: 73–88.

Couser, G. Thomas. 1988. "Black Elk Speaks with Forked Tongue." In *Studies in Autobiography*, edited by James Olney, 73–88. New York: Oxford Univ. Press.

———. 1996. "Indian Preservation: Teaching *Black Elk Speaks*." In *Teaching American Ethnic Literature: Nineteen Essays*, edited by John R. Maitino and David R. Peck, 21–36. Albuquerque: Univ. of New Mexico Press.

Cunningham, Leo. 1928. "The Great Spirit." *Indian Sentinel* 8 (spring): 60.

Curtis, Edward. 1970. *The North American Indian*. Vol. 3. New York: Johnson Reprint.

d'Aquili, Eugene. 1983. "The Myth-Ritual Complex: A Biogenetic Structural Analysis." *Zygon* 18, no. 3: 247–69.

Daugherty, George H., Jr. 1927. "The Technique of Indian Composition." *Open Court* 41: 150–66.

Deleuze, Gilles. 1993. *The Deleuze Reader*, edited by Constantin Boundas. New York: Columbia Univ. Press.

Deloria, Ella C. 1929. "The Sun Dance of the Oglala Sioux." *Journal of American Folklore* 42: 354–413.

———. c. 1937. *Teton Myths* [The George Bushotter coll.], MS 30 (x8c.3), (Boas Coll., American Philosophical Society, Philadelphia), 56: 1.

———. 1944. *Speaking of Indians*. New York: Friendship Press.

———. 1954. "Short Dakota Texts, Including Conversations." *International Journal of American Linguistics* 20: 17–22.

———. 1961. "Some Notes on the Santee." *Museum News of the W. H. Over Museum* 22: 1–7.

———. 1972. *Dakota Texts*. 1932. New York: DaCapo.

———. 1974. *Dakota Texts*. 1932. New York: AMS Press.

———. 1988. *Waterlily*. Lincoln: Univ. of Nebraska Press.

Deloria, Philip. 1998. *Playing Indian*. New Haven: Yale Univ. Press.

Deloria, Vine, Jr. 1969. *Custer Died for Your Sins: An Indian Manifesto*. New York: Macmillan.

———. 1970a. "Some Criticisms and a Number of Suggestions." In *Anthropology and the American Indian: A Symposium,* edited by J. Henry, 93–99. San Francisco: Indian Historical Press.

———. 1970b. *We Talk, You Listen: New Tribes, New Turf.* New York: Macmillan.

———, ed. 1972. *Of Utmost Good Faith.* New York: Bantam Books.

———. 1974a. *Behind the Trail of Broken Treaties: An Indian Declaration of Independence.* New York: Delacorte Press.

———. 1974b. *The Indian Affair.* New York: Friendship Press.

———. 1975. *God Is Red.* New York: Dell.

———. 1976. "This Country Was a Whole Lot Better Off When Indians Were Running It." In *Solving "The Indian Problem": The White Man's Burdensome Business,* edited by M. L. Wax and R. W. Buchanan, 177–90. New York: New Viewpoints/Franklin Watts.

———. 1978. "The Indian Student Amid American Inconsistencies." In *The Schooling of Native America,* edited by T. Thompson, 9–27. Washington, D.C.: American Association of Colleges for Teacher Education.

———. 1979a. Introduction to *Black Elk Speaks.* Lincoln: Univ. of Nebraska Press.

———. 1979b. *The Metaphysics of Modern Existence.* New York: Harper and Row.

———. 1980. "Our New Research Society: Some Warnings to Social Scientists." *Social Problems* 27, no. 3: 265–71.

———. 1982. Introduction to *The Vanishing Race and Other Illusions.* New York: Pantheon Books, in association with the Smithsonian Institution Press.

———, ed. 1984. *A Sender of Words: Essays in Memory of John G. Neihardt.* Salt Lake City: Howe Brothers.

———. 1992. "Is Religion Possible? An Evaluation of the Present Efforts to Revive Traditional Tribal Religions." *Wicazo Sa* 8 (spring 1992): 35–39.

———. 1995. *Red Earth, White Lies: Native Americans and the Myth of Scientific Fact.* New York: Scribner.

———. 1997. "Conclusion: Anthros, Indians and Planetary Reality." In *Indians and Anthropologists: Vine Deloria, Jr. and the Critique of Anthropology,* edited by T. Biolsi and L. J. Zimmerman, 204–21. Tucson: Univ. of Arizona Press.

———. 1999. *For This Land: Writings on Religion in America.* New York: Routledge.

Deloria, Vine, Jr., and Sandra Cadwalader, eds. 1984. *The Aggressions of Civilization: Federal Indian Policy since the 1880s.* Philadelphia: Temple Univ. Press.

Deloria, Vine, Jr., and Clifford Lytle. 1984a. *The Nations Within: The Past and Future of American Indian Sovereignty.* New York: Pantheon Books.

———, eds. 1984b. *American Indians, American Justice.* Austin: Univ. of Texas Press.

Deloria, Vine, Sr. 1987. "The Establishment of Christianity among the Sioux." In *Sioux Indian Religion*, edited by Raymond J. DeMallie and Douglas R. Parks, 91–111. Norman: Univ. of Oklahoma Press.

Delpit, Lisa. 1995. *Other People's Children: Cultural Conflict in the Classroom.* New York: New Press.

DeMallie, Raymond J. 1970. "A Partial Bibliography of Archival Manuscript Material Relating to the Dakota Indians." In *The Modern Sioux*, edited by E. Nurge, 312–43. Lincoln: Univ. of Nebraska Press.

———. 1971. "Teton Dakota Kinship and Social Organization." Ph.D. diss., Univ. of Chicago.

———. 1976a. "Nicollet's Notes on the Dakota." In *Joseph N. Nicollet on the Plains and Prairies*, edited by Edmund C. Bray and Martha Coleman Bray, 250–81. St. Paul: Minnesota Historical Society.

———. 1976b. "Teton Dakota Time Concepts: Methodological Foundations for the Writing of Ethnohistory." *Folklore Forum, Bibliographic and Special Series* 5: 7–17.

———. 1977. "Lakota Classifications of Peoples." Paper read at the Thirty-fifth Plains Conference, Lincoln, Nebr.

———. 1978a. "George Bushotter, Teton Sioux, 1864–1892." In *American Indian Intellectuals*, edited by M. Liberty, 91–102. St. Paul: West Publishing.

———. 1978b. "Pine Ridge Economy: Cultural and Historical Perspectives." In *American Indian Economic Development*, edited by Sam Stanley, 237–312. The Hague: Mouton.

———. 1979. "American Indian Kinship Systems: The Dakota." In *Currents in Anthropology: Essays in Honor of Sol Tax*, edited by R. Henshaw, 221–41. The Hague: Mouton.

———. 1982. "The Lakota Ghost Dance: An Ethno-historical Account." *Pacific Historical Review* 51: 385–405.

———. 1983. "Male and Female in Traditional Lakota Culture." In *The Hidden Half*, edited by P. Albers and B. Medicine, 237–61. Lanham, Md.: Univ. Press of America.

———, ed. 1984a. *The Sixth Grandfather: Black Elk's Teachings Given to John G. Neihardt.* Lincoln: Univ. of Nebraska Press.

———. 1984b. "John G. Neihardt's Lakota Legacy." In *A Sender of Words: Essays in Memory of John G. Neihardt*, edited by Vine Deloria Jr., 110–34. Salt Lake City: Howe Brothers.

———. 1984c. Introduction to *The Sixth Grandfather: Black Elk's Teachings Given to John G. Neihardt*, edited by Raymond J. DeMallie, 3–74. Lincoln: Univ. of Nebraska Press.

———. 1986. "The Sioux in Dakota and Montana Territories: Cultural and Historical Background of the Ogden B. Read Collection." In *Vestiges of a Proud Nation: Ogden B. Reid Collection of Western Art,* edited by Glenn Markoe, 19–64. Burlington, Vt.: Robert Hull Fleming Museum.

———. 1987. "Lakota Belief and Ritual in the Nineteenth Century." In *Sioux Indian Religion,* edited by Raymond J. DeMallie and Douglas R. Parks, 25–43. Norman: Univ. of Oklahoma Press.

———. 1988. "Lakota Traditionalism: History and Symbol." In *Native North American Interaction Patterns,* edited by R. Darnell and M. Foster, 2–21. Hull, Quebec: Canadian Museum of Civilization, National Museum of Canada.

———. 1995. "Black Elk." In *A Companion to American Thought,* edited by Richard Wrightman Fox and James T. Koppenberg, 78–81. Oxford: Blackwell.

———. 1997. Review of *Black Elk's Religion,* by Clyde Holler. *Journal of American History* 84, no. 1 (June): 245.

DeMallie, Raymond J., and Douglas R. Parks, eds. 1987. *Sioux Indian Religion.* Norman: Univ. of Oklahoma Press.

DeMallie, Raymond J., and Robert H. Lavenda. 1977. "Wakan: Plains Siouan Concepts of Power." In *The Anthropology of Power: Ethnographic Studies from Asia, Oceania and the New World,* edited by R. Fogelson and R. Adams. New York: Academic Press.

Densmore, Frances. 1916. "Music in Relation to the Religious Thought of the Teton Sioux." In *Holmes Anniversary Volume, Anthropological Essay.* Washington, D.C.

———. 1918. *Teton Sioux Music.* Vol. 61, "Bulletin of the Bureau of American Ethnology." Washington, D.C.: Government Printing Office.

———. 1920a. "The Rhythm of Sioux and Chippewa Music." *Art and Archaeology* 9, no. 2: 58–67.

———. 1920b. "The Sun Dance of the Teton Sioux." *Nature* 104: 437–40.

———. 1992. *Teton Sioux Music and Culture.* 1918. Reprint, Lincoln: Univ. of Nebraksa Press.

Derrida, Jacques. 1978. *Writing and Difference.* Chicago: Univ. of Chicago Press.

Dewing, Rolland. 1995. *Wounded Knee II.* Chadron, Nebr.: Great Plains Network.

Digmann, Florentine. 1886–1922. Diary. Unpublished manuscript in Marquette Univ. Archives.

———. 1924. "I Want to See the Great Spirit." *Indian Sentinel* 4 (Jan.): 26.

Dippie, Brian W. 1982. *The Vanishing American: White Attitudes and U.S. Indian Policy.* Middletown, Conn.: Wesleyan Univ. Press.

Doll, Don, S.J. 1994. *Vision Quest: Men, Women, and Sacred Sites of the Sioux Nation*. New York: Crown.

———. 1996. *Vision Quest: Men, Women and Sacred Sites of the Sioux Nation*. Omaha: Magis Press. CD ROM.

Doll, Don, S.J., and Jim Alinder, eds. 1976. *Crying for a Vision: A Rosebud Sioux Trilogy, 1886–1976: Photographs by John A. Anderson, Eugene Buechel, S.J., Don Doll, S.J.* Dobbs Ferry, N.Y.: Morgan and Morgan.

Dombrowski, Daniel A. 1987. "Black Elk's Platonism." *North Dakota Quarterly* 55, no. 1: 56–64.

Dooling, D. M. 1984. *The Sons of the Wind: The Sacred Stories of the Lakota*. New York: Harper.

Dooling, D. M., and Paul Jordan-Smith, eds. 1989. *I Become Part of It: Sacred Dimensions in American Life*. New York: Parabola Books.

Dorsey, George A. 1906. "Legend of the Teton Sioux Medicine Pipe." *Journal of American Folk Lore* 19: 326–29.

Dorsey, James Owen. 1884. "Siouan Folk-Lore and Mythologic." *American Antiquarian and Oriental Journal* 6: 174–76.

———. 1885. "Siouan Folk-Lore and Mythologic Notes." *American Antiquarian and Oriental Journal* 7: 105–8.

———. 1889a. "Camping Circles of the Siouan Tribes." *American Anthropologist* 2: 175–77.

———. 1889b. "Teton Folk-Lore." *American Anthropologist* 2: 143–58.

———. 1889c. "Teton Folk-Lore Notes." *Journal of American Folklore* 2: 133–39.

———. 1891a. "Games of Teton Dakota Children." *American Anthropologist* 4: 329–45.

———. 1891b. "The Social Organization of Siouan Tribes." *Journal of American Folk-Lore* 4: 257–63.

———. 1892. "Nanibozhu in Siouan Mythology." *Journal of American Folklore* 5: 293–304.

———. 1894. "A Study of Siouan Cults." *Bureau of American Ethnology, Annual Reports* 11: 351–544.

———. 1897. "Siouan Sociology." *U.S. Bureau of American Ethnology, Annual Reports* 15: 205–44.

Douglas, Frederic H., and Rene D'Harncourt. 1941. *Indian Art of the United States*. New York: Museum of Modern Art.

Downey, Anne M. 1994. "A Broken and Bloody Hoop: The Intertextuality of *Black Elk Speaks* and Alice Walker's *Meridian*." *Melus* 19: 37–45.

Drewermann, Eugen. 1990. *Tiefenpsychologie und Exegese, Band 1: Traum, Mythos, Märchen, Sage und Legende*. Freiberg: Walter-Verlag.

Drinnon, Richard. 1980. *Facing West: The Metaphysics of Indian-Hating and Empire-Building*. New York: New American Library.

Dudley, Joseph Iron Eye. 1992. *Choteau Creek: A Sioux Reminiscence*. Lincoln: Univ. of Nebraska Press.

Dunsmore, Roger. 1977. "Nickolaus Black Elk: Holy Man in History." *Kuksu: Journal of Backcountry Writing* 6: 4–29.

Duratschek, Sister Mary Claudia. 1947. *Crusading along Sioux Trails: A History of the Catholic Indian Missions of South Dakota*. Yankton, S.D.: Grail.

Dyck, Paul. 1971. *Brulé: The Sioux People of the Rosebud*. Flagstaff, Ariz.: Northland Press.

Eastman, Charles. 1894. *The Sioux Mythology*. Vol. 46, *Popular Science Monthly*.

———. 1898. *Sioux Mythology*. Edited by H. Bassett and F. Starr. Vol. 1, *The International Folk-Lore Congress of the World's Columbian Exposition*. Chicago: Charles Sergel.

———. 1902. *Indian Boyhood*. New York: McClure, Phillips.

———. 1904. *Red Hunters and the Animal People*. New York: Harper.

———. 1907. *Old Indian Days*. New York: McClure, Phillips.

———. 1910. *Smoky Days, Wigwam Evenings: Indian Tales Retold*. Boston: Houghton Mifflin.

———. 1911. *The Soul of the Indian: An Interpretation*. Boston: Houghton Mifflin.

———. 1913. *Indian Child Life*. Boston: Little, Brown.

———. 1914. *Indian Scout Talks: Guide for Boy Scouts and Campfire Girls*. Boston: Little, Brown.

———. 1915. *The Indian Today: The Past and Future of the First American*. Garden City, N.Y.: Doubleday, Page.

———. 1916. *From the Deep Woods to Civilization: Chapters in the Autobiography of an Indian*. Boston: Little, Brown.

———. 1918. *Indian Heroes and Great Chieftains*. Boston: Little, Brown.

———. 1977. *From Deep Woods to Civilization*. 1916. Lincoln: Univ. of Nebraska Press.

———. 1980. *The Soul of the Indian: An Interpretation*. 1911. Lincoln: Univ. of Nebraska Press.

———. 1991a. *Indian Heroes and Great Chieftains*. Lincoln: Univ. of Nebraska Press.

———. 1991b. *Old Indian Days*. 1907. Lincoln: Univ. of Nebraska Press.

Eastman, Charles A., and Elaine Goodale Eastman. 1909. *Wigwam Evenings: Sioux Folk Tales Retold*. Boston: Little, Brown.

———. 1919. *Indian Tales Retold*. Boston: Little, Brown.

———. 1930. *Wigwam Evenings: Animal Tales*. Boston: Little, Brown.

———. 1990. *Wigwam Evenings: Sioux Folk Tales Retold.* 1909. Lincoln: Univ. of Nebraska Press.

Eastman, Elaine Goodale. 1945. "The Ghost Dance War and Wounded Knee Massacre of 1890–91." *Nebraska History* 26: 26–42.

———. 1978. *Sister to the Sioux: The Memoirs of Elaine Goodale Eastman, 1885–91.* Edited by K. Graber. Lincoln: Univ. of Nebraska Press.

Ebersole, Gary. 1995. *Captured by Texts: Puritan to Postmodern Images of Indian Captivity.* Charlottesville: Univ. of Virginia Press.

Eco, Umberto. 1979. *The Role of the Reader: Explorations in the Semiotics of Texts.* Bloomington: Indiana Univ. Press.

Ehler, Sidney, and John Morrall. 1967. *Church and State Through the Centuries: A Collection of Historic Documents with Commentaries.* New York: Biblo and Tannen.

Eisley, Loren. 1969. *The Unexpected Universe.* New York: Harcourt, Brace and World.

Eliade, Mircea. 1961. *The Sacred and the Profane: The Nature of Religion.* Translated by Willard R. Trask. New York: Harper and Row.

———. 1964. *Shamanism: Archaic Techniques of Ecstasy.* Princeton: Princeton Univ. Press.

———. 1978. *A History of Religious Ideas, Vol 1.* Translated by Willard R. Trask. Chicago: Univ. of Chicago Press.

Ellenberger, H. 1970. *The Discovery of the Unconscious.* New York: Basic Books.

Emerson, Ralph Waldo. 1983. "Nature." In *Essays and Lectures,* edited by Joel Porte, 5–49. 1836. New York: Library of America.

Enochs, Ross. 1996. *The Jesuit Mission to the Lakota Sioux : Pastoral Theology and Ministry, 1886–1945.* Kansas City: Sheed and Ward.

Erdoes, Richard. 1972. *The Sun Dance People.* New York: Knopf.

———. 1973. "My Travels with Medicine Man John Lame Deer." *Smithsonian* 4: 30–37.

———. 1976. *The Sound of Flutes and Other Indian Legends Told by Lame Deer, Jenny Leading Cloud, Leonard Crow Dog, and Others.* New York: Pantheon Books.

———. 1990. *Crying for a Dream: The World Through Native American Eyes.* Sante Fe, N.M.: Bear.

Erdoes, Richard, and Archie Fire Lame Deer. 1992. *Gift of Power: The Life and Teachings of a Lakota Medicine Man.* Santa Fe, N.M.: Bear.

Erdoes, Richard, and John Lame Deer. 1972. *Lame Deer: Seeker of Visions.* New York: Simon and Schuster.

Erdoes, Richard, and Leonard Crow Dog. 1995. *Crow Dog: Four Generations of Sioux Medicine Men.* New York: HarperCollins.

Erdoes, Richard, and Mary Brave Bird. 1993. *Ohitika Woman*. New York: Grove Press.

Erdoes, Richard, and Mary Crow Dog. 1990. *Lakota Woman*. New York: Grove Weidenfeld.

Erikson, Erik Homburger. 1939. "Observations on Sioux Education." *Journal of Psychology* 7: 101–56.

Evans, Wayne. 1995. Glossary to *Wounded Warriors*. Edited by Doyle Arbogast. Omaha, Nebr.: Little Turtle.

Ewers, John C. 1938. *Teton Dakota*. Berkeley: United States Department of the Interior, National Parks Service.

Feraca, Stephen. 1957. "The Contemporary Teton Sioux Sun Dance." Master's thesis, Columbia Univ.

———. 1961. "The Yuwipi Cult of the Oglala and Sicangu Teton Sioux." *Plains Anthropologist* 6, no. 13: 155–63.

———. 1962. "The Teton Sioux Eagle Medicine Cult." *American Indian Tradition* 8, no. 5: 195–96.

———. 1963. *Wakinyan: Contemporary Teton Dakota Religion*. Vol. 2, *Studies in Plains Anthropology and History*. Browning, Mont.: Museum of the Plains Indian.

———. 1990. *Why Don't They Give Them Guns?: The Great American Indian Myth*. Lanham, Md.: Univ. Press of America.

———. 1994. *The Wounded Bear Winter Count*. Kendall Park, N.J.: Lakota Books.

———. 1998. *Wakinyan: Lakota Religion in the Twentieth Century*. Lincoln: Univ. of Nebraska Press.

Finster, David. 1968. "The Hardin Winter Count." *Museum News, Univ. of South Dakota* 29, no. 3–4: 1–59.

Fish, Stanley. 1980. *Is There a Text in This Class?* Cambridge: Harvard Univ. Press.

Fletcher, Alice. 1882. "The Shadow or Ghost Lodge: A Ceremony of the Oglala Sioux." *Peabody Museum Papers* 3: 3–4.

———. 1883. "The Sun Dance of the Oglala Sioux." Proceedings of the American Association for the Advancement of Science 31: 580–84.

———. 1884a. "The Elk Mystery or Festival of the Ogallala." *Peabody Museum Report* 3: 4.

———. 1884b. "Indian Ceremonies." *Report of the Peabody Museum of American Archaeology and Ethnology* 16: 260–333.

———. 1891. "The Indian Messiah." *Journal of American Folk-Lore* 4, no. 12: 55–57.

———. 1896. "The Emblematic Use of the Tree in the Dakota Group." Paper read at American Association for the Advancement of Science.

Flood, Renee Sansom. 1995. *Lost Bird of Wounded Knee: Spirit of the Lakota.* New York: Scribner.

Forché, Carolyn, ed. 1993. *Against Forgetting: Twentieth-Century Poetry of Witness.* New York: W. W. Norton.

Foucault, Michael. 1977. "What Is an Author?" In *Language, Counter-memory, Practice: Selected Essays and Interviews,* edited by Donald Bouchard, 113–38. Ithaca: Cornell Univ. Press.

———. 1980. *The History of Sexuality.* New York: Vintage Books.

Frazier, Ian. 1989. *Great Plains.* New York: Farrar, Straus, Giroux.

Fugel, Eugene. 1966. "The Nature and Function of the Lakota Night Cults." *(W. H. Over) Museum News, Univ. of South Dakota* 27, no. 3–4: 1–38.

Furlong, Jay. 1980. "The Occupation of Wounded Knee, 1973." Master's thesis, Univ. of Oklahoma.

Gadamer, Hans. 1994. *Truth and Method.* New York: Continuum.

Gallegher, Susan VanZanten. 1995. "Through Other People: Confession in South African Literature." In *Christianity and Literature* 45, no. 1 (autumn): 95–110.

Geertz, Clifford. 1957. "Ethos, World View, and the Analysis of Sacred Symbols." *Antioch Review* 17 no. 4: 421–37.

———. 1982. *Local Knowledge: Further Essays in Interpretive Anthroplogy.* New York: Basic Books.

Giago, Tim A., Jr. 1992. "Time to Guard Freedom for Everyone's Religion." *Indian Country Today* 17 Dec., sec. A, 4.

———. 1993. "Apply a Little Skepticism with the Phony 'Indians.' " *Indian Country Today* 14 Jan., sec. A, 4.

Goldfrank, E. 1943. "Historic Change and Social Character: A Study of the Teton Dakota." *American Anthropologist* 45: 67–83.

Gonzalez, Mario, and Elizabeth Cook-Lynn. 1999. *The Politics of Hallowed Ground: Wounded Knee and the Struggle for Indian Sovereignty.* Univ. of Illinois Press.

Goodman, Ronald. 1992. *Lakota Star Knowledge: Studies in Lakota Stellar Theology.* Rosebud, S.D.: Sinte Gleska Univ.

Grange, R. 1963. "The Garnier Oglala Winter Count." *Plains Anthropologist* 8: 74–79.

Grimes, Ronald L. 1996. "This May Be a Feud, But It's Not a War: An Electronic, Interdisciplinary Dialogue on Teaching Native Religions." *American Indian Quarterly* 20, nos. 3/4: 433–50.

Grobsmith, Elizabeth S. 1974. "Wakunza: Uses of Yuwipi Medicine Power in Contemporary Teton Dakota Culture." *Plains Anthropologist* 19, no. 64: 129–33.

———. 1976. "Lakota Bilingualism: A Comparative Study of Language Use in Two Communities on the Rosebud Sioux Reservation." Ph.D. diss., Univ. of Arizona, Tucson.

———. 1979a. "The Lakhota Giveaway: A System of Social Reciprocity." *Plains Anthropologist* 24: 123–31.

———. 1979b. "Styles of Speaking: An Analysis of Lakota Communication Alternatives." *Anthropological Linguistics* 21, no. 7: 355–61.

———. 1981a. "The Changing Role of the Giveaway in Contemporary Lakota Life." *Plains Anthropologist* 26: 75–79.

———. 1981b. *Lakota of the Rosebud: A Contemporary Ethnography.* New York: Holt, Rinehart and Winston.

Gugelberger, Georg. 1991. "Decolonizing the Canon: Considerations of Third World Literature." *New Literary History* 22: 505–24.

———, ed. 1996. *The "Real" Thing: Testimonial Discourse and Latin America.* Durham: Duke Univ. Press.

Gugelberger, Georg, and Michael Kearney. 1991. "Voices for the Voiceless: Testimonial Literature in Latin America." In *Latin American Perspectives* 18, no. 3 (summer): 3–14.

Habermas, Jürgen. 1985. *The Philosophical Discourses of Modernity.* Cambridge: MIT Press.

Hairy Shirt, LeRoy, Lloyd One Star, Victor Douville, Caroline Stands, Stanley Sosnowski, and Terry Brennan. 1973. *Lakota Woonspe Wowapi.* Aberdeen, S.D.: Northern Plains Press.

Hallowell, A. Irving. 1960. "Ojibwa Ontology, Behavior, and World View." In *Culture in History: Essays in Honor of Paul Radin,* edited by Stanley Diamond, 207–44. New York: Columbia Univ. Press.

Hamilton, Henry, and Hamilton Jean Tyree. 1971. *The Sioux of the Rosebud: A History in Pictures.* Norman: Univ. of Oklahoma Press.

Hand, Floyd Looks for Buffalo. 1998. *Learning Journey on the Red Road.* Toronto: Learning Journey Communications.

Handler, Richard, and Joycelyn Linnekin. 1984. "Traditions, Genuine or Spurious." *Journal of American Folklore* 97: 273–90.

Hardorff, Richard G. 1991. *Yellowstone Command: Colonel Nelson A. Miles and the Great Sioux War, 1876–1877.* Lincoln: Univ. of Nebraska Press.

———. 1993. *Hokahey! A Good Day to Die!: The Indian Casualties of the Custer Fight.* Spokane, Wash.: Arthur H. Clark.

———, ed. 1995. *Cheyenne Memories of the Custer Fight: A Source Book.* Spokane, Wash.: Arthur H. Clark.

———, ed. 1997. *Lakota Recollections of the Custer Fight.* Lincoln: Univ. of Nebraska Press.

————. 1998. *Lakota History*. Spokane, Wash.: Arthur H. Clark.

Hassan, Ihab. 1971. *The Dismemberment of Orpheus: Toward a Postmodern Literature*. New York: Oxford Univ. Press.

Hassrick, Royal. 1964. *The Sioux: Life and Customs of a Warrior Society*. Norman: Univ. of Oklahoma Press.

Havelock, Eric A. 1967. *Preface to Plato*. New York: Gosset and Dunlap.

Hawthorne, Nathaniel. 1961. *The Marble Faun*. 1859. New York: Dell.

Heflin, Ruth J. 1997. "Examples for the World: Four Transitional Sioux Writers and the Sioux Literary Renaissance." Ph.D. diss., Oklahoma State Univ.

Heisig, James W. 1987. "Symbolism." In *Encyclopedia of Religion,* vol. 14, 198–208. New York: Macmillan.

Henry, James. 1986. "Religious Experience, Archetypes, and the Neurophysiology of Emotions." *Zygon* 21, no. 1 (Mar.): 47–74.

Hernández-Ávila, Inés. 1996. "Meditations of the Spirit: Native American Religious Traditions and the Ethics of Representation." *American Indian Quarterly* 20, nos. 3 and 4: 329–52.

Herskovits, Melville J. 1958. *Acculturation: The Study of Culture Contact*. Gloucester, Mass.: Peter Smith.

Hillman, James. 1979. *The Dream and the Underworld*. New York: Harper and Row.

Hinman, Eleanor H. 1976. "Oglala Sources on the Life of Crazy Horse." *Nebraska History* 57: 1–52.

Hinsley, Curtis M. 1981. *Savages and Scientists: The Smithsonian Institution and the Development of American Anthropology, 1846–1910*. Washington, D.C.: Smithsonian Institution Press.

Hobsbawm, Eric, and Terrence Ranger, eds. 1986. *The Invention of Tradition*. Cambridge: Cambridge Univ. Press.

Holler, Clyde. 1984a. "Lakota Religion and Tragedy: The Theology of *Black Elk Speaks.*" *Journal of the American Academy of Religion* 52, no. 1: 19–45.

————. 1984b. "Black Elk's Relationship to Christianity." *American Indian Quarterly* 8, no. 1: 37–49.

————. 1995. *Black Elk's Religion: The Sun Dance and Lakota Catholicism*. Syracuse: Syracuse Univ. Press.

Holly, Carol T. 1979. "*Black Elk Speaks* and the Making of Indian Autobiography." *Genre* 12, no. 1: 117–36.

Hoover, Herbert. 1979. *The Sioux: A Critical Bibliography*. Bloomington: Indiana Univ. Press.

Hoover, Herbert, and Jack Marken. 1980. *Bibliography of the Sioux*. Vol. 1, *Native American Bibliography Series*. Metuchen, N.J.: Scarecrow Press.

House, Julius T. 1920. *John G. Neihardt: Man and Poet.* Wayne, Nebr.: F. H. Jones and Son.

Howard, James H. 1950. "Notes on Dakota Archery." *Museum News, South Dakota Museum* 12, no. 2: 1–3.

———. 1951. "Dakota Fishing Practices." *Museum News, South Dakota Museum* 12, no. 5: 1–4.

———. 1954a. "The Dakota Heyoka Cult." *Scientific Monthly* 78, no. 4: 254–58.

———. 1954b. "Yanktonai Dakota Eagle Trapping." *Southwestern Journal of Anthropology* 10, no. 1: 69–74.

———. 1955a. "The Tree Dweller Cults of the Dakota." *Journal of American Folklore* 68, no. 268: 169–74.

———. 1955b. "Two Dakota Winter Count Texts." *Plains Anthropologist* 5: 13–30.

———. 1960a. "The Cultural Position of the Dakota: A Reassessment." In *Essays in the Science of Culture in Honor of Leslie A. White,* edited by G. Dole and R. Carneiro, 249–68. New York: Crowell.

———. 1960b. "Dakota Winter Counts as a Source of Plains History." *Anthropological Papers No. 61, Bureau of American Ethnology, Bulletin 173:* 335–416.

———. 1960c. "The Northern Style Grass Dance Costume." *American Indian Hobbyist* 7, no. 1: 18–27.

———. 1961. "A Note on the Dakota Water Drinking Society." *American Indian Tradition* 7, no. 3: 96.

———. 1962. "Peyote Jokes." *Journal of American Folklore* 75: 10–14.

———. 1966. "The Dakota or Sioux Indians: Part III: The Teton or Western Dakota." *Museum News, South Dakota Museum* 27, no. 9–10: 1–6.

———. 1968. *The Warrior Who Killed Custer: The Personal Narrative of Chief Joseph White Bull.* Lincoln: Univ. of Nebraska Press.

———. 1972. "Notes on the Ethnogeography of the Yankton Dakota." *Plains Anthropologist* 13: 281–307.

———. 1976. "Yanktonai Ethnohistory and the John K. Bear Winter Count." Part 2. *Plains Anthropologist, Memoir 11* 21, no. 73 (Aug.): 1–64.

———. 1980. *The Dakota or Sioux Indians: A Study in Human Ecology.* Lincoln, Nebr.: J and R Reprints.

———. 1984. *The Canadian Sioux.* Lincoln: Univ. of Nebraska Press.

Howard, Scott. 1999. "Incommensurability and Nicholas Black Elk: An Exploration." *American Indian Culture and Research Journal* 23, no 1: 111–36.

Hoxie, Frederick E., ed. 1996. *Encyclopedia of North American Indians.* New York: Houghton Mifflin.

Hultkrantz, Åke. 1998. Review of *Black Elk's Religion,* by Clyde Holler. *Journal of Religion* 77, no. 3, 505–7.

Hurt, Wesley R., and James H. Howard. 1960. "A Yuwipi Ceremony at Pine Ridge." *Plains Anthropologist* 5, no. 10: 48–52.

Hyde, George E. 1937. *Red Cloud's Folk: A History of the Oglala Sioux Indians.* Norman: Univ. of Oklahoma Press.

———. 1956. *A Sioux Chronicle.* Norman: Univ. of Oklahoma Press.

———. 1961. *Spotted Tail's Folk: A History of the Brulé Sioux.* Norman: Univ. of Oklahoma Press.

Irwin, Lee. 1994. *The Dream Seekers: Native American Visionary Traditions of the Great Plains.* Norman: Univ. of Oklahoma Press.

———. 1996. Review of *Black Elk's Religion,* by Clyde Holler. *American Indian Culture and Research Journal* 20, no. 4, 203–7.

Iverson, Peter. 1984. "Neihardt, Collier and the Continuity of Indian Life." In *A Sender of Words: Essays in Memory of John G. Neihardt,* edited by Vine Deloria Jr., 100–109. Salt Lake City: Howe Brothers.

Jahner, Elaine. 1977. "The Spiritual Landscape." *Parabola* 2, no. 3: 32–38.

———. 1983a. Introduction to *Lakota Myth.* Edited by E. Jahner. Lincoln: Univ. of Nebraska Press.

———. 1983b. "Stone Boy: Persistent Hero." In *Smoothing the Ground,* edited by Brian Swann, 1–40. Berkeley and Los Angeles: Univ. of California Press.

———. 1987. "Lakota Genesis: The Oral Tradition." In *Sioux Indian Religion,* edited by Raymond J. DeMallie and Douglas R. Parks, 45–65. Norman: Univ. of Oklahoma Press.

———. 1989. "The Spiritual Landscape." In *I Become Part of It: Sacred Dimensions in American Life,* edited by D. M. Dooling and Paul Jordan-Smith, 193–203. New York: Parabola Books.

Jameson, Fredric. 1972. *The Prison House of Language.* Princeton: Princeton Univ. Press.

———. 1981. *The Political Unconscious: Narrative as Socially Symbolic Act.* Ithaca: Cornell Univ. Press.

Jeltz, Patsy. 1991. "Elder Pete Catches Shares Wisdom." *Lakota Times* 24 July, sec. B, 1.

Jennings, Francis. 1975. *The Invasion of America: Indians, Colonialism and the Cant of Conquest.* Chapel Hill: Univ. of North Carolina Press.

Jensen, Richard E., R. Eli Paul, and John E. Carter. 1991. *Eyewitness at Wounded Knee.* Lincoln: Univ. of Nebraska Press.

Jocks, Christopher Ronwanien:te. 1996. "Spirituality for Sale: Sacred Knowledge in the Consumer Age." *American Indian Quarterly* 20 (summer): 415–31.

Josephy, Alvin M., Jr. 1984. "The Poet Beyond Black Elk." In *A Sender of Word: Essays in Honor of John G. Neihardt,* edited by Vine Deloria Jr., 25–29. Salt Lake City: Howe Brothers.

Jung, Carl. 1965. *Memories, Dreams, Reflections*. New York: Vintage Books.

———. 1966–1985. *The Collected Works of C. G. Jung*. 18 vols. Princeton, N.J.: Princeton Univ. Press.

Kaiser, Patricia. 1984. "The Lakota Sacred Pipe: Its Tribal Use and Religious Philosophy." *American Indian Culture and Research Journal* 8, no. 3: 1–26.

Karol, Joseph S., ed. 1969. *Red Horse Owner's Winter Count: The Oglala Sioux, 1786–1968*. Martin, S.D.: Booster Publishing.

Kehoe, Alice B. 1989. *The Ghost Dance: Ethnohistory and Revitalization*. Fort Worth, Tex.: Holt, Rinehart and Winston.

———. 1990. "Primal Gaia: Primitivists and Plastic Medicine Men." In *The Invented Indian: Cultural Fictions and Government Policies*, edited by J. A. Clifton. New Brunswick, N.J.: Transaction Publishers.

Keiser, Albert. 1933. *The Indian in American Literature*. New York: Oxford Univ. Press.

Kemnitzer, Louis. 1969a. "Whiteman Medicine, Indian Medicine and Indian Identity on the Pine Ridge Reservation." *Pine Ridge Research Bulletin* 8: 12–23.

———. 1969b. "Yuwipi." *Pine Ridge Research Bulletin* 10: 26–33.

———. 1970. "The Cultural Provenience of Objects Used in Yuwipi: A Modern Teton Dakota Healing Ritual." *Ethnos* 35: 40–75.

———. 1975. "A 'Grammar Discovery Procedure' for the Study of a Dakota Healing Ritual." In *Linguistics and Anthropology: In Honor of C. F. Voegelin*, edited by M. D. Kinkade, K. L. Hale, and O. Werner, 405–22. Lisse, Netherlands: Peter de Ridder Press.

———. 1976. "Structure, Content, and Cultural Meaning of Yuwipi: A Modern Lakota Healing Ritual." *American Ethnologist* 3, no. 2: 261–80.

———. 1978. "Yuwipi." *Indian Historian* 11, no. 2: 2–5.

Ketcham, William. 1908. Letters. Bureau of Catholic Indian Missions Collection, Marquette Univ., Dec. 12, 1-58-26.

Kibbey, Anne. 1986. *The Interpretation of Material Shapes in Puritanism: A Study of Rhetoric, Prejudice, and Violence*. New York: Cambridge Univ. Press.

Klein, Christina. 1994. " 'Everything of Interest in the Late Pine Ridge War Are Held by Us for Sale': Popular Culture and Wounded Knee." *Western Historical Quarterly* (spring): 45–68.

Krupat, Arnold. 1985. *For Those Who Come After: A Study of Native American Autobiography*. Berkeley and Los Angeles: Univ. of California Press.

———. 1987. *Recovering the Word : Essays on Native American Literature*. Berkeley and Los Angeles: Univ. of California Press.

———. 1989. *The Voice in the Margin: Native American Literature and the Canon*. Berkeley and Los Angeles: Univ. of California Press.

———. 1992. *Ethnocriticism: Ethnography, History, Literature.* Berkeley and Los Angeles: Univ. of California Press.

———. 1993. *New Voices in Native American Literary Criticism.* Washington, D.C.: Smithsonian Institution Press.

———. 1996. *The Turn to the Native: Studies in Criticism and Culture.* Lincoln: Univ. of Nebraska Press.

Krupat, Arnold, and Brian Swann. 1987. *I Tell You Now: Autobiographical Essays by Native American Writers.* Lincoln: Univ. of Nebraska Press.

Kurkiala, Mikael. 1997. "Building the Nation Back Up: The Politics of Identity on the Pine Ridge Indian Reservation." Ph.D. diss., Uppsala Univ., Uppsala, Sweden.

Lacan, Jaques. 1968. *The Language of the Self: The Function of Language in Psychoanalysis.* Translated by Anthony Wilden. New York: Dell.

Laeuchli, Samuel. 1980. *Religion and Art in Conflict.* Philadelphia: Fortress Press.

———. 1992. "The Expulsion from the Garden and the Hermeneutics of Play." In *Body and Bible: Interpreting and Experiencing Biblical Narratives,* edited by Bjïrn Krondorfer, 27–56. Philadelphia: Trinity International Press.

———. 1996. "Black Elk in Stüttgart." *Circle: Journal of the Mimesis Institute* (spring): 1–2.

Lakoff, George, and Mark Johnson. 1980. *Metaphors We Live By.* Chicago: Univ. of Chicago Press.

Landes, Ruth. 1968. *The Mystic Lake Sioux: Sociology of the Mdewakantonwan Santee.* Madison: Univ. of Wisconsin Press.

La Pointe, James. 1976. *Legends of the Lakota.* San Francisco: Indian Historian Press.

Larson, Robert W. 1997. *Red Cloud: Warrior-Statesman of the Lakota Sioux.* Norman: Univ. of Oklahoma Press.

Laubin, Gladys, and Reginald Laubin. 1977. *Indian Dances of North America: Their Importance to Indian Life.* Norman: Univ. of Oklahoma Press.

Lazarus, Edward. 1991. *Black Hills White Justice: The Sioux Nation Versus the United States, 1775 to the Present.* New York: HarperCollins.

Lee, Dorothy. 1959. *Freedom and Culture.* Englewood Cliffs, N.J.: Prentice-Hall.

Levi-Strauss, Claude. 1966. *The Savage Mind.* Chicago: Univ. of Chicago Press.

———. 1969. *Totemism.* Middlesex, Eng.: Penguin.

Lewis, Thomas. 1968. "The Oglala Sun Dance." *Pine Ridge Research Bulletin* 5: 52–64.

———. 1970. "Notes on the Heyoka, the Teton-Dakota 'Contrary' Cult." *Pine Ridge Research Bulletin* 11: 7–19.

——. 1972. "The Oglala (Teton Dakota) Sun Dance: Vicissitudes of Its Structures and Functions." *Plains Anthropologist* 17: 44–49.

——. 1974a. "The Heyoka Cult in Historical and Contemporary Oglala Sioux Society." *Anthropos* 69: 17–32.

——. 1974b. "An Indian Healer's Preventive Medicine Procedure." *Hospital and Community Psychiatry* 25, no. 2: 74–95.

——. 1975a. "Oglala (Sioux) Concepts of Homosexuality and the Determinants of Sexual Identification." *Journal of the American Medical Association* 225, no. 3: 312–13.

——. 1975b. "A Syndrome of Depression and Mutism in the Oglala Sioux." *American Journal of Psychiatry* 137, no. 7: 753–55.

——. 1980a. "The Changing Practice of the Oglala Medicine Man." *Plains Anthropologist* 25: 265–67.

——. 1980b. "An Ethnopharmacologic Search for the Identity of *Canli Icahiye.*" *Plains Anthropologist* 25: 87–88.

——. 1980c. "A Sioux Medicine Man Describes His Own Illness and Approaching Death." *Annals of Internal Medicine* 92: 265–67.

——. 1981. "Phallic Masks and Fear of Sexuality." *Journal of Operative Psychiatry* 12, no. 2: 100–104.

——. 1982a. "The Evolution of the Social Role of the Oglala Heyoka." *Plains Anthropologist* 27: 249–53.

——. 1982b. "Group Therapy Techniques in Shamanistic Medicine." *Journal of Group Psychotherapy, Psychodrama, and Sociometry* (spring): 24–30.

——. 1987. "The Contemporary Yuwipi." In *Sioux Indian Religion,* edited by Raymond J. DeMallie and Douglas R. Parks, 173–87. Norman: Univ. of Oklahoma Press.

——. 1990. *The Medicine Men.* Lincoln: Univ. of Nebraska Press.

Lincoln, Kenneth. 1983. *Native American Renaissance.* Berkeley and Los Angeles: Univ. of California Press.

——. 1991. Foreword to *American Indian Poetry: An Anthology of Songs and Chants.* Edited by George W. Cronyn. New York: George Braziller.

Linden, George W. 1977a. "Dakota Philosophy." *American Studies* 18, no. 2: 17–43.

——. 1977b. "Understanding Cultural Diversity." In *Perspectives on South Dakota: Addresses Presented During Humanities Conferences, Sponsored by the South Dakota Committee on the Humanities in 1975 and 1976.* Brookings, S.D.: The Committee.

——. 1984. "Warrior and Mystic: Nicholas Black Elk and John G. Neihardt." *Proceedings, Sixteenth Dakota History Conference:* 482–96.

——. 1994. "The Dethronement of Yata." *Wicazo Sa Review* 10, no. 2: 80–89.

Linden, George, and Fred Robbins. 1984. "*Black Elk Speaks* as a Failure Narrative." *Heritage of the Great Plains* 17, no. 2: 35–45.

Linderman, Frank. 1957. *Plenty-Coups, Chief of the Crows.* 1930. Lincoln: Univ. of Nebraska Press.

Little Eagle, Avis. 1991a. "After the Sweat: Caviar, Wine and Cheese." *Lakota Times* 24 July, sec. A, 1–2.

———. 1991b. "False Prophets Will Suffer." *Lakota Times* 31 July, sec. A, 1–2.

———. 1991c. "Lakota Rituals Being Sold." *Lakota Times* 2 July, sec. A, 1–2.

———. 1991d. "Oh Shinnah; Prophet for Profit." *Lakota Times* 7 Aug., sec. A, 1–2.

———. 1991e. "Paid Ads Call Her 'Medicine Woman.' " *Lakota Times* 14 Aug., sec. A, 1–2.

———. 1991f. "Sacred Pipe Keeper Fears Feds Will Step In." *Lakota Times* 17 July, sec. A, 1–2.

———. 1992a. "Lakota Discuss Exploitation of Religion, Preserving Culture." *Indian Country Today* 26 Nov., sec. B, 1–2.

———. 1992b. " 'Spiritual Orphans' Peddle Religion in Great Round." *Lakota Times* 21 Jan., sec. A, 8.

Looking Horse, Arval. 1987. "The Sacred Pipe in Modern Life." In *Sioux Indian Religion,* edited by Raymond J. DeMallie and Douglas R. Parks, 67–73. Norman: Univ. of Oklahoma Press.

Lowie, Robert H. 1913. "Dance Associations of the Eastern Dakota." *Anthropological Papers of the American Museum of Natural History* 11, no. 2: 101–42.

Luebke, Frederick C., ed. 1990. *A Harmony of the Arts: The Nebraska State Capitol.* Lincoln: Univ. of Nebraska Press.

Lurie, Nancy O. 1968. "Historical Background." In *The American Indian Today,* edited by Stuart Levine and Nancy O. Lurie, 49–81. Deland, Fla.: Everett-Edwards.

Luther, Joseph. 1924a. "High Lights from a Hundred Per Cent American Convention." *Jesuit Bulletin* 3 (Dec.): 13.

———. 1924b. "A Real One Hundred Percent American Convention." *Woodstock Letters* 53: 351.

Lyman, Stanley. 1991. *Wounded Knee, 1973: A Personal Account.* Lincoln: Univ. of Nebraska Press.

Lyon, William S. 1996. *Encyclopedia of Native American Healing.* Santa Barbara: ABC-CLIO.

Macgregor, Gordon. 1946. *Warriors Without Weapons: A Study of the Society and Personality Development of the Pine Ridge Sioux.* Chicago: Univ. of Chicago Press.

Mailloux, Stephen. 1982. *Interpretive Conventions: The Reader in the Study of American Fiction.* Ithaca: Cornell Univ. Press.

Mails, Thomas E. 1972. *Mystic Warriors of the Plains.* New York: Doubleday.

———. 1973. *Dog Soldiers, Bear Men and Buffalo Women: A Study of the Societies and Cults of the Plains Indians.* Englewood Cliffs, N.J.: Prentice-Hall.

———. 1978. *Sundancing at Rosebud and Pine Ridge.* Sioux Falls, S.D.: The Center for Western Studies.

———. 1979. *Fools Crow.* New York: Avon.

———. 1988. *Secret Native American Pathways: A Guide to Inner Peace.* Tulsa, Okla.: Council Oak Books.

———. 1991. *Wisdom and Power: Fools Crow.* Tulsa, Okla.: Council Oak Books.

Mails, Thomas E., and Dallas Chief Eagle. 1979. *Fools Crow.* New York: Doubleday.

Malan, Vernon. 1956. *Acculturation of the Dakota Indians.* Brookings, S.D.: Agricultural Experiment Station, South Dakota State College of Agriculture and Mechanical Arts.

———. 1958. *The Dakota Indian Family.* "Agricultural Extension Bulletin 470." Brookings, S.D.: Rural Sociology Department, South Dakota State College.

———. 1962. *The Social System of the Dakota Indians.* "Extension Circular 606, Cooperative Extension Service." Brookings, S.D.: Cooperative Extension Service, South Dakota State College, U.S. Department of Agriculture.

Malan, Vernon, and Clinton Jesser. 1959. *The Dakota Religion: A Study in Conflicting Values.* "Agricultural Extension Bulletin 473." Brookings, S.D.: Rural Sociology Department, South Dakota State College.

Malan, Vernon, and Ernest Schusky. 1962. *The Dakota Indian Community: An Analysis of the Non-Ranching Population of the Pine Ridge Reservation.* "Agricultural Extension Bulletin 505." Brookings, S.D.: Rural Sociology Department, South Dakota State College.

Malan, Vernon, and Joseph Powers. 1960. *The Crow Creek Indian Family.* "Agricultural Extension Bulletin 487." Brookings, S.D.: Rural Sociology Department, South Dakota State College.

Malan, Vernon, and R. C. McCone. 1960. "The Time Concept Perspective and Premise in the Socio-cultural Order of the Dakota Indians." *Plains Anthropologist* 5, no. 9: 12–15.

Mallery, Garrick. 1886. "The Dakota Winter Counts and the Corbusier Winter Counts." In *Pictographs of the North American Indians.* Washington, D.C.: Government Printing Office.

———, ed. 1893. "Winter Counts." In *Picture Writing of the American Indians. Tenth Annual Report, Bureau of American Ethnology, 1888–1889.* Washington, D.C.: Government Printing Office.

Manfred, Frederick. 1984. "Those Western American Darks." In *A Sender of*

Words: Essays in Memory of John G. Neihardt, edited by Vine Deloria Jr., 39–45. Salt Lake City: Howe Brothers.

Matthiessen, Peter. 1983. *In the Spirit of Crazy Horse.* New York: Viking Press.

May, Rollo, ed. 1960. *Symbolism in Religion and Literature.* New York: George Braziller.

McAllister, Mick. 1997. "Native Sources: American Indian Autobiography." *Western American Literature* 32, no. 1: 3–23.

McCluskey, Sally. 1972. "Black Elk Speaks: And So Does John Neihardt." *Western American Literature* 6: 231–42.

McGaa, Ed. n.d.-a. *Black Elk's Prayer on the Mountain.* Minneapolis: Four Directions. Audio Tape.

———. n.d.-b. *Finding Wakan Tanka.* Minneapolis: Four Directions. Audio Tape.

———. n.d.-c. *Native Wisdom.* Minneapolis: Four Directions. Video Tape.

———. 1990. *Mother Earth Spirituality.* San Francisco: Harper and Row.

———. 1992. *Rainbow Tribe.* New York: Harper San Francisco.

———. 1995. *Native Wisdom : Perceptions of the Natural Way.* Minneapolis: Four Directions.

———. 1998. *Eagle Vision: Return of the Hoop.* Minneapolis: Four Directions.

McGee, W. J. 1987. "The Siouan Indians." 1897. *Bureau of Ethnology, Annual Report* 15: 157–204.

McKinzie, Richard. 1972. *New Deal for Artists.* Princeton: Princeton Univ. Press.

McLaughlin, Marie. 1916. *Myths and Legends of the Sioux.* Bismark, N.D.: Bismark Tribune.

McLuhan, T. C. 1972. *Touch the Earth.* New York: Outerberg and Dienstfrey, distributed by E. P. Dutton.

McPherson, Dennis H., and J. Douglas Rabb. 1993. *Indian from the Inside: A Study in Ethno-Metaphysics.* Thunder Bay, Ont.: Lakehead Univ. Press, Center for Nothern Studies, Occasional Paper no. 14.

Means, Russell. 1980. "Fighting Words on the Future of the Earth." *Mother Jones* 10, no. 5 (Dec.): 23–38.

———. 1995. *Where White Men Fear to Tread.* New York: St. Martin's Press.

Medicine, Beatrice. 1969a. "The Changing Dakota Family and the Stresses Therein." *Pine Ridge Research Bulletin* 9: 1–20.

———. 1969b. "Warrior Women: Sex Role Alternative for Plains Indian Women." In *The Hidden Half: Studies in Plains Indian Women,* edited by P. Albers and B. Medicine, 267–80. Lanham, Md.: Univ. Press of America.

———. 1976. "The Schooling Process: Some Lakota (Sioux) Views." In *The Anthropological Study of Education,* edited by Craig J. Calhoun and Francis A. J. Ianni, 283–91. The Hague: Mouton.

———. 1978. "Native American Communication Patterns: The Case of the

Lakota Speaker." In *Handbook of Intercultural Communication: Theories, Research and Application*, edited by M. Asante, E. Newmark, and C. Blake, 373–81. Beverly Hills, Calif.: Sage.

———. 1981. "Native American Resistance to Integration: Contemporary Confrontations and Religious Revitalization." *Plains Anthropologist* 26: 277–86.

———. 1987. "Indian Women and the Renaissance of Traditional Religion." In *Sioux Indian Religion*, edited by Raymond J. DeMallie and Douglas R. Parks, 159–71. Norman: Univ. of Oklahoma Press.

Mekeel, Haviland S. 1932a. "A Discussion of Culture Change as Illustrated by Materials from a Teton-Dakota Community." *American Anthropologist* 34: 274–85.

———. 1932b. "A Modern American Community in the Light of Its Past." Ph.D. diss., Yale Univ.

———. 1936. "The Economy of a Modern Teton Dakota Community." *Yale Univ. Publications in Anthropology* 6: 3–14.

———. 1943. "A Short History of the Teton-Dakota." *North Dakota Historical Quarterly* 10: 137–205.

Menchú, Rigoberta. 1993. *I, Rigoberta Menchú: An Indian Woman in Guatemala*. Edited by Elsabeth Burgos-DeBray. 1984. London: Verso Publishers.

Merkur, Dan. 1992. *Becoming Half Hidden: Shamanism and Initiation among the Inuit*. New York: Garland Publishing.

Merleau-Ponty, Maurice. 1962. *Phenomenology of Perception*. New York: Humanities Press.

———. 1964. *Signs*. Evanston: Northwestern Univ. Press.

Meyer, Roy W. 1967. *History of the Santee Sioux: United States Indian Policy on Trial*. Lincoln: Univ. of Nebraska Press.

Miller, David Humphreys. 1985. *Ghost Dance*. Lincoln: Univ. of Nebraska Press.

Miller, Perry. 1970. *Roger Williams: His Contribution to the American Tradition*. New York: Athenaeum.

Milligan, Edward A. 1973. *Wounded Knee 1973 and the Fort Laramie Treaty of 1868*. Bottineau, N.D.: Bottineau Courant Print.

Momaday, N. Scott. 1973. *The Way to Rainy Mountain*. New York: Ballentine Books.

———. 1984. "To Save a Great Vision." In *A Sender of Words: Essays in Memory of John G. Neihardt*, edited by Vine Deloria Jr., 30–38. Salt Lake City: Howe Brothers.

Mongia, Padmini, ed. 1996. *Contemporary Postcolonial Theory: A Reader*. London: Arnold.

Mooney, James. 1896. *The Ghost-Dance Religion and the Sioux Outbreak of*

1890. "Fourteenth Annual Report of the Bureau of American Ethnology, Part 2."

———. 1973. *The Ghost-Dance Religion and the Sioux Outbreak of 1890*. 1896. New York: Dover.

———. 1991. *The Ghost-Dance Religion and the Sioux Outbreak of 1890*. 1896. Lincoln: Univ. of Nebraska Press.

Moore, James T. 1982. *Indian and Jesuit: A Seventeenth Century Encounter*. Chicago: Loyola Univ. Press.

Moore, William. 1939. "With the Sioux in Camp." *Indian Sentinel* 19 (Oct.): 118–19.

Mounce, Robert H. 1977. *The Book of Revelation*. Grand Rapids: Eerdmans.

Murray, David. 1991. "Autobiography and Authorship: Identity and Unity." In *Forked Tongues: Speech, Writing, and Representation in North American Indian Texts*, edited by David Murray, 65–97. Bloomington: Indiana Univ. Press.

Neihardt, Hilda. 1995. *Black Elk and Flaming Rainbow: Personal Memories of the Lakota Holy Man and John Neihardt*. Lincoln: Univ. of Nebraska Press.

Neihardt, John G. 1900. *The Divine Enchantment*. New York: James T. White.

———. 1907. *The Lonesome Trail*. New York: John Lane.

———. 1908. *A Bundle of Myrrh*. New York: Outing.

———. 1909. *Man-Song*. New York: Mitchell Kennerly.

———. 1910. *The River and I*. New York: Putnam.

———. 1911. *The Dawn Builder*. New York: Mitchell Kennerly.

———. 1912. *The Stranger at the Gate*. New York: Mitchell Kennerly.

———. 1913. *Death of Agrippina*. Chicago: Poetry Magazine.

———. 1914. *Life's Lure*. New York: Mitchell Kennerly.

———. 1915. *The Song of Hugh Glass*. New York: Macmillan.

———. 1919. *The Song of Three Friends*. New York: Macmillan.

———. 1920a. *The Splendid Wayfaring: The Exploits and Adventures of Jedediah Smith and the Ashley-Henry Men, 1822–1831*. New York: Macmillan.

———. 1920b. *Two Mothers*. New York: Macmillan.

———. 1925a. *Poetic Values: Their Reality and Our Need of Them*. New York: Macmillan.

———. 1925b. *The Song of the Indian Wars*. New York: Macmillan.

———. 1926. *Collected Poems*. New York: Macmillan.

———. 1928. *The Quest*. New York: Macmillan.

———. 1932. *Black Elk Speaks: Being the Life Story of a Holy Man of the Ogalala Sioux*. New York: William Morrow.

———. 1935. *The Song of the Messiah: A Cycle of the West*. New York: Macmillan.

———. 1941. *The Song of Jed Smith*. New York: Macmillan.

———. 1945. "Red Hail and the Two Suitors." *Indians at Work* 13 (May–June): 6–10.

———. 1951. *When the Tree Flowered: An Authentic Tale of the Old Sioux World.* New York: Macmillan.

———. 1953. *Eagle Voice: An Authentic Tale of the Sioux Indians.* London: Andrew Melrose.

———. 1965. *Lyric and Dramatic Poems.* Lincoln: Univ. of Nebraska Press.

———. 1970. *When the Tree Flowered: The Fictional Autobiography of Eagle Voice, a Sioux Indian.* 1951. New York: Macmillan.

———. 1971a. *Mountain Men.* Lincoln: Univ. of Nebraska Press.

———. 1971b. *Twilight of the Sioux.* Lincoln: Univ. of Nebraska Press.

———. 1972a. *All Is but a Beginning: Youth Remembered, 1881–1901.* New York: Harcourt Brace Jovanovich.

———. 1972b. "The Book That Would Not Die." *Western American Literature* 6 (winter): 227–30.

———. 1978. *Patterns and Coincidences: A Sequel to "All Is but a Beginning."* Columbia: Univ. of Missouri Press.

———. 1979. *Black Elk Speaks: Being the Life Story of a Holy Man of the Oglala Sioux.* 1932. Lincoln: Univ. of Nebraska Press.

———. 1988. *Indian Tales and Others.* Lincoln: Univ. of Nebraska Press.

Nichols, William. 1983. "Black Elk's Truth." In *Smoothing the Ground: Essays on Native American Oral Literature,* edited by Brian Swann, 334–43. Berkeley and Los Angeles: Univ. of California Press.

Nietzsche, Fredrich. 1956. *The Birth of Tragedy and the Geneology of Morals.* Garden City, N.Y.: Doubleday.

———. 1967. *The Will to Power.* Translated by Walter Kaufmann and R. J. Hollingdale. New York: Vintage.

northSun, nila. 1994. "stupid questions." In *Returning the Gift: Poetry and Prose from the First North American Native Writers Festival,* edited by Joseph Bruchac, 217–18. Tucson: Univ. of Arizona Press.

Nurge, Ethel, ed. 1970. *The Modern Sioux: Social Systems and Reservation Culture.* Lincoln: Univ. of Nebraska Press.

Obrian, Lynn Woods. 1973. *Plains Indian Autobiographies.* Vol. 10, *Boise State College Western Writers Series.* Boise, Idaho: Boise State College.

Olson, James C. 1965. *Red Cloud and the Sioux Problem.* Lincoln: Univ. of Nebraska Press.

Olson, James S., and Raymond Wilson. 1986. *Native Americans in the Twentieth Century.* Univ. of Illinois Press.

Olson, Paul A. 1982. "*Black Elk Speaks* as Epic and Ritual Attempt to Reverse History." In *Vision and Refuge: Essays on the Literature of the Great Plains,* edited by V. Faulkner and F. C. Luebke, 3–37. Lincoln: Univ. of Nebraska Press.

Ong, Walter. 1967. *The Presence of the Word*. New Haven: Yale Univ. Press.

Ortiz, Roxanne, ed. 1977. *The Great Sioux Nation: Sitting in Judgment on America—An Oral History of the Sioux Nation and Its Struggle for Sovereignty*. Berkeley, Calif.: Moon Books.

———. 1980. "Wounded Knee 1890 to Wounded Knee 1973: A Study in United States Colonialism." *Journal of Ethnic Studies* 8, no. 2: 1–15.

Osterreich, Shelley Anne. 1991. *The American Indian Ghost Dance, 1870 and 1890: An Annotated Bibliography*. Westport, Conn.: Greenwood Press.

O'Sullivan, Thomas. 1989. "Joint Venture or Testy Alliance? The Public Works of Art Project in Minnesota, 1933–34." *Great Plains Quarterly* 9 (spring): 89–99.

Otto, Rudolf. 1958. *The Idea of the Holy*. Translated by John W. Harvey. New York: Oxford Univ. Press.

Overholt, Thomas W. 1986. *Prophecy in Cross-Cultural Perspective*. Atlanta: Scholars Press.

———. 1989. *Channels of Prophecy: The Social Dynamics of Prophetic Activity*. Minneapolis: Fortress Press.

Owens, Lewis. 1992. *Destinies: Understanding the American Indian Novel*. Norman: Univ. of Oklahoma Press.

Paige, Harry. 1970. *Songs of the Teton Sioux*. Los Angeles: Westernlore Press.

———. 1987. *Land of the Spotted Eagle: A Portrait of the Reservation Sioux*. Photographs by Don Doll, S.J. Chicago: Loyola Univ. Press.

Parkhill, Thomas C. 1997. *Weaving Ourselves into the Land: Charles Godfrey Leland, 'Indians,' and the Study of Native American Religions*. Albany: SUNY Press.

Parks, Douglas R., and Raymond J. DeMallie. 1992. "Plains Indian Native Literatures." *Boundary 2* 19, no. 3 (fall): 105–47.

Paul, R. Eli. 1997. *Autobiography of Red Cloud: War Leader of the Oglalas*. Helena: Montana Historical Society Press.

Pearce, Roy Harvey. 1988. *Savagism and Civilization: A Study of the Indian and the American Mind*. Berkeley and Los Angeles: Univ. of California Press.

Peelman, Achiel. 1995. *Christ Is a Native American*. Ottawa: Novalis–St. Paul Univ.

Pendleton, Reece. 1995. "A Ghostly Splendor: John G. Neihardt's Spiritual Preparation for Entry into Black Elk's World." *American Indian Culture and Research Journal* 19, no. 4: 213–29.

Pommersheim, Frank. 1995. *Braid of Feathers: American Indian Law and Contemporary Tribal Life*. Berkeley and Los Angeles: Univ. of California Press.

Pond, Gideon H. 1854. "Power and Influence of Dakota Medicine Men." In *Historical and Statistical Information Respecting the History, Condition and*

Prospects of the Indian Tribes of the United States, edited by H. Schoolcraft, 4: 641–51. Philadelphia: Lippincott, Grambo.

———. 1857. "Religious and Mythological Opinions of the Mississippi Valley Tribes." In *Historical and Statistical Information Respecting the History, Condition and Prospects of the Indian Tribes of the United States,* edited by H. Schoolcraft, 6: 647–57. Philadelphia: Lippincott, Grambo.

———. 1889. "Dakota Superstitions." *Collection of the Minnesota Historical Society* 2: 215–55.

Pond, Peter. 1908. "The Journal of Peter Pond, 1740–1775." Edited by R. Thwaites. *Collections of the State Historical Society of Wisconsin* 18: 314–54.

Pond, Samuel W. 1908. "The Dakota or Sioux in Minnesota as They Were in 1834." *Collections of the Minnesota Historical Society* 12: 319–501.

———. 1986. *The Dakotas or Sioux in Minnesota as They Were in 1834.* 1908. St. Paul: Minnesota Historical Society Press.

Powers, Marla N. 1980. "Menstruation and Reproduction: An Oglala Case." *Signs: The Journal of Women in Culture and Society* 6, no. 1: 54–65.

———. 1986. *Oglala Women.* Chicago: Univ. of Chicago Press.

———. 1988. "Symbolic Representations of Sex Roles in the Plains War Dance." *European Review of Native American Studies* 2, no. 2: 17–24.

———. 1990a. "Mistress, Mother, Visionary Spirit: The Lakota Culture Heroine." In *Religion in Native North America,* edited by Christopher Vecsey, 36–48. Moscow: Univ. of Idaho Press.

———. 1990b. *The Star Quilt: Symbol of Lakota Identity.* Kendall Park, N.J.: Lakota Books.

———. 1991. *Lakota Naming: A Modern-day Hunka Ceremony.* Kendall Park, N.J.: Lakota Books.

Powers, William K. 1970. "Contemporary Oglala Music and Dance: Pan-Indianism Versus Pan-Tetonism." In *The Modern Sioux,* edited by E. Nurge, 268–90. Lincoln: Univ. of Nebraska Press.

———. 1975. *Oglala Religion.* Lincoln: Univ. of Nebraska Press.

———. 1979. "The Archaic Illusion." *American Indian Art Magazine* 5, no. 1: 58–71.

———. 1980a. "Oglala Song Terminology." In *Selected Reports in Ethnomusicology,* edited by C. Heth, vol. 3, no. 2, 23–42. Los Angeles: Univ. of California Press.

———. 1980b. "Plains Indian Music and Dance." In *Anthropology of the Great Plains,* edited by M. Liberty and W. R. Wood, 212–29. Lincoln: Univ. of Nebraska Press.

———. 1981a. "Bear Facts about Hanta Yo." *Lakota Eyapaha* 5, no. 2: 21.

———. 1981b. "On Mandalas and Native American World Views." *Current Anthropology* 25: 43.

———. 1982. *Yuwipi*. Lincoln: Univ. of Nebraska Press.

———. 1985. "Counting Your Blessings: Sacred Numbers and the Structure of Reality." *Zygon* 21, no. 1: 75–94.

———. 1986. *Sacred Language: The Nature of Supernatural Discourse in Lakota*. Norman: Univ. of Oklahoma Press.

———. 1987a. *Beyond the Vision: Essays on American Indian Culture*. Norman: Univ. of Oklahoma Press.

———. 1987b. "Cosmology and the Reinvention of Culture: The Lakota Case." *Canadian Journal of Native Studies* 7, no. 2: 165–80.

———. 1990a. *Voices from the Spirit World*. Kendall Park, N.J.: Lakota Books.

———. 1990b. *War Dance: Plains Indian Musical Performance*. Tucson: Univ. of Arizona Press.

———. 1990c. "When Black Elk Speaks, Everybody Listens." In *Religion in Native North America*, edited by Christopher Vecsey, 136–51. Moscow: Univ. of Idaho Press.

———. 1994. *A Winter Count of the Oglalas*. Kendall Park, N.J.: Lakota Books.

Powers, William K., and Marla N. Powers. 1984. "Metaphysical Aspects of an Oglala Food System." In *Food in the Social Order*, edited by M. Douglas, 40–96. New York: Russell Sage Foundation.

———. 1986. "Putting on the Dog." *Natural History* 95, no. 2: 6–16.

———. 1994. *Testimony to Wounded Knee: A Comprehensive Bibliography*. Kendall Park, N.J.: Lakota Books.

Praus, Alexis. 1962. "The Sioux, 1798–1922: A Dakota Winter Count." *Bulletin 44, Cranbrook Institute of Science*: 1–31.

Price, Catherine. 1996. *Oglala People, 1841–1879: A Political History*. Lincoln: Univ. of Nebraska Press.

Rahner, Karl. 1961–1991. *Theological Investigations*. 23 vols. New York: Seabury Press.

Read, Herbert. 1952. *English Prose Style*. Lincoln: Univ. of Nebraska Press.

Redfield, Robert, Ralph Linton, and Melville J. Herskovits. 1941. "Memorandum for the Study of Acculturation." *American Anthropologist* 38: 149–52.

Red Shirt, Delphine. 1997. *A Lakota Childhood*. Lincoln: Univ. of Nebraska Press.

Rennie, Bryan. 1996. *Reconstructing Eliade: Making Sense of Religion*. Albany: SUNY Press.

Reyer, Carolyn, Beatrice Medicine, and Debra Lynn White Plume. 1991. *Cante Ohitika Win (Brave-hearted Women): Images of Lakota Women from the Pine Ridge Reservation, South Dakota*. Freeman, S.D.: Pine Hill Press.

Rice, Julian. 1984. "How Lakota Stories Keep the Spirit and Feed the Ghosts." *American Indian Quarterly* 8, no. 4: 331–47.

———. 1985. "Akicita of the Thunder: Horses in Black Elk's Vision." *Melus* 12, no. 1: 5–23.

———. 1989. *Lakota Storytelling: Black Elk, Ella Deloria, and Frank Fools Crow.* New York: Peter Lang.

———. 1991. *Black Elk's Story: Distinguishing Its Lakota Purpose.* Albuquerque: Univ. of New Mexico Press.

———. 1992a. *Deer Women and Elk Men: The Lakota Narratives of Ella Deloria.* Albuquerque: Univ. of New Mexico Press.

———. 1992b. "Narrative Styles in Dakota Texts." In *On the Translation of Native American Literature,* edited by Brian Swann, 276–92. Washington, D.C.: Smithsonian Institution Press.

———. 1993. *Ella Deloria's "Iron Hawk."* Translated by Julian Rice. Albuquerque: Univ. of New Mexico Press.

———. 1994a. *Ella Deloria's "The Buffalo People."* Translated by Julian Rice. Albuquerque: Univ. of New Mexico Press.

———. 1994b. "A Ventriloquy of Anthros: Densmore, Dorsey, Lame Deer and Erdoes." *American Indian Quarterly* 18, no. 2: 169–96.

———. 1998. *Before the Great Spirit: The Many Faces of Sioux Spirituality.* Albuquerque: Univ. of New Mexico Press.

Ricoeur, Paul. 1978. "Image and Language in Psychoanalysis." In *Psychiatry and the Humanities.* Vol. 3, *Psychoanalysis and Language,* ed. J. Smith, 293–324. New Haven: Yale Univ. Press.

Ridington, Robin. 1996. "Voice, Representation, and Dialogue: The Poetics of Native American Spiritual Traditions." *American Indian Quarterly* 20, nos. 3/4: 467–88.

Riester, Albert. 1930–1931. "Sioux Trails All Lead to Big Road." *Indian Sentinel* 11 (winter): 7–8.

Riggs, Stephen Return. 1852. *A Grammar and Dictionary of Dakota.* Vol. 4, *Smithsonian Contributions to Knowledge.* Washington, D.C.: Government Printing Office.

———. 1890. *A Dakota-English Dictionary.* Edited by J. O. Dorsey. Vol. 7, *Contributions to North American Ethnology.* Washington, D.C.: Government Printing Office.

———. 1893. *Dakota Grammar, Texts and Ethnography.* Edited by J. O. Dorsey. Vol. 9, *Contributions to North American Ethnology.* Washington, D.C.: Government Printing Office.

———. 1992. *A Dakota-English Dictionary.* Edited by J. O. Dorsey. St. Paul: Minnesota Historical Society Press.

Robinson, Doane. 1956. *A History of the Dakota or Sioux Indians.* Minneapolis: Ross and Haines.

Rogers, Dilwyn. 1980. *Lakota Names and Traditional Uses of Native Plants by the Sicangu (Brule) People in the Rosebud Area, South Dakota.* St. Francis, S.D.: Rosebud Educational Society.

Rogin, Michael Paul. 1976. *Fathers and Children: Andrew Jackson and the Subjugation of the American Indian.* New York: Vintage Press.

Rood, David, and Alan Taylor. 1976a. *Beginning Lakhota.* 2 vols. Boulder: Univ. of Colorado Lakhota Project.

———. 1976b. *Elementary Bilingual Dictionary, English-Lakhota, Lakhota-English.* Boulder: Univ. of Colorado Lakhota Project.

———. 1976c. *Lakhota Wayawapi [Lakhota Readings].* Boulder: Univ. of Colorado Lakhota Project.

Ross, Allen C. 1989. *Mitakuye Oyasin "We Are All Related."* Fort Yates, N.D.: Bear.

———. 1992. *Ehanamani "Walks Among": The Winter Count of a Santee Dakota Educator, Historian, and Spiritual Guide.* Kyle, S.D.: Bear.

Ross, Virginia. 1986. "The Transcendent Function of the Bilateral Brain." *Zygon* 21, no. 2 (June): 233–47.

Ruby, Robert. 1955. *The Oglala Sioux.* New York: Vantage Press.

———. 1966. "Yuwipi: Ancient Rite of the Sioux." *Montana* 16, no. 4: 74–79.

Sandoz, Mari. 1961. *Crazy Horse: The Strange Man of the Oglalas.* 1942. Lincoln: Univ. of Nebraska Press.

Sarris, Greg. 1993. *Keeping Slug Woman Alive: A Holistic Approach to American Indian Texts.* Berkeley and Los Angeles: Univ. of California Press.

Sayre, Robert. 1971. "Vision and Experience in *Black Elk Speaks.*" *College English* 32, no. 5 (Feb.): 509–35.

———. 1977. *Thoreau and the American Indians.* Princeton: Princeton Univ. Press.

Schramm, Tim. 1992. "Bibliodrama in Action: Reenacting a New Testament Healing Story." In *Body and Bible: Interpreting and Experiencing Biblical Narratives,* edited by Bjîrn Krondorfer, 57–84. Philadelphia: Trinity Press International.

Schultz, Terry. 1973. "Bamboozle Me Not at Wounded Knee." *Harper's* 246, no. 1477 (June): 46–48, 53–56.

———. 1974. "Continuing Massacre at Wounded Knee: Election for Presidency of the Tribal Council." *Harper's* 248, no. 1489 (June): 30–34.

Schusky, Ernest. 1977. *The Forgotten Sioux.* Chicago: Nelson-Hall.

Scott, John. 1941. "Sun Dance in Dakota." *Jesuit Missions* 15 (June): 146–47, 167.

———. 1963. *High Eagle and His Sioux.* St. Louis, n.p. Pamphlet, Marquette Univ. Archives, Holy Rosary Mission Collection, series 7, box 17, folder 1.

————. 1992. Interview, Creighton Univ., Oct.

Shalinsky, Audrey C. 1986. "Ritual Pageantry in the American West: A Wyoming Case Study." *Great Plains Quarterly* 6 (winter): 21–33.

Sialm, Placidus. 1922a. "Holy Rosary Mission." *Jesuit Bulletin* 1 (Dec.): 12.

————. 1922b. *Woodstock Letters* 51: 305.

————. 1923. "A Retreat to Catechists." *Indian Sentinel* 3 (Apr.): 78.

————. 1931. "Left-hand Heron: Sioux Story Teller." *Indian Sentinel* 11 (spring): 54.

————. c. 1932. "Camp Churches." Marquette Univ. Archives, Holy Rosary Mission Collection, series 7, box 17, folders 5–7.

————. 1937. "Mary Kills Two's Party." *Indian Sentinel* 17 (May): 67–68.

Skinner, Alanson B. 1919. "A Sketch of Eastern Dakota Ethnology." *American Anthropologist* 21: 164–74.

Slotkin, Richard. 1973. *Regeneration Through Violence: The Mythology of the American Frontier, 1600–1860.* Middletown, Conn.: Wesleyan Univ. Press.

Smith, John L. 1967. "A Short History of the Sacred Calf Pipe of the Teton." *South Dakota University Museum News* 28: 1–37.

————. 1970. "The Sacred Calf Bundle: Its Effect on the Present Teton Dakota." *Plains Anthropologist* 15: 87–93.

Smith, Rex Allen. 1975. *Moon of the Popping Trees.* Lincoln: Univ. of Nebraska Press.

Sneve, Virginia Driving Hawk. 1974. *When Thunders Spoke.* Lincoln: Univ. of Nebraska Press.

————. 1977. *That They May Have Life: The Episcopal Church in South Dakota, 1859–1976.* New York: Seabury Press.

————. 1993. *The Chichi HooHoo Bogeyman.* Lincoln: Univ. of Nebraska Press.

————. 1995. *Completing the Circle.* Lincoln: Univ. of Nebraska Press.

————. 1997. *The Trickster and the Troll.* Lincoln: Univ. of Nebraska Press.

Spector, Janet D. 1993. *What This Awl Means: Feminist Archaeology at a Wahpeton Dakota Village.* St. Paul: Minnesota Historical Society Press.

————. 1994. "Collaboration at Inyan Ceyaka Atonwan (Village of the Rapids)." *Bulletin of the Society for American Archaeology* 12, no. 3: 8–10.

Sperber, Dan. 1974. *Rethinking Symbolism.* Translated by Alice L. Morton. Paris: Cambridge Univ. Press.

Spivak, Gayatri Chakravorty. 1988. "Can the Subaltern Speak?" In *Marxism and the Interpretation of Culture,* edited by Cary Nelson and Lawrence Grossberg, 271–313. Urbana: Univ. of Illinois Press.

Spresser, James Clarence. 1985. "Fantasy Theme Analysis as Applied to the Oglala Sioux Indian Text *Black Elk Speaks.*" *Journal of American Culture* 8: 75–78.

St. Pierre, Mark. 1991. *Madonna Swan: A Lakota Woman's Story.* Norman: Univ. of Oklahoma Press.

St. Pierre, Mark, and Tilda Long Soldier. 1995. *Walking in the Sacred Manner: Healers, Dreamers, and Pipe Carriers—Medicine Women of the Plains Indians.* New York: Simon and Schuster.

Standing Bear, Luther. 1975. *My People the Sioux.* Lincoln: Univ. of Nebraska Press.

———. 1978. *Land of the Spotted Eagle.* Lincoln: Univ. of Nebraksa Press.

———. 1988a. *Indian Boyhood.* Lincoln: Univ. of Nebraska Press.

———. 1988b. *Stories of the Sioux.* Lincoln: Univ. of Nebraska Press.

Starkloff, Carl J., S.J. 1984. "Renewing the Sacred Hoop." In *A Sender of Words: Essays in Memory of John G. Neihardt,* edited by Vine Deloria Jr., 159–72. Salt Lake City: Howe Brothers.

Starr, Edward. 1994. *A Dictionary of Modern Lakota.* Kendall Park, N.J.: Lakota Books.

Starr, Ivan. 1997. *Lakotiyapi: An Introduction to the Lakota Language.* Kendall Park, N.J.: Lakota Books.

Stauffer, Helen. 1981. "Two Authors and a Hero: Neihardt, Sandoz, and Crazy Horse." *Great Plains Quarterly* (winter): 34–66.

Steinmetz, Paul, S.J. 1970. "The Relationship Between Plains Indian Religion and Christianity: A Priest's Viewpoint." *Plains Anthropologist* 15: 83–86.

———. 1984a. *Meditations with Native Americans: Lakota Spirituality.* Santa Fe, N.M.: Bear.

———. 1984b. "The Sacred Pipe in American Indian Religions." *American Indian Culture and Research Journal* 8: 27–80.

———. 1990. "Shamanic Images in Peyote Visions." In *Religion in Native North America,* edited by Christopher Vecsey, 104–16. Moscow: Univ. of Idaho Press.

———. 1998a. *Pipe, Bible and Peyote among the Oglala Lakota: A Study in Religious Identity.* 1990. Syracuse: Syracuse Univ. Press.

———. 1998b. *The Sacred Pipe: An Archetypal Theology.* Syracuse: Syracuse Univ. Press.

Steltenkamp, Michael F. n.d. *No More Screech Owl.* Marquette Univ. Archives.

———. 1982. *The Sacred Vision.* New York: Paulist Press.

———. 1993. *Black Elk: Holy Man of the Oglala.* Norman: Univ. of Oklahoma Press.

———. 1997. "Black Elk." In *The Encyclopedia of American Catholic History,* edited by Michael Glazier and Thomas J. Shelly, 150–51. Collegeville, Minn.: Liturgical Press.

Stevens, Anthony. 1983. *Archetypes: A Natural History of the Self.* New York: Quill.

Stewart, Omar. 1987. *The Peyote Religion.* Norman: Univ. of Oklahoma Press.

Stocking, George W., Jr. 1968. *Race, Culture, and Evolution: Essays in the History of Anthropology.* New York: Free Press.

———, ed. 1989. *A Franz Boas Reader: The Shaping of American Anthropology, 1883–1911.* 1971. Chicago: Univ. of Chicago Press.

———, ed. 1996. *Volkgeist as Method and Ethic: Essays on Boasian Ethnography and the German Anthropological Tradition.* Madison: Univ. of Wisconsin Press, 1996.

Stoll, David. 1998. *Rigoberta Menchú and the Story of All Poor Guatemalans.* Boulder, Colo.: Westview Press.

Stolzman, William, S.J. 1986a. *How to Take Part in Lakota Ceremonies.* Pine Ridge, S.D.: Red Cloud Indian School.

———. 1986b. *The Pipe and Christ.* Pine Ridge, S.D.: Red Cloud Indian School.

Stone, Albert E. 1982a. "The Soul and the Self: Black Elk and Thomas Merton." In *Autobiographical Occasions and Original Acts: Versions of American Identity from Henry Adams to Nate Shaw,* 59–91. Philadelphia: Univ. of Pennsylvania Press.

———. 1982b. "Collaboration in Contemporary American Autobiography." In *Revue Française d'études Americaines* 7, no. 1: 151–65.

Storm, Hyemeyohsts. 1973. *Seven Arrows.* New York: Ballentine.

Stover, Dale. 1996. "The Other Side of the Story: Indigenous Interpretation of Contact with Europeans." In *The Age of Exploration: Spain and New Spain,* edited by Bryan F. LeBeau and Menachem Mor, 96–116. Omaha, Nebr.: Creighton Univ. Press.

———. 1997. "Eurocentrism and Native Americans." Review of *Black Elk's Religion,* by Clyde Holler. *Crosscurrents* 47, no. 3 (fall): 390–98.

———. 1998. "Religious Freedom, Native American: Legal and Philosophical Context." In *The Encyclopedia of Native American Legal Tradition,* edited by Bruce Johansen, 264–73. Westport, Conn.: Greenwood Press.

Sundstrom, Linea. 1996. "Mirror of Heaven: Cross-cultural Transference of the Sacred Geography of the Black Hills." *World Archaeology* 28, no. 2: 177–89.

Sword, George. 1892. "The Story of the Ghost Dance." *Folk-Lorist* 1: 28–36.

Tedlock, Dennis. 1980. "The Spoken Word and the Work of Interpretation in American Indian Religion." In *Myth, Symbol and Reality,* edited by Alan M. Olsen, 129–44. Notre Dame: Univ. of Notre Dame Press.

Theisz, Ron D., ed. 1975. *Buckskin Tokens: Contemporary Oral Narratives of the Lakota.* Rosebud, S.D.: Sinte Gleska College.

———. 1996. *Sending Their Voices: Essays on Lakota Musicology*. Kendall Park, N.J.: Lakota Books.

Tinker, George E. 1993. *Missionary Conquest: The Gospel and Native American Cultural Genocide*. Minneapolis: Fortress Press.

Tuan, Yi-Fu. 1977. *Space and Place: The Perspective of Experience*. Minneapolis: Univ. of Minnesota Press.

Turner, Victor. 1992. *From Ritual to Theatre: The Human Seriousness of Play*. New York: PAJ Publications.

Utley, Robert. 1963. *The Last Days of the Sioux Nation*. New Haven: Yale Univ. Press.

———. 1993. *The Lance and the Shield: The Life and Times of Sitting Bull*. New York: Henry Holt.

Vecsey, Chris. 1997. "A Century of Lakota Sioux Catholicism at Pine Ridge." In *Religious Diversity and American Religious History: Studies in Traditions and Cultures*, edited by Walter H. Conser Jr. and Sumner B. Twiss, 262–95. Athens: Univ. of Georgia Press.

Versluis, Arthur. 1992. *Sacred Earth: The Spiritual Landscape of Native America*. Rochester, Vt.: Inner Traditions International.

Vestal, Stanley. 1934. *New Sources of Indian History, 1850–1891*. Norman: Univ. of Oklahoma Press.

———. 1948. *Warpath and Council Fire*. New York: Random House.

———. 1957. *Sitting Bull, Champion of the Sioux*. 2d ed. Norman: Univ. of Oklahoma Press.

———. 1984. *Warpath: The True Story of the Fighting Sioux Told in a Biography of Chief White Bull*. Edited by Raymond J. DeMallie. Lincoln: Univ. of Nebraska Press.

Waggoner, Hyatt H. 1966. "*The Marble Faun*." In *Hawthorne: A Collection of Critical Essays*, edited by A. N. Kaul. Englewood Cliffs, N.J.: Prentice-Hall.

Walker, James. 1905. "Sioux Games." *Journal of American Folk-Lore* 18: 277–90.

———. 1906. "Sioux Games." *Journal of American Folk-Lore* 19: 29–36.

———. 1914. "Oglala Kinship Terms." *American Anthropologist* 16, no. 1: 96–109.

———. 1917. "The Sun Dance and Other Ceremonies of the Oglala Division of the Teton Sioux." *Anthropological Papers of the American Museum of Natural History* 16, no. 2: 51–221.

———. 1937. "Legends of the Oglala Sioux." Comments and annotation by Ella Deloria. In *Dakota Commentary on Walker's Texts*. MS 30 (X8.5), Boas Collection. Philadelphia: American Philosophical Society.

———. 1980. *Lakota Belief and Ritual*. Edited by Raymond J. DeMallie and E. Jahner. Lincoln: Univ. of Nebraska Press.

————. 1982. *Lakota Society.* Edited by Raymond J. DeMallie. Lincoln: Univ. of Nebraska Press.

————. 1983. *Lakota Myth.* Edited by E. Jahner. Lincoln: Univ. of Nebraska Press.

Walsh, Roger. 1997. "The Psychological Health of Shamans: A Reevaluation." *Journal of the American Academy of Religion* 65, no. 1: 101–24.

Waters, Frank. 1984. "Neihardt and the Vision of Black Elk." In *A Sender of Words: Essays in Memory of John G. Neihardt,* edited by Vine Deloria Jr., 12–24. Salt Lake City: Howe Brothers.

Wax, Murray, Rosalie Wax, and Robert Dumont. 1989. *Formal Education in an American Indian Community: Peer Society and the Failure of Minority Education.* Prospect Heights, Ill.: Waveland Press.

Wax, Rosalie, and Murray Wax. 1968. "Indian Education for What?" In *The American Indian Today,* edited by Stuart Levine and Nancy O. Lurie, 257–67. Deland, Fla.: Everett-Edwards.

Weisenhorn, Charles. 1920a. "Sioux Congress on Pine Ridge Reservation." *Indian Sentinel* 2 (Oct.): 169–73.

————. 1920b. "A Missionary Trip in South Dakota." In *Woodstock Letters,* edited by George Zorn, 49: 151–63. Woodstock, Md.: Woodstock College Press.

West, Louis J., and Paul R. Martin. 1996. "Pseudo-identity and the Treatment of Personality Change in Victims of Captivity and Cults." *Cultic Studies Journal* 13, no. 2: 125–52.

Weston, Jesse L. 1993. *From Ritual to Romance.* 1920. Princeton: Princeton Univ. Press.

Westropp, Henry. Letters. Bureau of Catholic Indian Missions Collection, Marquette Univ. Archives. 8 Nov. 1908, BCIM 1-58-26; 2 Feb. 1910, BCIM 1-67-16. Undated letter c. 1909, BCIM 1-63-4, written on the back of Ketcham letter dated 14 Oct. 1909.

————. c. 1910. "In the Land of the Wigwam." Pamphlet. Holy Rosary Mission Folders, Missouri Province Archives of the Society of Jesus in St. Louis.

White Bull, Joseph. 1998. *Lakota Warrior.* Lincoln: Univ. of Nebraska Press.

Whitney, Blair. 1976. *John G. Neihardt.* New York: Twayne.

Williams, Patrick, and Laura Crisman, eds. 1994. *Colonial Discourse and Postmodern Theory.* New York: Columbia Univ. Press.

Williams, Robert. 1990. *The American Indian in Western Legal Thought.* New York: Oxford Univ. Press.

Williamson, John P. 1902. *An English-Dakota Dictionary.* New York: American Tract Society.

————. 1992. *An English-Dakota Dictionary.* 1902. St. Paul: Minnesota Historical Society Press.

Winquist, Charles. 1983. "Theology, Deconstruction, and Ritual Process." In *Zygon* 18, no. 3 (Sept.): 295–309.

"Wiping the Tears of Seven Generations." 1991. Native American Relations Series. A Kifaru Production in association with Eagle Heart Productions.

Wise, Christopher, and R. Todd Wise. 1998. "Mary Brave Bird Speaks: A Brief Interview." *American Indian Literatures* 10, no. 4 (winter): 1–8.

Wise, R. Todd. 1995a. "Native American Testimonio: The Shared Vision of Black Elk and Rigoberta Menchú." *Christianity and Literature* 45, no. 1: 111–27.

————. 1995b. "An Empirical-Phenomenological Examination of the Rite of Reconciliation from the Perspective of the Penitent." Ph.D. diss., Union Institute Graduate School of Psychology. UMI, Bell and Howell.

————. 1999. "A Neocomparative Investigation of the Orpheus Myth as Found in the European and Native American Traditions." Ph.D. diss., Temple Univ. Graduate School of Religion. UMI, Bell and Howell.

Wissler, Clark. 1904. "Decorative Art of the Sioux." *Anthropological Papers of the American Museum of Natural History* 18: 231–78.

————. 1907a. "Some Dakota Myths I, II." *Journal of American Folk Lore* 20: 121–31, 195–206.

————. 1907b. "Some Protective Designs of the Dakota." Part 2. *Anthropological Papers of the American Museum of Natural History* 1: 21–53.

————. 1912. "Societies and Ceremonial Associations in the Oglala Division of the Teton-Dakota." Part 1. *Anthropological Papers of the American Museum of Natural History* 11: 1–99.

Witkin–New Holy, Alexandra. 1998. "The Heart of Everything That Is: *Paha Sapa*, Treaties, and Lakota Identity." *Oklahoma City University Law Review* 23, nos. 1 and 2: 317–52.

————. 1999. "Possibilities for Accommodating Contradictions: Developing Lakota Theology and Its Classroom Applications." *AYAANGWAAMIZIN: The International Journal of Indigenous Philosophy* 3, no. 1 (forthcoming).

Wong, Hertha D. 1992a. *Sending My Heart Back Across the Years: Tradition and Innovation in Native American Autobiography.* Oxford: Oxford Univ. Press.

————. 1992b. "Oral and Written Collaborative Autobiography: Nicholas Black Elk and Charles Alexander Eastman." In *Sending My Heart Back Across the Years: Tradition and Innovation in Native American Autobiography,* 117–52. Oxford: Oxford Univ. Press.

Wong, Joseph H. 1994. "Anonymous Christian: Karl Rahner's Pneuma-Christocentrism and an East-West Dialogue." *Theological Studies* 55: 609–37.

Wright, Ronald. 1993. *Stolen Continents.* Penguin Books of Canada.

Yuasa, Yasuo. 1987. *The Body: Toward an Eastern Mind-Body Theory.* New York: SUNY Press.

Zimmerman, Bill. 1975. *Airlift to Wounded Knee.* Chicago: Swallow Press.

Zimmerman, Joseph. 1927. "Great Sioux Chief Passes Away." *Indian Sentinel* 7 (fall): 180–81.

———. 1940. "Sioux Virtues." *Indian Sentinel* 20 (Jan.): 11–12.

———. 1944. "The True Faith Versus Paganism." *Calumet* (May): 16–17.

Zitkala-Sa. 1901. *Old Indian Legends.* Boston: Ginn.

———. 1921. *American Indian Stories.* Washington, D.C.: Hayworth Publishing House.

———. 1985a. *American Indian Stories.* 1921. Reprint, Lincoln: Univ. of Nebraska Press.

———. 1985b. *Old Indian Legends.* 1901. Reprint, Lincoln: Univ. of Nebraska Press.

Zuesse, Evan M. 1979. *Ritual Cosmos: The Sanctification of Life in African Religions.* Athens: Ohio Univ. Press.

Index

Acterberg, Jeanne, 250n
Adorno, Theodor Wiesengrund, 19
Alexander, Hartley Burr, 155
Aly, Lucile, 91
Amiotte, Arthur: on Lakota metaphor,
192; on Lakota universe, 197; on the
Sun Dance, 200
assimilation studies, 316
Ayquichi, Alberto Orozco, 38

Bachelard, Gaston, 245
Barnet, Miguel, 21
Bataille, Gretchen M.: on *Black Elk Speaks,*
85
Benjamin, Walter, 23
Bergson, Henri, 218n, 240
Beverley, John, 21, 28
Black Elk, Ben, 8–9, 98, 171
Black Elk, Charlotte, 32, 188, 192
Black Elk, Nicholas: adopted the Neihardts,
87–88; as archetypal Indian, 135–39;
belief in importance of vision, 45; biographical sources, xxin; challenge to
study of religion of, xvi; challenge to
Western thought, xvi; choice of collaborator, 3–4; compared to other *Oyate*
writers, 17; conversion, 268–69; cre-
ativity of, 175; date of birth of, xxii; at
Custer Fight, xxii–xxiii; death of, xxvi;
debate over religious allegiances of,
xv–xvi; describes missionary trip,
290–91; dual religious stance of, 32–33;

and Duhamel Sioux Pageant, xxv–xxvi,
271–72; as Ecumenist II, 267–68, 280;
effect of Sun Dance ban on, xxiii–xxiv;
enacts Horse Dance, xxiii; as Episcopalian, 118n, 270; and Ghost Dance,
xxiv–xxv, 118–19, 275–76; and ghost
shirts, 10–12; Great Vision of, 86, 201,
213, 245, 253–59, 261n, 280; as Indian
intellectual, 139–43; influence of, xiv,
45; influence on AIM activists, 42–43;
involvement in Catholicism, 29–32,
81–82, 106–9, 124–25, 161, 256–60,
268–71; letters affirming Catholicism,
97–98, 292–93; life and times, xxi–xxvi;
member of St. Joseph Society, 269–70;
as mythological figure, 127; oral tradition, xv; on pipe religion, 100; as postcolonial Indian, 143–46; religion, 56,
81–82, 108, 161, 256–60, 268–81; on
the Sacred Pipe, 277–78; and soldier
weed, 17, 68–69, 72, 96; as stereotype,
104; as Sun Dance intercessor, 90, 271;
as theologian, 57–58; as traditionalist or
Christian, xviin, 157; use of Sacred Pipe,
278n; use of Two Roads Map,
100–102, 257–58, 274–75; as vanishing Indian, 131–35; wake of, 125; and
Wild West Show, xxiv, 118, 156–57; at
Wounded Knee, 12–13. *See also* De-
Mallie, Raymond J.; Holler, Clyde;
Rice, Julian; Steltenkamp, Michael F.
Black Elk, Wallace, 113, 161